WORD, OBJECT,
AND CONCEPTUAL
DEVELOPMENT

Jeremy M. Anglin

WORD, OBJECT, AND CONCEPTUAL DEVELOPMENT

 W · W · Norton & Company · Inc · New York

BF
723
.C5
A53
1977

First Edition

Library of Congress Cataloging in Publication Data
Anglin, Jeremy M
  Word, object, and conceptual development.
  Bibliography: p.
  Includes index.
  1. Cognition (Child psychology) 2. Children—
Language. I. Title.
BF723.C5A53 1977   155.4′13   76–45428
ISBN 0–393–01132–1

1 2 3 4 5 6 7 8 9 0

Contents

For Margaret

Preface

This book is concerned with the relation between thought and language. More specifically it presents a study of the relation between cognitive development and language development.

Theories of cognitive development have often tended not to focus on those aspects of the young child's intellectual growth which highlight his considerable competence. Thus many accounts of the child's intellectual progress characterize that growth as an upward journey through a pyramid of qualitatively different and increasingly sophisticated periods or phases or stages. Almost every major theory of cognitive development postulates an important transition in intellectual development between the ages of five and seven. While there is debate about the mechanism which brings about the transition in the child's cognitive capacities there has been little disagreement about whether there is in fact a transition in this period, at least in North American and European children. One of the tacitly accepted implications of this view has often been that the preschool child's thought processes are unsophisticated, immature, and "primitive" relative to what they will eventually become.

The study of language development has also produced a picture of growth and transition. However, language development has not so often been characterized as a progression of qualitatively different stages as has cognitive development. Moreover, although language development is by no means over by the time the child enters school, the study of psycholinguistic development has revealed that a great deal has been achieved by the child before he enters primary school in one performance system at least, namely language. Indeed, the child's progress in language development in the first five or six years seems almost astounding in comparison with his progress in some other areas of cognitive development.

Human language of course is one of man's first and most essential means of communication and therefore its acquisition is part of a larger process of social development. At the same time, however, language will eventually become an important instrument of thought and from the outset it reveals underlying cognitive predispositions and processes in the child who acquires it. For these reasons language acquisition has implications for cognitive development as well as social development.

This book represents one approach to the study of the relation between thought and language. The investigations to be described have examined one aspect of language development as a window through which to view conceptual processes in the child's preschool years. Specifically this book presents a scientific inquiry into the acquisition of English nomenclature, common nouns which refer to classes of objects. The assumption, and indeed I would want to argue, insight, underlying the entire inquiry has been that an examination of the child's production, comprehension, and description of this symbolic system will illuminate processes of conceptual development in early childhood.

While the present inquiry concerns only one facet of the total process of language development it will be argued that this facet is basic to the enterprise as a whole. It will also be argued that the approach undertaken here to the study of conceptual development has the advantage of focusing on the child at his best since it is concerned with language and, in particular, with a linguistic domain which the child shows both precocity and speed in learning. The reader will discover that the picture of conceptual development that has emerged from the inquiry bears some affinity to the theories of cognitive development referred to at the beginning of the Preface in that it characterizes development as involving progress and change. At the same time, however, it has revealed that the preschool child has at his disposal mechanisms of categorization and conceptualization which while not identical with those of adults are nonetheless quite remarkable in their own right, remarkable in the apparent ease with which they are used, in the extent of their application, and in their adaptiveness. Thus, while it is not denied that there is change in development, it is also hoped that the present inquiry gives the preschool child credit for his considerable competence in categorizing the world through language, more credit perhaps than other accounts of intellectual growth which have not studied the child at his best.

This book is based upon a program of research begun in the summer of 1971 when I became an assistant professor at Harvard University and completed there in the summer of 1975. I have been aided immensely in the execution of the research upon which this book is based by several students and colleagues to whom my debt is greatest. Without their very able help in interviewing young children, in analyzing the resultant findings, and in making things clearer to the writer, this book would not have been possible. In particular, I would like to thank three students who worked as research assistants on the project over the course of the last few years. Maryellen Ruvolo, who was my research assistant during the summer of 1972, helped greatly with both the design and execution of the studies to be reported in the second chapter. Marc Fiedler worked on the project during the summer of 1975 and helped enormously with both the research described in Chapter 7 and with a number of statistical analyses. Perhaps my greatest single debt is to Elizabeth Smith who worked hard and skillfully on the project from the spring of 1973 until the fall of 1974. The other students who helped conduct the studies reported in this book were: Marvin Cohen, Ruth Berger, Laure De Broglie, Janet Zeller, Daniel Klett, Sophia Cohen, Kay Tolbert, David Rubin, Judith Burton, Joy Skon, Yvette Sheline, Martha Finn, Sara Weiss, Sally Weiskopf, Martha Bronson, and Judy Ungerer. To each of them I am deeply indebted. I would also like to express my gratitude to four people for their expert advice on a number of statistical analyses applied to various portions of the data reported in this book: Professors Basil Kalymon, Roberta Dihoff, Reid Hastie, and David Kenny.

The Department of Psychology and then of Psychology and Social Relations at Harvard University where the research reported in this book was conducted and the book itself was written provided an excellent intellectual environment in which to pursue the kinds of questions addressed in the pages that follow. Moreover, the Department of Psychology and Social Relations provided material support (in the form of financial aid) in the later phases of the project in addition to spiritual support. I am most grateful for both. During the past four years I have benefited greatly from conversations with colleagues both at Harvard and elsewhere about various issues raised in our research. In particular, I would like to mention Sheldon White, Nelson Goodman, George Miller, Susan Carey, Roger Brown, Richard Herrnstein, Peter and Jill de Villiers, Jerome Bruner, Jane Platt, Katherine Nelson, Fred Morrison, Catherine Lord, Carol Smith, Gail Ross, Dianne Lusk, Ellen Winner, Bella De Paulo, Odile Jacob, Robert Campbell, Helene Boyd, and Nathan Stemmer. Unfortunately I cannot pin the blame for whatever problems remain in the book on any of the above.

I am indebted to the children who allowed us to interview them and to their parents and teachers. Their cooperation was obviously essential to the enterprise and I am most grateful to them for it. This is the second time I have worked on a project with Donald S. Lamm of W. W. Norton and Company, the publisher of this book. As in the case of the first project, he has made many valuable suggestions and has encouraged and supported the enterprise from its inception. I would also like to thank Mary Shuford and Geraldine Stevens for their expert advice on details concerning the editing of this book. Finally, I would like to thank my wife, Margaret, for her help with the project, her support of it, and her perseverance through it. This book is dedicated to her with love and gratitude.

The research upon which this book is based was supported in part by a grant [No. 1–0624–A, Grant No. OEG–1–71–111(508)] from the National Institute of Education to the author.

WORD, OBJECT,
AND CONCEPTUAL
DEVELOPMENT

Chapter 1

Words, Categories, and Concepts

When we use a word to refer to an object, whether consciously or unconsciously, we categorize that object together with others to which we have applied and could apply the same term. Thus the production of terms of reference implies an underlying conceptual mechanism which is capable of guiding the application of the same term to a variety of different objects. It is this premise which motivates the present inquiry, the goal of which is to illuminate the nature of the child's early concepts by investigating the ways in which he uses, misuses, understands, and describes the symbolic system known technically as English nomenclature. Thus this book presents a scientific investigation of conceptual structure in early childhood, an investigation which exploits the child's remarkable facility with language as a window through which to view underlying conceptual processes in his preschool years.

A book which purports to illuminate the nature of the child's concepts owes its reader at least a preliminary definition of *concept,* since this elusive term clearly denotes a hypothetical construct, and quite a vague one at that. In this introductory chapter therefore I shall attempt to define the term *concept* as well as a number of related notions as they will be used in this book and to indicate the ways in which conceptual development can be studied in view of these definitions.

Whatever else it may be, a concept is a mechanism which enables categorization, the grouping together of different stimuli into the same category or class, the treatment of those different stimuli as equivalent. Actually, the different stimuli which are categorized may in fact be different forms

1

of the same thing, as when a child identifies his mother as *Mommy* regardless of whether she is near or far, partially occluded or in full view. In such cases one speaks of an identity category. More often, however, as in the present inquiry, the concern is with the treatment of discriminably different objects as the same kind of thing, as when a child identifies a variety of different dogs as *doggie*. In these cases one speaks of an equivalence category. Granting the distinction between identity and equivalence categories most psychologists, including this writer, would agree with Bourne (1966) that "a concept exists whenever two or more distinguishable objects or events have been grouped or classified together and set apart from other objects [or events]," that is, whenever they have been categorized. The psychological study of conceptual behavior has therefore most often involved the scientific investigation of categorization.

A great deal of work has been done on the problem of classification or categorization, an amount which is justified by the importance of this fundamental human cognitive activity. There are a number of interrelated reasons why the process of categorization is important which give clues to the nature of the conceptual knowledge which mediates it. These have been pointed out by a number of experts in the field of conceptual behavior, such as Bourne (1966), Nelson (1974), Johnson (1972), and especially by Bruner, Goodnow, and Austin (1956). The following are most significant for our purposes. First, the process of categorization is a ubiquitous cognitive activity which, it has been argued convincingly, is implicated not only in concept formation, but also in perception (see for example Neisser, 1967; Bruner, 1957), in memory (see for example Bousfield, 1953; Miller, 1956), in problem solving (see for example the literature on functional fixedness in Wason and Johnson-Laird, 1968), and in almost every aspect of linguistic behavior (see for example Labov, 1973), including language development, a claim that the present volume, among others, should substantiate. Second, the ability to categorize allows us to reduce the complexity of the world to make it manageable. If we were to respond to every object we encountered as unique, we would soon be overwhelmed by the diversity of our environment. Fortunately, however, the ability to categorize allows us to group together the immense number of objects and events we experience into a smaller number of categories or classes and thus to respond to those objects in terms of their category membership. Third, the ability to categorize provides us with a mechanism for rendering the unfamiliar familiar. If a novel object can be assigned to a category it can be treated accordingly. Fourth, and of greatest significance, when an individual categorizes an object he can go beyond what is perceptually given, can draw inferences about the object so categorized, and can attribute to it properties which are true of the category as he knows it. For example, if I categorize a four-legged furry thing seen in a forest as a mammal (and if I am correct) I know that it has a heart, has lungs, respires, is probably capable of spontaneous movement, of reproduction, of nursing its young, of digestion, and so on. Thus, to categorize is to know, and in particular, to know more than is available to one's senses. The most fundamental kinds of such inferences are functional in nature. For example, if I see something which is red, round, and shiny and if I therefore categorize it as an apple, I can infer that it is edible and I can use this inference as a guide to my future actions with respect to that object. If I am hungry, for example, I may pick it up and eat it. Thus the capacity to categorize provides one with direction for future instrumental activity.

While it is agreed that concepts underlie the process of categorization, it is not correct to simply equate a concept with the process of categorization as is often done. Concepts mediate categorization but concepts are not the resultant categories. Moreover, there is more to a concept than a mechanism for categorization. As noted above, a crucial benefit to be derived from the ability to categorize is that it provides a means of going beyond the perceptual information given to other kinds of knowledge about the objects or events so categorized, the most basic of which are functional in nature. These other kinds of knowledge are as much a part of one's concept, and as important, as the perceptual knowledge which permits identification.

Thus a concept is all of the knowledge possessed by an individual about a category of objects or events. Part of this knowledge is primarily perceptual in nature and permits the assignment of objects or events to categories or classes. But in the most important cases (i.e., "natural" concepts), perceptual knowledge is only a subset of all of the knowledge possessed by an individual about that category of things, and therefore, only a part of the concept's meaning for him. In addition to knowing what the instances of categories look like, sound like, feel like, taste like and so on, one also knows other nonperceptible attributes about those instances, such as their origins, their internal constituents, their relations to other things in the world, and most fundamentally, the uses to which they can be put, their implications for him.

This view of conceptual knowledge is related to the fundamental distinction to be used throughout the entire analysis of the child's concepts to be presented in this book, the distinction between extension and intension. Both in studies of concepts and of word meanings, philosophers, linguists, and psychologists have often distinguished between the extension of a concept or a word and its intension (see for example Goodman, 1972; Brown, 1958a; Nelson, 1973a; Miller, 1975; Johnson, 1972; Inhelder and Piaget, 1964; Fodor, 1975; Anglin, 1976; Miller and Johnson-Laird, 1976). By extension is meant the set of objects which are instances of the concept or word. By intension is meant the properties which define the concept or word. So for example, if in a study of concept attainment the experimenter decides that the subjects' task is to discover a concept such as ALL FIGURES CONTAINING A RED TRIANGLE SURROUNDED BY TWO BORDERS, the extension of the concept to be attained is the set of figures which satisfy those specifications, while the intension of the concept is the conjunctive set of properties or, as they are called, defining attributes, red, triangle and two borders, which constitute the specifications. To take another example, the extension of the more natural concept ANIMAL is the set of dogs, cats, fish, birds, insects, and so forth, which are its instances. The intension of the concept ANIMAL is the set of properties—lives, breathes, digests, is capable of spontaneous motion, and the like—which define it. When applied to verbal concepts the distinction between extension and intension is the same as the distinction between reference and meaning. A term can be used to refer to or denote a given set of objects, those included in its extension. Moreover, a term has a meaning above and beyond the objects denoted by it, that is, its intension.

Thus a concept is a hypothetical construct which consists of all of the knowledge an individual possesses about a category of objects or events. This knowledge includes both information about what objects or events are instances of the concept, that is, knowledge of its extension, and also information about the properties which can be predicated of the instances of that concept, that is, knowledge of its intension. A complete account of conceptual structure must deal with both of these kinds of knowledge, with both extension and intension.

To really understand the process of concept formation it is necessary to study it scientifically. A variety of methods have in the past been adopted to scrutinize this cognitive activity, and to some extent the methods chosen have determined the ways in which concept formation and conceptual structure have been described. That is to say, the presuppositions implicit in the materials and procedures employed in the investigation of conceptual behavior, the particular windows through which it has been observed, have often forced a particular view of that behavior. Before the approach to the study of concept formation which has been adopted here is set forth, it will be helpful to characterize the way in which this notion has been previously studied, since the present approach both builds upon and diverges from earlier approaches to the problem. Specifically, I shall present an overview of three approaches to the study of concept formation which are of most relevance to the present inquiry.

The Traditional Approach to Concept Formation

Typically in the research which I am calling the traditional approach to concept formation, an array of stimuli is used which represents every possible combination of a number of simple sensory invariants or perceptual properties. As an example, an investigator might use a set of twenty-seven figures, with each figure showing either a circle, a triangle, or a square, which is either black, white, or red and which is surrounded by either one, two, or three borders. The experimenter decides at the outset that the members of some subset of these are to be instances of the concept while the remainder are noninstances. Most often the concept is defined in terms of a conjunctive set of some of the sensory invariants displayed by the stimuli. To pursue our example, the concept might be defined as the class of all stimuli which contain a circle and are surrounded by two borders. Thus, of the set of twenty-seven stimuli, three would be instances (the black, white, and red circles which are surrounded by two borders) and the remaining twenty-four would be noninstances.

There are two basic paradigms which have been used to study the attainment of concepts in this literature. The first is the reception paradigm in which the experimenter presents a stimulus to the subject who is asked to guess whether or not it is an instance of the concept. After his guess the experimenter tells him whether he is correct or not. Then the experimenter presents another stimulus and the subject again guesses whether or not it is an instance. This procedure continues until the subject has satisfied some criterion for having attained the concept, such as a certain number of errorless consecutive responses or the verbalization of the relevant attributes and their rule of combination. The second is the selection paradigm which is similar except that the subject is presented with the array of stimuli and he chooses one, guessing whether or not it is an instance of the concept, after which the experimenter gives him feedback. Then the subject chooses another stimulus, guesses again, is given feedback, and so on until he has satisfied the criterion. The important difference between the two methods is that in the selection paradigm the subject has the freedom to choose which stimuli he wants to test, whereas in the reception paradigm the order of presentation is entirely under the experimenter's control.

Notice that in such research, because of the choice of materials used, a concept is "well defined" as a group of objects which share a common set of features, that there is an explicit rule characterizing the necessary relation among the features which is usually conjunction, and that the features themselves are most often simple sensory invariants. The properties which actually determine whether or not a given object is an instance of the concept are called defining attributes. The properties which the subject thinks determine whether or not an object is an instance of the concept at any given time are called criterial attributes. In a sense, the process of attaining a concept is a process of socialization in which the defining attributes become criterial for the individual. The subject is often described as deliberately modifying his own criteria through the appropriate use of feedback until they conform to the ones the experimenter has in mind. Thus, according to a procedure that is akin to analysis by synthesis or the hypothetico-deductive method, the subject is often characterized as abstracting a set of defining attributes in the process of discovering a concept.

The resultant view of conceptual structure as a conjunctive set of sensory invariants has been with us since Aristotle's time at least and characterizes much of the psychological literature on concept formation or concept attainment (e.g., Hull, 1920; Heidbreder, 1946a, b; Vygotsky, 1962; Bruner, Goodnow, and Austin, 1956; Bourne, 1966; see also Levine, 1969, 1971). Probably the most extensive and influential series of studies in this tradition were performed by Bruner and his colleagues (Bruner, Goodnow, and Austin, 1956). Readable summaries of this work have been presented by Bourne (1966), by Johnson (1972), and by Posner (1973, Chapter 4).

To be sure, the preceding description of this tradition has been somewhat oversimplified. For example, in addition to concepts defined by conjunctive rules, researchers have occasionally studied concepts defined by disjunctive rules in which stimuli are instances if they possess any one of a number of defining attributes (see for example, Chapter 6 in Bruner, Goodnow, and Austin, 1956) and concepts defined by a relation between or among the defining attributes (see especially Smoke, 1932, 1933). Moreover, the research has not always used geometrical figures (see for example, Heidbreder, 1946a, b; Vygotsky, 1962). Nonetheless, it is fair to say that in this research a concept is almost always well defined in terms of the presence of one or more sensory invariants and when more than one sensory invariant is involved the rule of combination is usually that of conjunction.

The result of a great deal of investigation in this tradition has been a detailed and often elegant description of the strategies adopted by subjects when confronted with this sort of problem (see especially Bruner, Goodnow, and Austin, 1956) and the effects of a variety of task variables which facilitate or impede its solution (see Bourne, 1966, Chapter 4). However, the relevance of such work to the formation of "natural" concepts in everyday life has recently been questioned by a variety of authors (see for example Fodor, 1972; Rosch, 1973, 1975; Anglin, 1973; Nelson, 1974; Bransford, 1970; Labov, 1973; Herrnstein and Loveland, 1964; Herrnstein et al., 1976; see also Wittgenstein, 1953; Cassirer, 1923, 1946). In general the criticisms almost all claim that the model of concepts implicit in such work does not accurately reflect the structure of real or natural concepts. The argument is that concepts such as ALL BLACK FIGURES WITH ONE BORDER or ALL RED TRIANGLES WITH TWO DOTS are not the kinds of concepts we learn in everyday life and, what is worse, they are not even like such concepts.

Of the various specific criticisms of this kind seven are most relevant for our purposes. First, several authors have pointed out that most natural concepts are ill-defined (Neisser, 1967; Rosch, 1973; Fodor, 1972; Herrnstein and Loveland, 1964; Herrnstein et al., 1976; Labov, 1973). Recall that in the classic literature the assumption is that concepts are well defined, usually as a conjunctive set of perceptual attributes such as "black" and "circle." Yet in the case of such natural concepts as PERSON or TREE it has been pointed out that there is usually no such simple set of sensory attributes whose conjunction determines all and only the instances of those concepts. Rather it is argued, such concepts are fuzzy around the edges and exceedingly difficult to define precisely. It may seem that a reasonable definition of PERSON is "a featherless biped," but such a definition fails to exclude such nonpersons as monkeys and plucked chickens. Moreover, most observers would agree that the possession of feet is not really essential to personhood. In his *Philosophical Investigations* the philosopher Wittgenstein (1953) has an extended discussion of how natural language concepts cannot be specified in terms of a set of features shared by all of the members of those concepts. One of the examples which he uses to illustrate his point is the word *game*. He points out that there is no single characteristic nor a set of characteristics which all and only games share in common. Not all games involve boards (e.g., tennis), or winning and losing (e.g., ring around the roses), or competition between teams (e.g., checkers), or even more than one person (e.g., solitaire). The first definition of the word *game* given in Webster's dictionary is "amusement or diversion." The problem with this definition is that it is too broad since it would include such activities as playing a musical instrument, square dancing, or painting for pleasure, activities which are not usually thought of as games.

It might seem that it would be easier to construct a precise definition for terms referring to concrete objects as compared to terms denoting more abstract notions such as *game*. However, even the names of objects are more often than not difficult to define exactly. Consider for example the term *chair*. Webster defines *chair* as "a seat with four legs and a back for one person." However, not all chairs in fact have four legs or backs, as in the case of beanbag chairs. One might drop the perceptual criteria and define *chair* primarily in terms of function as "an object whose normal function is for seating one person." Such a definition, since it is primarily based upon use, has many advantages but still there would seem to be problems with it. For example, under this definition a stool would count as a chair. But is a stool really a chair?

This example suggests the real problem with attempts to construct definitions which include all and only the instances denoted by a given class name. If one could decide exactly which things are in fact instances of the class, then it would be possible to generate a precise definition. However, it is sometimes not clear whether certain things are or are not to be included in the class—they straddle the border as it were, making classifications difficult and therefore pre-empting the possibility of forming a perfectly precise definition. Is a stool a chair or not? Is coffee food? Is a virus an animal? The point is that there are, in the case of most natural concepts, objects which seem to lie on the borders and for which it is often difficult to decide whether or not they are, or are not, to be considered instances. Some objects are clearly instances, some are clearly not, but for some objects it is not at all clear. In the classic literature on concept formation concepts are assumed to be well defined such that any stimulus is clearly either an instance or it is not. The resulting model of conceptual structure does not therefore mirror the nature of natural concepts which, as argued above, are often fuzzy around the edges and therefore ill-defined.

Second, not only are the boundaries of natural concepts fuzzy but also not all the instances of a given natural concept are equally good as instances of that concept. Even though adults will agree that both dogs and praying mantises are animals, they will also agree that dogs are better, or more typical, animals than are praying mantises. Similarly, although they will agree that both robins and penguins are birds, they will also point out that robins epitomize the category, whereas penguins are somewhat atypical birds. Such intuitions show up in the way we sometimes modify our statements, in which we assign various instances to superordinate categories. For example, we would say that "a robin is a *true* bird," but not that "a penguin is a *true* bird," since we recognize penguins as somehow deviant; we would say that *"technically speaking,* a penguin is a bird," but not *"technically speaking,* a robin is a bird," since a robin is the quintessence of what it means to be a bird (Lakoff, 1972; see also Smith, Shoben, and Ripps, 1974).

Rosch has recently validated such arguments empirically (see Rosch, 1973, 1975). She has argued that most natural concepts have internal structure such that they consist of certain central or prototypical instances which are "surrounded by" other more peripheral less typical instances. She has found that adults find it a meaningful task to rate instances with respect to their degree of centrality to a given concept and that they tend to agree in their judgments. Moreover, she has found that such judgments are correlated with the performance of adults and of children in certain information-processing tasks, suggesting the psychological reality of a construct such as centrality (see also Smith, Shoben, and Ripps, 1974).

In the traditional approach, a concept is usually defined as a conjunctive set of perceptual attributes. Thus an object either is an instance (if it possesses all of the attributes) or it is not (if it does not) and there is no question of degree of membership. Thus the notion of concepts which emerges from the classic approach does not model more natural concepts since it fails to acknowledge the fact that they usually have the kind of internal structure described above.

Third, in describing a concept as a list of perceptual attributes abstracted from its instances, psychologists have tended to disregard certain kinds of conceptual knowledge which we surely have about those instances. An important part of our conceptual knowledge includes relational and configurational characteristics of the instances of a concept in addition to the sensory attributes taken alone. For example, a red triangle is different from a red patch and a triangle but this difference is not captured by the usual account of concepts as being a list of perceptual invariants (Bransford, 1970). Similarly, in addition to knowing that a dog has a mouth, a nose, eyes, a head, a torso, a tail, and four legs, we also know that the mouth is slightly below the nose, which is slightly below the eyes, and that the body is between the head and the tail, above the legs, and so on. Of course one could add to one's description of a concept a list of such relational or configurational characteristics, but this has not typically been done. Moreover, it is not clear that it would be wise to do so since the resultant list would become extremely long and unwieldy and the proposition that such a list would be stored in memory for each and every natural concept should not be accepted uncritically given the limits of human memory. It would seem to be more economical to postulate that people are capable of conjuring up something like an "image" of an instance of a concept and can read such configurational characteristics from the "image."

Fourth, typically in the literature which I have dubbed the traditional approach to concept formation, every possible combination of the values of attributes is represented in the stimulus array from which the subject must construct a concept. For example, if the stimuli in such an array were based on three dimensions (form, color, number of borders) with two attributes along each dimension (circle vs. square, black vs. white, and one vs. two borders), every one of the possible eight (2^3) combinations of the values would be present in the array. This however is not really the way the world is. The attributes of real objects do not occur in every possible combination with equal probability; that is, they are not orthogonal. Rather, there are definite correlations among attributes as they occur in real objects. For example, an object with a beak and two legs is far more likely to have wings and feathers than an object with no beak and four legs. An animal which speaks is far more likely to wear clothing, to have two legs, and to live in a house than an animal which does not. In this sense the stimuli used in the classic literature do not mirror the nature of the objects and events actually encountered in everyday life from which natural concepts are formed.

Fifth, notice that in the typical study in the classic literature an important problem has already been solved for the subject. The set of stimuli from which he must abstract a set of defining attributes has been chosen by the experimenter. If one is presented a set of objects and if required to do so it is often a relatively easy matter to infer a set of properties which make those objects similar. However, in the formation of natural concepts the question arises of why and how the objects are grouped together in the first place. There must be some reason for choosing as instances a particular group of objects before one can abstract out a set of defining attributes. This process which is fundamental to concept formation and a prerequisite for the abstraction of predictive attributes has been most often tacitly presupposed in the classic literature (Cassirer, 1923, 1946; Nelson, 1974). While some authors, and in particular Bruner, Goodnow, and Austin (1956), have acknowledged the difference between the abstraction of predictive attributes (concept attainment) and a prior process of concept formation, others have not and in general only the abstraction process has in fact been studied.

Sixth, the answer that Cassirer and Nelson both suggest to the question of why we group together a certain set of objects in the first place is that the grouping is based upon function. While their ultimate definitions of *function* differ somewhat perhaps, both authors have argued that the essence of a concept resides in the function of its instances. This seems to be especially true of concepts of man-made objects, such as CHAIRS, TOYS, MONEY, and so on. The critical aspect of the instances of the concept CHAIR is not that chairs have a back or four legs but rather that one can sit on them. The critical aspect of a ball is not that it is round, but rather that you can roll it and throw it and bounce it. The critical aspect of a door is not that it is rectangular or that it is made of wood, but rather that you can open it and close it. Thus the defining properties of natural concepts are often functional in nature and not so much a question of perceptual attributes as the traditional literature might lead one to believe. It is true that although the essential attributes of the instances of a concept are often functional it is not correct to say that the perceptual attributes of the instances of a concept are accidental. Function and form are definitely correlated. For example, in order for an object to be rollable, bounceable, and throwable (i.e., to be a ball) it must be spherical, made of resilient material, and small enough to be grasped by the hand. In spite of this correlation, however, the essential aspect of the instances of a natural concept is often function, for regardless of the perceptual similarity of two objects, if they do not serve the same function, they do not usually belong to the same natural concept.

Finally, consider an empirical criticism. It has been shown that children are particularly deficient in abstracting out a set of sensory invariants that make a group of objects similar. For example, Vygotsky (1962) has found that it is not until adolescence that an individual is capable of forming what he calls "true concepts," a capacity which was measured in terms of the child's ability to use certain perceptual attributes such as "tall" and "fat" consistently as a basis for grouping the famous Vygotsky blocks (see also Inhelder and Piaget, 1964). However, there is some suggestive evidence that even the prelinguistic infant may be able to form concepts (Piaget, 1963; Riccuiti, 1965; Nelson, 1973a) and certainly before they go to school children have learned certain terms like *dog, apple,* and *flower* which by five or six years of age they use to refer to roughly the same set of objects as those denoted by the corresponding adult terms. Since preschool children appear to be deficient in abstracting criterial attributes, it would seem that some other conceptual mechanism must be at work to account for such observations.

In view of the many criticisms which have been levied at the traditional approach it is not surprising that alternative approaches to the study of concept formation have recently been developed. Of these, two are of greatest relevance for the present inquiry.

One Alternative to the Traditional Approach: Prototype or Schema Formation

The first alternative to the traditional theory of concept formation to be considered has been called prototype theory or schema theory. The basic idea underlying this approach is that when an individual is presented with several instances of a concept he tends to form an internal representation of the central tendency of the instances to which he has been exposed which can then be used as a guide in classifying new instances. The idea of a prototype goes back to Galton's work with composite photographs in which, for example, he superimposed several faces of the members of a particular family. Galton had found that such a composite photograph served as an especially good representation of the family as a whole.

Much of the recent work on prototype formation has been done with visual stimuli such as random dot patterns or geometrical figures. Consider briefly two recent lines of investigation which should convey the basic findings in the prototype research. In one series of studies Posner and Keele (1968, 1970) generated a set of distortions from each of a set of what they called prototype dot patterns. The prototypes consisted of nine dots arranged in a random fashion on a two dimensional surface. For each of four prototypes four distortions were generated by subjecting the dots in the prototype to a "random walk." Distortions were generated such that the prototype from which they were generated represented the central tendency of the group of distortions as a whole.

In an experiment subjects were trained to respond to the four different distortions of each prototype by pressing the same key. There were four keys in all, one for each set of distortions of each of the four different prototypes. A series of slides showing the distortions were presented one at a time, each slide remaining in view until the subject had pressed one of the four buttons. Then a feedback light came on indicating the appropriate button for that slide which informed the subject whether or not his choice had been correct. This part of the experiment continued until the subject had correctly responded to two complete series in a row. Thus the training phase of the experiment involved a standard paired association technique but notice that the prototypes themselves were not presented during this phase of the study.

In the next phase of the experiment subjects were shown a set of patterns made up of the following kinds: (1) the prototypes which they had never seen before; (2) the old distortions which they had just learned to classify, and; (3) control patterns which were transformations of the prototypes but which had not been seen by the subjects before. Subjects were required to classify them into the correct categories again by pushing the appropriate buttons. Recall that the prototypes represented the central tendency of each of the sets of transformations which had been classified earlier but had not themselves ever been seen before. The old distortions were the stimuli which subjects had learned to correctly classify in the first phase of the experiment. The control patterns were distortions of the same basic set of four prototypes but ones which the subjects had not seen before.

It was found that prototype patterns were correctly classified significantly more than any of the control patterns and in some experiments as well as the old already learned distortions. Moreover, with a delay of a week after the learning task, classification of the memorized distortions declined, whereas there was no decline in the accuracy of classifying the prototype patterns. In a related experiment involving a test of recognition memory Posner (1969) asked subjects to classify patterns as either "old" (i.e., they had seen it before) or "new" (i.e., they had not seen it before). Posner states that in this study "the subjects tended to classify the prototype pattern as 'old' as if they had actually experienced it in the list. The experience of seeing different distortions produced a trace system which misled the subjects into thinking they had seen the prototype of that series when they had not" (Posner, 1973).

The foregoing is actually a simplified overview of this work. The reader is referred to Posner and Keele (1968, 1970) and to Posner (1969, 1973, Chapter 3) for details. It is hoped, however, that the description presented above is sufficient to convey the main theoretical implication of this work which is that when exposed to a series of distortions of the prototype people behaved as though they had formed a schema or prototype which represented the central tendency of those distortions even though they had never actually seen the prototype itself before.

As a second example, consider a related series of experiments performed by Franks and Bransford (1971). The materials they used were not patterns of dots but rather geometrical forms. For example, in their first experiment they used as a prototype or base a rectangular card on the left of which appeared a small red triangle superimposed on a large blue square and on the right of which appeared a small yellow diamond superimposed on a large green circle. They then subjected the base to a number of discrete transformations such as a permutation of the pair of figures on the left of the rectangle with the pair of figures on the right of the rectangle (major constituent permutation), or a change of the large square with a superimposed triangle to a large triangle with a superimposed square (minor constituent permutation), or a deletion of one of the figures, or a substitution of one of the figures (for example a heart for the diamond). By applying one, two, three, or more transformations to the base they generated a set of sixteen stimuli with the major constraint being that the base would be the central tendency or prototype of the set of transformations. Specifically this meant that the base was "the least transformational distance" from the whole set of distortions such that the sum of the numbers of transformations necessary to yield the set of sixteen transformations from the base would be less than the sum of the numbers of transformations which would have to be applied to any other configuration in the set to yield the set of transformations (including the base).

During the training phase of the experiment subjects were presented the sixteen transformations but not the base or prototype. Each of the sixteen transformations was shown to the subjects for five seconds after which they attempted to draw what they had just seen. After each attempt to draw a figure subjects were again shown the configuration so that they could check the accuracy of their reproduction. Subjects were shown and were required to draw each of the sixteen figures twice.

After the training phase of the experiment and a five-minute break subjects were shown a set of thirty-six configurations and were supposed to indicate whether or not they thought they had seen each configuration in the training phase of the experiment and to provide confidence ratings to indicate how certain they felt about whether or not they had seen each one before. Unbeknownst to the subjects all thirty-six configurations shown in this part of the experiment were new. They had not seen any of them before. One of the new configurations was the base or prototype. The remaining thirty-five were transformations of the base but ones which had not been seen before.

The major finding in this and related studies was that recognition ratings were inversely related to a configuration's transformational distance from the prototype, with the base or prototype getting by far the highest rating. In general subjects felt quite confident that they had seen the prototype before even though they had not.

Related studies have been done by Attneave (1957), Dukes and Bevan (1967), and by Reed (1972). Helpful reviews of this literature have been written by Evans (1967) and by Posner (1973, Chapter 3). The gist of the studies is that when subjects are exposed to a set of instances of a concept they tend to form and store in memory a representation of the central tendency of the instances to which they have been exposed which guides them in recognizing new instances of the concept. Generally speaking researchers in the field are not explicit about the form of representation involved although some have hinted that it might take the form of an "abstract image" (e.g., Reed, 1972) or a set of features in semantic space (cf. Smith, Shoben, and Ripps, 1974). It is important to note that what is stored is thought not only to be the central tendency or the prototype but also information about specific instances previously seen as well. Recall that in Posner and Keele's research, subjects were better able to classify old transformations than control patterns which would not have been the case had they only stored prototypes.

In addition to the prototype and information about specific instances subjects also seem to make inferences about the amount of variability of which the instances of a given concept are susceptible. For example, in Posner and Keele's (1968) experiment some subjects were taught either "tight" concepts involving only small transformations of the prototype while others were taught "loose" concepts involving large transformations of the prototype. Following learning both groups of subjects were asked to classify severely distorted transformations. Subjects who had been taught the "loose" concepts based on highly variable transformations did better on the severe distortions than subjects who had learned the "tight" concepts based on transformations of small variation. Thus, in addition to forming a representation of the central tendency of the instances of a concept, they also appear to have formulated some conception of the boundaries or breadth of the concept on the basis of their exposure to specific instances.

Posner (1973), in reviewing this work, calls concepts based on prototype or schema formation "iconic," which he distinguishes from "symbolic" concepts based upon the abstraction of defining attributes. He argues that lower animals are capable of forming such iconic concepts and that they have their basis in more primitive kinds of processes than the conscious, analytic, and reflective processes involved in what I have been calling the traditional research on concept formation.

The picture of conceptual structure which emerges from the prototype research appears to have at least some advantages over the model of conceptual structure suggested by the traditional literature. The idea that a concept consists of a prototype and some notion of a boundary might be used to account for some of the problems plaguing the view that a concept is a conjunctive set of sensory invariants. The idea of a prototype is consistent with the argument that some instances are better or more typical instances of a concept than others. Specifically, the closer the instance to the prototype, the better or more typical it would be. Similarly, such a view is consistent with the idea that certain stimuli straddle the borders of concepts making the decision as to whether or not they should be included in the concept difficult. Under the prototype conception these would be those peripheral stimuli at or near the boundaries of the concept. If the prototype took the form of an abstract image as has sometimes been implied, then configurational and relational characteristics could be read from the image. Finally, the fact that prototype formation appears to be a more primitive process than the abstraction of defining attributes may well imply that preschool children, although not capable of consciously abstracting sensory invariants, are capable of forming concepts through a process similar to prototype formation.

Nonetheless, most of the studies on prototypes have employed such visual stimuli as random dot patterns and geometrical figures which are not the natural kinds of objects we experience in everyday life. In particular, they lack the functional significance which as pointed out earlier is so important to natural concepts. We turn now, therefore, to a consideration of another alternative to the traditional approach to concept formation which is explicitly based on function.

A Second Alternative to the Traditional Approach: Function

Although others have implicated function in the process of concept formation (see especially Piaget, 1952, 1962), the most explicit recent statement of the importance of function in the process of concept formation is contained in the work of Nelson (1973a, b; 1974). Unlike the other theories thus far considered, Nelson's theory of concept formation is developmental, in that she tries to account for the way in which the child forms concepts as he grows up.[1] Indeed, according to Nelson the child forms con-

[1] In discussing conceptual development in the child in general I have at times used masculine pronouns such as *he* and *his* with reference not just to boys but to both girls and boys. This is a conventional practice although it is regrettable that there do not exist pronouns in English which are neutral with respect to gender.

cepts even prior to his learning of language and when he does first learn to speak the words of the language he simply affixes them to concepts which have already been well formed (see also Macnamara, 1972). Such a view differs from earlier interpretations of the relation between the child's first words and his concepts, the old view being that the child forms concepts to match the word, or that the word is an invitation to form a concept.

Nelson (1974) suggests that there are four steps in forming a concept which take place in the following order: First the child identifies an object as an object rather than as a picture or image or collection of features. The second step is "the identification of important relationships of objects and assigning individuals on the basis of their functional relations to a synthesized 'chunk' or concept" (Nelson, 1974). This is the crucial step in concept formation according to Nelson and is the step that implicates the functions of objects in the process. In Nelson's work function is defined in two ways: (1) the uses to which objects are put and, (2) what the objects themselves do. Thus a concept like APPLE might be initially conceptualized in terms of the operation of eating that the child can perform on apples whereas a concept like DOG might be initially conceptualized in terms of the actions the child has experienced a dog engaging in, such as barking, running, scratching, and tail wagging. This twofold definition of function in terms of both use and action is somewhat unorthodox and perhaps it should be pointed out here that in the research to be presented later in this book which concerns function (see especially Chapters 6 and 7), function has been defined in terms of use but not in terms of action. At any rate, conceptualization in terms of function according to Nelson "does not require more than one member; a single object in its relations may be conceptualized as readily as (perhaps more readily than) a collection of objects" (Nelson, 1974).

The third step in the process involves the "identification of new concept instances by noting the salient stable characteristics of members included in the concept on functional grounds and forming a hierarchy of identificational attributes therefrom" (Nelson, 1974). Thus this step involves the abstraction of sensory invariants as in the traditional model and the difference between this step and the preceding one corresponds to the distinction between concept formation and concept attainment (see Bruner, Goodnow, and Austin, 1956).

Fourth and finally, the child attaches a name to the concept so formed. Notice that this implies that the meaning of a word is basically correct from the outset.

Nelson illustrates her theory of conceptual development in terms of the way in which a particular child might form the concept BALL. The process might begin, for example, when the child directs his attention to a ball with which his mother and he are playing. Initially according to Nelson, the concept BALL is conceptualized in terms of all of the salient relationships and acts which the ball is observed to enter into, such as "in the living room," "on the porch," "Mommy throws, picks up, bounces," "I hold, pick up, bounce," and so on. Later, however, when the child experiences another ball, for example, one that another child is playing with in the playground, he notices that certain relationships are identical to the first ball he had experienced, specifically, the functional ones such as rolling, bouncing, and throwing, while other aspects of the experience are different, such as the agent, the location, and so on. As a result of these different experiences, the child is thought to "synthesize" a functional core such as rolls, bounces, throws, which is the essence of the concept BALL, and to replace other kinds of specific information with more general and abstract specifications that acknowledge that the agent, the location, and so on can differ. Notice therefore that what Nelson calls a synthesis of the functions actually involves abstraction, a process which she believes to be in contrast to her approach, although what is abstracted is not a set of perceptual attributes but rather a set of functions. At any rate, the child is now in a position to recognize new instances of the concept BALL provided those new instances are engaged in one of the functions in the core, that is, rolling, bouncing, throwing, and so forth.

However, in order for the child to be able to recognize instances of the concept which are stationary the child eventually is thought to abstract perceptual attributes such as "roundness" which different balls share in common which can then be used to identify new instances even though they may not be engaged in their normal functions. Thus, ultimately the concept includes both functional information and perceptual information. Finally, the child may learn a name for his concept—that is, *ball*.

The functional core is presumed to be not only the first component of the concept to be acquired by children, but also the most important in full-fledged concepts. For example Nelson states, "Thus the minimal statement 'X is a ball' implies the functional core but no more" (Nelson, 1974). And although she had earlier argued that instances are identified on the basis of form, whereas they are formed on the basis of function (Nelson, 1973a), she later argued that in identifying new instances of a concept the functional core relationships are most reliable (Nelson, 1974).

Nelson's interesting theory of conceptual development has the advantage of dealing directly with the ways in which the child forms concepts in his day-to-day encounters with the real world as he grows up and therefore seems more pertinent to concept formation as it normally occurs than either criterial attribute theory or prototype theory. The kinds of concepts she is concerned with (e.g., BALL, DOG, CAR, etc.) seem far more natural than the geometrical figures and random dot patterns with which the other theories are concerned. In particular, they seem to possess the functional significance so important to natural concepts and her point that the essence of full-fledged concepts is often a question of the functions of the instances of those concepts is well taken. Nonetheless her proposal that children initially form concepts on the basis of function should not be accepted uncritically. In order to evaluate her theory of conceptual development it will be necessary to examine the sources of evidence which she offers to support it.

Apart from arguments that functional core theory is consistent with the writings and theories of Piaget (1952) and of Cassirer (1923) there appear to be four major empirical sources of evidence which she has offered as support for the theory. Two of these were experiments performed by herself and her colleagues on young children (Nelson, 1973a). The first was a grouping study which was similar to a previous experiment conducted by Riccuiti (1965) with one major difference. While Riccuiti had investigated the ability of one-to-two-year-old children to group together geometrical forms such as ellipses versus diamonds or cubes versus spheres, Nelson's study included more realistic objects such as (toy) animals versus eating utensils and cars versus planes. Seven infants between nineteen and twenty-two months were studied in Nelson's experiment. Each child was seated in a high chair and presented a variety of sets of eight objects on the tray of the high chair, one set at a time. In each set of eight objects four were of one kind and four were of another kind. The contrasting dimension that distinguished the objects within each set varied from set to set. For example, the basis for classification in one set made up of four large blue plastic planes and four small blue plastic planes was size, while in another set made up of four small green plastic animals and four small yellow plastic animals it was color. In another critical set made up of four small plastic green animals and four small plastic green eating utensils the basis for classification was supposed to be function, while in still another set made up of four small yellow plastic cars and four small blue plastic planes the basis for classification according to Nelson could have been form, color, or function or any combination of these factors. The children were encouraged to play with the objects and their manipulative behavior was recorded. Following Riccuiti (1965) two kinds of measures were used to assess whether or not the children evinced categorization behavior: (1) sequential choice behavior, in which evidence for categorization was suggested if a child having manipulated one member of a subset (e.g., a small green animal), then proceeded to manipulate another member of the same subset (e.g., another small green animal) more often than a member of the other subset (e.g., a small green eating utensil) than would be expected by chance; (2) grouping behavior, in which evidence for categorization was suggested if the child spatially ·separated one subset (e.g., the animals) from the others (e.g., the eating utensils). The finding was that the children demonstrated categorization behavior according to these two measures for the set in which the basis for classification was supposed to have been function and for the set in which it was supposed to have been color, form, and function but not for the other sets.

This study, like Riccuiti's earlier study, does suggest that children of less than two years will show categorization behavior with certain kinds of materials. However, it does not provide unequivocal support for Nelson's claim that "the function or use of objects is a salient principle of categorizing behavior with children less than two years of age" (Nelson, 1973a) since it is not clear that the sole basis for categorizing the small plastic green animals and the small plastic green eating utensils was function as it was supposed to be. Although the objects which were used in the study were not shown, it nonetheless seems quite clear that the animals would have been more perceptually similar to one another and that the utensils would have been more perceptually similar to one another than the animals would have been to the eating utensils and therefore the basis for categorization may well have been differences in form rather than differences in function.

The same sort of problem crops up in another interesting experiment by Nelson (1973a) which was also taken as support for her "functional core" theory. In this study adults were asked to rate twenty-seven objects with respect to their degree of similarity in either form or function to instances of the concept BALL. On the basis of these ratings ten objects were chosen to be used in an experiment with children. One of these was a ball. Three were like a ball in function but unlike in form according to the adult ratings (an oval-shaped block covered in soft plastic, a small soft rubber football, a large hard plastic whiffle football). Three were like a ball in form but unlike in function according to the adult ratings (the 8 ball—a heavy black ball of hard plastic used in a fortunetelling game, the bulletin ball—a rotating cork sphere on a stand with holes for holding pencils, and a spherical rattle orbiting within a round flat stand). Finally, three were unlike a ball in both form and function according to the adult ratings (a small frisbee, a square block, and a cylindrical-shaped rattle).

The child was seated either on a chair or on his mother's lap and the ten objects were spread out in front of him in a random order. The child was asked to give the experimenter the "ball." After he had picked one of the objects up that object was removed and the request was repeated until ultimately five choices had been made. Following this the five objects were then put back on the table and the child was allowed to play with all of them. After ten minutes of free play the objects were again spread out in front of the child who was again asked for the "ball" until five choices had been made as before.

The basic findings were that on the first test children chose the objects alike in form about equally often as the objects alike in function. On the second test they chose the objects alike in function more often than those alike in form. Nelson concludes her discussion of the experiment by stating that "the results indicate that in this experiment at least function was as potent as form in identifying new concept members and it was more potent than form when the child was given the opportunity to manipulate the objects" (Nelson, 1973a).

The problem with the experiment which Nelson in fact acknowledges concerns the choices of stimuli, especially the three which were supposed to be alike in function but unlike in form—the oval-shaped block covered in hard plastic and the two footballs. These stimuli are actually at least somewhat perceptually similar to instances of the concept BALL, certainly more so than the stimuli which were unlike in both form and function. Thus, it seems possible that the determinant of the child's overgeneralization in the case of these objects was the result of perceptual similarity as opposed to or in addition to functional similarity. Even more problematic was the fact that, as Nelson reports, the two footballs were often called *balls* by the children.

The problem with this and the preceding study is a result of the fact that it is often difficult to find objects which are functionally similar to instances of a concept but not perceptually similar, for function often determines form. As pointed out earlier, if an object is to be rollable, throwable, and bounceable it must be somewhat rounded, resilient, and small enough to be grasped by the hand.

If it were not for these problems the studies described above would seem to indicate that young children generalize and overgeneralize on the basis of function. Although Nelson herself predicts at least in one place that the child "generalizes to new instances on the basis of form" (Nelson, 1973a), the experiments summarized above taken at face value would seem to indicate that function was equally effective as form in enticing the child to generalize. However, as noted above, this may not have been the case because of the problems with the choice of materials in these experiments. Other studies have indicated that overgeneralization is most often the result of perceptual similarity rather than functional similarity (see for example E. Clark's [1973] analysis of the diary literature; also see Chapter 6 of the present volume).

A third kind of evidence mentioned, although not emphasized, by Nelson in support of her theory concerns the nature of the child's definitions of verbal concepts. In my opinion this is the strongest source of evidence implicating function in the child's early concepts. As Nelson points out, children often provide definitions in terms of use or action, for example "a hole is to dig," "a dog goes ruff" (see Feifel, 1949; Feifel and Lorge, 1950; Wolman and Barker, 1965; Al-Issa, 1969; Campbell, 1975). While the child's inclination to define words in terms of use or action is striking it should nonetheless be pointed out that most of the studies examining children's definitions have dealt with children of five years or older and that they have also often revealed a tendency in the child to provide definitions in terms of concrete perceptual properties as well (e.g., "straw is yellow," "a puddle is mud," "a flower looks like a star"). It should also be noted that children are not really so much more likely than adults to define verbal concepts in terms of use even though the literature on the subject often describes the child's definitions as being in terms of use as opposed to the adult's which are described as "abstract." In fact both children and adults often mention use in their definitions with the difference being that children mention only use (e.g., gown: "you wear it") whereas adults mention a superordinate category as well as use (e.g., gown: "a beautiful dress that women wear").

Finally, the fourth kind of empirical evidence which Nelson offers to support her theory and the one stressed by her most, concerns the nature of the child's first terms of reference. She points out correctly that these words usually denote objects which the child either acts upon (e.g., *ball, apple*) or which move and change in interesting ways (e.g., *dog, car*) in his environment. Other studies (see for example Leopold, 1939; Stern, 1930), including the present one (see Chapter 2), confirm that these are in fact the kinds of words which the child acquires first. Nonetheless, knowledge of the words learned first by children does not directly indicate the conceptual structure underlying those words. Although they are known to be somewhat selective in sampling vocabulary from their linguistic environment (Leopold, 1939; Nelson, 1973b), nonetheless the actual words acquired by children are to some extent dependent on the naming practices of others and in their early preschool years of their parents in particular (Brown, 1958b; Chapter 3 of the present volume). In order to really understand the nature of the conceptual structure underlying these first words it is necessary to study their meaning for the child, which requires an analysis of their extension and their intension. Nelson's (1973b) study of the first words acquired by children was based upon records kept by mothers of the words occurring in the child's spontaneous speech but did not involve an examination of either their extension or their intension. In the later chapters of this book (in particular Chapters 4–7) both the extension and the intension of the child's first terms of reference will be studied in detail in the hope of revealing the nature of the conceptual structure underlying their use in his preschool years.

The Present Approach

As indicated in the opening paragraph of this chapter, the approach taken
to investigate conceptual structure in early childhood in this book has been
to examine the ways in which the child uses, misuses, understands, and
describes his first terms of reference, specifically, the common nouns he
acquires before his entry into school. Of the approaches considered in the
preceding pages the present approach is closest to Nelson's with the difference being, as noted above, that the emphasis here is on the extension
and the intension of the child's first terms of reference, in addition to their
entry into his vocabulary. The fundamental assumption underlying this approach is that beneath every term of reference acquired by the child is a
concept, however rudimentary and however different from the corresponding concept underlying the same term of reference in adults. Thus this book
shares the assumption stated by Ayn Rand in her little-read book *Introduction to Objectivist Epistemology* (1966–67) that "a word is merely a
visual-auditory symbol used to represent a concept; a word has no meaning
other than that of the concept it symbolizes." Thus, for example, underlying a word such as *dog* there is a concept DOG which represents all of the
knowledge that any given individual possesses of dogs. The concept includes both knowledge of extension (what things he believes to be dogs)
and knowledge of intension (the properties which he believes to be true of
the dogs which comprise the extension of the concept). The concept is
thought to mediate both linguistic categorization, for example, to guide the
application of the term *dog* to collies, terriers, retrievers, and so on, and to
allow inference about the objects so categorized above and beyond what is
perceptually apparent.

Of course the concepts underlying English nomenclature are only one
kind of concept which humans are capable of forming. For example, under
laboratory conditions adults are capable of attaining concepts such as all
red triangles surrounded by two borders and all green circles possessing
five dots (see Bruner, Goodnow, and Austin, 1956; Bourne, 1966). However, as argued earlier, such concepts are not the natural kinds of concepts which children tend to learn as they grow up. Thus far, although I
have often referred to "natural" concepts and have contrasted them with
the kinds of artificial concepts studied in the traditional literature, I have
not explicitly stated what a natural concept is. Similarly, in other critiques
of the traditional approach psychologists have often also contrasted "natural concepts" or "natural categories" with artificial concepts and categories,
but again have not usually been explicit about what a natural concept or
category is. However, when one examines the kinds of natural concepts to
which these authors refer they often (though not always) seem to be such

concepts as PEOPLE, TREES, WATER (Herrnstein and Loveland, 1964; Herrnstein et al., 1976), TOYS, BIRDS, FRUIT (Rosch, 1973), BALLS, CARS, and DOGS (Nelson, 1974). That is to say, they are often concepts of classes of objects denoted by terms of reference.

Other arguments can be made to support the contention that the concepts labeled by terms of reference are more natural than the kinds of artificial concepts often studied by psychologists. For example, the point has been made that natural concepts are part of a system of hierarchically related concepts (Vygotsky, 1962; Bruner, Olver, and Greenfield, 1966; Anglin, 1970, 1973; Fodor, 1972). Such a hierarchic system is not an evident property of the concepts which have been studied in the traditional approach. However, English nomenclature clearly constitutes this kind of system. A given object can be named in several different ways and each name serves to classify it at a certain level of generality. For example, this particular dog might be called *Lassie,* a *collie,* a *dog,* an *animal,* an *organism,* an *object,* or an *entity.* The name *Lassie* is very specific and like all proper names focuses on the uniqueness of the object being named. It is a generic term only in that it applies to the same object over transformations in space and time. *Collie* is a relatively specific or concrete term which groups this dog together with the members of a certain breed of dogs and distinguishes it from other breeds such as pointers, spaniels, and chihuahuas. *Dog* is a more inclusive name which groups together this dog with several breeds of dogs and distinguishes it from other kinds of animals such as cats, cows, horses, and men. The name *animal* groups this dog with a great variety of living things such as cats, people, birds, fish, and insects and distinguishes it from other forms of life such as trees, flowers, and shrubs as well as from the inanimate things of the world. The word *organism* serves to group it with all living things and to distinguish it from inanimate matter. The word *object* is extremely general and serves to group it with the other things in the physical world and to distinguish it from the concepts of a mental world such as IDEA, TRUTH, or JUSTICE, which can neither be pointed to nor touched. This is only one example which could be used to illustrate that English nomenclature constitutes an interrelated hierarchic system.

Another fact which suggests that concepts labeled by terms of reference are natural is the apparent ease with which they are learned by children. As noted before, the child seems particularly deficient in forming concepts based upon a conjunctive set of sensory invariants (Vygotsky, 1962; Inhelder and Piaget, 1964). On the other hand, the one-year-old child produces several terms of reference in his spontaneous speech (see Leopold, 1939; Stern, 1930; Lewis, 1959; Moore, 1896), can comprehend even more (Huttenlocher, 1974; Leopold, 1939; Stern, 1930; Lewis, 1959), and by the time he is ready to go to school it has been estimated that he has a vocabulary in the neighborhood of seventy-five hundred words, many of which are terms of reference (Nelson, 1973b). While the meanings of these terms may not yet be fully developed, he often applies them appropriately and often to instances which he has never before encountered. The child's apparent facility in acquiring such concepts in contrast to his difficulty with others (such as Vygotsky blocks) again suggests that they are more natural in some sense than the others.

At any rate, the present approach has the advantage of being explicit about what is being studied—namely, the child's first terms of reference— an explicitness that has often been lacking in previous discussions of "natural" concepts. It also has the advantage of studying the child at his best. Recently several authors have noted that the situation in which a child is studied will often determine whether or not a developmental psychologist will be willing to attribute to him a given ability or skill (see for example, Fodor, 1972; Bower, 1974; de Villiers and de Villiers, 1974; Brown, 1973; Cole and Bruner, 1971; Anglin, 1970; see also Cole and Scribner, 1974; Labov, 1970). It now appears that it is often a mistake to conclude that a child either has a given ability or that he does not. Rather, very young children will often demonstrate the kinds of skills once believed to be beyond their ken, provided one looks in the right places for them. The argument here is that the right place to look in the preschool child is at his linguistic behavior. The child's progress in learning language in his first five years is a truly remarkable feat. This is so for both grammatical development and semantic development. In the case of syntax, children by the age of five are capable of using a complex system of rules to produce novel grammatical sentences seemingly without effort. One example of their grammatical ability is that before they go to school children are quite able to append tag questions to the ends of sentences, the little rhetorical questions which ask for confirmation as in "Mother and I are going to the store, *aren't we?*" (Brown and Hanlon, 1970). As simple as they may seem, tags are grammatically extremely complex, involving four transformations—pronominalization of the subject, negation, interrogation, and predicate ellipsis. Progress in semantic development is also quite astounding. For example, as noted above children of five years of age have as many as seventy-five hundred words in their working vocabularies (Nelson, 1973b). This is not of course to say that grammatical or semantic development is by any means complete by the time the child goes to school (see for example, Chomsky, 1969; Anglin, 1970), but nonetheless, the linguistic skills that are accomplished by this time are quite remarkable especially when contrasted with the child's apparent difficulty with other kinds of cognitive tasks such as conservation (Piaget, 1965), seriation (Inhelder and Piaget, 1964), and of course mastery of Vygotsky's blocks (Vygotsky, 1962).

The present inquiry of course involves only one aspect of the entire process of language learning, the acquisition of English nomenclature. Nonetheless, arguments can be made that this part of language learning is basic to the enterprise as a whole. For it can be argued that content words (nouns, verbs, adjectives, etc.) must be learned before grammatical inflections (since one needs content words to which to apply the inflections) and that among the content words terms of reference are most basic in the sense that they denote objects "directly" whereas the others refer to actions of objects (verbs), to qualities of objects (adjectives), to qualities of actions of objects (adverbs), and so on. Such an argument is borne out empirically by the findings that grammatical inflections are acquired after content words (Brown, 1973) and that among the content words, terms of reference are acquired first (Stern, 1930; Moore, 1896; Leopold, 1939; however, see Bloom, 1973). At a minimum it is fair to say that such terms of reference are the most numerous class of words acquired by young children (Rescorla, 1976), although individual differences have been noted (Nelson, 1973b), and that the proportion of such words in the child's vocabulary is greater than it is in the vocabulary of adults (Brown, 1958b).

This is not the first psychological investigation to define concepts in terms of word meanings. For example, Vygotsky (1962) had done so previously. However, his experimental studies with the Vygotsky blocks carried with them certain presuppositions about the nature of word meanings and in particular that word meanings or concepts are a conjunctive set of sensory invariants (see Fodor's [1972] critique of Vygotsky [1962]), which, as argued earlier, may well be inappropriate as a model for either concepts or word meanings. Rather than make assumptions about the structure of word meanings, it would seem to be preferable to study the ways in which real words are produced, comprehended, and described and to infer their underlying structure from such behavior.

Recently a number of other investigators have in fact studied the meanings of terms of reference in preschool children. In fact each of the three models of conceptual structure discussed earlier in this chapter has its counterpart in recent theories of what words mean to children. Specifically E. Clark in her semantic feature theory, has proposed that the child's terms of reference can be characterized as a conjunctive set of perceptual attributes or sensory invariants (E. Clark, 1973, 1974). Although most of her work is not developmental, Rosch has hypothesized that children might initially define a category (i.e., a word) in terms of its central instances rather than in terms of abstract criterial attributes (Rosch, 1973). While not exactly an argument for a prototype, such a view is more akin to the model of conceptual structure emerging from the prototype research than that emerging from say the traditional approach. Others have been more explicit in implicating prototypes beneath the child's words (see Palermo, 1976; Anglin, 1976). Finally, as we have seen, Nelson has argued that the child's first verbal concepts are based upon function. Although Nelson's theory has been considered already at length, I have not described either Clark's work or Rosch's work in any detail. This will be done in later sections of the book. Their theories are only mentioned here to indicate that others have been concerned with the child's terms of reference and that a number of different theoretical positions have been developed to account for them.

It is, however, not necessary at the outset to assume the validity of any model of conceptual structure underlying the child's first terms of reference. Rather it is possible to actually study the child's ability to produce, comprehend, and describe them; to compare their linguistic behavior with the linguistic behavior of adults under the same circumstances; and to be guided by the resulting observations in making inferences about their underlying conceptual structure. It may be that one of the models thus far considered is most able to account for the resulting facts; it may be that some sort of synthesis is required; or it may be that some completely different model will be necessary. Ultimately it is an empirical question.

Thus in this inquiry the nature of what words mean to children is to be determined by studying how they produce, comprehend, and describe those words. Moreover, the nature of what those words mean to adults is also to be determined in the same way. It has been argued that words do not have a single fixed meaning but rather a multiplicity of meanings dependent upon their context of use (see for example Olson, 1970).[2] Some philosophers have gone so far as to deny that words have meanings at all or at least that the construct is of little value (see for example, Quine, 1953; see also Goodman, 1972). Others have pointed out that adults often do not know the true extension or intension of many words as defined in terms of the most recent scientific knowledge (Putnam, 1975). In view of such arguments it would be a mistake to presuppose what words mean to adults. Thus in most of the experiments to be described such assumptions are not made about adults. Rather adults are studied in the same way as children are. For example, a question with which we shall be concerned in Chapter 4 has to do with the differences between the extension of the child's terms of reference as compared to the extension of the same terms as used and understood by adults. In order to make such comparisons it is necessary to establish the range of referents encompassed by such terms in both children and adults since it would not do to presuppose either.

---

[2] It is well taken that many words are polysemous. However, in the studies to be presented in this book we have attempted to choose words for which one meaning was in our judgment primary. For example, one word we used in many studies was *dog*. While Webster's dictionary lists ten definitions for the word *dog*, in our judgment it had one primary meaning—the domesticated mammal.

Basic Definitions

At the risk of being redundant with what has already been described, I shall now attempt to define the important terms that will be used (as they will be used) throughout the entire analysis of the child's first terms of reference to be presented in this book. Other terms of lesser importance will be defined in later sections.

1. TERM OF REFERENCE: *A term of reference is a word and in particular a common noun which denotes or refers to real objects. They are units of speech which, it is assumed, become associated with meanings as the child develops.* Examples are *dog, flower, food,* and *money.*

2. EXTENSION: *The extension of a term of reference includes all of the objects which an individual is willing to denote with that term of reference.* The group of objects comprising the extension of a term of reference will sometimes be called the category of objects denoted by that term. The extension of a term of reference is assumed also to be the extension of the concept underlying that term of reference.

3. INTENSION: *The intension of a term of reference is the set of properties which an individual believes to be true of the instances of the category denoted by that term.*[3]

4. CONCEPT: *The concept underlying a term of reference is all of the knowledge possessed by an individual about the category of objects denoted by that term. This knowledge includes both knowledge of extension and knowledge of intension.*[4]

Throughout this book when a term of reference is being discussed italics are used (e.g., *dog*); when the concept underlying a term of reference is being discussed, small capital letters are used (e.g., DOG).[5]

Notice that the make-up of the extension, of the category, of the intension. and of the concept associated with any given term of reference

[3] In this book intension is defined broadly to include not only properties believed to be true of all and only the instances of a category (i.e., properties which are "defining" of the category for the individual) but also properties believed to be true of only some of the instances of the category and properties believed to be true of more than just the instances of the category (i.e., properties which are "characteristic" of the category for the individual).

[4] This knowledge of course may be generative in nature, and it may have focus, organization, and structure. For example, it may have occurred to the reader that the intension of a concept determines its extension. While it will be argued that this is not always the case, intension and extension are often coordinated, at least in the adult. However, the nature of conceptual knowledge will not be specified here, since much of the rest of this book represents an attempt to characterize its nature in different phases of development.

[5] The use of italics to indicate words in print is a standard convention. Since there is no standard convention for indicating concepts, small capital letters were chosen for certain practical reasons and used for this purpose, a procedure which may be unique to this book.

depends upon the particular individual concerned as they are here defined. There is nothing to prevent differences in the composition of any of these constructs for any given term of reference across individuals and, in particular, between adults and children. Sometimes constructs like extension and intension are defined in terms of some absolute (i.e., scientific) standard. For example, Putnam (1975) defines the extension of a term like *gold* as the set of substances which are truly gold according to the most recent scientific knowledge—that is, those which would be identified as gold by a metallurgist. As he argues, most people will not on their own be able to determine the true extension of many such terms. He goes on to make the interesting point that in our society (and perhaps in all societies) there is a "division of linguistic labor" such that a certain select group of experts knows how to decide whether or not a given metal is gold (i.e., determine its true extension) while the rest of us get by with a certain stereotype of what gold is such as that it is yellow in color, softer than most metals, fairly heavy, and so on. When it is important to know whether or not something really is gold we can consult one of the experts.

At any rate, for Putnam the extension of a term in one's "idiolect" is the true extension of the term, not the objects which he believes to be instances of the category denoted by the term. Similarly, for Putnam meanings (intensions) "are not in the head" but again rather defining properties according to the most recent scientific knowledge. It is well taken that often even adults will not know the "true" extension or intension of a given term of reference. However, in this inquiry extension, intension (or meaning), category, and concept are all defined from the point of view of a particular individual. Thus, for example, the meaning of a word for that individual is taken to be what that word means to him. This may seem like psychologism, but after all this is a psychological investigation (see Katz's [1975] distinction between lexicographical or phenomenological meaning and scientific meaning).

Fundamental Questions about the Child's First Terms of Reference

In the following chapters a series of related investigations will be described whose intent has been to provide answers to three sets of questions considered to be basic to an understanding of the conceptual structure underlying the child's first terms of reference. The first set of questions concerns the first terms of reference to be learned by children. What are the child's first terms of reference? Of the thousands of such category labels, which are among the first to enter the child's vocabulary? What is the order of acquisition of English nomenclature in children and why this particular order? Is the order in which different children acquire these terms invariant or is there variation from child to child? Are the naming practices of mothers related to the order in which children learn English nomenclature? If so what determines the ways in which mothers name objects for their children?

Answers to this first set of questions would seem to be a prerequisite for the investigation of conceptual structure underlying the child's first terms of reference since for such an investigation it is necessary to know which terms to study. However, knowledge of the words acquired first by children does not by itself reveal the nature of the concepts underlying those words since it should not be assumed that they necessarily mean to the child what they might mean to the adult who observes him. Thus the remaining two sets of questions both concern the nature of the concepts underlying the child's category labels. Specifically they are concerned with the extension and the intension of the child's terms of reference respectively.

Therefore the second set of questions deals with the scope or the extension of the child's terms of reference. What is the extension of the child's terms of reference? Does the category of objects to which the child applies a given term differ from the category of objects to which an adult applies the same term? Does the child overgeneralize or undergeneralize his first terms of reference relative to adult standards or both? If he overgeneralizes, what factors entice him to do so? If he undergeneralizes what factors entice him to do so? Does the tendency to overgeneralize or undergeneralize depend upon the particular term of reference being used and if so how? Are these tendencies the same in both studies of comprehension and production or are they different?

The third set of questions concerns the intension of the child's terms of reference. What is the intension of the child's category labels? What properties is the child inclined to ascribe to common nouns? How do these properties differ from those which adults ascribe to the same terms? How does the preschool child verbally define such words? And finally, what is the relation between the intension and the extension of the child's first terms of reference?

The research we have undertaken to attempt to answer these questions will be presented in the next six chapters. Specifically, in Chapters 2 and 3 research will be presented which has been concerned with the order of acquisition of terms of reference in preschool children. In Chapters 4, 5, and 6 a series of studies will be described whose purpose has been to determine the extension of his terms of reference. In Chapter 7 the concern is with the intension or meaning of these words for the child above and beyond their extension and with the relation between intension and extension. Finally, in the last chapter of the book an attempt will be made to draw some conclusions regarding the child's concepts in view of the findings reported in Chapters 2 through 7.

Chapter 2

On the Order of
Acquisition of Category Labels[1]

In thinking about the possible determinants of the order of acquisition of category labels I have found it useful, if somewhat simplistic, to distinguish between horizontal development and vertical development.[2] By horizontal development I mean the acquisition of category labels which classify the world at roughly the same level of generality. Preliminary investigations had revealed that the child is better able to name correctly a picture of an apple than a picture of a persimmon, or a picture of a dog than a picture of an aardvark. These observations are hardly surprising and they suggest simply that the child will learn category labels first for objects which are familiar and important to him in his day-to-day dealings with the world and only later will he learn names for less familiar and less important objects. But what about vertical development, by which I mean the acquisition of category labels at different levels of generality? The child may need a term to refer to his pet collie but the English language, in fact, contains several valid possible names at different levels of generality—for example, *Lassie, collie, dog, mammal, animal, being, thing, entity.* Is it possible to predict the order of acquisition of such hierarchically related category labels?

[1] The experiments reported in this chapter were conducted with great care by Maryellen Ruvolo and Elizabeth Smith. I am very grateful to them and to Marc Fiedler for help with the analysis of the results.
[2] The terms *horizontal development* and *vertical development* as they are used here should not be confused with the same terms as used by other developmental psycholinguists such as McNeill (1970) or Nelson (1973b) although roughly synonymous definitions of these terms have been given by others (e.g., Berlin, 1972).

In his recent book on language development Roger Brown (1973) has dealt with a related problem—how to predict the order in which the child will acquire various grammatical morphemes. Brown's conclusions are that while frequency of occurrence of the morphemes in parental speech to the child is not a good predictor, a metric of semantic complexity (as well as one of grammatical complexity) is predictive of their order of acquisition (see also de Villiers and de Villiers, 1973; Slobin, 1971; H. Clark, 1973a; Haviland and E. Clark, 1974). Is it possible that there exists a definition of semantic complexity for English nomenclature which might allow us to predict the order in which the child will acquire terms of reference at different levels of generality? What are the semantic relationships among category labels which can be ordered along a specific to general dimension such that the category denoted by one word is a proper subset of the category denoted by another word? Consider for example the terms *collie, dog,* and *animal.* Is there some sense in which one of these terms might be considered to be semantically more complex than the others, and might this metric of semantic complexity be a predictor of the order of acquisition of such category labels?

It was pointed out in Chapter 1 that the fundamental distinction to be used throughout the entire analysis of the child's terms of reference to be presented in this book is between the extension of a term and the intension of that term. As it turns out, it is possible to define a metric of semantic complexity for nested category labels either in terms of extension or in terms of intension. Consider first a definition in terms of extension. Semantic complexity might be defined in terms of extension such that a term that refers to a set of objects is semantically more complex than a term which refers to only a subset of those objects. That is to say, according to this definition the more diversity in the referent class for a given category label the more semantically complex it is. If semantic complexity were defined in this fashion and if the resulting metric were the sole predictor of the order of acquisition of category labels, then the order would be *collie* first, *dog* second, and *animal* third, as the arrows in Figure 2.1 illustrate.

Consider now a definition of semantic complexity in terms of intension, that is, the set of properties that defines the word. It is the case that for nested category labels every property which is true of all instances of the superordinate term is also true of all instances of the subordinate term. For example, the properties "live," "breathe," "digest," "is capable of spontaneous motion," and so on, which are the defining properties of the class of ANIMALS are also all true of the class of DOGS. However, there are certain properties which are true of all instances denoted by the subordinate term which are not true for all instances denoted by the superordinate term. For example, "is a mammal" is a predicate which applies to all dogs but not to all animals, and "has four legs," "has fur," "barks," and so on, are predicates which apply to virtually all dogs, but by no means to all animals. If semantic complexity were defined solely in terms of a word's intension such that the term defined by a set of properties was semantically simpler than a term defined by those properties and other properties as well, then according to this definition of semantic complexity *animal* would be simpler than *dog* which would be simpler than *collie*. If this definition of semantic complexity were the sole predictor of the order of acquisition of category labels such that simpler terms are acquired before more complex ones, then the order would be *animal* first, *dog* second, and *collie* third (for this particular hierarchy of terms) as the arrows to the left of Figure 2.2 indicate.

As a matter of fact, several arguments can be offered at the outset

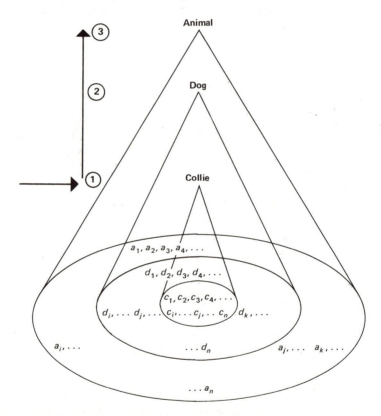

FIGURE 2.1 Schematic representation of the relations among the extensions of the words *collie*, *dog*, and *animal*. If semantic complexity were defined solely in terms of a word's extension and if this definition of semantic complexity were the sole predictor of the order of acquisition of category labels then the order would be *collie* first, *dog* second, and *animal* third, as the arrows indicate.

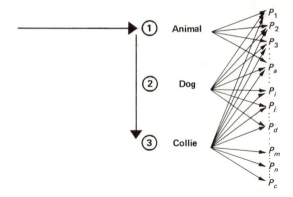

FIGURE 2.2 Schematic representation of the relations among the intensions of the words *collie, dog,* and *animal.* If semantic complexity were defined solely in terms of a word's intension and if this definition of semantic complexity were the sole predictor of the order of acquisition of category labels, then the order would be *animal* first, *dog* second, and *collie* third, as the arrows to the left indicate.

against the plausibility that either of these definitions of semantic complexity will provide a good predictor of the order of acquisition of category labels. First, each definition makes exactly the opposite prediction of the other. Thus, unless one definition is all-important and the other is totally irrelevant neither of the hypothesized progressions will be followed exactly.

Second, the definitions have been formulated in terms of the true extension and the true intension of the terms. It should not be assumed that the child who acquires those terms will instantly understand either the exact scope (extension) or the full meaning (intension) of them. Indeed, it would be a mistake to do so, as later chapters of this book will show. This line of argument of course begs the question of what is meant by the acquisition of a given term of reference. One might insist that a term of reference had not been acquired until its exact extension and full intension had been mastered. However, such stringent criteria would carry with them the implication that most adults let alone children never acquire many simple terms of reference. A more reasonable criterion of acquisition is simply that they can be used to denote at least some objects appropriately.[3] If some such criterion were used then it would not be necessary for a child to have completely mastered either the true extension or the true intension of a given term of reference to satisfy the criterion and the relevance of either in generating predictions about order of acquisition would become more suspect.

---

[3] The exact criterion which we have used to establish that a given term of reference has been acquired by a given child will be described in more detail later in this chapter.

Third, considerations of the capacities of the child and the functions of language would seem to argue against the unidirectional progressions suggested by the two definitions of semantic complexity which have been discussed. If the child were to begin to learn the most specific possible names for every object he encountered the result would be a vast number of terms which taken together might well impose too heavy a burden on memory. On the other hand it seems clear that the child would not initially be taught and therefore learn an extremely general term such as *thing* to refer to every object he encountered since such a term would be of little communicative value in that it would fail to discriminate a given object from any other object. Thus there would seem to be a pull in the direction of generality to reduce the number of terms to be committed to memory and a pull in the direction of specificity to increase the communicative value of the terms learned by the child. If both factors were operative the result would be that the child would often first learn to categorize a given object linguistically at some intermediate level of generality rather than at a very specific level or a very general level.

Finally, neither unidirectional progression is suggested by the literature on the child's vocabulary. It does seem to be true that among the very first words often learned by children are proper nouns (e.g., Moore, 1896; Huttenlocher, 1974) and names for particular people such as *Mommy, Daddy,* and *baby.* Such observations while immediately ruling out the predictive power of the definition of semantic complexity in terms of intension, are consistent with the hypothesis that the definition of semantic complexity in terms of extension is predictive of the order of acquisition of category labels. Moreover, the child's vocabulary has often been described as concrete compared to the vocabulary of adults (e.g., Brown, 1958b; Anglin, 1970). However, it does not seem to be the case that there is a unidirectional specific to general progression in vocabulary development since it has been pointed out by others (e.g., Brown, 1958b) that children will sometimes learn to categorize a given object at some intermediate level of generality and beyond that learn both more specific and more general terms to categorize that object. Such a trend was suggested by some of our preliminary investigations. The child, when shown a picture of a sandal and asked, "What is this?" would call it a *shoe* rather than a *sandal* or *clothing.* He would call a rose a *flower* rather than a *rose* or a *plant;* a collie a *dog* rather than a *collie* or an *animal;* a Volkswagen a *car* rather than a *Volkswagen* or a *vehicle;* and so on. The problem with this sort of observation (and most of the literature on the child's vocabulary) is that since each of the terms *collie, dog,* and *animal* is actually correct for a picture of a collie, we cannot say for sure that children are not capable of producing the specific or the general terms—perhaps they simply prefer to produce the intermediate term for some reason. This is especially problematic for more general terms such as *animal, plant, food,* and so on, since when asked to give a name for a single object, adults certainly, and probably children as well, tend to produce relatively specific names, since these convey more information. Thus the task of naming single pictures will rarely evoke these more general terms even though they may be part of the child's linguistic competence. What is needed therefore is a task which will make the production of specific terms, and general terms, obligatory (see Brown, 1973; de Villiers and de Villiers, 1973).

In puzzling about this problem, Maryellen Ruvolo and I came up with the following solution. We decided to present to the child not a single picture of an object, but rather a set of pictures of objects, and ask him to name each picture in the set with a different name and also to produce a name that applies to all of the objects in that set by asking, "What are they all?" In this way we hoped to provide a context which for an adult makes the use of both differentiated terms and of general terms obligatory.

Experiment 2.1

METHOD

The purpose of the present study was to examine the child's ability to produce names of objects for several different domains and at different levels of generality within any given domain. Since one of the goals of this experiment was to examine the child's ability to produce class names at different levels of generality, a set of eight hierarchies of terms were chosen to be studied. With these hierarchies in mind we constructed a set of twenty-six posters with four pictures on each poster.[4] Pictures were chosen

---

[4] In this study and in many of the others reported in this book pictures of objects have been used. While our interest is ultimately in the ways in which children classify the real objects they encounter as they grow, pictures of real objects have been employed in many of the studies for obvious practical reasons (e.g., it would not have been especially feasible to bring elephants or cars or trees into the laboratory). Pictures of objects rather than real objects have been used by many other developmental psychologists interested in the kinds of questions which concern us here. Students of early language development have in fact often pointed out that the child can name pictures of real objects with the same kind of facility that he shows when he names real objects (see for example the diary literature discussed in Chapters 4–6; see also Inhelder and Piaget, 1964). Molly Potter at M.I.T. once conducted a study comparing the preschool child's ability to name real objects with his ability to name pictures of real objects and found that he was equally adept at both (personal communication). Moreover, in some cases, such as when the child learns the names of animals other than household pets he often first learns to name pictures of instances rather than real instances. For these reasons our studies have employed pictures of real objects as an approximation to the kinds of real objects the child learns to classify linguistically. Whenever possible an attempt has been made to corroborate the findings based upon pictures with the findings of others who have observed and recorded the speech of children in the presence of real objects.

for each poster so that, we suspected, the class name elicited from adults for the four pictures on one poster would be one of the terms in our reference hierarchies. So, for example, our first hierarchy was

I

people
children
boys

On the first poster for this hierarchy there were four pictures of boys. On the second there were four pictures of children, two girls and two boys. On the third poster there were pictures of four different people—a boy, a girl, a man, and an elderly woman. The other three-term reference hierarchies were as follows:

II	*III*	*IV*	*V*	*VI*	*VII*
food	plants	vehicles	money	animals	animals
fruit	flowers	cars	coins	dogs	fish
apples	roses	Volkswagens	dimes	collies	sharks

Finally, we decided to study an eighth hierarchy with five levels in it:

VIII

living things
animals
mammals
primates
chimpanzees

It should be pointed out that these words were our reference words only and were not actually an integral part of the experiment.

The pictures mounted on the posters were clear black and white photographs. Figure 2.3 shows the three sets of four pictures corresponding to the collie-dog-animal hierarchy which were used in this experiment. Our design was such that posters constructed to elicit a more general class name for adults always included an instance of the most specific class name. For example, as can be seen in Figure 2.3, there was a picture of a collie on the posters for *dogs* and for *animals*.

There were three groups of subjects in the experiment. There was one group of ten children between two and three and a half years of age, one group of twenty children between four and five and a half years of age,

See facing page
FIGURE 2.3 Three sets of four pictures used in Experiment 1. For each picture in a set children were asked, "What is this?" and then for each set they were asked, "What are they all?"

Collies

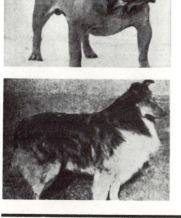

Dogs

Animals

and one group of twenty adults, half of whom were mothers of ten of the children and half of whom were graduate students at Harvard.

The three posters for the first hierarchy (boys, children, people) were used as a demonstration and subjects were helped if they had trouble. They were not given hints or feedback on the rest of the posters however. The posters for hierarchies II through VII were presented in a different random order for each subject. For each poster the subject was asked to name each object depicted in the four pictures and then to give a class name for all the pictures on a given poster. In order to elicit individual names for each picture *E* would point to each in turn and say, "What is this?" In order to elicit class names, after the subject had attempted to name each picture, *E* would ask him, "What are they all?" Except for the posters which correspond to the lowest level in each hierarchy, if a subject gave a name for a given picture of an object which was not specific enough to differentiate it from the other objects (e.g., *dog* for each of the four dogs), then he was encouraged to give a more specific name for each of the objects if he could. Children in particular were praised for giving a correct name but were asked if they could think of "another name," a "different name," a "special name," and the like. Also, if the subject gave a class name which was more general than our reference word (e.g., *food* rather than *fruit* for pear, apple, banana, and pineapple), he was again asked for a more differentiated name for all the objects. Finally, the eighth hierarchy was presented as a unit, beginning with the poster for *living things* and working down toward *chimpanzees*. Children were given lollipops and little toys as rewards at the end of an experimental session, which usually took about an hour. Adult subjects usually spent about half an hour at the task and were paid for their services.

RESULTS

Not surprisingly, adults were better able than children to produce more correct differentiated names for individual pictures and more correct class names for all four pictures on a given poster. In one analysis we computed the percentage of correct differentiated responses as a function of age group. In this analysis we excluded the pictures on the posters for the lowest level in each hierarchy since for these pictures we did not expect nor did we press for differentiated names. For each picture on every other poster we calculated the percentage of subjects within each age group who gave a correct response which was specific enough to differentiate it from the names for the other pictures on that poster. So, for example, in the case of the poster with four flowers on it, if the subject could only say that each picture was of a *flower*, these were not counted as correct differentiated responses since he failed to distinguish them. However, if the subject correctly named them *daisy, rose, carnation,* and *tulip,* these were counted as correct differentiated responses. If a subject named them *daisy, rose, flower,* and *flower,* he was scored as having given a correct differentiated response for the daisy and rose but not for the carnation and tulip. When the analysis was done in this way our youngest group of subjects was capable of producing less than 30 percent correct differentiated responses, the older children were capable of producing about 50 percent correct differentiated responses, and the adults were capable of producing more than 80 percent correct differentiated responses.

In a second analysis we computed the percentage of correct class names as a function of age. In this analysis we calculated for each age group the percentage of posters for which subjects in that age group were capable of giving some class name (at any level of generality) which was superordinate to all of the objects depicted on a given poster. So, for example, for the four pictures of dogs names such as *dogs, mammals, animals,* and so on were counted as correct, whereas *collies* or *flowers,* and the like were counted as incorrect. When the analysis was done in this way it was found that our youngest group of children was capable of giving correct class names for less than 20 percent of the posters, whereas the older children were capable of giving more than 60 percent correct class names and the adults gave close to 100 percent correct class names.

These trends are not surprising nor especially informative. The question of real interest is for which pictures and for which classes the responses of children and adults diverged the most. We have calculated for each picture the percentage of children and of adults giving correct differentiated names and for each poster the percentage of children and of adults giving correct class names. In these analyses (and most of the others that follow) we combined the younger and older children into one group called "children" and compared their performance with the adults.

A comparison of the percentage of children who were capable of giving correct differentiated responses for each picture with the corresponding percentages for adults revealed that adults gave more correct differentiated responses for almost all pictures than children. Excluding the person hierarchy, which was used mainly as a demonstration, there were in fact only two exceptions (out of sixty-four) to this general rule and they both appeared to be instances of the same phenomenon. Many adults, in the cases of a picture of a dog (a pointer) on the mammal poster for hierarchy VIII and of a fish (a piranha) on the animal poster for hierarchy VIII, attempted to give specific names (e.g., *retriever, flounder*) and were in fact wrong, whereas children were satisfied with the more general terms (*dog* and *fish*) and therefore did better according to our criterion. Apart from these two discrepant cases adults did better than children at giving differentiated responses for all pictures, although children had relatively less difficulty with some pictures than with others. For example, they did relatively well with food terms—they often distinguished a pineapple from a banana from an apple from a lemon (although they did not do too well on the lemon) and they often distinguished an apple from lettuce from bread from a walnut (although they did not do too well on the walnut). By comparison, they were less adept at distinguishing specific makes of cars (a Model-T Ford from a Cadillac from a Volkswagen from a Jaguar) or at distinguishing specific kinds of dogs (a bulldog from a German shepherd from a collie from a poodle). In most cases they were better (as were adults) at distinguishing among objects in a higher level category than objects in a lower level category. For example, they were better at distinguishing a bicycle from a VW from an airplane from a train than at distinguishing a Model-T from a Cadillac from a VW from a Jaguar. Or, to take another example, they were better at distinguishing among animals —a duck from a frog from a collie from a leopard—than they were at distinguishing among various breeds of dogs—a bulldog from a German shepherd from a collie from a poodle.

Now consider the ability of children and adults to give some class name which is appropriate for all four pictures on a given poster. For the moment we are concerned with the ability of children (or adults) to produce any class name which is appropriate for all of the pictures on a poster. For example, for the four pictures of collies the responses *collies, dogs, animals,* and so on are all considered to be correct class names in this analysis. In later analyses we shall be concerned with the ability of children to give just the term *collies* which is the response most often given by adults as a class name for the four collies, but here we shall be using the much less stringent criterion of any appropriate class name. One hundred percent of the adults gave some correct class name to all of the posters except for one. The one exception was the poster with pictures of a monkey, a chimpanzee, a man, and an orangutan on it. Eighteen out of twenty adults gave a correct class name for these pictures but two of them gave as responses *a man and three monkeys* which we did not count as correct since it was not a single superordinate term. Apart from this one exception adults had no trouble at all in generating class names for the posters.

Children had much more difficulty in producing correct class names. Generally children were better at giving some appropriate class name for the posters which corresponded to the lowest level in our reference hierarchies. For example, 67 percent of the children gave a correct class name for four apples, 47 percent for four fruits, and 40 percent for four different kinds of foods. Or to take another example, 63 percent gave a correct class name for four roses, 47 percent for four different kinds of flowers, and 30 percent for four different kinds of plants. This, however, definitely does not mean that children gave the response *roses* for four roses more often than they gave the response *flowers* for four flowers, but only that they gave an appropriate class name for the four roses (which was usually *flowers*) more often than they did for the four flowers. There was only one exception to the general rule of a monotonically nonincreasing ability to give some appropriate class name with increasing level in a given hierarchy. This exception occurred for a poster in hierarchy VIII which had pictures of a monkey, a chimpanzee, a man, and an orangutan on it. Most children gave as a class name *one (a) man and three monkeys* which was not counted as correct. In both this study and in later studies children consistently refused to classify human beings as animals and this, I believe, is the reason why they had such difficulty in generating a class name for that particular poster.

The fact that children are usually best at giving some appropriate class name for the most specific category in a hierarchy, next best for the next highest, and so on, reminds me very much of a major finding in my monograph (Anglin, 1970) that in a variety of tasks children can see and exploit a similarity between two words such as *boy* and *girl* or *boy* and *horse* before they can do so for a similarity between two less related words such as *boy* and *flower* or *boy* and *chair*. I argued that this was evidence of a concrete-to-abstract progression in the development of the appreciation of the relations among words. Although it is somewhat tempting to describe the patterns of results obtained in the study described here as reflecting a "concrete-to-abstract" progression as well, it should be pointed out that it is not clear what is causing this progression, or to put it another way, what the variable is that would be called "concreteness."

One variable that probably does change systematically with increasing levels of generality in a given hierarchy is the perceptual similarity of the instances on a given poster, although we have not scaled these pictures for perceptual similarity. That is to say, if we had scaled the pictures for perceptual similarity we would probably have found that adults would have rated the four roses as being more perceptually similar to one another than the four flowers which would have been rated as being more perceptually similar than the four plants, and so on. Perhaps it is easier for children to name a category comprised of perceptually homogeneous instances than to name one comprised of perceptually dissimilar instances. Another dimension that does vary with increasingly general levels in a given hierarchy is the number of appropriate names that the English language provides as possible responses to our request for a class name. The terms *roses, flowers,* and *plants* are all appropriate for four roses, whereas *roses* is not appropriate for four different kinds of flowers and neither *roses* nor *flowers* is appropriate for four different kinds of plants. Whatever the reasons for this trend, however, the following analyses will show that it does not mean that children necessarily acquire specific terms invariably before more general terms. There may be something which it is appropriate to call a concrete-to-abstract progression in cognitive development, but, as will be seen, there is not a unidirectional specific-to-general progression in vocabulary development.

Our primary goal in conducting this study was to learn about the actual names that children use both for individual objects and for classes of objects. As an aid in achieving this goal we have computed the adult modal word (*AMW*) and the child modal word (*CMW*) for each picture and for each set of four pictures. By adult modal word is meant that single name that the twenty adults produced most often for a picture or set of pictures. By child modal word is meant that single name that children produced most often. We calculated the percentage of children and of adults producing the *AMW* and the *CMW* by means of a procedure which I shall illustrate by describing how we arrived at the percentage of children producing the *CMW* for an individual picture. First, a frequency distribution showing the frequency of every name produced by the children for each picture was extracted from the raw data. Then that single name which occurred most frequently in this distribution was called the *CMW*. The number of children who gave the *CMW* included both the children who used the *CMW* exactly and the children who used the *CMW* embedded in a longer word or phrase. So, for example, if the *CMW* was *dog* for a given picture, all those children who said *dog* or some word or phrase which included *dog* (e.g., *doggie, big dog,* etc.) were scored as having produced the *CMW*. The percentage of children giving the *CMW* was simply calculated by dividing this number by thirty (the total number of children in the study). The percentages of adults producing the *CMW* and of children and adults producing the *AMW* were computed similarly.

Appendix 1 shows the adult modal words and the child modal words for each individual picture used in this experiment, and the percentage of adults and children giving each. Sometimes the adult modal word was the same as the child modal word. For example, the *AMW* and *CMW* for a picture of an apple were both *apple;* for a picture of a banana they were both *banana;* for a picture of a bicycle they were both *bicycle;* for a picture of a frog they were both *frog;* and so on. However, for many pictures the adult modal word was different from the child modal word and when it was, in every case but one, it was a more differentiated term, a more specific name. Some examples are *rose* for adults but *flower* for children; *cactus* for adults, but *plant* for children; *Cadillac* for adults, but *car* for children; *shark* for adults, but *fish* for children; *seagull* for adults, but *bird* for children. The one instance in which the child modal word was more specific than that of the adults was for the picture of an elderly lady, for which the adult modal word was (*old*) *woman* and the child modal word was *grandmother*. Whether this particular woman was a grandmother or not I do not know, but the specificity of the children's modal word was not in fact justified by the visual information in the photograph.

In what cases is the child likely to produce the adult modal word for a given picture? We suspected that frequency of occurrence might be a good predictor of the order of acquisition of terms of reference for reasons that will become clearer later. To test this idea we calculated rank order correlations (Spearman's rho) between the percentage of children giving the *AMW* and the frequency of occurrence of the *AMW* according to six different measures of frequency of occurrence. The results will be more fully presented later but let me note here that we obtained highly significant correlations ($p < .0005$ for five of them; $p < .005$ for the sixth) for all measures. The highest correlations were for Rinsland (1945) which gives the frequency of occurrence of English words in child speech (Grade 1) and writing (Grade 2), ($r_s = .74$ for Grade 1; $r_s = .76$ for Grade 2).

So far I have been comparing adult modal words and child modal words for individual pictures. We also calculated adult modal words and child modal words for each set of four pictures. We were gratified to discover that adults did by and large produce as modal words for categories (i.e., for sets of four pictures) our reference words. That is, for the four pictures of apples the *AMW* was *apples;* for the four pictures of fruits the *AMW* was *fruit(s)*; for the four pictures of foods the *AMW* was *food(s)*; and so on. There were only four cases out of twenty-six possible where the actual *AMW* for a class name was different from our reference words. These were (1) *transportation* for *vehicles;* (2) *monkeys* for *chimpanzees;* (3) *animals* for *mammals;* and (4) for our reference word *coins, coins* and *money* were given equally often by adults. In all other cases the adult modal words were our reference words. What this means is that adults clearly gave class names at different levels of generality for each hierarchy, the level of generality being determined by the set of pictures being classified.

Examination of the child modal words for categories revealed that children did not produce as many different correct class names for a given domain. Consider the plant hierarchy (III), for it reveals a pattern that was most typical. Figure 2.4 presents two tree diagrams showing the child modal words and the adult modal words for each set of pictures and for each individual picture in the plant hierarchy. The child and adult modal words for sets of pictures are represented at the nodes of the tree diagrams whereas the modal words for individual pictures are represented at the ends of the twigs. As Figure 2.4 shows, the *CMW* for four different kinds of flowers is *flowers* which is also the *AMW* for four different kinds of flowers. However, for four roses the *CMW* is *flowers* whereas the *AMW* is *roses*. Children generally did not give the more differentiated class name even though they did recognize the pictures of roses as being flowers. Moreover,

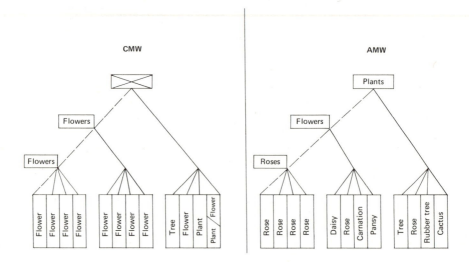

FIGURE 2.4 Trees showing adult modal words and child modal words for each individual picture and for each set of pictures in the plant hierarchy. Data based on first order of acquisition experiment.
NOTE: *AMW* = adult modal word; *CMW* = child modal word; ⊠ indicates that no response ("don't know") was the modal response.

the children's most frequent response when shown the poster with pictures of a tree, a rose, a rubber plant, and a cactus to the question "What are they all?" was "I don't know," whereas for adults it was "plants." This suggests that of the three nested category labels *roses, flowers,* and *plants,* children first are able to produce the intermediate term *flowers* in a context that requires this term, and only later can they produce the more differentiated term *roses* and the more general term *plants.* The pattern is the same for the transportation hierarchy, and the two animal hierarchies. With respect to the transportation hierarchy the *AMW*s for four VWs, four cars, and four different means of transportation were *Volkswagens, cars,* and *transportation* respectively, whereas the *CMW*s were *cars, cars,* and *don't know.* With respect to the animal hierarchies the *AMW*s were *collies, dogs,* and *animals,* whereas for children the corresponding *CMW*s were *dogs, dogs,* and *don't know;* and where the *AMW*s were *sharks, fish,* and *animals,* the corresponding *CMW*s were *fish, fish,* and *don't know.* Thus it appears that most children can produce the word *dogs* in a context that requires it before *collies* or *animals* and *fish* before *sharks* or *animals.*

For these sets of nested category labels there is neither a specific-to-general progression nor a general-to-specific progression, but rather children usually begin by learning an intermediate term and beyond that learn both more specialized terms and more general terms. This is not always the case in our hierarchies of course. For example, children were better able to produce the term *apples* than *fruit* or *food*. But, even though in this hierarchy children do seem to start at the most specific level with respect to the terms we were testing for, it is nonetheless safe to assume that had our lowest level been *Delicious apples* or *MacIntosh apples,* children would not have been able to produce names at that level of specificity. Similarly, in one set of terms children most often gave evidence of having acquired *money* before *dime* or *coin*. Again however, even though *money* was the most general term in this particular hierarchy, it is safe to assume that had we tested for the more general term *currency* children would not have given evidence of productive control over this word before *money*.

These trends are revealed perhaps more clearly in Table 2.1 which shows the percentage of children who produced the adult modal word for each set of four pictures for each hierarchy studied in this experiment.[5] On the assumption that the percentage of children who can produce the adult modal words in a context that requires them is directly correlated with the modal order of acquisition of those words in development, the arrows to the right of the words in Table 2.1 suggest that for the food hierarchy the modal order of acquisition is *apple* first, *food* second, and *fruit* third; that for the plant hierarchy the order is *flower* first, *plant* second, and *rose* third; that for the transportation hierarchy the order is *car* first, *Volkswagen* second, and *transportation* third; that for the money hierarchy the order is *money* first, *dime* second, and *coin* third; that in the two animal hierarchies the order is *dog* first, *animal* second, and *collie* third and *fish* first, *animal* second, and *shark* third; that for the living thing hierarchy the order is *animal* first, *monkey* second, and *primate* and *living thing* later; and that for the people hierarchy the order is *boy* first, *children* second, and *people* third. The arrows to the right of the words in Table 2.1 indicate our best guess as to the modal order of acquisition of the words within each of the eight hierarchies of terms we have studied in this experiment. However, two cautionary points should be made. The first is that while the procedure employed in this experiment may have indicated

---

[5] In the case of class names (names for sets of four pictures) children were scored as having produced the adult modal word regardless of whether their responses were singular or plural provided they produced the appropriate stem. For example, the *AMW* for four flowers was *flowers*. The percentage of children producing the *AMW* was based on not only those children who produced the term *flowers* but also on those children who gave as a response to this set of stimuli *flower*. Occasionally children did not pluralize the words they produced as class names but their failure to do so was not held against them since our interest was in their ability to produce the stems and not in their ability to pluralize. At this point in the narrative, therefore, I shall switch to discussing the singular forms of the terms of reference which were studied.

TABLE 2.1 *Percent of children who produced the adult modal word for each set of pictures for each hierarchy studied in the first order of acquisition experiment. Frequency of occurrence of each word according to Rinsland (1945) is also shown.*

F(R)	AMW		% AMW	F(R)	AMW		% AMW
(139)	2 | Food	| 2	(40.0)	(156)	2 ↑ Animal	↑ 2	(36.7)
(66)	3 ↓ Fruit	↓ 3	(23.3)	(1309)	1 → Dog	← 1	(63.3)
(561)	1 → Apple	← 1	(46.7)	(0)	3 ↓ Collie	↓ 3	(3.3)
(55)	2 ↑ Plant	↑ 2	(26.7)	(156)	1 → Animal	↑ 2	(43.3)
(263)	1 → Flower	← 1	(43.3)	(146)	2 | Fish	← 1	(50.0)
(39)	3 ↓ Rose	↓ 3	(13.3)	(4)	3 ↓ Shark	↓ 3	(13.3)
(0)	2 ↑ Transportation ↑ 3		(0.0)	(28)	3 ↑ Living Thing	↑ 3	(0.0)
				(156)	1 → Animal	← 1	(50.0)
(566)	1 → Car	← 1	(63.3)	(156)	1 → Animal	← 1	(66.7)
				(0)	4 | Primate	↑ 3	(0.0)
(0)	2 ↓ Volkswagen	↓ 2	(13.3)	(92)	2 ↓ Money	| 2	(33.3)
(105)	1 → Money	← 1	(40.0)	(209)	3 ↑ People	↑ 3	(0.0)
(0)	3 ↑ Coin	↑ 3	(3.3)	(346)	2 | Children	| 2	(13.0)
(34)	2 | Dime	| 2	(16.7)	(1433)	1 → Boys	← 1	(39.1)

NOTE: *F(R)* = frequency of occurrence according to Rinsland, Grade 1; *AMW* = adult modal word; *% AMW* = percent of children who use the adult modal word.

an absence of the ability in a given child to produce a given word in an obligatory context, other procedures might well have indicated some appreciation of or control over the use of that word. Both naturalistic observation and psycholinguistic experiments comparing production and comprehension skills have often shown that comprehension precedes production (see for example, Moore, 1896; Leopold, 1939, 1949a; Lewis, 1959; Huttenlocher, 1974; see also Brown, Fraser, and Bellugi, 1963; Ingram, 1974). Our studies of the comprehension of terms (see Chapters 4 and 5) have also suggested that children in general may well be able to recognize instances of a concept (e.g., when asked for example, "Is this an animal?") before they are able to produce the term (e.g., *animal[s]*) in an obligatory context, as was required in this study. A related and quite interesting phenomenon was observed among a few of the youngest children in this experiment. That is, they were sometimes able to name each of the four pictures within a set appropriately with the same name but unable to answer the question "What are they all?" even though the name that they had just used for the specific instances was totally appropriate as a class name. For instance, one two-year-old child, when asked, "What is this?" for each of the four individual pictures of apples, responded "apple" with no hesitation but when asked, "What are they all?" drew a blank. Another two year old, when asked of each of the four individual pictures of dogs, "What is this?" answered "doggie" in each case, but when asked, "What are they all?" said that he did not know. In such cases, it is clear that even though the child was incapable of producing a correct class name in the experimental situation employed here, he nonetheless had the word in his productive vocabulary. Such observations confirm that the situation in which the child is studied may affect the willingness of a psychologist to attribute any given ability to him (see Labov, 1970; Cole and Scribner, 1974; Cole and Bruner, 1971; de Villiers and de Villiers, 1974; Brown, 1973). However, even though other criteria might well indicate a somewhat different time scale for the acquisition of the kinds of terms studied in this experiment, I do feel that the arrows to the right of the words in Table 2.1 accurately reflect the modal order of acquisition of those words. This is because the criterion used here was the same for each word in a given hierarchy. That is to say, in each case the child was required to produce the term in the context of exactly four instances and in response to the question "What are they all?" A variety of additional kinds of evidence will be presented in later sections of this book consistent with the claim that the modal order of acquisition of the terms presented in Table 2.1 is as it is there indicated.[6]

The second cautionary point to be made is that although the arrows to the right of the words in Table 2.1 indicate our best guess as to the modal order of acquisition of those words, there are undoubtedly children who

---

[6] In the next experiment to be presented in this chapter a similar analysis again suggests that *apple* is acquired before *food* which is acquired before *fruit;* that *dog* is acquired before *animal* which is acquired before *collie;* and that *flower* is acquired before *plant* which is acquired before *rose.* In Chapter 3 it will be seen that mothers when they name objects for children usually choose those terms within the hierarchies which this study suggests that children learn first. In a study of comprehension to be described in Chapter 4 more children indicated that they had some knowledge of the word *dog* than *animal,* and more indicated that they had some knowledge of *animal* than *collie;* more indicated that they had some knowledge of *flower* and of *plant* than *tulip;* and more indicated that they had some knowledge of *apple* than *food,* and of *food* than *fruit.* In a study described in Chapter 7 children were engaged in conversations about a number of the words studied in this experiment and it was found that more children in their conversations indicated some knowledge of *dog* and of *animal* than of *collie;* that more indicated some knowledge of *flower* than of *plant* and of *rose;* and that more children indicated some knowledge of *car* than of *Volkswagen,* and of *Volkswagen* than *vehicle.* Finally, the order of acquisition of the terms suggested by our experiments is consistent with the studies of others who have recorded the spontaneous speech of children when they first learn to talk (e.g., Leopold, 1939; Nelson, 1973b; Rescorla, 1976).

deviate from those modal patterns. That is to say, there are some individual differences in the order of acquisition of English nomenclature. It is possible to get a feeling for the extent of individual differences in the order of acquisition of the words within each hierarchy studied in this experiment by examining the performance of each child in response to our request for a class name for each of the posters for a given hierarchy. Consider for example, the collie-dog-animal hierarchy. According to Table 2.1 the modal order of acquisition within this hierarchy is *dog* first, *animal* second, and *collie* third. Any given child was able to produce either zero, one, two, or all three of these terms in an obligatory context. Cases in which a child produced none of the terms are uninformative concerning whether or not that individual child will conform to the modal order of acquisition. Similarly, cases in which a child produced all of the terms are again uninformative with respect to the question of whether or not that particular child acquired the words in the modal order. However, cases in which a child produced either one or two of these terms are somewhat informative with respect to the issue of whether or not that child is conforming to the modal order. This is so since, if the child produces just one of the words, it should be *dog* (not *collie* and not *animal*) if he is conforming to the modal order. And if the child produces just two of the words then they should be *dog* and *animal* (not *dog* and *collie* and not *animal* and *collie*) if he is conforming to the modal order. In the case of the collie-dog-animal hierarchy, of the thirty children studied in this experiment, ten produced none of the three terms as class names, ten produced one, nine produced two, and one produced all three. Thus, nineteen of our thirty children produced responses which were informative with respect to the question of whether or not their performance was consistent with the modal order of acquisition or not, as outlined above. Of these nineteen subjects, eighteen produced responses consistent with the modal order of acquisition, whereas one did not. The one child whose behavior violated the modal pattern was able to produce *animal* but not *dog* or *collie* as class names. The other nine children who produced only one class name, all produced *dog*. The nine children who produced two class names each, all produced *dog* and *animal*. Thus it can be seen that for this particular hierarchy nearly every child who produced data which was informative with respect to the issue of the order of acquisition of the terms *collie, dog,* and *animal* generated responses consistent with the modal order of *dog* first, *animal* second, and *collie* third.

Table 2.2 shows the number and percentage of individual children whose performance was consistent with the modal order of acquisition of terms within each hierarchy studied in this experiment. Cases in which a child produced none or all of the terms in a given hierarchy have not been included in this table since, as noted above, such cases are uninformative

TABLE 2.2 Number and percentage of individual children whose performance was consistent with the modal order of acquisition of terms within each hierarchy studied in the first order of acquisition experiment.

AMW	Number of informative cases	Number consistent with modal pattern	% consistent	AMW	Number of informative cases	Number consistent with modal pattern	% consistent
Food ↓2				Animal ↑2			
Fruit ↱3 ←1	14	7	50	Dog ←1 ↓3	19	18	95
Apple ↓3				Collie			
Plant ↑2				Animal ↑2			
Flower ←1 ↓3	15	10	67	Fish ←1 ↓3	19	12	63
Rose				Shark			
Transportation ↑3				Living thing ↑3			
Car ←1 ↓2	20	19	95	Animal ←1 ↑3	21	20	95
Volkswagen				Primate ↑2 Monkey			
Money ←1				People ↑3			
Coin ↱3 ⌐2	15	11	73	Children ⌐3 ⌐2	11	9	82
Dime				Boys ←1			

with respect to the issue of conformity to the modal order of acquisition. Table 2.2 reveals that for some of the hierarchies of terms more children deviate from the modal pattern than was the case for the collie-dog-animal hierarchy considered above. Only 50 percent (seven out of fourteen) of the children whose performance was informative with respect to the order of acquisition of terms within the apple-fruit-food hierarchy was consistent with the modal pattern of *apple* first, *food* second, and *fruit* third. There were, in fact, six children who could produce *food* in an obligatory context but not *apple* and one child who could produce *apple* and *fruit* (vs. *apple* and *food*) which means that the performance of seven out of fourteen children was inconsistent with the modal order of acquisition of the terms in this hierarchy. This suggests that individual differences in the order of acquisition of terms within this hierarchy are substantial and that, in particular, some children seem to have acquired the term *food* before *apple* according to our criteria. Other studies which bear on the question of the order of acquisition of these terms (see especially pp. 52–67) have not suggested this degree of departure from the modal pattern across children but there are undoubtedly individual children who do not acquire these terms in the modal order.

For none of the other hierarchies of terms is the performance of individual children this inconsistent with the modal order. As Table 2.2 shows, 67 percent of the performance of individual children is consistent with the modal pattern of *flower* first, *plant* second, and *rose* third; 95 percent is consistent with the modal pattern of *car* first, *Volkswagen* second, and *transportation* third; 73 percent is consistent with the modal pattern of *money* first, *dime* second, and *coin* third; as described above, 95 percent is consistent with the modal pattern of *dog* first, *animal* second, and *collie* third; 63 percent is consistent with the modal pattern of *fish* first, *animal* second, and *shark* third; 95 percent is consistent with the modal pattern of *animal* first, *monkey* second, and *primate* and *living thing* later; and finally, 82 percent is consistent with the modal pattern of *boy* first, *children* second, and *people* third.

It is clear from Table 2.2 that there are some individual differences in the order of acquisition of the terms and the extent of the individual differences appears to depend upon the particular set of terms in question. For some hierarchies such as collie-dog-animal or Volkswagen-car-transportation, it would appear that most children (for whom our children were a representative sample) learn the words in the same order. For other hierarchies such as apple-fruit-food or dime-coin-money it would appear that there is more variation in the order in which children learn those terms. At any rate, what is clear from Table 2.2 is that the modal order of acquisition of the terms indicated in Table 2.1 is just that—the modal order—and not an invariant order to which all children necessarily conform.

The modal order of acquisition of the terms within each hierarchy is obviously compatible with neither of the definitions of semantic complexity outlined in the introduction to this experiment (see pp. 31–33) which raises the question "What is a good predictor of these orderings?" It turns out that a very good predictor is provided by the frequency of occurrence of these words in child speech according to Rinsland (1945), Grade 1. To demonstrate the power of this measure of frequency of occurrence to predict the order of acquisition of category labels we have included the frequencies of the adult modal words according to Rinsland (1945), Grade 1, in Table 2.1. For every hierarchy but one it can be seen that there is a perfect correspondence between the modal order of acquisition of these category labels and the rank order of the corresponding frequencies according to Rinsland. This one exception occurs in hierarchy VII in which children do a little better on *fish* than on *animal*, whereas the frequency for *animal* is slightly higher than for *fish*.

A test of the relation between frequency of occurrence according to Rinsland and the percentage of children who are capable of giving the adult modal word does not have to be restricted to a single hierarchy. Whereas it would be difficult to order words from the different hierarchies according to either definition of semantic complexity, it is a simple matter to order them according to frequency of occurrence. Table 2.3 presents the adult modal words for each poster ordered according to their frequency of occurrence in Rinsland (1945), Grade 1 (middle column). Table 2.3 also shows in the right-hand column the percentage of children who were capable of producing the *AMW*. As Table 2.3 shows there is a very strong positive relationship (although it is not perfect) between the frequency of occurrence of the word according to Rinsland and the percentage of children who can produce it in an obligatory context. The rank order correlation coefficient (Spearman's rho) between the frequency of occurrence according to Rinsland of the *AMW* and the percentage of children who can produce it is .96 ($p. < .0005$).[7]

We have investigated the relation between frequency of occurrence (according to Rinsland and according to various other frequency tables) and the order of acquisition suggested by the results of this experiment (and also by the one to be described next) in much greater detail than has been described here. However, I shall postpone the presentation of these results and my interpretation of them until after a more refined version of the experiment described above has been presented.

[7] In calculating this correlation coefficient the terms *boys, children,* and *people* were not included in the analysis since the posters intended to elicit these terms were presented first and used partly as a demonstration. The term *Volkswagens* was not included either since Rinsland's tables were published in 1945 before Volkswagens were common in North America. All of the other 19 terms were included in this analysis, however.

TABLE 2.3 *Frequency of occurrence according to Rinsland (1945) of the adult modal word for each set of pictures and the percent of children giving that adult modal word in the first order of acquisition experiment.*

Adult modal word	F(R)	% AMW
Dogs	1309	63.33
Cars	566	63.33
Apples	561	46.67
Flowers	263	43.33
Animals	156	49.18
Fish(es)	146	50.00
Food(s)	139	40.00
Money	105	40.00
Monkeys	92	33.33
Fruit(s)	66	23.31
Plants	55	26.67
Roses	39	13.33
Dimes	34	16.67
Living, life	28	0.00
Sharks	4	13.33
Transportation	0	0.00
Coins	0	3.33
Collies	0	3.33
Primates	0	0.00
Volkswagens	—	13.33
Boys	1433	39.13
Children	346	13.04
People	209	0.00

NOTE: $F(R)$ = frequency of occurrence according to Rinsland, Grade 1. Frequency count for Rinsland, Grade 1, includes singular and plural. *% AMW* = the percentage of children who were capable of producing the *AMW*. *% AMW* for *animal* is the average of the percentages of children who produced *animal* in four different contexts. *Volkswagen* does not appear in Rinsland at all.

Experiment 2.2

What worried us most about Experiment 2.1 was the possible objection that the test of the child's ability to produce category labels was not equally fair across concepts. As noted in the first chapter the various instances of a concept are not all equally good as instances of that concept. Rather, as Rosch (1973, 1975) has argued, natural concepts have "internal structure," by which she means that they are instantiated by different exemplars to varying degrees. Thus, instances of a concept vary along a dimension she calls centrality, with the best instances being very central and the worst instances being very peripheral. She has found that adult subjects find it a meaningful task to rate instances according to their degree of centrality to a certain concept and that they tend to agree in their judgements of centrality. For example, adults tend to agree that a robin and a sparrow are central instances of the concept BIRD, whereas a chicken and a duck are peripheral.

Moreover, in another study (see Chapter 5) we have found that adult judgments of the centrality of pictures to concepts is a good predictor of the likelihood that the child will not include an instance in a concept. Specifically, children will often not include in a concept an instance which adults do include but which they rate as being peripheral. In fact, the centrality-peripherality dimension proves to be much more predictive of underextension in the child than a familiarity-unfamiliarity dimension. So, for example, children will count as instances of the concept ANIMAL either a picture of a horse (familiar-central) or of an aardvark (unfamiliar-central) but will often not include a butterfly (familiar-peripheral) or a crustacean (unfamiliar-peripheral). This suggests that a fair test of the order of acquision of category labels done in the style of Experiment 2.1 would involve sets of pictures which were equally central to the concepts being tested. That is to say, if we are interested in the order of acquisition of the category labels *collie, dog,* and *animal,* the instances (i.e., pictures) of collies should be equally central to the concept COLLIE as the pictures of dogs are to DOG and the pictures of animals are to ANIMAL. We had noticed in Experiment 2.1 that children were more likely to give the response *animal* to four mammals (66.7 percent) than to four animals which included a bird, a fish, an insect, and a chimpanzee (50 percent). This finding is consistent with the idea that children are somewhat better able to produce a given category label when the instances are central to that category than when they are peripheral.

To get an estimate of the extent to which the sets of pictures used in Experiment 2.1 varied in terms of their centrality to the concepts being tested we had adult judges rate each picture in each set for its degree of centrality to the concept that that set was intended to test.[8] We found that there was in fact a weak but discernible tendency for the centrality ratings for pictures to decrease with increasing level in a hierarchy. For example, the four foods (an apple, lettuce, a walnut, and bread) received an average centrality rating of only 5.78 to FOOD whereas the four apples received an average centrality rating of 6.6 to APPLE and the four fruits received an average centrality rating of 6.55 to FRUIT. Similarly, the four plants (a tree, a rose, a rubber plant, and a cactus) received an average centrality rating

---

[8] A seven-point scale was used with a 7 representing extremely central and a 1 representing extremely peripheral. The exact method used to obtain judgments of centrality from adults is described in detail in Chapter 5 (pp. 137–138).

of only 5.93 to PLANT whereas the four roses received an average centrality rating of 6.58 to ROSE and the four flowers received an average centrality rating of 6.63 to FLOWER. To take a third example, the four animals (leopard, collie, frog, and duck) received an average centrality rating of only 5.83 to the concept ANIMAL whereas the four collies received an average centrality rating of 6.70 to COLLIE and the four dogs received an average centrality rating of 6.48 to DOG. While these differences are not large they were enough to make us wonder if children might not have been able to do better on the more general terms if we had conducted a fairer test with instances of each concept being equally central to their concepts. Therefore, we decided to conduct a replication of Experiment 2.1 but this time making the test as fair as possible by seeing to it that the instances of each concept being tested were equally central to their respective concepts.

METHOD

We chose three representative hierarchies of terms from Experiment 2.1 to test again. Specifically, these were:

I	*II*	*III*
animal	plant	food
dog	flower	fruit
collie	rose	apple

We collected a picture pool of approximately two hundred and sixty-five pictures of objects which were instances of these nine concepts. From these we selected one hundred and forty-six pictures which we thought were clear and useful for our purposes. We then asked ten adult judges (five males and five females; ages eighteen to twenty-eight; seven students at Harvard and three working in Cambridge) to rate the pictures according to how central they were to the nine concepts under study. They were given an instruction sheet explaining what was meant by centrality and how to use a seven-point scale. Then they were asked to rate the one hundred and forty-six pictures according to how central the objects depicted were to our nine reference concepts. Specifically they were asked to rate twelve pictures of collies according to how central these were to the concept COLLIE; eighteen dogs to DOG; twenty-four animals to ANIMAL; eight roses to ROSE; eighteen flowers to FLOWER; eighteen plants to PLANT; twelve apples to APPLE; thirteen fruits to FRUIT; and twenty-three foods to FOOD. If they did not consider the object in a picture to be an instance of the concept in question they were asked to indicate this by putting an *X* in their response sheet rather than choosing a number from the seven-point scale. (This was to check to see that all of the pictures were, in fact, considered to be instances by adults.) The pictures were rated by concept with a separate rating sheet for each concept which included the seven-point rating scale at the top of

TABLE 2.4 Adult centrality ratings for each picture to each concept and average centrality ratings for all pictures on a single poster for the stimuli used in the second experiment on the order of acquisition of category labels.

Concept	Picture	Centrality to COLLIE	Picture	Centrality to DOG	Picture	Centrality to ANIMAL	Picture	Centrality to ANIMAL
	$Collie_1$	6.3	Dog_1 (fox terrier)	6.4	$Animal_1$ (Prince Charles spaniel)	6.2	$Animal_4$ (bullfrog)	4.0
	$Collie_2$	6.1	Dog_2 (Belgian sheepdog)	6.0	$Animal_2$ (African elephant)	6.2	$Animal_5$ (monarch butterfly)	3.2
	$Collie_3$	6.3	Dog_3 (Siberian husky)	6.3	$Animal_3$ (cat)	6.3	$Animal_6$ (marsh hawk)	3.8
		$\bar{x} = 6.23$		$\bar{x} = 6.23$		$\bar{x} = 6.23$		$\bar{x} = 3.67$

Concept	Picture	Centrality to ROSE	Picture	Centrality to FLOWER	Picture	Centrality to PLANT	Picture	Centrality to PLANT
	$Rose_1$	6.0	$Flower_1$ (white daisy)	6.0	$Plant_1$ (mullier)	5.7	$Plant_4$ (monkey puzzle tree)	3.9
	$Rose_2$	6.2	$Flower_2$ (snowball)	5.7	$Plant_2$ (castor bean)	5.8	$Plant_5$ (cactus)	4.8
	$Rose_3$	5.6	$Flower_3$ (calendula)	6.1	$Plant_3$ (jade)	6.3	$Plant_6$ (poppies)	3.9
		$\bar{x} = 5.93$		$\bar{x} = 5.93$		$\bar{x} = 5.93$		$\bar{x} = 4.20$

Concept	Picture	Centrality to APPLE	Picture	Centrality to FRUIT	Picture	Centrality to FOOD	Picture	Centrality to FOOD
	$Apple_1$	6.5	$Fruit_1$ (apple)	6.5	$Food_1$ (steak)	6.0	$Food_4$ (candy bar)	3.0
	$Apple_2$	6.2	$Fruit_2$ (banana)	6.1	$Food_2$ (round bread)	6.4	$Food_5$ (cake)	4.0
	$Apple_3$	5.5	$Fruit_3$ (strawberries)	5.6	$Food_3$ (corn)	5.8	$Food_6$ (onion)	3.9
		$\bar{x} = 6.07$		$\bar{x} = 6.07$		$\bar{x}' = 6.07$		$\bar{x} = 3.63$

Scale used:

PERIPHERAL	1	2	3	4	5	6	7	CENTRAL
	extremely	very	quite	moderate	quite	very	extremely	

each sheet. The session lasted about half an hour and subjects found it a meaningful task and were eager to discuss its implications.

Adult ratings were then averaged for each picture. From the one hundred and forty-six pictures we then chose twenty-seven (three for each of the nine concepts) such that within any given hierarchy the average centrality ratings for each set of three pictures were exactly equal. We also tried to choose pictures which would result in a high average centrality rating and with as little variability around the mean centrality as possible. Moreover, we tried to make the average centrality ratings across hierarchies as close as possible. Finally, for each of the most general concepts in the three hierarchies we chose three pictures which were rated by our adult judges as being peripheral to their respective concepts. (We decided to include some peripheral sets in order to get a feeling for the strength of the central-peripheral effect.) Thus, we had selected a total of thirty-six pictures which we proceeded to mount on posters with three pictures per poster. The result was a total of twelve posters, three for each of our three reference hierarchies with pictures being high and equal in centrality and three containing peripheral instances of the concepts ANIMAL, PLANT, and FOOD.

Table 2.4 shows the average adult centrality ratings for each picture to each concept and the average centrality ratings for all pictures on a single poster for the stimuli used in the second experiment on the order of acquisition of category labels. Figure 2.5 shows the four sets of three pictures from the collie-dog-animal hierarchy that were used in this experiment. By comparing the set of three central animals in Figure 2.5 with the set of four animals in Figure 2.3 the reader can get a feeling for the major difference between this experiment and the preceding one.

In the actual experiment there were two groups of subjects. First, there was a group of twenty children (nine females and eleven males) from the Living and Learning School in Woburn, Massachusetts. Their ages ranged from two to five years. The children were all from a middle-class background, and all of them had watched some television, and some "Sesame Street" in particular. The children were tested in a private staff room of the school. The second group of subjects comprised ten adults (six females and four males), nine of whom were Harvard students and one of whom was a nonworking woman.

The procedure was the same as for Experiment 2.1. *E* began by explaining to *S* what would take place in the experiment and then turned on a tape

---

See facing page
FIGURE 2.5 Four sets of three pictures used in the second order of acquisition experiment. For each picture in a set children were asked, "What is this?" and then for each set they were asked, "What are they all?" The pictures of collies, of dogs, and of central animals were chosen such that according to adult ratings they are very central and equally central to their respective concepts.

Collies

Dogs

Animals (central)

Animals (peripheral)

recorder and began the session. The subject was shown three posters from Experiment 2.1 (from the boy-child-person hierarchy) which were used again as a demonstration and for which they were helped if they had trouble. Then they were shown the twelve test posters in a different random order for each subject. For each poster the subject was asked to name each object in the three pictures and then to give a class name for all three pictures on a given poster. In order to elicit individual names for each picture, *E* would point to each in turn and ask, "What is this?" In order to elicit class names, after the subject had attempted to name each picture, *E* would ask him "What are they all?" Except for the posters corresponding to the lowest level in each hierarchy, if a subject gave a name for a given picture of an object which was not specific enough to differentiate it from the other objects (e.g., *dog* for each of the three dogs), then he was encouraged to give a more specific name if he could. Children in particular were praised for giving a name but were asked if they could think of "another name," a "special name," a "different name," and the like. Also, if a subject gave a class name for a set of pictures which was more general than our reference word (e.g., *dog* rather than *collie* for three collies), he was again asked for a more differentiated name for all of the objects. Children seemed to enjoy the session which usually lasted about half an hour and they were given lollipops and little toys as rewards. Adult subjects took about ten minutes at the task and were paid for their services.

RESULTS

In discussing the results of this experiment, I would like to focus on the nine posters which contained pictures equated for centrality. Suffice it to say here that with respect to the posters containing peripheral instances children were not quite as good at producing a class name for these as they were for posters containing central instances, although the differences were not as great as anticipated. Specifically, 30 percent of the children gave the class name *animals* for the three peripheral animals, whereas 50 percent of the same children gave the class name *animals* for the three central animals; 10 percent gave the class name *plants* for the three peripheral plants, whereas 15 percent gave the class name *plants* for the three central plants; and 30 percent gave the class name *food* for the three peripheral foods, whereas 40 percent gave the class name *food* for the three central foods. We suspect that these differences would have been larger had we used instances such that the differences between the peripherality and centrality of the instances were greater than they were. (It is worth noting that the central-peripheral variable was least effective in the case of plants, and in fact, the differences between the average adult ratings for the central plants [5.93] and that for the peripheral plants [4.20] was smallest in this case.)

For each of the pictures on the nine central posters and for each of these

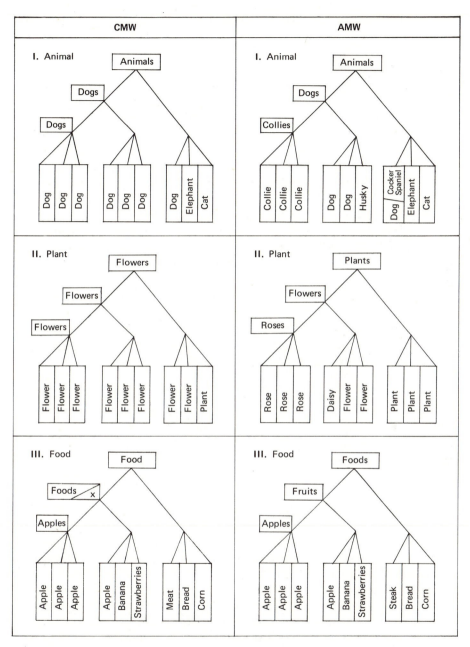

FIGURE 2.6 Trees showing adult modal words and child modal words for each individual picture and for each set of pictures used in the second experiment on the order of acquisition of category labels.

NOTE: *AMW* = adult modal word; *CMW* = child modal word; ⊠ indicates that no response ("don't know") was the modal response; ◿ indicates that there were two names given equally.

sets of three pictures we calculated the adult modal word and the child modal word in exactly the same way as we had in Experiment 2.1. Figure 2.6 presents tree diagrams showing the child modal words (left column) and the adult modal words (right column) for each individual picture and for each set of pictures used in Experiment 2.2 (except for the peripheral stimuli). With respect to the individual pictures, just as was the case in Experiment 2.1, whenever there is a difference, the *AMW* is always a more differentiated term than the *CMW*. So, for example, the *AMW* for a picture of a collie is *collie* whereas the *CMW* is *dog,* the *AMW* for a picture of a Siberian husky is *husky* whereas the *CMW* is *dog,* the *AMW* for a picture of a rose is *rose* whereas the *CMW* for that picture is *flower,* the *AMW* for a picture of a steak is *steak* whereas the corresponding *CMW* is *meat,* and so on.

With respect to class names (i.e., for sets of three pictures) it can be seen that the adult modal words correspond exactly to our reference words. That is, the *AMW* for three collies is *collies,* for three dogs is *dogs,* for three animals is *animals,* for three roses is *roses,* for three flowers is *flowers,* for three plants is *plants,* for three apples is *apples,* for three fruits

TABLE 2.5 Percent of children who produced the adult modal word for each set of pictures for each hierarchy studied in the second order of acquisition experiment. Frequency of occurrence of each word according to Rinsland (1945) is also shown.

F(R)			AMW			% AMW
(156)	2	↑	Animal	↑	2	(50.0)
(1309)	1	→	Dog	←	1	(100.0)
(0)	3	↓	Collie	↓	3	(0.0)
(55)	2	↑	Plant	↑	2	(15.0)
(263)	1	→	Flower	←	1	(70.0)
(39)	3	↓	Rose	↓	3	(10.0)
(139)	2		Food		2	(40.0)
(66)	3	↓	Fruit	↓	3	(20.0)
(561)	1	→	Apple	←	1	(95.0)

NOTE: *F(R)* = frequency of occurrence according to Rinsland, Grade 1; *AMW* = adult modal word; *% AMW* = percent of children who use the adult modal word.

is *fruits,* and for three foods is *foods.* The *CMWs* for class names follow roughly the same pattern as they had in Experiment 2.1 but these children seem to be a little more advanced—in particular, they are better in this experiment at producing two of the general terms *animal* and *food.* Still, it can be seen that the children do not have command of the variety of class names at different levels of generality for a given domain that the adults do. Three collies for children are all *dogs* rather than the specific *collies;* the three roses are all *flowers* for children rather than the more discriminating *roses;* the three fruits are all *foods* or *don't know* for children rather than the more discriminating *fruit.* It is interesting that the child modal word for the three plants is *flowers* (vs. *plants* for adults). In this study and in others we have found that the child's tendency to overgeneralize the word *flower* (to other kinds of plants) is more striking than for any other verbal concept we have investigated (see, for example, Chapter 4 "On the Extension of the Child's First Terms of Reference"). This also usually involves undergeneralization of the concept PLANT.

Table 2.5 shows the percentage of children who produced the adult modal word for each concept for each hierarchy studied in the second order of acquisition experiment. This analysis has been done in the same way as it was for the first experiment (see Table 2.1) and the trends are the same as well. Again, on the assumption that the percentage of children who can produce the adult modal words in a context that requires them is directly correlated with the modal order of acquisition of those words in development, Table 2.5 suggests that for the animal hierarchy the order of acquisition is *dog* first, *animal* second, and *collie* third; that for the plant hierarchy the order is *flower* first, *plant* second, and *rose* third; and that for the food hierarchy the order is *apple* first, *food* second, and *fruit* third. These are exactly the same orderings that emerged from the first experiment and again, therefore, each ordering is predicted by the rank order of the frequency of occurrence of the adult modal word in Rinsland (1945), Grade 1, as the arrows on the left in Table 2.5 indicate.

We have again examined the performance of each individual child in this experiment to see whether or not his performance was consistent with the modal order of acquisition of the three terms within each of the three hierarchies studied in this experiment. The rationale behind this analysis is the same as that behind the analysis of individual differences in the order of acquisition of category labels in the first experiment (see pp. 47–50). Table 2.6 shows the number and percentage of those children studied in the second experiment whose performance was informative with respect to the question of conformity to the modal pattern who were in fact consistent with that modal pattern. As Table 2.6 suggests the performance of most individual children was consistent with the modal order of acquisition suggested in Table 2.5. In the case of the collie-dog-animal hierarchy

TABLE 2.6 *Number and percentage of individual children whose performance was consistent with the modal order of acquisition of terms within each hierarchy studied in the second order of acquisition experiment.*

AMW			Number of informative cases	Number consistent with modal pattern	% consistent with modal pattern
Animal	↑	2			
Dog	←	1	20	20	100
Collie	↓	3			
Plant	↑	2			
Flower	←	1	14	12	86
Rose	↓	3			
Food		2			
Fruit	↓	3	17	16	94
Apple	←	1			

the performance of all children was consistent with the modal order of *dog* first, *animal* second, and *collie* third. Ten children produced only one of these three class names each, and everyone of them produced *dog* (vs. *collie* or *animal*). The remaining ten children produced two of these three class names each, and everyone of them produced *dog* and *animal* (vs. *dog* and *collie* or *animal* and *collie*). Thus all twenty of the children tested in this experiment generated responses which were consistent with the modal order of *dog* first, *animal* second, and *collie* third. This finding confirms the implication drawn from a similar analysis in Experiment 2.1 that most children for whom our sample of children is representative usually acquire the word *dog* before *animal* and *animal* before *collie*. There are likely to be few such children who acquire these terms in a different order.

In the case of the rose-flower-plant hierarchy, 86 percent of the children whose performance was informative with respect to the issue of whether or not they were conforming to the modal order generated responses which were in fact consistent with that order. Nine children produced as class names just one of the terms *rose, flower, plant,* and in every case the term produced was *flower.* Five of the children produced exactly two of these class names. Three of these produced *flower* and *plant,* while two of them produced *flower* and *rose.* Thus the performance of all of the indivdual children is consistent with the notion that *flower* is the first term acquired in this hierarchy; but beyond that although three children appear to have acquired *plant* before *rose,* two of them appear to have acquired *rose* before *plant,* at least according to our criterion.

In the case of the apple-fruit-food hierarchy a higher percentage (94 percent) of the performance of individual children is consistent with the modal pattern of *apple* first, *food* second, and *fruit* third than was the case in Experiment 2.1 (50 percent). Twelve children were capable of producing just one of these terms as a class name and all twelve of them produced the term *apple.* Five children were capable of producing exactly two of these terms as class names. Four of them produced *apple* and *food,* while one produced *fruit* and *food.* This one child was the only child whose performance in this experiment was inconsistent with the modal pattern of *apple* first, *food* second, and *fruit* third.

One thing that worried us about this experiment is that when asked to name the individual pictures children were sometimes unable to in certain cases and gave incorrect responses which were inconsistent with the class name that we were testing. This was most notable in the case of two of our food pictures, specifically, the picture of a steak and the picture of bread. The pictures were quite unambiguous to our adult subjects but were ambiguous for a few of our children. One child, for example, called the picture of a steak a *rock* and one child called the picture of some bread a *shell.* If this child really saw the picture of a steak as a rock then one could argue that he could not be expected to give the class name *food* for pictures of the steak, bread, and a piece of corn on the cob, since a rock is not a kind of food. For this reason we reanalyzed the data calculating the percent of children who produced the adult modal word based only on children who gave responses to the individual pictures which were consistent with (i.e., instances of) the category word. We were not sure whether we should count the response "don't know" as consistent or inconsistent with the category word so we did the analysis both ways, in one case counting "don't know" as consistent with the category word and in the other case counting "don't know" as inconsistent. Table 2.7 shows the percentage of children giving the adult modal word for each concept for each of the three hierarchies studied in the second experiment according to these two methods of analysis (Method 2 and Method 3) and also, for comparison, for the straightforward method (Method 1) reported in Table 2.5. Table 2.7 also shows the results of these three methods of analysis for these three hierarchies based on data from Experiment 2.1. As Table 2.7 shows, the rank order of the percentage of children who can produce the *AMW* for the three terms within a given hierarchy is the same for all three methods of analysis and is predicted by the rank order of frequency of occurrence of the words in Rinsland (1945), Grade 1. The only case for which there is a slight discrepancy is for the food hierarchy where

TABLE 2.7 Percentage of children giving the adult modal word for each concept for each hierarchy studied in Experiment 2.2 according to three different methods of analysis. Results of the same three methods of analysis for these three hierarchies are also shown based on the data from Experiment 2.1.

| | | Experiment 2.2 % AMW | | | | | | Experiment 2.1 % AMW | | | | | |
| | | Method 1 | | Method 2 | | Method 3 | | Method 1 | | Method 2 | | Method 3 | |
F(R)	AMW												
(156)	2 ↑ Animal	50.0 ↑	2	50.0 ↑	2	50.0 ↑	2	36.7 ↑	2	36.7 ↑	2	38.5 ↑	2
(1309)	1 → Dog	100.0 ↓	1	100.0 ↓	1	100.0 ↓	1	63.3 ↓	1	67.9 ↓	1	78.3 ↓	1
(0)	3 → Collie	0.0 →	3	0.0 →	3	0.0 →	3	3.3 →	3	3.6 →	3	3.7 →	3
(55)	2 ↑ Plant	15.0 ↑	2	15.0 ↑	2	15.8 ↑	2	26.7 ↑	2	31.0 ↑	2	36.0 ↑	2
(263)	1 → Flower	70.0 ↓	1	87.5 ↓	1	87.5 ↓	1	43.3 ↓	1	43.3 ↓	1	52.0 ↓	1
(39)	3 → Rose	10.0 →	3	11.8 →	3	12.5 →	3	13.3 →	3	13.8 →	3	11.1 →	3
(139)	2	Food	40.0 →	2	47.1 →	2	61.5 →	2	40.0 →	2	39.3 →	2	50.0 ↔	2
(66)	3 ↘ Fruit	20.0 →	3	21.1 →	3	21.4 →	3	23.21 ↓	3	26.9 ↓	3	50.0 ↙	2
(561)	1 → Apple	95.0 ↓	1	95.0 ↓	1	95.0 ↓	1	46.7 ↓	1	52.0 ↓	1	52.0 ↓	1

NOTE: $F(R)$ = frequency of occurrence according to Rinsland (1945), Grade 1; AMW = adult modal word; $\%AMW$ = percent of children who use the adult modal word, computed by three methods: *Method 1*: total number of children who gave the adult modal word divided by the total number of children; *Method 2*: total number of children who gave the adult modal word divided by the total number of children who gave three (Experiment 2.2) or four (Experiment 2.1) names for the individual pictures which were consistent with the category word, when "don't know" is considered *consistent*, and a child's data was deleted if he gave any inconsistent response for any of the individual pictures; *Method 3*: total number of children who gave the adult modal word divided by the total number of children who gave three (Experiment 2.2) or four (Experiment 2.1) names for the individual pictures which were consistent with the category word, when "don't know" is considered *inconsistent*, and a child's data was deleted if he gave any inconsistent response for any of the individual pictures.

Method 3 in Experiment 2.1 results in equal percentages of children producing the *AMW*s *food* and *fruit* whereas in the other five cases the percentage of children producing *food* is higher than the percentage producing *fruit*.

Since we had approximately equated for the average centrality of instances to the concepts being tested not only within but also across hierarchies we decided to see how good a predictor frequency of occurrence according to Rinsland (1945) was for the percentage of children capable of giving each of the nine words. Table 2.8 shows the nine words ordered

TABLE 2.8 *Relationship between frequency of occurrence of words according to Rinsland (1945) and percentage of children and adults who produce those words in a context that requires them. Data from Experiment 2.2.*

			% AMW (children)		
AMW	*F(R)*	*%A*	Method 1	Method 2	Method 3
Dogs	1309	100.0	100.0	100.0	100.0
Apples	561	100.0	95.0	95.0	95.0
Flowers	263	100.0	70.0	87.5	87.5
Animals	156	80.0	50.0	50.0	50.0
Foods	139	100.0	40.0	47.1	61.5
Fruits	66	90.0	20.0	21.1	21.4
Plants	55	100.0	15.0	15.0	15.8
Roses	39	90.0	10.0	11.8	12.5
Collies	0	70.0	0.0	0.0	0.0

NOTE: $F(R)$ = frequency of occurrence according to Rinsland, Grade 1; AMW = adult modal word; $\%A$ = percent of adults who gave the adult modal word; $\%AMW$(children) = percent of children who gave the adult modal word, computed by three methods: *Method 1:* total number of children who gave the adult modal word divided by the total number of children; *Method 2:* total number of children who gave the adult modal word divided by the total number of children who gave three names for the individual pictures which were consistent with the category word, when "don't know" is considered *consistent*, and a child's data was deleted if he gave any inconsistent response for any of the individual pictures; *Method 3:* total number of children who gave the adult modal word divided by the total number of children who gave three names for the individual pictures which were consistent with the category word, when "don't know" is considered *inconsistent*, and a child's data was deleted if he gave any inconsistent response for any of the individual pictures.

according to frequency of occurrence in Rinsland (the left column) and the percentage of children capable of producing those words in a context that requires them according to the three methods of analysis. As Table 2.8 shows, the percentage of children capable of producing the word is a perfectly decreasing monotonic function of the frequency of occurrence of that word for Methods 1 and 2, and only one point is out of line for Method 3. This means that for Methods 1 and 2 the rank order correlation coefficient (Spearman's rho) between frequency of occurrence of the word in

TABLE 2.9 *Rank order correlations between the percentage of children giving an adult modal word and the frequency of occurrence of that word. Correlation coefficients were computed for the two experiments for category data and individual pictures data for six different measures of frequency of occurrence.*

		Rinsland Grade 1	Rinsland Grade 2	Thorndike and Lorge G Count	Thorndike and Lorge J Count	Kucera and Francis	Howes
Experiment 2.1	Category data N = 19	$r_s = +0.96$ (******)	$r_s = +0.92$ (******)	$r_s = +0.41$ (*)	$r_s = +0.45$ (**)	$r_s = +0.38$ (NS)	$r_s = +0.39$ (*)
	Individual pictures N = 44	$r_s = +0.74$ (******)	$r_s = +0.76$ (******)	$r_s = +0.60$ (******)	$r_s = +0.55$ (******)	$r_s = +0.53$ (******)	$r_s = +0.45$ (***)
Experiment 2.2	Category data N = 9	$r_s = +1.0$ (******)	$r_s = +0.97$ (******)	$r_s = -0.05$ (NS)	$r_s = +0.16$ (NS)	$r_s = +0.17$ (NS)	$r_s = +0.26$ (NS)
	Individual pictures N = 15	$r_s = +0.62$ (**)	$r_s = +0.67$ (***)	$r_s = -0.26$ (NS)	$r_s = +0.28$ (NS)	$r_s = +0.17$ (NS)	$r_s = +0.04$ (NS)

NOTE: Significance levels of r_s are represented in the following way: (*) $= p < .05$; (**) $= p < .01$; (***) $= p < .005$; (****) $= p < .001$; (*****) $= p < .0005$; (NS) = not significant.

Rinsland and the percentage of children capable of producing those words is equal to 1.00.

Since frequency of occurrence was proving to be a good predictor of the percentage of children capable of giving the adult modal word in both Experiments 2.1 and 2.2, we decided to calculate correlation coefficients for both experiments for both the individual pictures data and for the category data between the percentage of children giving an adult modal word and the frequency of occurrence of that word based on six different measures of frequency of occurrence. Specifically, the measures of frequency of occurrence were taken from Rinsland (1945), Grade 1; Rinsland, Grade 2; Thorndike and Lorge (1944), General Count; Thorndike and Lorge, Juvenile Count; Kucera and Francis (1967); and Howes (1966). Table 2.9 shows the rank order correlation coefficients between the frequency of occurrence of the *AMW* for each of these measures and the percentage of children who produced the *AMW*. It can be seen from Table 2.9 that in Experiment 2.1 the correlation coefficients are highest for Rinsland Grades 1 and 2 ($r_s = +.96$, $+.92$ for category data; $r_s = +.74$, $+.76$ for individual pictures data; $p < .0005$ for all of them). The correlations for the other measures of frequency of occurrence, while not as high as these, are all positive and all but one of them are significant at at least the .05 level. In Experiment 2.2 again the correlation coefficients are highest for Rinsland Grades 1 and 2 ($r_s = +1.0$, $+.97$ for category data; $p < .0005$ for both; $r_s = +.62$, $+.67$ for individual pictures data; $p < .01$ and $p < .005$ respectively). The correlations for the other measures of frequency for Experiment 2.2 are small and not statistically significant.

DISCUSSION

There is neither a unidirectional specific-to-general progression in vocabulary development nor a unidirectional general-to-specific progression. Rather, the child usually first learns common nouns which categorize a given domain at some intermediate level of generality and only later learns more specific terms and more general terms. Thus vocabulary development is characterized by the trends of differentiation and hierarchic integration which may be processes of cognitive development more generally (see Werner, 1948).

This means that neither of the definitions of semantic complexity in terms of intension or of extension outlined in the introduction to this chapter is a good predictor of the order of acquisition of category labels. This may, of course, mean that those definitions of semantic complexity were misguided and there is still the possibility that some alternative definition of semantic complexity, possibly one that acknowledges the existence of "natural kinds", is predictive. However, I remain doubtful of this possibility for reasons that will become clear.

What does appear to be a good predictor of the order of acquisition of category labels is frequency of occurrence, in general, and frequency of occurrence in child speech, in particular (e.g., according to Rinsland, 1945). It may strike the reader as not especially surprising that the words used most often by another generation of children are, in fact, the words learned first by children today, but it is not a tautologous finding and the realization that frequency of occurrence is predictive may provide clues as to the determinants of the order of acquisition of category labels.

Frequency of occurrence has emerged as a predictor of the order of acquisition of vocabulary not only in the studies reported in this chapter but in others as well. (See, for example, Chapters 3, 4, and 7.) Frequency of occurrence is also correlated with the difficulty of vocabulary items on the Stanford-Binet Intelligence Scale (Terman and Merrill, 1960). Table 2.10 shows rank order correlation coefficients (Spearman's rho) between

TABLE 2.10 *Rank order correlations between frequency of occurrence and the difficulty of vocabulary items on the Stanford-Binet test. Correlation coefficients are shown for all forty-five words, for the twenty-one names of objects, and for the twenty-four other words. The results for three different measures of frequency are shown.*

	Rinsland	Thorndike and Lorge	Kucera and Francis
45 Words	$r_s = {}^+0.78$(*****)	$r_s = {}^+0.80$(*****)	$r_s = {}^+0.68$(*****)
21 Names of objects	$r_s = {}^+0.82$(*****)	$r_s = {}^+0.78$(*****)	$r_s = {}^+0.77$(*****)
24 Other words	$r_s = {}^+0.88$(*****)	$r_s = {}^+0.90$(*****)	$r_s = {}^+0.79$(*****)

NOTE: Significance level of r_s is represented in the following way: (*****) $p < .0005$.

the difficulty of vocabulary items on the Stanford-Binet Intelligence Scale and the frequency of occurrence of those items according to Rinsland (1945), Thorndike and Lorge (1944), and Kucera and Francis (1967). Correlations with frequency were computed for all forty-five words in the Stanford-Binet vocabulary test, for the twenty-one names of objects, and for the twenty-four other words which were not names of objects. As Table 2.10 shows, each correlation coefficient is high and statistically significant ($p < .0005$ for each of the nine values of r_s). The correlations between frequency of occurrence and the order of acquisition of category labels based on data from the two experiments presented in this chapter were of greatest magnitude and most statistically significant when they were based on Rinsland's tables of frequency of occurrence. In the present analysis, again the frequency of the words in Rinsland (Grade 1) appears to be highly correlated with the order of acquisition of terms of reference (and other content words as well), on the assumption that difficulty of vocabulary items provides a measure of their order of acquisition. However, the correlations are also strong and highly significant when based on the adult measures of frequency, as Table 2.10 shows. Thus it appears that frequency of occurrence is highly correlated with the difficulty of vocabulary items on the Stanford-Binet IQ test, a principle which holds for both a measure of frequency based primarily on child language (Rinsland, 1945) and measures of frequency based on material written by and for adults (Thorndike and Lorge, 1944; Kucera and Francis, 1967). The strength of these correlations suggests that frequency of occurrence is correlated with and therefore provides a predictor of the order of acquisition of terms by children beyond the age of five which is the age at which definitions are first tested on the Stanford-Binet scale.

Although there appeared to be some degree of correlation between frequency of occurrence and the order of acquisition of English nomenclature in the experiments that have been reported in this chapter, the correlations were definitely stronger when the frequency measure used was Rinsland (1945), the one measure of frequency that was based upon children's speech and written material. Therefore, on the basis of these studies it appears that frequency of occurrence according to Rinsland is more powerful as a predictor of the order of acquisition of category labels in the two-to-five-year age range than measures based on adult usage whether based on conversations (Howes, 1966) or on material written by adults (Thorndike and Lorge, 1944, General Count; Thorndike and Lorge, Juvenile Count; Kucera and Francis, 1967).

To argue that there is a high correlation between frequency of occurrence of words in child speech and the order of acquisition of those words is not terribly surprising, nor, of course, equivalent to explaining the order of acquisition of those words. For one thing, we lack a clear understanding of exactly why some words are more frequently occurring (i.e., used more often) than others. Nonetheless, identification of frequency of occurrence according to Rinsland (1945) as a predictor of the order of acquisition of category labels gives us a clear hypothesis as to which words are the first category labels acquired by children and which are acquired only later. Specifically, according to this hypothesis, among the very first category labels to be acquired by children are the *n* most frequently occurring names of objects in Rinsland (1945). Is it not possible that by examining these first *n* words we can make some progress toward discerning the origins of the child's first verbal concepts?

As a first step in this direction, we took from Rinsland (1945), Grade 1, the two hundred and seventy-five most frequently occurring names of objects and sorted them into semantic categories on the basis of similarity of meaning (see Miller, 1967, 1969; Anglin, 1970). Elizabeth Smith and I took turns sorting these words into semantic categories until we finally agreed on a single classification scheme. For comparison we also sorted the two hundred and seventy-five most frequently occurring words in the Thorndike and Lorge (1944) General Count and the two hundred and seventy-five most frequently occurring words in Howes (1966). The results of each analysis are shown in full in Appendix 2. Figure 2.7 presents a histogram showing the total number of words among the two hundred and seventy-five most frequently occurring words in Rinsland (1945) which we classified into each of twenty-two semantic categories.

As it turned out, the words from the three frequency of occurrence tables fell into twenty-two semantic categories although there were a few words from each frequency table which were "difficult to categorize" (#23 in Appendix 2). These categories we labeled "animals"; "people"; "food"; "toys, games, and sports"; "body parts"; "clothing"; "furniture, parts of the house"; "elements"; "buildings, places of occupation"; "geographic terms"; "tools"; "vehicles"; "vegetation"; "terms of quantity"; "currency"; "school items"; "written communication"; "kitchenware"; "media for travel"; "media for communication, amusement"; "general terms"; and "weapons." As Figure 2.7 shows, there were words from Rinsland which fell into each of these categories except "weapons." The majority of the words (i.e., more than 60 percent) from Rinsland fell into the seven categories "animals" (thirty-six); "people" (thirty-five); "food" (twenty-seven); "toys, games, and sports" (twenty-four); "body parts" (sixteen); "clothing" (fifteen); "furniture, parts of the house" (fifteen). These categories accord well with classifications of the nouns in the child's early spontaneous vocabulary (see, for example, Leopold, 1939; Nelson, 1973b, pp. 29–34, Rescorla, 1976). The fact that there are so many words in certain domains (e.g., animals, people, food, etc.) suggests that for these domains children very early learn a great number of words for classifying them and are not restricted to just a few terms.

A lot of the most frequently occurring words in child speech are the same as the most frequently occurring words taken from the adult counts. As noted earlier, there were words from each list which fell into each of the twenty-two semantic domains except for one. Another point of similarity across lists was that within these domains the list for children was just as likely to include a class name for that domain (e.g., *animal, food, money, plant, clothes, place, building, toy, game*) as were the lists for adults. Nonetheless, there were differences and these may be instructive. For example, the list for children contained many more words in certain domains (e.g., animals—thirty-six for children, seven and five for adults; toys—twenty-four for children, three and eight for adults) than did the lists for adults. On the other hand, the list for children contained far fewer terms for other domains than the lists for adults (e.g., geographic terms— only ten for children versus forty and forty-three for adults; buildings—

Category

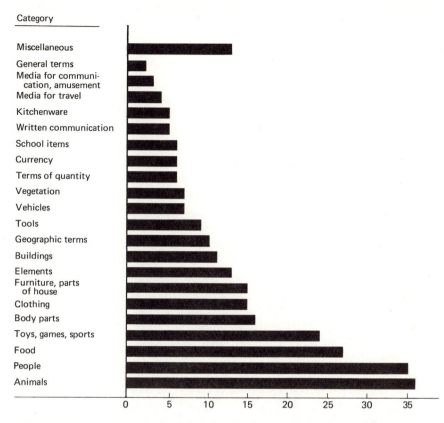

FIGURE 2.7 Histogram of a breakdown of the two hundred and seventy-five most frequently occurring names of objects in Rinsland (1945), Grade 1, into twenty-two semantic categories.

only eleven for children versus fifteen and twenty-eight for adults; general terms—only two for children versus eight and eight for adults). The distribution of words in the people category was especially interesting. The list for children included more kin terms (sixteen) than the lists for adults (ten and twelve). Notably lacking among the kin terms in the child's list, however, but present in both lists for adults were the terms *wife* and *husband*. Apart from kin terms, other kinds of terms for people (nonkin descriptions, occupations, groups, and proper names) were more frequent in the lists for adults than the list for children.

As a first approximation both the distribution of the most frequently occurring words in the list for children and the differences between this list and the lists for adults suggest that the most frequently occurring words for children are names of objects which are likely to be important to them in their day-to-day transactions with the world. Many of the categories which include the greatest number of terms in the children's list cover basic activities which are presumably important to the child in his early years (e.g., social interaction [people], eating [food], play [toys], etc.). Moreover, it seems reasonable that since children do not normally work for a living or travel as much as adults that they would not know as many occupational terms or geographic terms. Thus the distribution of words in the list for children, by and large, seems to be consistent with the notion that these words denote objects that serve important functions in the child's life. That is to say, a large number of the most frequently occurring names of objects according to Rinsland (1945) are words which denote objects which are likely to be important to the child in his daily activities.

Not all of the terms in the list for children, of course, fit neatly into an interpretation in terms of function, especially if function is narrowly defined in terms of biological needs. Particularly it is unclear why there were so many animal terms in the list for children according to the narrow interpretation. But animals may be especially salient in the child's world because he experiences them either as household pets or as toys or in picture books and so on.[9] Thus the child's first terms of reference appear to be names of objects with which he will interact whether the interaction serves basic biological needs (such as eating food) or whether the interaction is less intimately related to survival (such as playing with toys or simply paying attention to salient objects).

These conclusions are quite consistent with the findings of others (see Leopold, 1939, p. 174; Stern, 1930, p. 167; Lewis, 1959, p. 87) and are strengthened by the recent work of Nelson (1973b). In an extensive study of the first words acquired by children between the ages of one and two she found that most of their category labels refer either to objects which the child can act upon (e.g., shoes, toys, food, etc.) or to things which are likely to change in his environment (e.g., dogs, cars, etc.). She emphasizes the point that the child seldom learns terms for objects which are simply "there" such as houses, walls, or tables. Thus Nelson's work confirms the argument presented above and further pinpoints the notion of salience by identifying it with movement and change.

This discussion suggests a solution, although admittedly not a very surprising one, to the problem of horizontal vocabulary development. The child will learn first names of objects which he is likely to act upon or which are salient in his world and only later will he learn names for objects which he does not act upon and objects which are less salient. But what about the problem of vertical vocabulary development, the problem of at what level of generality the child will first categorize the useful and salient objects in his world. The studies described in this chapter have established

---

[9] Or on television, although this would not apply to the children whose spoken and written speech Rinsland tabulated.

the level of generality at which the child will first learn to categorize a number of different domains. However, an explanation of these findings will require an analysis of the naming practices of mothers when they transmit vocabulary to their children. Such an analysis is the topic of the next chapter.

Chapter 3

The Naming Practices
of Mothers[1]

In Chapter 2 it was observed that adults, when asked to name pictures of objects, often produce very specific names such as *rose, Volkswagen,* and *collie.* Children, however, when asked to name the same pictures usually produce somewhat more general and less discriminating responses such as *flower, car,* and *dog.* It seems reasonable that often children will learn the names of objects from adults in general and at least in their early preschool years, from their parents in particular. This speculation raises the question of why it is that the child does not learn the specific words which adults seem to use when they name objects. Is it possible that parents tailor their naming practices for their children in a way which accords with the character of the child's vocabulary?

There is at the moment a rapidly growing literature on the subject of "baby talk", which concerns the modifications parents make in the speech they address to children. While much of this work deals with grammatical and phonological modifications, some studies have been concerned, at least in part, with the vocabulary provided to the child (for example, Ferguson, 1964; Berko-Gleason, 1973; Broen, 1972; Phillips, 1973; Weeks, 1971; Drach, 1969; De Paulo and Bonvillion, 1975). In general it has been found

[1] I am very grateful to Ruth Berger, Kay Tolbert, Janet Zeller, David Rubin, Judith Burton, and Laure DeBroglie for their help in running the experiments reported in this chapter and to Marc Fiedler for his help with the analysis of the results.

that, in comparison to the vocabulary supplied by adults to other adults, the vocabulary transmitted by mothers to their children is less diverse, more repetitious, more concrete, and contains a greater proportion of diminutives. Baby talk vocabulary most often includes terms of reference which are kin names, animal names, the names of body parts, and the names of games and playthings—in other words, the kinds of terms which are most frequently occurring in the speech of young children (see Chapter 2).

Of most direct relevance to the investigations described in this chapter are arguments made by Roger Brown some time ago (see especially Brown, 1958, 1965). In 1958 Brown pointed out that parents will in fact sometimes name objects differently for their child than they might for another adult. One of his examples was that some parents will, at first, call every sort of coin *money* for their children presumably since the young child does not need to know specific denominations of coins until he gets into the business of buying and selling. Brown pointed to three factors which may be of importance in determining the choice of a word by an adult for a child. The first he called the brevity principle by which he meant that the parent will tend to supply the child with shorter rather than longer words. The second was the frequency principle by which he meant that adults will tend to use names which are commonly occurring. For example, an adult will probably label a spoon with the more frequently occurring term *spoon* for the child rather than the less frequently occurring term *silverware,* since the child may find it useful to distinguish spoons from knives and forks at the dinner table. There is of course a correlation between frequency and brevity (Zipf's law, 1935). Words which are commonly occurring tend to be short. Sometimes, however, the frequency-brevity principle, as Brown called it, will not hold even for the names provided by adults for their children. For example, an adult will tend to name a pineapple *pineapple* rather than *fruit, food,* or *thing* even though *pineapple* is longer (has more syllables) and less frequent (according to Thorndike and Lorge, 1944) than the alternatives. That is to say, there is sometimes a tendency to use a more specific or concrete term even though it involves a cost in frequency and length. While frequency and brevity are positively related, specificity or concreteness is often negatively correlated with frequency and brevity.

The purpose of the following two experiments was to see whether or not mothers actually do tailor their choice of names of objects for their children and whether they do sometimes name objects differently for their children than for other adults. Frequency, brevity, and concreteness have been systematically pitted against one another in every possible combination in order to determine the relative contributions of these three factors in determining the vocabulary supplied by adults to their children.

Experiments 3.1 and 3.2

METHOD

A total of twenty-five pictures was used in both of the following experiments. The pictures had been selected so that in the writer's judgment at least two names were appropriate for each picture. The pair of names fell into four different types: (1) In the first, the choice was between a specific, long, infrequent word versus a general, short, frequent word. (A word was considered to be more specific than another if it was subordinate to it; longer if it contained more syllables; less frequent if it had a lower general frequency count according to Thorndike and Lorge [1944]). For example, *collie* is specific, long, and infrequent relative to *dog* which is by comparison general, short, and frequent. (2) In the second, the choice was between a specific, short, and infrequent word versus a general, long, and frequent word—for example, *mint* versus *candy* or *dime* versus *money*. *Mint* is specific, short, and infrequent relative to *candy* which is general, long, and frequent by comparison. (3) In the third, the choice was between a specific, short, frequent word versus a general, long, infrequent word— for example, *knife* versus *silverware* or *gun* versus *weapon*. (4) In the fourth set of word-pairs the choice was between a specific, long, and frequent word versus a general, short, and infrequent word. It should be pointed out that these particular word pairs took a long time to think of since brevity and generality are both usually signs of high frequency. Nonetheless, we did manage to come up with five such word pairs—for example, *refrigerator* versus *appliance* or *elephant* versus *mammal*. These four categories of word pairs exhaust the possible combinations of the three variables under study. Table 3.1 shows the vital statistics for the words being studied in this investigation.[2]

In Experiment 3.1 twenty mothers from the Cambridge area named the twenty-five pictures both for their two-year-old children and for the experimenter. The pictures were placed in a loose-leaf binder one per page,

---

[2] In addition to showing whether a word in a pair was relatively specific or general, the number of syllables in each word, and the frequency of each word according to Thorndike and Lorge's General Count (1944), Table 3.1 also shows the frequency of each word according to Rinsland (1945), Grade 1. As it turned out, for twenty-one of the word pairs, if one word of a pair was more frequent according to Thorndike and Lorge (1944) then it was also more frequent according to Rinsland (1945). However, for four of the word pairs being tested for in these experiments the more frequent word according to Thorndike and Lorge was actually less frequent according to Rinsland. These four word pairs are *hammer-tool, grasshopper-insect, ant-insect,* and *cat-animal.* For example, *cat* is infrequent relative to *animal* according to Thorndike and Lorge (*A* vs. *AA*), but it is frequent relative to *animal* (1,366 vs. 32) according to Rinsland.

TABLE 3.1 *Vital statistics of words being studied in the mother-naming experiments.*

Specific-long-infrequent

	S/G?	#Syllab.	F(T-L)	F(R)
Pineapple	S	3	15	3
Sandal	S	2	5	0
Pigeon	S	2	34	2
Collie	S	2	3	0
Carnation	S	3	1	1
Cantaloupe	S	3	—	1
Typewriter	S	3	12	3
Hammer	S	2	34	15
Grasshopper	S	3	14	5
Pomegranate	S	4	2	9

General-short-frequent

	S/G?	#Syllab.	F(T-L)	F(R)
Fruit	G	1	AA	57
Shoe	G	1	AA	46
Bird	G	1	AA	240
Dog	G	1	AA	1,198
Flower	G	2	AA	73
Fruit	G	1	AA	57
Machine	G	2	AA	29
Tool	G	1	40	5
Insect	G	2	40	1
Fruit	G	1	AA	57

Specific-short-infrequent

	S/G?	#Syllab.	F(T-L)	F(R)
Mint	S	1	13	0
Dime	S	1	11	33
Ant	S	1	38	8
Cat	S	1	A	1,366
Mints	S	1	13	0

General-long-frequent

	S/G?	#Syllab.	F(T-L)	F(R)
Candy	G	2	32	269
Money	G	2	AA	105
Insect	G	2	40	1
Animal	G	3	AA	32
Candy(ies)	G	2	32	269

TABLE 3.1 (*continued*)

Specific-short-frequent

	S/G?	#Syllab.	F(T-L)	F(R)
Knife	S	1	A	31
Ring	S	1	AA	31
Table	S	2	AA	187
Gun	S	1	A	104
Snake	S	1	28	47

Specific-long-frequent

	S/G?	#Syllab.	F(T-L)	F(R)
Elephant	S	3	35	64
Refrigerator	S	5	11	3
Automobile	S	4	A	36
Ruler	S	2	32	4
Record	S	2	AA	1

General-long-infrequent

	S/G?	#Syllab.	F(T-L)	F(R)
Silverware	G	3	2	0
Jewelry	G	3	12	0
Furniture	G	3	A	33
Weapon	G	2	42	0
Reptile	G	2	8	0

General-short-infrequent

	S/G?	#Syllab.	F(T-L)	F(R)
Mammal	G	2	6	0
Appliance	G	3	1	—
Vehicle	G	3	13	0
Gauge	G	1	5	—
Disk	G	1	8	0

NOTE: #*Syllab.* = number of syllables; *F(T-L)* = frequency of occurrence of word per million according to Thorndike and Lorge's General Count (1944); *F(R)* = frequency of occurrence of word according to Rinsland (1945); *S/G?* = specific or general?; *A* = a frequency of at least fifty per million but not so many as one hundred per million in Thorndike and Lorge's General Count; *AA* = a frequency of one hundred or more per million.

and the mothers were asked to name the first picture, to turn the page, to name the next picture, to turn the page, and so on until they had named each of the pictures. A mother was asked to go through this procedure twice, once naming the pictures for her child and once naming them for the experimenter. As she named them for either her child or the experimenter she was to be sure that the person for whom she was naming them could see the pictures and was paying attention. Ten of the mothers named the pictures first for the experimenter and then for their children. The other ten mothers named the pictures first for their children and then for the experimenter.

In Experiment 3.2, twenty different mothers from the Cambridge area were interviewed. The procedure was comparable to that of Experiment 3.1 except that this time the two names for a picture were written on a small slip of paper which was placed underneath the picture for which they were appropriate. Rather than naming the pictures spontaneously the mothers were asked to choose one of the pair of names in telling either the child or the experimenter what the object in the photograph was. Again, half of the mothers chose names for the experimenter first and then for their child; the other half chose names for their child first and then for the experimenter.

To see whether or not children's names for this set of pictures would correspond to the way the mothers had named them for their children in Experiments 3.1 and 3.2, we asked eighteen different children to name the objects depicted in the pictures. These eighteen children were between the ages of three and five and were from homes in Cambridge, Massachusetts.

RESULTS

The results for Experiments 3.1 and 3.2 are presented in Tables 3.2 through 3.5 which show the number of times mothers chose either of the words in a pair for all the word pairs under study when naming the pictures for the experimenter and for their children. Also shown in these tables is the number of times the eighteen different children named the pictures with either of the words in a pair for each of the word pairs.

Consider each of the four types of word pairs under study in turn. Table 3.2 shows the results for pictures for which the names could be either specific, long, and infrequent or general, short, and frequent. For five of these pictures mothers clearly chose the specific, long, infrequent name more often for both the experimenter and their children. Thus, even though *pineapple* is both longer and less frequent than *fruit,* mothers almost always called a picture of a pineapple a *pineapple* rather than *fruit* (see Brown, 1958b). So too for pictures of a cantaloupe, a typewriter, a hammer, and a grasshopper. These were called *cantaloupe, typewriter, hammer,* and *grasshopper* much more often than the alternatives (*fruit, machine, tool,*

TABLE 3.2 *Number of times mothers chose the words under study for the experimenter and for their children in the two experiments on mothers' naming practices when the choice was between a specific, long, infrequent word versus a general, short, frequent word. Also shown are the number of times eighteen different children named the pictures with the words under study.*

Specific-long-infrequent vs. General-short-frequent	Adult-adult		Adult-child		Child-adult
	Exp't. 3.1	Exp't. 3.2	Exp't. 3.1	Exp't.3.2	N = 18
Pineapple	20	20	20	18	11
Fruit	0	0	0	2	0
Other	0	—	0	—	7
Sandal	13	15	4	3	5
Shoe	7	5	16	17	12
Other	0	—	0	—	1
Pigeon	15	16	8	5	3
Bird	5	4	12	15	15
Other	0	—	0	—	0
Collie	6	10	2	0	0
Dog	14	10	18	20	14
Other	0	—	0	—	4
Carnation	9	11	0	1	0
Flower	11	9	20	19	18
Other	0	—	0	—	0
Cantaloupe	14	19	10	15	1
Fruit	0	1	0	5	0
Other	6	—	10	—	17
Typewriter	20	19	20	19	18
Machine	0	1	0	1	0
Other	0	—	0	—	0
Hammer	20	19	19	20	18
Tool	0	1	1	0	0
Other	0	—	0	—	0
Grasshopper	20	19	19	18	12
Insect	0	1	0	2	0
Other	0	—	1	—	6
Pomegranate	11	11	10	6	0
Fruit	3	9	4	14	0
Other	6	—	6	—	18

TABLE 3.3 Number of times mothers chose the words under study for the experimenter and for their children in the two experiments on mothers' naming practices when the choice was between a specific, short, infrequent word versus a general, long, frequent word. Also shown are the number of times eighteen different children named the pictures with the words under study.

Specific-short-infrequent vs. General-long-frequent	Adult-adult Exp't. 3.1	Exp't. 3.2	Adult-child Exp't. 3.1	Exp't. 3.2	Child-adult $N = 18$
Mint	7	13	4	1	0(1)*
Candy	7	7	9	19	0(4)*
Other	6	—	7	—	18(9)*
Dime	15	18	5	7	1
Money	1	2	11	13	2
Other	4	—	4	—	15
Ant	18	17	16	19	3
Insect	0	3	1	1	0
Other	2	0	3	—	15
Cat	18	19	9	20	18
Animal	0	1	0	0	0
Other	2	—	11	—	0
Mints	8	16	4	4	4
Candies	9	4	14	16	2
Other	3	—	2	—	12

* Fourteen of the eighteen children who were asked to name the pictures in this study were also asked to name a real mint. The numbers in parentheses indicate how many children named the mint with the terms *mint*, *candy*, and others.

insect) even though the alternatives are shorter and more frequent according to Thorndike and Lorge. Thus it can be seen that mothers will sometimes supply their children with a specific word even at a cost in length and frequency. In these five cases mothers usually name the objects depicted in the pictures in the same way for both adults and children. However, there are systematic differences between the way in which mothers named four of the pictures for an adult and for their children. Mothers most often called a picture of a sandal a *sandal* for an adult but a *shoe* for their child. They most often called a picture of a pigeon a *pigeon* for an adult but a *bird* for their child. They often called a picture of a collie a *collie* for an adult although they virtually never called it a *collie* for their children, but rather either *dog* or *doggie*. And half of them called a picture of a carnation a *carnation* for an adult whereas they almost invariably called it a *flower* for their child. In the case of the picture of the pomegranate a few mothers chose the term *fruit* to name it for their children but chose *pomegranate* for the adult. Thus it can be seen that in some cases mothers will choose a shorter and more frequent term as a name for their children, thereby sacrificing specificity, whereas they tend to choose the most specific name for an adult.

A gain in both frequency and brevity will sometimes be sufficient to sway a mother to choose a less specific term for her child. How about a gain in frequency alone? The answer to this question is suggested by Table 3.3, which shows the results for pictures for which the names could be either specific, short, and infrequent or general, long, and frequent. The pattern of results here is similar to the pattern of results just considered. For two of the pictures mothers clearly chose the specific, short, and infrequent (at least according to Thorndike and Lorge) term more often for both the experimenter and their children. Thus mothers called a picture of an ant an *ant* and a picture of a cat a *cat* far more often than *insect* and *animal* for both the experimenter and their children. However, the other three pictures revealed again differences between the mothers' naming practices for adults and for their children. A picture of a mint was more often called a *mint* for adults but more often called *candy* for children. The picture of a dime was more often called *dime* for adults but *money* for children

TABLE 3.4 *Number of times mothers chose the words under study for the experimenter and for their children in the two experiments on mothers' naming practices when the choice was between a specific, short, frequent word versus a general, long, infrequent word. Also shown are the number of times eighteen different children named the pictures with the words under study.*

Specific-short-frequent vs. General-long-infrequent	Adult-adult		Adult-child		Child-adult $N = 18$
	Exp't. 3.1	Exp't. 3.2	Exp't. 3.1	Exp't. 3.2	
Knife	20	20	20	20	18
Silverware	0	0	0	0	0
Other	0	—	0	—	0
Ring	20	20	20	20	10
Jewelry	0	0	0	0	0
Other	0	—	0	—	8
Table	20	20	20	20	17
Furniture	0	0	0	0	0
Other	0	—	0	—	1
Gun	16	19	20	19	15
Weapon	0	1	0	1	0
Other	4	—	0	—	3
Snake	18	19	20	20	17
Reptile	0	1	0	0	0
Other	2	—	0	—	1

TABLE 3.5 Number of times mothers chose the words under study for the experimenter and for their children in the two experiments on mothers' naming practices when the choice was between a specific, long, frequent word versus a general, short, infrequent word. Also shown are the number of times eighteen different children named the pictures with the words under study.

Specific-long-frequent vs. General-short-infrequent	Adult-adult Exp't. 3.1	Adult-adult Exp't. 3.2	Adult-child Exp't. 3.1	Adult-child Exp't. 3.2	Child-adult N = 18
Elephant	20	20	20	20	18
Mammal	0	0	0	0	0
Other	0	—	0	—	0
Refrigerator	19	20	18	20	15
Appliance	0	0	0	0	0
Other	1	—	2	—	3
Automobile	0	20	0	20	0
Vehicle	0	0	0	0	0
Other	20	—	20	—	18
Ruler	20	20	20	20	1
Gauge	0	0	0	0	0
Other	0	—	0	—	17
Record	19	20	19	20	17
Disc	0	0	0	0	0
Other	1	—	1	—	1

(see Brown, 1958b). And the picture of a number of mints was most often called *mints* for adults but *candy(ies)* for children. Thus it seems that in some cases a gain in just frequency will be sufficient to sway a mother in her choice of a name for her child even though it involves a cost in both specificity and brevity.

Table 3.4 shows the results for pictures for which the names could either be specific, short, and frequent or general, long, and infrequent. It should come as no surprise that for all pictures in this set mothers almost invariably chose the specific, short, frequent name over the general, long, and infrequent name for both the experimenter and their children. The specific, short, frequent names have everything going for them (i.e., specificity, brevity, and frequency) and indeed it would have come as a surprise if mothers had not chosen these terms for either the experimenter or their child.

Finally, consider Table 3.5 which shows the results for pictures for which the names could either be specific, long, and frequent or general, short, and infrequent. For this set of pictures mothers never chose the general, short, infrequent name for either the experimenter or their children. For four out of five pictures they almost invariably produced the specific, long, and frequent names (*elephant, refrigerator, ruler,* and *record*) in both Experiments 3.1 and 3.2. For the picture of a car when they were asked to name it spontaneously in Experiment 3.1 they always said *car* rather than *automobile* but in Experiment 3.2, when forced to choose between *automobile* and *vehicle,* they always chose *automobile.* Thus, at least for these word pairs, a gain in brevity alone was never enough to sway a mother to sacrifice specificity and frequency in choosing a name for her child.

To assess the statistical significance of the tendency of mothers to use more frequent, more general, and shorter words for their children than for the experimenter we began by making a record of the number of times a mother used a more frequent, more general, or shorter term for her child and the number of times she used a less frequent, less general, or a longer term for her child for each word pair tested in these experiments. In this analysis we were only concerned with cases in which there was a difference in the frequency, generality, or length of the word an individual mother provided her child as compared with the word that same mother provided the adult. Table 3.6 summarizes our findings. The grand totals in Table 3.6 show that out of 183 cases in which a mother named a picture with a word of different frequency for her child as compared to the adult, 160 times she used a more frequent term for the child and only 23 times did she use a less frequent term for the child;[3] that out of 174 cases in which she named a picture with a word at a different level of generality for her child as compared to the adult, 157 times she used a more general term for the child and only 17 times did she use a more specific term for the child; and finally, that out of 182 cases in which she named a picture with a word of different length for her child as compared to the adult, 104 times she used the shorter term for the child whereas 78 times she used a longer term for the child. Using one-tailed sign tests (see Siegel, 1956, pp. 68–75) we found that the tendency of mothers to use more frequent words for their children in these experiments was highly significant ($p < .0005$) and also that the tendency of mothers to use more general terms for their children was as well ($p < .0005$). The tendency of mothers to use shorter terms for their children in these experiments was only marginally significant ($p < .05$). Thus we can with confidence assume that if this experiment (with the same word pairs) were replicated with another set of mothers (sampled from the same population of mothers), we would again find that with respect to differences in the ways in which they would name these pictures for their children as compared to adults they would tend to use more frequent and more general terms for their children.

What if we were to run the experiment again, but this time testing a different set of words. In other words, are these findings true of English

---

[3] Again Thorndike and Lorge's General Count (1944) was the measure of frequency of occurrence used in the analysis.

TABLE 3.6 Number of times mothers used more frequent, more general, or longer terms for their child (than for an adult) and the number of times they used less frequent, less general, and shorter terms for their child (than for an adult) for each word-pair tested for in the experiments on the naming practices of mothers.

Word pairs	Frequency ↑	Frequency ↓	Generality ↑	Generality ↓	Length ↑	Length ↓
Specific-long-infrequent/General-short-frequent						
Pineapple/Fruit	2	0	2	0	0	2
Sandal/Shoe	21	0	21	0	0	21
Pigeon/Bird	18	0	18	0	0	16
Collie/Dog	14	0	14	0	5	13
Carnation/Flower	19	0	19	0	0	19
Cantaloupe/Fruit	9	1	9	1	1	9
Typewriter/Machine	1	1	1	1	1	1
Hammer/Tool	1	1	1	1	1	1
Grasshopper/Insect	2	2	2	1	1	3
Pomegranate/Fruit	6	0	6	0	0	6
TOTALS	93	5	93	4	9	91
Specific-short-infrequent/General-long-frequent						
Mint/Candy	19	4	16	1	19	2
Dime/Money	23	0	23	0	22	1
Ant/Insect	1	3	2	2	2	1
Cat/Animal	0	9	0	9	9	0
Mints/Candies	17	0	17	0	16	1
TOTALS	60	16	58	12	68	5
Specific-short-frequent/General-long-infrequent						
Knife/Silverware	0	0	0	0	0	0
Ring/Jewelry	0	0	0	0	0	0
Table/Furniture	0	0	0	0	0	0
Gun/Weapon	4	0	4	0	0	4
Snake/Reptile	2	0	2	1	0	3
TOTALS	6	0	6	1	0	7
Specific-long-frequent/General-short-infrequent						
Elephant/Mammal	0	0	0	0	0	0
Refrigerator/Appliance	0	1	0	0	0	1
Automobile/Vehicle	0	0	0	0	0	0
Ruler/Gauge	0	0	0	0	0	0
Record/Disk	1	1	0	0	1	0
TOTALS	1	2	0	0	1	1
GRAND TOTALS	160	23	157	17	78	104

NOTE: ↑ = more frequent, more general, or longer word for child; ↓ = less frequent, less general, or shorter word for child.

nomenclature in general above and beyond the twenty-five word pairs which were studied in these experiments (see H. Clark, 1973b)? It is difficult to argue with certainty about this issue for a reason which will become clear shortly, but I will suggest that probably the frequency and generality effects would hold even for different word pairs. There were a total of fifteen word pairs for which either the more or the less frequent member of the pair was transmitted more often to the child. Of these, there were twelve cases in which the more frequent member of the pair was transmitted to the child more often and only three cases in which the less frequent member of the pair was transmitted to the child more often. If these word pairs had been drawn at random from some larger population of word pairs and given the null hypothesis of no tendency on the part of the mother to provide her child with the more frequent member of the pair, it can be shown again by a one-tailed sign test that the probability of finding twelve or more word pairs out of fifteen consistent with the alternative hypothesis of a frequency effect is statistically significant ($p < .02$). Similarly there were a total of fourteen word pairs for which either the more general or the less general member of the pair was transmitted more often to the child. Of these, there were thirteen cases in which the more general member of the pair was transmitted more often to the child and only one case in which the more specific member of the pair was transmitted to the child more often. Again, if these word pairs had been drawn at random from some larger population of word pairs and given the null hypothesis of no tendency on the part of a mother to provide her child with the more general member of the pair, it can be shown again by a one-tailed sign test that the probability of finding thirteen or more word pairs out of fourteen consistent with the alternative hypothesis of a generality effect is statistically significant ($p < .001$). A similar treatment of the data on length [4] would not allow us to reject the null hypothesis of no tendency on the part of a mother to provide a shorter word for the child ($p < .16$).

The problem with the above argument is that the word pairs which were tested in these experiments were not deliberately drawn at random from some larger population of word pairs (e.g., English nomenclature in general) but were chosen for a variety of other practical reasons. Thus it is not clear what population of word pairs the set of twenty-five used in this experiment is representative of, which is why, as noted above, it is difficult to argue with certainty that these findings are generalizable to English nomenclature as a whole. Nonetheless, it is not at all clear that the word pairs that were studied in this experiment are more likely to show the frequency and

[4] Out of seventeen word pairs for which either the longer or the shorter member of the pair was provided more often to the child, there were eleven cases in which the shorter member was provided more often and six cases in which the longer member was provided more often.

generality effects than other word pairs which might have been used, and therefore, as stated above, it seems likely that these effects would hold for word pairs other than those sampled in this study.

In the immediately foregoing discussion the frequency and generality effects were considered separately. It should be pointed out, however, that usually when a mother named an object differently for her child she used a term that was both more frequent and more general for the child. Thus mothers were more inclined to use the term *shoe* than *sandal,* the term *bird* than *pigeon,* the term *dog* than *collie,* the term *flower* than *carnation,* the term *candy* than *mint,* the term *money* than *dime,* and the term *candies* than *mints* when naming for their children than when they were naming for the experimenter. In each of these cases the term which mothers tended to use for their children was both more frequent and more general than the term they tended to use for the experimenter. Thus usually when there is a difference in the way in which a mother will name an object for her child and an adult it will be in the direction of both greater frequency and greater generality for the child.

To give the reader a feeling for the kinds of pictures which were named by mothers with more general and more frequent terms for their children than for an adult, Figure 3.1 is presented. Figure 3.1 shows the pictures of the collie, the sandal, the carnation, and the dime, each of which tended to elicit more frequent and more general names from mothers to children than from those mothers to the experimenter.

When the eighteen three-to-five-year-old children were asked to name the pictures, they sometimes had difficulty. This was probably due to two factors: (1) their limited vocabulary, and (2) the ambiguity for them of certain pictures, especially the pictures of a single mint and of a group of mints. Nonetheless, in twenty-four out of twenty-five cases they used most often the same names as the ones that the mothers had used most often when naming the pictures for their children. This of course means that for some of the pictures they did not use the names that the mothers had used most often when naming the pictures for the experimenter. Thus, for example, mothers tended to name a picture of a sandal a *sandal* for adults but a *shoe* for children, or a picture of a pigeon a *pigeon* for adults but a *bird* for children. The children's words for these pictures were most often *shoe* and *bird,* thus corresponding with the mothers' names for children rather than their names for adults. The one exception to this general rule was in the case of the picture of several mints for which four children gave the name *mints* whereas only two used the word *candies,* which had been the preferred name of mothers for their children. Apart from this one slight exception the children's names for the pictures accord better with the way in which mothers named them for their children than with the way they named them for an adult.

Collie

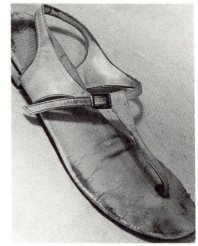

Sandal

Dime

Carnation

DISCUSSION

Although the child's vocabulary is often described as "concrete" (see Brown, 1958b; Anglin, 1970), it is in fact only relatively so. It is true that the child lacks very general terms such as *object, article, matter,* and so forth, which are frequently occurring in the vocabulary of adults. But at the same time he also lacks very specific terms such as *collie, carnation, Volkswagen,* and so forth. His first common nouns tend to cluster at some intermediate level of generality which classifies the world into categories which are not too big, but then again, not too small.

When an adult names an object for another adult she often uses as specific a term as possible, presumably because a specific term conveys more information. It seems reasonable to assume that the child will learn many of his category labels from listening to his mother name the various objects in his world. This raises the question of why the child does not learn the very specific terms (e.g., *collie, pigeon, sandal*) that mothers often use when they name objects. At least part of the answer seems to be that when naming objects for their children mothers will not as often use these specific terms. Rather, a mother will sometimes tailor her choice of a name of an object for her child, thus supplying him with vocabulary at an intermediate level of generality.

A mother will not always choose the most frequently occurring word when naming objects for her child. In some cases she will favor a more specific term over a more frequently occurring alternative (e.g., *pineapple* versus *fruit*). But usually when there is a difference between the way in which a mother names an object for her child and for an adult, it is in the direction of the more frequently occurring but less specific word for the child and of the less frequently occurring but more specific term for the adult.

In addition to the tendency to supply a child with more frequent and more general words there may also be a tendency to supply the child with shorter words rather than longer words, as Brown (1958b) has argued; but on the basis of this study it would not appear to be as strong a factor.

See facing page

FIGURE 3.1 Pictures of objects which tend to be named by mothers with more frequent and more general terms for their children than for an adult. Mothers often called the picture of a collie *collie* for an adult but they called it *dog* or *doggie* for their children. They usually called the picture of a sandal *sandal* for the experimenter but *shoe* for their children. While half of the mothers called the picture of a carnation *carnation* for the experimenter, in all cases but one they called this picture *flower* for their children. They usually called the picture of a dime *dime* when addressing the experimenter but more often than not they used the term *money* for their children.

Usually of course, frequency and brevity are correlated and so when an adult names a particular object, a *car* rather than an *automobile,* for example, it is not clear whether this preference is related to a preference for frequently occurring words or for short words or for both. However, in this study, which attempted to disentangle the relative contribution of these factors, it was seen that mothers would sometimes choose a word whose only advantage seemed to be that it was frequently occurring when naming objects for their children (e.g., *money* over *dime, candy* over *mint*) whereas they never chose a word whose only advantage was brevity.

The child's first common nouns are, in fact, relatively frequently occurring names of objects in English, objects which are often classified at some intermediate level of generality. It would seem likely that children will often acquire these common nouns from the ways in which their mothers name objects for them, at least initially. The present study addressed the question of whether or not there is a tendency, in fact, on the part of mothers to supply children with those words that children seem to learn first. The answer appears to be yes, which simply means that the child's first terms of reference are consistent with the kinds of terms a mother transmits to her child in the original naming process.

Behavioral Equivalence

The studies described thus far in this chapter have established that there is some correspondence between the way in which mothers name objects for children and the order in which children acquire English nomenclature. But why should mothers name objects for children in the particular ways that they do? Why should mothers name a carnation a *flower,* a dime *money,* or a collie *dog(gie)* when first transmitting vocabulary to their children? Why do they choose these particular terms and not more specific or more general terms?

As an answer to these questions I would like to present an argument which is very similar to one suggested by Brown in his paper "How Shall a Thing Be Called" (1958b) and elaborated in Chapter VII of his text *Social Psychology* (1965). Brown argued that a mother will provide children with names that will categorize objects at their "usual level of utility" (1958b), which he later defined as their "level of probable non-linguistic equivalence" (1965). The objects named by the same common noun are linguistically equivalent since the same name can be applied to each of them. These objects are also "non-linguistically equivalent" in some degree since the objects named by the same word can be treated in the same way; that is, they are equivalent in terms of the actions which it is appropriate to take toward them. This will be more true of the sets of objects denoted by some terms than those denoted by others. For example, the term *flower* would seem to have a higher degree of nonlinguistic equivalence than either *tulip* or *plant* since there are certain actions which it is appropriate to take toward flowers in general—you can smell them, you can (but perhaps should not) pick them, and so on—which are not appropriate for all of the things we call *plants* (you don't usually smell trees or pick trees) or exclusively appropriate to just the objects we call *tulips*. When a mother names an object for her child she may choose a term which will be applicable to all of those objects which the child should behave toward in the same way. Thus in the above example a mother may name this particular tulip a *flower* as a first step in enticing the child to group this particular object with all of those other objects called *flowers* which are pickable, smellable, and in general equivalent in terms of the actions which are appropriate to all of the objects normally called *flowers*.

Such an argument might make sense out of some individual differences which have been observed in the order in which children acquire category labels at different levels of generality. For most English-speaking children the terms *dog* and *cat* are among the very first words they acquire (see for example Nelson, 1974, and also Chapter 2 of this book). However, when there is a pet at home children are often observed to acquire a specific name of the pet before the more generic classifications. For example, Huttenlocher (1974) observed that the three children whose comprehension skills she had studied who had pets, learned the specific names of the pets (e.g. *Candy*) before they learned any other words, including such terms as *dog* and *cat*. Such observations are consistent with the argument outlined above since when a child has a specific dog, for example, as a pet that animal is important in its uniqueness in the sense that the child's treatment of it should be different from his treatment of dogs in general. The pet should be fed, played with, taken care of, and in general treated in a way that is different from the behavior appropriate to all other dogs. Since the pet is to be treated in a way which is unique, the fact that the child learns a proper name for it, presumably from his parents, is consistent with the argument that parents will provide, and that therefore children will learn, names which group together objects toward which the child should behave in the same way. In this case the pet is important in its uniqueness and to be treated differently from all of the other objects in the child's world and therefore it is named in a way which distinguishes it from all of those other objects, with a proper noun.

Consider another example. We found in the previous studies that when mothers were asked to name a picture of a dime for their two-year-old child, more often than not they called it *money,* whereas when naming it for an adult they almost invariably called it a *dime*. Such a difference may seem somewhat surprising in view of the fact that *dime* seems, to some observers at least, like the obvious and natural name for this particular object.

However, this finding becomes comprehensible in view of the arguments outlined above. While it is important for adults to know the specific denominations of currency, it is not so important for the two-year-old child since he has not yet become entangled in the world of buying and selling. Rather for him it is only important to treat all of the things called *money* with due respect—he should not eat them, nor lose them, but rather put them away safely in Mummy's purse, Daddy's wallet, or his piggy bank.

The purpose of the studies to be presented now has been to lend some empirical support to this line of argument. In these studies we have called the variable under investigation "behavioral equivalence" rather than non-linguistic equivalence but the basic idea is the same. In the studies to be presented we have tried to lend empirical support to the position that the names that children learn first are ones which group together objects toward which they should behave in the same way.

Experiment 3.3

METHOD

The specific purpose of the present study was to obtain judgments of the behavioral equivalence for the two-year-old child of a set of hierarchically related words and to see whether the word rated highest in behavioral equivalence within a given hierarchy was also the word that children learned first. Since we had already established the order of acquisition by children of the words within a set of hierarchically related terms (see Chapter 2 Experiment 2.1), we decided to obtain judgments of the behavioral equivalence of the objects grouped together by the words within those word hierarchies. Thus the seven three-term hierarchies which we chose to investigate were:

I	*II*	*III*	*IV*	*V*	*VI*	*VII*
people	food	plants	vehicles	money	animals	animals
children	fruit	flowers	cars	coins	dogs	fish
boys	apples	roses	Volkswagens	dimes	collies	sharks

We decided also to obtain judgments of behavioral equivalence for the five-term hierarchy which we had also studied in that investigation. Thus the eighth hierarchy which was investigated in the present study was:

VIII
living things
animals
mammals
primates
chimpanzees

Subjects were forty-eight male and female kindergarten teachers in Providence, Rhode Island. Although not all of these adults were parents, they were, because of their vocation, all familiar with young children. Each subject was given the following directions in written form:

Please read carefully:
Common nouns such as *dog, animal, car, money,* etc. refer not to one but rather to a group of objects. The objects named by the same word are linguistically equivalent because the same name applies to each of them. These objects are also "behaviorally equivalent" in some degree because behavior which is appropriate to one of the objects named by a word will also be appropriate to all of the other objects named by that word. In this study we would like to obtain your judgments of the behavioral equivalence for the two-year-old child of the objects named by different words. The more appropriate behaviors (or responses) that the child can direct toward all of the instances and only the instances named by a particular word, the greater its "behavioral equivalence." Conversely, the fewer the behaviors (or responses) the child can exhibit to all of the instances and only the instances named by a particular word, the less its "behavioral equivalence." Consider the following two examples: (1) *Rain* has a higher behavioral equivalence than does *weather* because the child has many behaviors appropriate to (and only to) rain—he must wear rubber boots, he must use an umbrella, he must not play in the puddles, etc.—but few behaviors exclusively appropriate to (and only to) weather since *weather* refers to any prevailing atmospheric condition (sunny, rainy, snowy, windy, muggy, hot, foggy, etc.), each of which requires a different set of behaviors. In judging the degree of behavioral equivalence of a word, it is important to remember that the behaviors which you think of should be appropriate to *only* the instances named by that word. Consider a second example: (2) There are a number of behaviors which the young child can exhibit toward tennis balls— he can roll them, bounce them, throw them, catch them, etc. However, each of these behaviors (rolling, bouncing, catching, throwing) is appropriate to various other kinds of balls (such as baseballs, footballs, rubber balls, etc.). Therefore, in this example *ball* would have a greater degree of behavioral equivalence than *tennis ball*.

When judging the degree of behavioral equivalence of a word, please consider both the "do's" (appropriate behaviors) and "don'ts" (inappropriate behaviors) which the child learns in relation to the objects denoted by each word. Please use the numbers 1 to 3 (1 to 5 in the last case) to indicate the word which has the highest (1), the next highest (2), and the lowest (3) degree of behavioral equivalence.

After subjects felt they understood the instructions (which sometimes took a while) they were given an answer sheet which presented the eight hierarchies of terms described above. Each hierarchy was separate from the others on the answer sheet and within each hierarchy the words were arranged so that the most general term was at the top, the next most general term was immediately below it, and so on. Beside each word within a hierarchy was a space in which subjects were to assign a number—1 beside the term which they thought was highest in behavioral equivalence, 2 beside the word which they thought was next highest and so on. It took about ten minutes for subjects to complete the task.

RESULTS

In order to obtain orderings of the words within each hierarchy of terms along the dimension of behavioral equivalence and in order to make use of all of the data provided by subjects in this study, we computed a weighted measure of behavioral equivalence for each word in each hierarchy according to the following method. For each word within each of the three-term hierarchies we counted the number of adults who had rated that word as being highest in behavioral equivalence and multiplied this number by 3; then we counted up the number of adults who had rated that word as being next highest in behavioral equivalence and multiplied this number by 2; finally, we multiplied the number of remaining adults who had rated that word as being least behaviorally equivalent by 1. Then we added these three products, giving the weighted measure of behavioral equivalence for that word. The procedure was the same for the five-term hierarchy except that we multiplied the number of adults rating a given word within it as being highest in behavioral equivalence by 5, the number of adults rating that word as being next most behaviorally equivalent by 4, and so on, before adding the products to obtain the weighted measure of behavioral equivalence for that word.

The results of these calculations are presented in Table 3.7, which shows the weighted estimates of behavioral equivalence for each word within each of the eight hierarchies of terms (left-hand column) and also the modal order of acquisition of those terms suggested by the studies described in Chapter 2 (right-hand column). The question which we were seeking to answer in conducting this study was whether adult judgments of behavioral equivalence predict the first term in the various hierarchies that our other studies had shown children acquired first. As Table 3.7 shows, in seven out of eight hierarchies the term which received the highest weighted measure of behavioral equivalence was the term that children were shown to acquire first. Thus, within the food hierarchy, *apples* received a higher rating than *fruit* or *food;* within the plant hierarchy *flowers* received a higher rating than *roses* or *plants;* within the vehicle hierarchy *cars* received a higher rating than *Volkswagens* or *vehicles;* within the money hierarchy *money* received a higher rating than *dimes* or *coins;* within the two three-term animal hierarchies *dogs* received a higher rating than *collies* or *animals,* and *fish* received a higher rating than *sharks* or *animals;* and within the five-term hierarchy *animals* received a higher rating than the other four terms.

TABLE 3.7 Weighted estimates of behavioral equivalence for the words within each of eight sets of hierarchically related terms and the modal order of acquisition of those terms. Estimates of behavioral equivalence are based on data from Experiment 3.3. Estimates of the modal order of acquisition are based on the results of Experiment 2.1.

	Weighted measure of behavioral equivalence	RANK ORDER	Words	Modal order of acquisition
I**	75	↑ 3	Food	2 |
	87	| 2	Fruit	3 ↓
	126	→ 1	Apples	1 ←
II**	73	↑ 3	Plants	2 ↑
	129	→ 1	Flowers	1 ←
	86	↓ 2	Roses	3 ↓
III*	51	↑ 3	Vehicles	3 ↑
	130	→ 1	Cars	1 ←
	107	↓ 2	Volkswagens	2 ↓
IV*	112	→ 1	Money	1 ←
	74	↑ 3	Coins	3 ↑
	102	| 2	Dimes	2 |
V**	74	↑ 3	Animals	2 ↑
	133	→ 1	Dogs	1 ←
	81	↓ 2	Collies	3 ↓
VI*	92	↑ 2	Animals	2 ↑
	109	→ 1	Fish	1 ←
	87	↓ 3	Sharks	3 ↓
VII**	136	3	Living things	2
	188	→ 1	Animals	1 ←
	115	4	Mammals	2
	97	5	Primates	2
	184	2	Chimpanzees	2
VIII	65	↑ 3	People	3 ↑
	116	→ 1	Children	2 |
	107	↓ 2	Boys	1 ←

NOTE: * indicates identical ordering of terms; ** indicates agreement at level of first word only.

As the right-hand column of Table 3.7 indicates it was just those words receiving the highest ratings (*apple, flower, car, money, dog, fish,* and *animal*) which our previous experiments had indicated that most children acquire first among the terms within the hierarchies. The one case in which the measure of behavioral equivalence failed to predict the level at which children first learn to categorize objects linguistically was the boys-children-people hierarchy. *Children* received the highest behavioral equivalence rating in this study, whereas the earlier experiments had suggested that children generally learn *boy* before *children*.

Is this degree of correspondence statistically significant? Under the null hypothesis that this measure of behavioral equivalence is not predictive of the term within a hierarchy which children tend to acquire first, the probability by chance of a correspondence at the first level in any three-term hierarchy is $\frac{1}{3}$, and the probability by chance of a correspondence at the first level in the five-term hierarchy is $\frac{1}{5}$. The probability by chance of a correspondence in six out of seven three-term hierarchies and the one five-term hierarchy or better can be shown to be $[(\frac{7}{6})\ (\frac{1}{3})^{6}\ (\frac{2}{3}) + (\frac{1}{3})^{7}]\ (\frac{1}{5})$ which equals .0014. Thus the null hypothesis of no correspondence between judgments of behavioral equivalence and the level at which children first learn to categorize objects linguistically can be rejected ($p < .002$ for a one-tailed test). While adult judgments of behavioral equivalence are good at predicting the first term within a given hierarchy that the child will learn, they are not especially good at predicting the order of acquisition of terms beyond the first level. As Table 3.7 shows, in only three out of eight hierarchies is there an exact correspondence between the ordering of the words according to judgments of behavioral equivalence and the order in which children tend to acquire those words. But it was really the first level with which we were concerned in this study. The results are in fact consistent with the argument outlined in the introduction to this study, that children will first learn to categorize objects with names (provided by caretakers) which group together those objects with others toward which they should behave in the same way.

Experiment 3.4

METHOD

We decided to try to replicate the preceding experiment but with three refinements. First, recall that in the preceding study the answer sheet presented the words in each hierarchy such that the most general word was immediately above the next most general word, and so on. It might be objected that there was something about our instructions which would encourage subjects to choose as most behaviorally equivalent the middle term within any given hierarchy. If the subject somewhat mechanically chose the middle term in each hierarchy the result would have been a correspondence in five out of eight hierarchies between the term judged most behaviorally equivalent and the term learned first by children, since our previous investigations had shown that in five of these hierarchies children tend to acquire the middle term first. We therefore decided to replicate the study, but this time presenting the words within each hierarchy in a random order. Thus in this study the three-term hierarchies on the answer sheet were presented as follows:

I	II	III	IV	V	VI	VII
boys	food	flowers	Volkswagens	dimes	collies	fish
people	apples	plants	vehicles	money	animals	animals
children	fruit	roses	cars	coins	dogs	sharks

Finally, the five-term hierarchy was presented as follows:

VIII
mammals
chimpanzees
animals
living things
primates

The second refinement concerned the make-up of the adult judges whose services we enlisted to rate the words. The argument that we wanted to confirm was that mothers of young children, in particular, judge as most behaviorally equivalent for their children the objects grouped together by that word within each of the hierarchies that our other studies had suggested children learn first. Our interest was primarily in mothers since presumably it is mothers who most often first transmit vocabulary to children. In the previous study, although all of the adult judges were familiar with children, not all of them were parents. Therefore in this study, ten mothers of young children between the ages of two and five were asked to give their ratings of behavioral equivalence for each of the words within each of the hierarchies. For comparison purposes we also ran ten adults who were not parents. All of the adult judges who were run in the study lived in the Cambridge area.

The third refinement was that in this study subjects were tested individually, whereas in the preceding study they had been run as a group.

Apart from these three refinements the procedure for this study was the same as it had been in the preceding one. Each subject was given the exact same directions as had been used before (see p. 93). After they felt they understood the instructions they were given the modified answer sheets on which they proceeded to write their ratings beside each of the words within each hierarchy. Again it took about ten minutes for subjects to complete the task.

RESULTS

We computed weighted measures of behavioral equivalence for each word within each hierarchy based on the responses of the ten mothers in exactly the same way as we had in the previous study (see p. 94). We also computed such measures based on the responses of the ten nonmothers. The results of these calculations are presented in Table 3.8. Consider the estimates of behavioral equivalence based on the mothers' data. Again in this study, in seven out of eight hierarchies the term which received the

TABLE 3.8 *Weighted estimates of behavioral equivalence for the words within each of eight sets of hierarchically related terms and the modal order of acquisition of those terms. Estimates of behavioral equivalence are based on data from ten mothers in Experiment 3.4. The weighted estimates of behavioral equivalence for ten nonmothers are also shown in parentheses.*

	Weighted measure of behavioral equivalence		RANK ORDER	Words	Modal order of acquisition
	Others	*Mothers*			
I**	(26)	15	↑ 3	Food	2 ⎤
	(19)	19	│ 2	Fruit	3 ↓
	(15)	26	→ 1	Apples	1 ←
II**	(22)	16	↑ 3	Plants	2 ↑
	(23)	26	→ 1	Flowers	1 ←
	(15)	18	↓ 2	Roses	3 ↓
III*	(24)	12	↑ 3	Vehicles	3 ↑
	(22)	29	→ 1	Cars	1 ←
	(14)	19	↓ 2	Volkswagens	2 ↓
IV*	(24)	25	→ 1	Money	1 ←
	(21)	17	↑ 3	Coins	3 ↑
	(15)	18	│ 2	Dimes	2 │
V*	(24)	19	↑ 2	Animals	2 ↑
	(20)	27	→ 1	Dogs	1 ←
	(16)	14	↓ 3	Collies	3 ↓
VI*	(22)	20	↑ 2	Animals	2 ↑
	(19)	26	→ 1	Fish	1 ←
	(19)	14	↓ 3	Sharks	3 ↓
VII**	(32)	32	3	Living things	2
	(38)	44	→ 1	Animals	1 ←
	(27)	20	4	Mammals	2
	(22)	12	5	Primates	2
	(31)	42	2	Chimpanzees	2
VIII	(20)	14	↑ 3	People	3 ↑
	(23)	24	→ 1	Children	2 │
	(17)	22	↓ 2	Boys	1 ←

NOTE: As in Table 3.7, * indicates identical ordering of terms and ** indicates agreement at level of first word only for estimates based on mothers' responses.

highest weighted measure of behavioral equivalence was the term which most children were shown to acquire first in Chapter 2. The one case in which the measure of behavioral equivalence failed to predict the level at which children first learn to categorize objects linguistically was again the boys-children-people hierarchy. *Children* received the highest behavioral equivalence rating in this study, whereas the experiment described in Chapter 2 had suggested that children generally learn *boy* before *children*. Since these results are identical to the results of the previous study in terms of the power of judgments of behavioral equivalence to predict the level at which children first learn to categorize objects, they are again statistically significant ($p < .002$ for a one-tailed test).

Table 3.8 also shows in parentheses to the left of the estimates of behavioral equivalence based on mothers' judgments the estimates based on the ratings of nonmothers. It can be seen that these estimates are not nearly as good at predicting the first term within each of the hierarchies that children learn first (they are in fact predictive of only three out of eight hierarchies). Thus, not really surprisingly, for adults not familiar with children, judgments of behavioral equivalence for the child may not be predictive of the order of acquisition of English nomenclature.[5] However, for adults familiar with children (the previous experiment) or better yet, for parents of young children (this experiment), such judgments are quite predictive.

CONCLUSIONS

Parental and teacher ratings of behavioral equivalence of these terms of reference have proved to be more consistent with their order of acquisition than a variety of other dimensions along which we have asked adults to scale them. While this is not a definitive study, it is suggestive confirmation of the validity of the hypothesis outlined above that mothers will initially label objects with names, and that therefore children will initially learn names, which classify the world into groups of things which will be behaviorally equivalent for the child.

Combining the results and arguments presented in this chapter with those of Chapter 2 we can see that the functions served by objects are implicated in the growth of vocabulary in determining both horizontal development and vertical development (see also Brown, 1958b, 1965; Nelson, 1973a, 1973b, 1974). The child will learn first the names of objects with which he interacts whether this interaction fulfills basic biological needs, as in the

[5] Two other studies have indicated that judgments of behavioral equivalence made by nonparents are somewhat more consistent with the order of acquisition of the words within these hierarchies, at the first level at least, than the results of this experiment suggest. In one study there was agreement in five out of eight cases, and in another in six out of eight cases.

case of eating food, or whether the interaction is less intimately related to survival, as in the case of playing with toys or simply looking at salient objects (see Chapter 2). Moreover, as the studies described in this chapter suggest, because of the ways in which parents will name these objects for him, he will initially learn terms which classify them at a maximally useful level of generality in the sense that they categorize together objects which he should behave toward in the same way.

Chapter 4

On the Extension
of the Child's First
Terms of Reference[1]

The vocabulary of a child (i.e., words used or understood) is not a direct index of his concepts, for it would be a mistake to presuppose that a given term of reference has the same meaning for the child as for the adults who transmit language to him. In order to cast some light on the nature of the conceptual structure underlying the child's terms of reference, it is necessary to examine carefully both the extension and the intension of these words for him. Only a direct examination of the range of objects which the child thinks are comprehended by a term of reference (i.e., extension) will reveal the nature of the child's natural tendency to categorize the world linguistically. And only a scientific investigation of the meaning of such words to the child, above and beyond the set of objects comprehended by the term (i.e., intension), will reveal the conceptual knowledge underlying the child's use and understanding of English nomenclature. Thus in this and the following three chapters we shall be concerned with the concepts underlying the child's first terms of reference. The present chapter, Chapter 5, and Chapter 6 will present the results from a number of studies examining the extension of the child's category labels. In Chapter 7 the focus will be on the intension of these words for the child and on the relation between intension and extension.

[1] I am grateful to Marvin Cohen, Joy Skon, and Yvette Sheline for their help in conducting the study described in this chapter.

One can imagine several possible relationships between the extension of a child's term and of the corresponding adult term, seven of which are illustrated in the form of Venn diagrams in Figure 4.1. (1) Underextension: The child might use the term to apply to only a subset of the objects included in the corresponding adult concept. For example, the child might think that only four-legged, furry mammals are ANIMALS. (2) Overextension: The child might use the term to apply to a broader range of referents than the adult does. For example, he may initially apply the term *dog* to all quadrupeds. (3) Overlap: The child might use the term to apply to some of the same objects that an adult does, not apply it to some objects denoted by the adult term, and apply it to some objects not encompassed by the adult term. For example, the child might apply the term *flower* to most flowers but not to roses and daisies and, in addition, might apply it to other kinds of plants. (4) Nonoverlap: The child might use the term to apply to a completely different range of referents from the range of referents denoted by the adult term. This particular relationship would seem to be unlikely but would prevail, for example, if the child used the term *dog* to refer only to cats. (5) The child might not use the word to apply to any referent. This is the case for terms which have not yet entered the child's vocabulary. For example, he may never use the term *philodendron* to refer to anything. (6) The child might use a word which does not exist in the adult's vocabulary to apply to some range of referents. For example, the child might invent a word such as *psee* to apply to flowers, trees, and other forms of vegetation, or *dee-dee* to apply to cars, trucks, and other vehicles. (7) Concordance: The child might use the term to apply to exactly the same range of referents as is encompassed by the adult term. For example, the child might use the term *person* to apply to exactly the same set of featherless bipeds as the adult does. This state of concordance presumably represents the end state toward which development progresses.[2]

The psychological literature on the subject has often characterized the relationship as one of overextension—the child is portrayed as using a term of reference to apply to a broader range of objects than the adult does (Brown, 1958b; Anglin, 1970; E. Clark, 1973). The corresponding developmental process is therefore viewed as differentiation—the child who begins with overly general categories gradually narrows these down until they focus on the same range of referents as is encompassed by the adult terms.

Many of the protagonists of this point of view offer as the primary

---

[2] This discussion of the possible relations between the extension of the child's terms and those of adults and the ensuing analysis and critique of theories based upon diary studies which stress only overgeneralization have been previously presented by the writer (Anglin, 1974, 1975, 1976). A similar line of argument has been made, in part, more recently by Reich (1976).

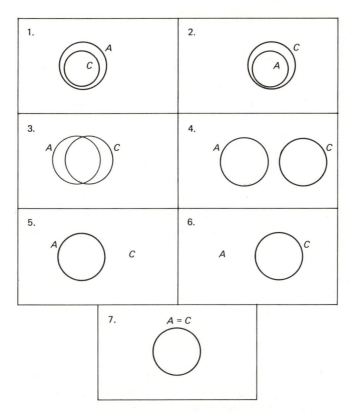

FIGURE 4.1 Venn diagrams illustrating possible relationships between the extension of a child's word and of the corresponding adult term.

NOTE: (1) Underextension: $C \subset A$: The child uses the term to apply only to a subset of the objects included in the adult concept. (2) Overextension: $A \subset C$: The child uses the term to apply to a broader range of referents than the adult does. (3) Overlap: $A \not\subset C$; $C \not\subset A$; $A \cap C > O$: The child uses the term to apply to some of the same objects as an adult does but overextends the term to some objects and does not apply the term to some objects covered by the adult term. (4) Nonoverlap: $A \cap C = O$ where $A > O$; $C > O$: The child uses the term to apply to a completely different range of referents from the range of referents covered by the adult term. (5) $A > O$; $C = O$: The child does not use the word to refer to any referent. (6) $C > O$: The child uses the word to refer to a range of referents whereas the adult does not. (7) Concordance: $A = C$: The adult and the child use the term to apply to exactly the same range of referents.

source of evidence for their hypothesis (i.e., that the child's early concepts are overly general) the results of diary studies in which the words used by the child are recorded along with the contexts in which they are used (see for example Leopold, 1939, 1948, 1949a, b; Moore, 1896; Stern, 1930; Lewis, 1959; Chamberlain and Chamberlain, 1904a, b; Piaget, 1962). Eve

Clark (1973) has recently written a valuable review of the diary literature (although I disagree with her theoretical position). The point often stressed by these writers is that the child often overextends a term to objects which are not included in the adult concept. For example, children have been observed to use the term *papa* to apply to men other than their fathers (Moore, 1896); the term *bird* to apply to cows, dogs, cats, and other animals (Moore, 1896); the term *fly* to apply to specks of dirt, dust, small insects, toes, bread crumbs, and a toad (Moore, 1896); the term *bottle* to apply to various glass containers (Leopold, 1939); the term *train* to apply to an airplane, a wheelbarrow and a streetcar (Leopold, 1939); the term *mama* to apply to many different women (Leopold, 1948); the term *carrot* to apply to a carrot, a turnip, a plum, and a watermelon (Luria and Yudovich, 1959); and so on. Eve Clark has argued that overextension is language independent and universal. Furthermore, she argues that the determinant of overextension is perceptual similarity between the object which evokes the overextension and the instances of the class denoted by the term which is overgeneralized. "The majority of overextensions seem to be based on the perceived similarities among objects or events included referentially in a single category. The principle characteristics can be classified into several categories such as 'movement,' 'shape,' 'size,' 'sound,' 'taste' and 'texture' " (Clark, 1973). According to Clark, the child narrows down the meaning of an originally overextended term as he adds new features to the word and as new words are introduced to take over subareas of the semantic domain. Furthermore, according to Clark, the child is thought to add general features to a lexical entry first and only later increasingly specific features.

Undoubtedly there are instances of overgeneralization in the child's early use of words. However, the evidence from diaries is systematically biased to suggest oxerextension only and, because of the way it is collected and interpreted, does not tend to reveal underextension if it occurs. The problems with diaries revolve around the fact that they are based upon the spontaneous production of words by the child. It is not just that the child's limited vocabulary forces him to overgeneralize when he wants to refer to an object for which he does not have a name, although this is a factor. The deeper problem concerns the fact that when the child does not think that an instance is to be included in a concept (i.e., when his concept is narrower than that of an adult) his spontaneous speech will not reveal it. Consider the way these data are collected in terms of a specific example:

Referent	Name	Error
collie	*dog*	No error
cat	*dog*	Overextension
Chihuahua	—	—(not recorded)

If in the presence of a collie the child uses the word *dog,* he is using the term as an adult would and is therefore considered to be correct. Now suppose that in the presence of a cat the child says *dog.* This is viewed as an overextension because the child is referring to an object by means of a term that is more restricted in adult use. Notice that if the word *cat* is in the child's vocabulary, then this could be considered to be an example of underextension of the word *cat* although it is rarely interpreted as such. Now suppose the same child sees a Chihuahua but does not realize that this particular creature is an instance of the concept DOG and therefore does not use the term. This sort of occurrence is not recorded since the child has not spoken. In other words, the child either uses a word appropriately or he does not. Whenever he uses the word appropriately his response is thought of as correct. Whenever he does not use the word appropriately his response is thought of as incorrect and an instance of overextension. In this way diary studies are systematically biased to suggest overextension and differentiation (narrowing down categories) as the developmental process. They do not as directly suggest underextension and therefore they do not illuminate the process of generalization (filling out categories) if it occurs in the development of verbal concepts. It is possible, therefore, that overgeneralization is like the tip of an iceberg, the most visible but neither the only nor necessarily the most prevalent component of the child's referential problems.

A careful examination of the diary literature, in fact, does reveal some cases of what can plausibly be interpreted as underextension in spite of the biases against them described above. Daniel Klett and I reviewed a number of diaries in search of such cases. Consider some of the examples of underextension we found: (1) Moore, (1896, p. 140) describes the case of her son calling a dog *bird* after he had already been using the word *dog* in his productive vocabulary. Thus while this can be considered to be a case of overgeneralization of *bird* it can also be considered to be a case of undergeneralization of *dog.* (2) Lewis's son suggested that he did not consider pictures of flowers to be instances of the concept "flower" because he did not respond to directions concerning the *fa-fa* (his word for flowers) when they were directed toward a picture of flowers, but did respond when the directions referred to real flowers (Lewis, 1959, p. 127). (3) Lewis's son also used *hosh* (horse) to refer to a large dog, not the word *goggie* (doggie) which he had been using for all dogs (Lewis, 1959, p. 127). Thus this appears to be a case of undergeneralization of *goggie* as well as overgeneralization of *hosh.* (4) Bloom (1973, p. 72) describes the case of her daughter restricting the use of the word *car* to cars moving on the street below when watched from her living room window and failing to use it when she was in a car, saw a car standing still, or saw pictures of cars (Bloom, 1973, p. 72). (5) Leopold's bilingual daughter, Hildegard, limited the word *"baU"* (*baum* is German for "tree") to pictures of trees, although by comprehension she indicated that she knew it referred to real trees as well (Leopold, 1939, p. 50). (6) Hildegard also limited the use of the word *bi* (her word for *bild* which is German for "picture") to refer to just pictures of people (Leopold, 1939, p. 54). (7) Hildegard once failed to call her toy duck a *duck,* the word she typically used to refer to it, instead calling it an *auto* (Leopold, 1939, p. 69). (8) At the age of one year, eight months Hildegard used the word *"haUS"* for houses she built with blocks and then for pictures of houses but it was not until she was one year, eleven months that she used the word for real houses (Leopold, 1939, p. 90). (9) Even though *baby* was the first word she obviously understood and one of the first she produced (*bebi*) at one year, seven months, Hildegard greeted her baby picture with *waUwaU,* her word for dogs (Leopold, 1939, p. 52). (10) Hildegard limited the use of the word *man* which she pronounced *mã* only to pictures of men (Leopold, 1939, p. 98). (11) Hildegard did not use the word *frau* (German for "woman") which she pronounced *waU* to refer to women in pictures, although she used the word in other contexts (Leopold, 1939, p. 130). (12) Hildegard limited the use of the word *building* (*biltin*) only in referring to an apartment house (Leopold, 1949b, p. 59). (13) Chamberlain and Chamberlain (1904a, p. 269) observed that their daughter called a rabbit a *dog* even though she had the word *rabbit* in her productive vocabulary at the time. (14) Chamberlain and Chamberlain (1904b, p. 461) recorded a case in which their daughter called her father *mama* even though she had called him *papa* earlier. (15) Piaget (1962, p. 224) reported that on seeing Lucienne in a new bathing suit Jacqueline asked, "What's the baby's name?" persistently even though she knew full well that her name was *Lucienne* when she was not dressed in the new bathing suit.

These cases and others like them show that a case can be made for underextension, as well as overextension, even on the basis of the spontaneous language production recorded in the diary literature. Moreover, some of the authors of the diaries did note that undergeneralization occurred as well as overgeneralization. For example, in summarizing his son's linguistic development, Lewis (1959, p. 140) states that the child "learns to classify things as we classify them, to limit the meaning of some words, and to extend the meaning of others." Similarly, Leopold (1949a, pp. 153–54) states, "Sometimes the child used standard words in a more restricted application, which was later extended to the standard range. More commonly, words were used in a variety of applications which the standard did not allow. The process of learning to conform to standard usage then required a later reduction of the scope of applicability. Sometimes these two processes were combined."

Nonetheless, in considering the range of application of their childrens' first words the authors of diaries have emphasized overgeneralization and in some cases have not even mentioned undergeneralization. Similarly, in recent accounts of the child's first words, overextension has often been stressed to the exclusion of underextension and theories of semantic structure in the child have been developed resting on the premise that only overgeneralization occurs (see especially E. Clark, 1973, 1974; also see Brown, 1958b). While others have noted the possibility that underextension also occurs (e.g., Bloom, 1973; Nelson, 1973b; Huttenlocher, 1974; Stemmer, in press), the phenomenon has been given virtually no attention, especially in comparison with the attempt to scrutinize the determinants of overextension in the child. This state of affairs is undoubtedly a result of the fact that the spontaneous production of language in the child recorded in the diaries tends to suggest overextension but not nearly so clearly underextension for reasons that have been described. While a careful examination of those diaries does reveal some suggestive evidence of underextension, the evidence for overextension is much more striking. In the study reported below, we have tried to improve upon the diaries by creating an equal opportunity for the child to both overgeneralize and undergeneralize his first terms of reference. Rather than relying upon the child's spontaneous production of such words the following study involves a controlled examination of his comprehension of them, for only a test of comprehension clearly allows one to circumvent the biases inherent in the diaries that have been discussed.

Experiment 4.1

METHOD

There were three groups of subjects with eighteen subjects in each group. The youngest group consisted of children between two and a half and four years of age; the next oldest group consisted of children between four and a half and six years of age; the oldest group consisted of undergraduates from Harvard and Radcliffe. Every subject was shown a total of one hundred and twenty pictures and was asked one question for each picture. The verbal concepts that were tested were as follows:

I	*II*	*III*
ANIMAL	FOOD	PLANT
DOG	FRUIT	FLOWER
COLLIE	APPLE	TULIP

We chose concepts at different levels of generality because we suspected that perhaps the tendency to undergeneralize (in particular) might vary with the generality of the concept in question. Specifically, it seemed quite possible that children would make more undergeneralization responses for rather general concepts such as ANIMAL, FOOD, and PLANT since these concepts include a broad and varied set of instances.

There were several pictures representing instances of each of these nine concepts as well as several pictures of inanimate objects. A given subject was shown ten instances of a concrete concept in one hierarchy and ten noninstances; he was shown twenty instances of an intermediate concept from a different hierarchy and twenty noninstances; finally, he was shown thirty instances of the general concept in the remaining hierarchy as well as thirty noninstances. Each time the subject was shown an instance or a noninstance of a given concept he was asked whether it was an instance of the concept being tested. For example, one child was shown ten pictures of collies and was asked, "Is this a collie?" and also 10 noncollies (three other dogs, three other animals, and four inanimate objects) for which he was also asked, "Is this a collie?" The same child was also shown twenty pictures of fruits (ten apples and ten other fruits) and twenty pictures of nonfruits for which the question was asked, "Is this a fruit?" Finally, he was shown thirty pictures of plants and thirty pictures of inanimate objects for which the question was asked, "Is this a plant?" The design was such that within each age group six subjects were tested on each of the nine concepts.

The one hundred and twenty pictures were presented one at a time in a different random order to each subject. Underextension was operationally defined as having occurred in cases in which the subject, having been shown an instance of a concept, declined to assign it to a category. For example, if a child said "no" when asked of a picture of a dog, "Is this a dog?" then this was taken as evidence of underextension since such responses imply either that the child did not think of the dog shown in the photograph as a dog or at least that he was not sure. Overextension responses were similarly operationally defined as "yes" responses to the question, "Is this a _____?" when the photograph showed a noninstance. Since the number of instances was equal to the number of noninstances for each verbal concept tested in this study, there was, in theory at least, an equal opportunity for both overextension and underextension.

RESULTS

Subject-by-Subject Breakdown of Extension Errors for Each Concept

There was ample evidence in the responses of the young children of both overextension and underextension. Table 4.1 shows a subject-by-subject breakdown of both kinds of responses for each child for each of the nine concepts investigated in this experiment. Recall that an underextension response is a "no" to an instance; an overextension response is a "yes" to a noninstance. When a child responded "I don't know" rather than "yes" or "no" his response was counted as neither an overextension nor an underextension. Such responses were surprisingly infrequent in this experiment, although they did occur occasionally. Table 4.1 consists of nine panels arranged vertically, with each of the nine panels showing the number of underextensions (upper row in panel) and the number of overextensions (lower row in panel) made by the children on each of the nine concepts tested in this experiment. With the aid of Table 4.1, I would now like to consider the number of each kind of response made by each subject on each concept in turn.

Animal

The uppermost panel in Table 4.1 shows the number of both kinds of responses made by each child when tested on the concept ANIMAL. One child (*S*7) appeared to have no notion of what the word *animal* means and said "no" in answer to the question "Is this an animal?" for every picture, regardless of whether or not it was an animal. The other eleven children did seem to have some conception of what an animal is, for they identified some animals as animals and uniformly never identified an inanimate object as an animal. However, none of these eleven children identified all of the pictures of animals as animals whereas, as we shall see, every adult who was tested on the concept ANIMAL identified each and every picture of an animal as an instance. One child (*S*1) correctly identified every picture of an animal as an animal except for the picture of a woman saying, "That's not an animal, that's a person." This child's pattern of responses was closest to the adult pattern for this particular concept. As we shall see in a picture-by-picture analysis, no child was willing to classify the picture of a woman as an instance of the concept ANIMAL. Many children (*S*s 2, 21, 22, 23, 24) identified all of the pictures of animals as animals with the exception of two instances, the woman and one other, which was usually either a praying mantis or the caterpillar. One child (*S*19), for each of the pictures of a dog, when asked, "Is this an animal?" said, "No, it's a dog, not an animal," apparently implying that for him the two classes were mutually exclusive. This behavior which we have come to call the dominant name response was also notable in another child (*S*8) who insisted that eight of the dogs were not animals ("They are dogs"). This child did not treat every picture of a dog in this way, but rather classified twelve of them correctly as animals. For most of the children, however, dogs were definitely animals but usually some other instances were not. One child (*S*25) classified all of the dogs as animals but not four of the noncanine animals.

Thus it can be seen from Table 4.1 that children are somewhat variable with respect to the instances they include in the concept ANIMAL. All of them undergeneralize to some extent, but many of them only in the cases of

TABLE 4.1 *Number (#) and percentage (%) of underextension and overextension responses made by the children on each of the nine concepts tested in the extension experiment. An underextension response is a "no" to an instance. An overextension response is a "yes" to a noninstance.*

I. Animal hierarchy

Is this an animal?

	Ages 2½–4 years						Ages 4½–6 years						Total	
	S_1	S_2	S_3	S_7	S_8	S_9	S_{19}	S_{21}	S_{22}	S_{23}	S_{24}	S_{25}	#	%
Underextension responses	1/30	2/30	3/30	30/30	11/30	5/30	23/30	2/30	2/30	2/30	2/30	4/30	87/360	24.2
Overextension responses	0/30	0/30	0/30	0/30	0/30	0/30	0/30	0/30	0/30	0/30	0/30	0/30	0/360	0.0

Is this a dog?

	Ages 2½–4 years						Ages 4½–6 years						Total	
	S_4	S_5	S_6	S_{10}	S_{11}	S_{12}	S_{20}	S_{34}	S_{35}	S_{26}	S_{27}	S_{36}	#	%
Underextension responses	2/20	0/20	0/20	0/20	0/20	4/20	1/20	0/20	1/20	0/20	0/20	1/20	9/240	3.8
Overextension responses	2/20	0/20	0/20	6/20	2/20	0/20	0/20	0/20	0/20	0/20	0/20	0/20	8/240	3.3

Is this a collie?

	Ages 2½–4 years						Ages 4½–6 years						Total	
	S_{13}	S_{14}	S_{15}	S_{16}	S_{17}	S_{18}	S_{28}	S_{29}	S_{30}	S_{31}	S_{32}	S_{33}	#	%
Underextension responses	10/10	10/10	0/10	0/10	8/10	0/10	10/10	0/10	10/10	10/10	0/10	5/10	63/120	52.5
Overextension responses	0/10	1/10	8/10	2/10	1/10	3/10	0/10	3/10	0/10	0/10	0/10	5/10	23/120	19.2

II. Plant hierarchy

Is this a plant?

	Ages 2½–4 years						Ages 4½–6 years						Total	
	S_4	S_5	S_6	S_{13}	S_{14}	S_{15}	S_{20}	S_{34}	S_{35}	S_{28}	S_{29}	S_{30}	#	%
Underextension responses	3/30	1/30	4/30	20/30	6/30	0/30	3/30	2/30	3/30	1/30	24/30	1/30	70/360	19.4
Overextension responses	0/30	0/30	0/30	0/30	0/30	4/30	1/30	0/30	1/30	1/30	0/30	0/30	7/360	1.9

TABLE 4.1 (continued)

Is this a flower?

	S_1	S_2	S_3	S_{16}	S_{17}	S_{18}	S_{19}	S_{21}	S_{22}	S_{31}	S_{32}	S_{33}	#	%
Underextension responses	0/20	0/20	2/20	1/20	2/20	0/20	0/20	0/20	1/20	3/20	0/20	0/20	9/240	3.8
Overextension responses	3/20	9/20	0/20	2/20	0/20	3/20	7/20	5/20	7/20	6/20	1/20	2/20	45/240	18.8

Is this a tulip?

	S_7	S_8	S_9	S_{10}	S_{11}	S_{12}	S_{23}	S_{24}	S_{25}	S_{26}	S_{27}	S_{36}	#	%
Underextension responses	0/10	9/10	9/10	7/10	0/10	9/10	2/10	4/10	4/10	3/10	9/10	8/10	55/120	45.8
Overextension responses	4/10	0/10	0/10	3/10	9/10	3/10	3/10	0/10	0/10	0/10	4/10	0/10	26/120	21.8

III. Food hierarchy

Is this a food?

	S_{10}	S_{11}	S_{12}	S_{16}	S_{17}	S_{18}	S_{26}	S_{27}	S_{36}	S_{31}	S_{32}	S_{33}	#	%
Underextension responses	12/30	1/30	29/30	5/30	28/30	1/30	20/30	0/30	1/30	6/30	0/30	2/30	105/360	29.2
Overextension responses	10/30	1/30	0/30	0/30	0/30	0/30	0/30	1/30	0/30	0/30	0/30	0/30	12/360	3.3

Is this a fruit?

	S_7	S_8	S_9	S_{13}	S_{14}	S_{15}	S_{23}	S_{24}	S_{25}	S_{28}	S_{29}	S_{30}	#	%
Underextension responses	16/20	19/20	16/20	12/20	3/20	8/20	3/20	1/20	4/20	0/20	5/20	2/20	89/240	37.1
Overextension responses	0/20	0/20	0/20	0/20	7/20	2/20	0/20	3/20	0/20	7/20	2/20	2/20	23/240	9.6

Is this an apple?

	S_1	S_2	S_3	S_4	S_5	S_6	S_{19}	S_{21}	S_{22}	S_{20}	S_{34}	S_{35}	#	%
Underextension responses	1/10	0/10	0/10	0/10	0/10	0/10	0/10	0/10	0/10	1/10	1/10	0/10	3/120	2.5
Overextension responses	2/10	1/10	0/10	2/10	2/10	1/10	1/10	1/10	0/10	1/10	1/10	2/10	14/120	11.7

a couple of the instances used in this experiment. Other children exclude more animals from the concept ANIMAL which often seems intuitively to be in the case of two kinds of instances: (1) atypical or noncentral (see Rosch, 1973, 1975) instances of animals and (2) very familiar animals for which they have a preferred dominant name (e.g., *dog*).

Dog

The next panel in Table 4.1 shows the results for each of the twelve children on the concept DOG. Children are very good at identifying instances of this concept and at excluding noninstances. *Dog* is a word which is often used as an illustration of overextension in the diary literature, but in this experiment these children by and large appear to have basically the same extension of the concept as adults.[3] There were two children (out of twelve) who overgeneralized the word *dog* to other kinds of animals (*S*s 10 and 11), but there were also children who undergeneralized, not counting a few dogs as DOGS while correctly identifying the others (e.g., *S*s 4 and 12). Most subjects neither overgeneralized nor undergeneralized this particular concept, however.

Collie

The next panel in Table 4.1 shows the results for each child who was tested on the concept COLLIE. Many children seemed to have no idea of what a collie is, responding "no" to both instances and noninstances (e.g., *S*s 13, 14, 28, 30, 31) or "yes" to both instances and noninstances (e.g., *S*15). Other children seemed to know that a collie is some kind of dog, but not exactly which dogs are collies. Thus some children said that all or most of the pictures of dogs were *collies* (*S*s 16, 18, 29), while one child identified two out of ten collies and one other dog as *collies*. The reader may wonder whether or not during the course of the experiment a child might learn what *collie* means and might show improvement in identifying the instances of collies as collies after a number of collies had been presented. Subjects were given no feedback as to the correctness of their responses during the experiment but it might still seem possible that seeing a number of collies for which the question was "Is this a collie?" might encourage them to adopt a correct or partially correct hypothesis concerning the concept during the course of the study. To check on this possibility we examined the responses of each subject to see whether or not there was a tendency to improve at identifying collies over trials. It turned out that for this concept only one child (*S*32) apparently improved. In general, for this and for the other concepts which we tested in this study, there was

---

[3] Of course, this may be a result of the fact that the children in this experiment were somewhat older (two and one-half–six years) than the children discussed in diaries, who are usually between one and three years of age.

very little improvement at identifying instances as the experiment progressed—usually, subjects either knew a concept at the beginning of the experiment or not at all.

Plant

The next panel of Table 4.1 shows the pattern of responses for each child for the concept PLANT. All children except one (S15) made some underextension responses when asked to identify pictures of plants. The one subject who made no underextension responses overgeneralized PLANT to four out of thirty inanimate objects. For the other children however, overextension of the concept was very rare to the thirty inanimate objects which were used as noninstances, while underextension was the rule. Two children (Ss 13 and 29) did not include most of the flowers and various other plants in the concept PLANT. The other children made fewer underextension responses (from one to six) with the most common mistakes being for the two trees (a sycamore tree and a traveler's tree). Children were often observed to say for a picture of a tree something like, "That's a tree, not a plant," again suggesting the role played by what we have been calling a dominant name.

Flower

The next panel of Table 4.1 shows the number of each kind of response made by each child on the concept FLOWER. Underextension responses to the concept FLOWER were relatively infrequent, although they did occur. On the other hand, overgeneralizations of the concept FLOWER to other kinds of plants were quite common. Ten of the twelve children made some overextension responses to other plants, with a third of the children (Ss 2, 19, 22, 31) overgeneralizing FLOWER to more than half of the plants. In this study as well as others (see, for example, Chapter 2), we have found the child's tendency to overextend the concept FLOWER (to other plants) to be more prevalent than for any other concept we have investigated. Conversely, as we have seen, children will also usually undergeneralize in the case of PLANT. For adults PLANT is clearly superordinate to the concept FLOWER, whereas children lack this appreciation of the hierarchic relation between these two concepts. For them it often appears that PLANT and FLOWER reside at roughly the same level of generality (see Vygotsky, 1962).

Tulip

The next panel of Table 4.1 shows the pattern of underextension and overextension for each child for the concept TULIP. As was the case for the concept COLLIE, some children seemed to have no notion of what a tulip is, since they responded "no" indiscriminately to both instances and noninstances (Ss 8, 9, 10, 12, 36) or "yes" to both instances and noninstances (*S*11). Other children seemed to realize that tulips are flowers, but they were not sure which flowers were tulips. Two of these children (*S*s 7 and 27) identified each instance of a tulip as a *tulip,* but overgeneralized the concept TULIP to other kinds of flowers and plants. Other children (*S*s 24, 25, 26) did not overgeneralize the concept TULIP to noninstances, but rather undergeneralized the concept so that only some instances of tulips were identified as TULIPS. Finally, one subject (*S*24) both undergeneralized and overgeneralized when tested on the concept TULIP.

Food

The next panel of Table 4.1 shows the pattern of underextension and overextension for each child when tested on the concept FOOD. One child (*S*10) overgeneralized FOOD to ten inanimate objects. This was the only child who demonstrated a tendency to overgeneralize FOOD to the noninstances of FOOD in this study. On the other hand, most subjects, including this one, tended to undergeneralize FOOD, declining to count some of the instances as examples of FOOD. Two subjects (*S*s 12 and 17) gave the response "no" to almost every instance of food when asked "Is this food?" usually identifying the kind of food with a more particular name—e.g., "That's not a food; it's an apple." Since these two subjects gave the response "no" indiscriminately to both instances and noninstances of FOOD it cannot be assumed that they had the word in their vocabulary at all. The other children, however, indicated that they had some notion of what *food* means since they did correctly identify some instances as FOOD and rarely overextended the concept to noninstances. For example, *S*26 correctly responded "no" to all noninstances, and "yes" to ten instances, but was incorrect in responding no to twenty instances. Similarly, *S*s 16 and 31 made no overextension responses but made five and six (out of thirty possible) underextension responses respectively.

It should be noted that these and other subjects who made underextension responses did not necessarily treat the same kind of food uniformly in their classification behavior. For example, *S*16 identified seven out of ten apples as *food* but excluded three apples from the food category. Two of these underextensions were associated with dominant name responses ("No, it's an apple"), whereas one was associated only with the response "no." Similarly, *S*26 identified two out of ten apples as *food* but excluded the other eight apples from the food category. This particular child simply said yes to two of the apples and no to the other eight with no overt dominant name coming into play in his responses, although it is quite possible that the negative responses were mediated by covert dominant naming. This inconsistency on the part of an individual subject in classifying apples as foods is puzzling and suggests that the child does not always use a single fixed criterion for classification, but rather vascillates from instance to instance between different, probably vaguely formulated, criteria. (For example, in response to the question "Is this a food?" the child might be thinking "Yes, because I can eat it," but later "No, it's an apple," and might respond inconsistently according to the two different criteria.)

This behavior also raises the question of how consistent an individual child would be in his underextensions or overextensions if he were tested on the same instance at different times. Although we did not include a test for consistency in this particular experiment, later studies have shown that when a child makes either an overextension response or an underextension response on a given instance he will usually, though not always, make the same response again. In one study, Judy Ungerer found that 85 percent of the times that a child makes an underextension response he will persist in his "mistake" if tested on it again immediately, and 81 percent of the time if he is tested on it sometime later. In another study Elizabeth Smith and I found that overall, 92 percent of the time a child will persist in his overextension response when he is tested again on the same noninstance some time after his initial "mistake."

Fruit

The next panel of Table 4.1 shows the pattern of underextension and overextension responses for each child for the concept FRUIT. Apart from *Ss* 7, 8, and 9 who made so many errors that it cannot be assumed that they have any idea of the concept FRUIT, it can be seen that some subjects (*Ss* 14, 28) tend to overgeneralize the concept FRUIT to other kinds of food, whereas other subjects tend to undergeneralize the concept FRUIT (*Ss* 13, 15, 23, 25, 29), although many of these subjects do make both overextension and underextension responses. Again, some of the younger subjects (e.g., *Ss* 13, 15) are inconsistent in the way they respond to the pictures of apples when asked, "Is this a fruit?" sometimes saying "yes" and sometimes saying "no." When these children said "no" they usually gave the dominant name reaction—e.g., "No, (it's an) apple."

Apple

The final panel of Table 4.1 shows the subject-by-subject breakdown of responses for the concept APPLE. Children are very good at identifying instances and rejecting noninstances of this concept. They make virtually no underextension responses, although they make some overextension responses, usually to a picture of a tomato or a pomegranate.

Table 4.2 shows a subject-by-subject breakdown of the underextension and overextension responses made by the adults tested in this experiment. This table is provided for comparison with Table 4.1 for children. Again, an underextension response is a "no" to an instance and is represented in the upper part of each panel of Table 4.2. An overextension response is a "yes" to a noninstance and is represented in the lower part of each panel.

TABLE 4.2 *Number and percentage of underextension and overextension responses made by the adults on each of the nine concepts tested in the extension experiment. An underextension response is a "no" response to an instance. An overextension response is a "yes" response to a noninstance.*

I. Animal hierarchy

Is this an animal?

	S_1	S_2	S_3	S_7	S_8	S_9	#	%
Underextension responses	$\frac{0}{30}$	$\frac{0}{30}$	$\frac{0}{30}$	$\frac{0}{30}$	$\frac{0}{30}$	$\frac{0}{30}$	$\frac{0}{180}$	0.0
Overextension responses	$\frac{0}{30}$	$\frac{0}{30}$	$\frac{0}{30}$	$\frac{0}{30}$	$\frac{0}{30}$	$\frac{0}{30}$	$\frac{0}{180}$	0.0

Is this a dog?

	S_4	S_5	S_6	S_{10}	S_{11}	S_{12}	#	%
Underextension responses	$\frac{0}{20}$	$\frac{0}{20}$	$\frac{0}{20}$	$\frac{0}{20}$	$\frac{0}{20}$	$\frac{0}{20}$	$\frac{0}{120}$	0.0
Overextension responses	$\frac{0}{20}$	$\frac{0}{20}$	$\frac{0}{20}$	$\frac{0}{20}$	$\frac{0}{20}$	$\frac{0}{20}$	$\frac{0}{120}$	0.0

Is this a collie?

	S_{13}	S_{14}	S_{15}	S_{16}	S_{17}	S_{18}	#	%
Underextension responses	$\frac{1}{10}$	$\frac{1}{10}$	$\frac{1}{10}$	$\frac{1}{10}$	$\frac{0}{10}$	$\frac{1}{10}$	$\frac{5}{60}$	8.3
Overextension responses	$\frac{1}{10}$	$\frac{0}{10}$	$\frac{1}{10}$	$\frac{0}{10}$	$\frac{0}{10}$	$\frac{0}{10}$	$\frac{2}{60}$	3.3

II. Plant hierarchy

Is this a plant?

	S_4	S_5	S_6	S_{13}	S_{14}	S_{15}	#	%
Underextension responses	$\frac{1}{30}$	$\frac{0}{30}$	$\frac{0}{30}$	$\frac{0}{30}$	$\frac{0}{30}$	$\frac{0}{30}$	$\frac{1}{180}$	0.6
Overextension responses	$\frac{0}{30}$	$\frac{0}{30}$	$\frac{0}{30}$	$\frac{0}{30}$	$\frac{0}{30}$	$\frac{1}{30}$	$\frac{1}{180}$	0.6

Is this a flower?

	S_1	S_2	S_3	S_{16}	S_{17}	S_{18}	#	%
Underextension responses	$\frac{0}{20}$	$\frac{0}{20}$	$\frac{1}{20}$	$\frac{0}{20}$	$\frac{0}{20}$	$\frac{0}{20}$	$\frac{1}{120}$	0.8
Overextension responses	$\frac{1}{20}$	$\frac{1}{20}$	$\frac{0}{20}$	$\frac{1}{20}$	$\frac{0}{20}$	$\frac{0}{20}$	$\frac{3}{120}$	2.5

Is this a tulip?

	S_7	S_8	S_9	S_{10}	S_{11}	S_{12}	#	%
Underextension responses	$\frac{4}{10}$	$\frac{6}{10}$	$\frac{4}{10}$	$\frac{4}{10}$	$\frac{4}{10}$	$\frac{2}{10}$	$\frac{24}{60}$	40
Overextension responses	$\frac{1}{10}$	$\frac{0}{10}$	$\frac{1}{10}$	$\frac{0}{10}$	$\frac{1}{10}$	$\frac{1}{10}$	$\frac{4}{60}$	6.7

TABLE 4.2 (continued)

III. Food hierarchy

Is this a food?

	S_{10}	S_{11}	S_{12}	S_{16}	S_{17}	S_{18}	#	%
Underextension responses	$\frac{1}{30}$	$\frac{0}{30}$	$\frac{1}{30}$	$\frac{1}{30}$	$\frac{0}{30}$	$\frac{1}{30}$	$\frac{4}{180}$	2.2
Overextension responses	$\frac{0}{30}$	$\frac{0}{30}$	$\frac{1}{30}$	$\frac{0}{30}$	$\frac{0}{30}$	$\frac{0}{30}$	$\frac{1}{180}$	0.6

Is this a fruit?

	S_7	S_8	S_9	S_{13}	S_{14}	S_{15}	#	%
Underextension responses	$\frac{0}{20}$	$\frac{1}{20}$	$\frac{1}{20}$	$\frac{2}{20}$	$\frac{2}{20}$	$\frac{0}{20}$	$\frac{6}{120}$	5.0
Overextension responses	$\frac{0}{20}$	$\frac{0}{20}$	$\frac{0}{20}$	$\frac{0}{20}$	$\frac{0}{20}$	$\frac{0}{20}$	$\frac{0}{120}$	0.0

Is this an apple?

	S_1	S_2	S_3	S_4	S_5	S_6	#	%
Underextension responses	$\frac{1}{10}$	$\frac{1}{10}$	$\frac{0}{10}$	$\frac{0}{10}$	$\frac{0}{10}$	$\frac{0}{10}$	$\frac{2}{60}$	3.3
Overextension responses	$\frac{0}{10}$	$\frac{0}{10}$	$\frac{0}{10}$	$\frac{0}{10}$	$\frac{0}{10}$	$\frac{0}{10}$	$\frac{0}{60}$	0.0

This table reveals that, unlike children, adults undergeneralize and overgeneralize very little, except for the concept TULIP, for which they tend to make a fairly large number of underextension responses. We were curious about why adult subjects had trouble with the pictures of tulips. It seemed possible that either there was something wrong with our pictures of tulips (e.g., perhaps they were visually ambiguous) or that the average adult cannot identify all instances of tulips as *tulips*. We therefore decided to test some experts on the pictures of tulips, specifically, four florists in the Cambridge area. Each of the florists was shown the ten tulips and the ten other kinds of flowers in a random order. For each picture he was asked, "Is this a tulip?" Three of the four florists made no errors (overextension or underextension) in the task, while the fourth expressed uncertainty ("I don't know") for two of the tulips. In their spontaneous explanations of their responses, they mentioned criteria such as leaf structure, the stamen, petal number, and shape. Their decisions were based on extensive knowledge of plant families and the distinctive characteristics of the botanical classification, including unusual and extinct varieties, regardless of whether or not they had ever actually seen each particular kind of tulip. Our typical adult, however, seemed to judge the pictures pretty much by the shape and general looks of the flower in comparison to their central notion of what a tulip looks like, and did not know the range well enough to include peripheral instances. At any rate, apart from the case of tulips, adults do on the whole correctly identify the instances of the concepts tested in this study as instances and reject the noninstances.

Picture-by-Picture Breakdown of Underextension Responses

We have also examined in detail the number of underextension responses made by children on each instance (i.e., picture) for each of the nine concepts tested in this experiment. The purpose of this analysis was to see if certain instances of a given concept were more likely to promote underextension responses than others and if we could formulate hypotheses concerning the determinants of underextension responses which we could then subject to further tests. In the present discussion I would like to focus on the most general concepts in each of the three hierarchies tested: ANIMAL, PLANT, and FOOD.

Consider first the concept ANIMAL. One of the instances of the concept ANIMAL evoked an underextension response from every child—the picture of the woman. In this study and in others (see, for example, Chapter 2) we have found that preschool children almost invariably refuse to classify people as ANIMALS. No other instance produced nearly such a high frequency of underextension responses, but some did produce more than others. For example, the picture of a praying mantis and the picture of a caterpillar produced more underextension than the other stimuli. Why should children be less likely to classify these insects as animals than a dog or a hedgehog, for example?

On the assumption that typical animals are four-legged, furry mammals, insects would seem to be rather atypical instances of the animal category. That is to say, although we have not scaled these instances for their degree of centrality (see Rosch, 1973, 1975) to the concept ANIMAL, it is safe to assume that adults would rate these insects as being less central to the concept than dogs or hedgehogs. Of course this is not the only possible explanation. Praying mantises and caterpillars are probably less familiar to the child than are dogs and cats, and so the child's general lack of experience with such creatures may be related to his inability to classify such instances as animals. Other considerations make lack of familiarity seem less likely to be an important determinant of underextension responses in children, however. For example, only one child (out of twelve) made an underextension response when shown a picture of a hedgehog. A hedgehog is presumably not a very familiar kind of animal in the child's world, but it is a four-legged, furry mammal, and therefore presumably central to the concept ANIMAL. Indeed, familiar stimuli, it could be argued, may be associated with more underextension responses than unfamiliar stimuli of equal centrality. For as we have seen, the young child will sometimes exclude a familiar instance from a general category when he has another name for that instance ("That's a dog, not an animal"). In fact, in this study children made fewer underextension responses to the presumably less familiar hedgehog than to the more familiar dogs and, as we saw previously, a failure to classify a dog as an animal was often associated with the use of a dominant name (e.g., *dog*). At any rate in a later study (see Chapter 5) we have tried to tease apart the roles played by lack of centrality and lack of familiarity in determining underextension responses.

Now consider the concept PLANT. The instances of plants which produced the greatest number of underextension responses were the pictures of two trees—the sycamore tree (eight out of twelve possible underextensions) and the traveler's tree (six out of twelve possible underextensions). Although trees are plants, intuitively they do not seem to be typical or central instances of the concept PLANT and this lack of centrality again may be the determinant of the large number of underextension responses made to these stimuli. Another factor which may also be operative in producing these responses, at least in some children, is their use of a dominant name ("That's a tree, not a plant").

Now consider the underextension responses made to the various instances of the concept FOOD. Each of the food stimuli evoked between two and five underextension responses. With this small a range it is difficult to establish with confidence that some of these stimuli produce more underextension than others, let alone to discern the determinants of such responses. However, here are some speculations on the subject.

The apples in general produced a relatively large number of errors (a total of forty-one out of one hundred and twenty), which may be related to the fact that apples are not central to the concept FOOD (they are not "meat, bread and potatoes"), and/or to the fact that in the presence of an apple children often give the dominant name reaction ("That's an apple, not a food"). Among the foods which are not fruits children did best on the pictures of bread, cheese, and an egg and worst on the pictures of a cookie, caviar, and lettuce. These latter instances are probably less typical of or less central to the concept FOOD than are the bread, cheese, and the egg. Caviar, of course, is probably quite unfamiliar to most preschool children, but cookies and lettuce are probably fairly familiar. Again, therefore, it would appear that instances which are not typical of or central to the concept FOOD are the ones most likely to be excluded from the concept by children and, again, the role played by familiarity is unclear. This analysis is of course *ad hoc,* speculative, and intuitive, but it has provided some hypotheses about the determinants of underextension which we have tested more objectively in a later study (see Chapter 5). So that the reader might get a feeling for the kinds of instances which promoted underextension responses in this study, three of the pictures which produced a relatively large number of such responses have been presented in Figure 4.2.

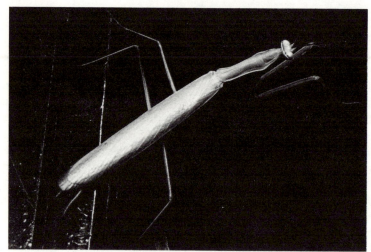

Praying mantis

Sycamore tree

Cookie

Picture-by-Picture Breakdown of Overextension Responses

Just as in the case of underextension, we have also studied in detail the number of overextension responses made by children on each noninstance for each concept tested in this experiment. Again our intention was to see if certain noninstances were more likely to promote overextension than others and, if so, whether we could infer hypotheses about the determinants of such responses which we could then subject to further tests.

A picture-by-picture breakdown of the noninstances revealed that no noninstance produced overextension in all children and, indeed, most noninstances produced very few overextensions. Nonetheless, some noninstances did produce more such responses than did others.

Although the task of discerning the relation between the noninstances for which there was a relatively high degree of overextension and the concepts which were being tested is complex and difficult, most overextension responses seemed consistent with the hypothesis that they were often a result of a perceptual similarity between the object depicted in the picture and some idealized visual representation of the concept or some visual memory of a particular instance of the concept. Intuitively this was borne out by the fact that far more overextension responses were made by children to pictures of other animals versus inanimate objects when the concept DOG was being tested; to pictures of other dogs versus other animals versus inanimate objects when the concept COLLIE was being tested; to pictures of other plants versus inanimate objects when the concept FLOWER was being tested; to pictures of other flowers versus other plants versus inanimate objects when the concept TULIP was being tested; to pictures of other foods versus inanimate objects when FRUIT was the concept being tested; and to pictures of other fruits versus other foods versus inanimate objects when APPLE was the concept being tested. Occasionally, there were overgeneralization responses to pictures of inanimate objects bearing little visual similarity to either an idealized or particular instance of the concepts TULIP and COLLIE, suggesting to us that in these cases the child did not really know the word at all and was just guessing. With the exception of these few cases, there was a strikingly small number of overextension responses to inanimate objects.

Although perceptual similarity suggests itself as a determinant of overextension, examination of the individual pictures raises the possibility that

---

See facing page
FIGURE 4.2 Three pictures of objects which produced a relatively large number of underextension responses in this experiment. A relatively large number of children said "no" when asked if the praying mantis was an *animal,* when asked if the sycamore tree was a *plant,* and when asked if the cookie was *food.*

other factors may be playing a role as well. For example, seven out of twelve children, when shown the picture of a tomato and asked, "Is this an apple?" said "yes." The tomato was clearly perceptually similar to an apple, but it was also functionally similar (you eat both apples and tomatoes), and tomatoes may be associated through contiguity with apples (since they are both found in the supermarket, in the refrigerator, or on the dinner table). Thus functional similarity or association through contiguity may be determinants of overextension responses in this case in addition to or, possibly, rather than, perceptual similarity. We were aware of the possible role played by association through contiguity since in another study conducted with great care by Judy Ungerer she found that children, when shown a picture of a vase and asked, "Is this a plant?" would often respond "yes." This vase did not look especially like a plant, but since vases often contain plants and therefore are contiguous to plants, this suggests that association through contiguity may play a role in producing overextension at least in some cases. Functional similarity seemed less likely to be a factor since we have not come across cases where objects which are used for the same purpose as instances of the concept being tested produce a great number of overextension responses unless those objects are perceptually similar to or likely to be associated through contiguity with instances of the concept in question. For example, a banana serves the same function as an apple (both dessert foods), but a picture of a banana produced only one overextension response (out of twelve possible) of the concept APPLE. Actually, this example would make it seem that the case of the child's overextending the term *apple* to a picture of a tomato were the result of perceptual similarity rather than association through contiguity, since bananas are just as likely, if not more so, to be experienced with apples as are tomatoes.

In this and other studies (see, for example, Chapter 2) we have found that the child's tendency to overgeneralize the concept FLOWER (to other kinds of plants) to be more prevalent than for any other concept we have tested. For example, five out of twelve children agreed that a picture of an elephant's ear was a *flower;* nine out of twelve children agreed that a picture of a coconut was a *flower;* and seven out of twelve children agreed that a picture of a philodendron was a *flower.* Again it is not clear whether perceptual similarity or association through contiguity is the chief determinant of these overextension responses. Functional similarity seems less likely to be a factor since neither plants nor flowers serve important functions in the

---

See facing page
FIGURE 4.3 Three pictures of objects which produced a relatively large number of overextension responses in children. In this study many children said "yes" when asked if the tomato was an *apple,* and when asked if the philodendron was a *flower.* In another study children were often observed to say "yes" when asked of the vase if it was a *plant.*

Tomato

Philodendron

Vase

child's life. Figure 4.3 shows three pictures of objects which have produced a relatively large number of overextension responses in our studies.

Thus an examination of the pictures which produced the greatest number of overextension responses suggests that three factors may play a role in bringing about overgeneralization. In decreasing order of the likelihood of their importance these are: (1) perceptual similarity—the noninstance is perceptually similar to an instance of the concept; (2) association through contiguity—the noninstance (or something like it) has been seen by the child in the presence of an instance of the concept; and (3) functional similarity—the noninstance serves the same function as an instance of the concept. In this study it was often difficult to discern exactly which of these three factors was crucial since the noninstances which produced overextension responses were often both perceptually similar and contiguous to an instance of the concept or perceptually similar, contiguous, and functionally similar to an instance of the concept. In another study (see Chapter 6) we have tried to disentangle the role played by each of these factors in determining overextension in the child.

The Ratio of Underextension to Overextension

As we have seen in this experiment children make both underextension and overextension responses. A question of mild interest is: Which kind of response do children make most often? This question is answered by Figure 4.4, which shows the percentage of possible underextension responses and the percentage of possible overextension responses made by each of the three age groups tested in this study. The number of both kinds of responses is shown in Figure 4.4 to decrease systematically with age. For both of the youngest age groups (as well as for the adults) the number of underextension responses is greater than the number of overextension responses. Specifically, the two-and-a-half-to-four-year-old group made 28.9 percent of the possible underextension responses and only 8.4 percent of the possible overextension responses. The four-and-a-half-to-six-year-old group made 16.5 percent of the possible underextension responses and only 6.2 percent of the possible overextension responses. Figure 4.4 was calculated using all subjects who answered "no" to instances being counted as underextension responses and "yes" to noninstances being counted as overextension responses. It might well be objected that it is not fair to count all subjects on all concepts since some subjects might not have a given term in their vocabulary and their responses might be simply guesses. Children in this study rarely said they didn't know when asked if a given stimulus was an instance of a given concept, even though their pattern of responses at times indicated that they had no idea of what the concept means. If children were biased to give more "no" responses than "yes"

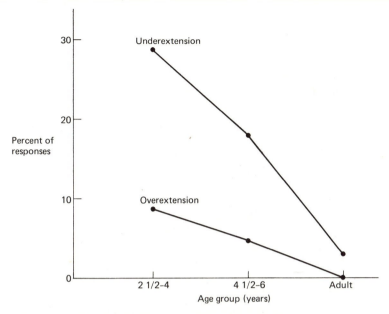

FIGURE 4.4 (1) The percentage of possible underextension responses and (2) the percentage of possible overextension responses made as a function of age. In this graph data from all subjects tested in the extension experiment were used. An underextension response is a "no" to an instance. An overextension response is a "yes" response to a noninstance.

responses to such stimuli, which seemed to be the case, then this would inflate the number of underextension responses relative to the number of overextension responses. For this reason we performed the analysis again, but this time only included subjects whose over-all pattern of responses indicated that they had some notion of the concept for which they were being tested. Our criteria for including a subject's performance on a given concept in this analysis were fairly stringent: (1) the subject had to identify more than 20 percent of the instances as instances, and (2) the ratio of the number of "yeses" to instances divided by the number of "yeses" to noninstances had to be equal to or greater than 2. The results are shown in Figure 4.5 which again shows the percentage of possible underextension responses and the percentage of possible overextension responses made by each age group, but this time the calculations are based only on subjects who met the aforementioned criteria for having the word in their vocabulary. Figure 4.5 shows that when the analysis is done in this way the percentages of both kinds of responses made by the children drops considerably, but still there is a decreasing tendency to make either kind of

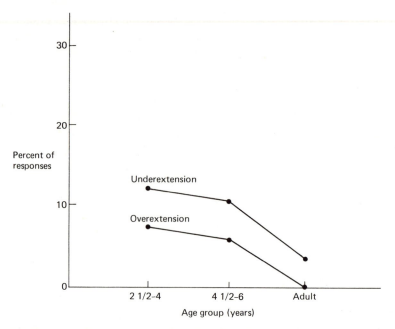

FIGURE 4.5 (1) The percentage of possible underextension responses and (2) the percentage of possible overextension responses made as a function of age. In this graph only data from subjects who met the criterion for having a word in their vocabulary have been included.

"mistake" with increasing age and still the number of underextension responses is greater for both groups of children than the corresponding number of overextension responses.

The question of which kind of response is made most often by children in this study is only mildly interesting because there is no guarantee that another study which employed different instances and noninstances would also show a greater number of underextension responses. It would be unwise to extrapolate from the findings of the present study to the conclusion that children more frequently undergeneralize than overgeneralize their first terms of reference, although it is certainly possible. The point is that by judicious choice of concepts, of instances and of noninstances, a clever experimenter could conduct a similar study which would show a preponderance of either kind of response.

In this particular study we did try to allow for the possibility of both kinds of responses not only by including an equal number of instances and noninstances of each concept but also by choosing instances which we thought might promote both kinds of responses. Specifically, in the case of the instances of a concept we attempted to cover a broad range of the denotative possibilities of the various concepts, including both typical and familiar instances (e.g., dog for ANIMAL, bread for FOOD) and unfamiliar and atypical instances (e.g., praying mantis for ANIMAL, caviar for FOOD). In the case of noninstances we included a relatively large number of cases which, based on our understanding of previous reports of overgeneralization in the child's first terms of reference, would be most likely to produce overextension (and indeed they did). For example, when the child was tested for COLLIE, three out of ten noninstances were other dogs, and three were other animals; when he was tested for DOG, ten out of twenty noninstances were other animals, and so on. Thus this study allowed for both kinds of responses and, indeed, both kinds of responses were made. It is notable that in this particular study children make more underextension responses, especially in view of the fact that the literature on the subject has so often stressed only overextension in the child's first terms of reference. However, I do not want to argue that underextension is necessarily more prevalent than overextension in the child's first terms of reference on the basis of this study. My position is rather that both kinds of phenomena do occur and whether you will observe more of one than the other depends upon the concepts being studied and the nature of the instances and the noninstances.

A more interesting question than "Which kind of responses do children make most?" is "How does the ratio of one type of response to the other change with increasing age?" The literature which emphasizes overgeneralization in the child is usually concerned with children between the ages of one and three years. The children in our study were between two and a half and four years and four and a half and six years. Is it possible that younger children are more likely to make relatively more overextension responses compared to underextension responses? The answer to this question is given by Figure 4.6, which shows the ratio of underextension to overextension for each group of children. The ratios of underextension to overextension responses were calculated by two different methods represented in Figure 4.6 as Method 1 and Method 2. Method 1 was based on all subjects with a "no" to an instance counting as an underextension response and a "yes" to a noninstance counting as an overextension response. The results of Method 1 suggest that, if anything, the two-and-a-half-to-four-year-old group makes proportionately more underextension responses than overextension responses compared to the four-and-a-half-to-six-year-old group. Again however, it might well be objected that we should not include subjects who have not demonstrated that they have a given word in their vocabulary. Therefore in Figure 4.6 we have also shown the results of Method 2 in which only data from those subjects who met the criteria mentioned above for having the word in their vocabulary have been used. When the analysis is done in this way it can be seen in Figure 4.6 that the ratio of underextension to overextension responses is 1.8 for both the

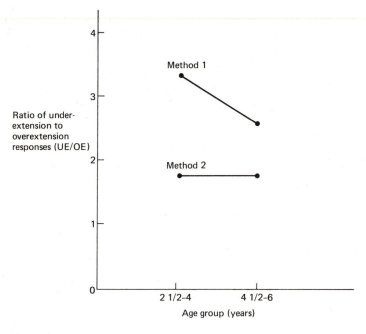

4

Method 1

3

Ratio of under-
extension to
overextension
responses (UE/OE)

2

Method 2

1

0

2 1/2–4   4 1/2–6

Age group (years)

FIGURE 4.6 Ratio of underextension responses to overextension responses made as a function of age by the two groups of children. In Method 1 data from all subjects have been used. In Method 2 only data from those subjects who met the criterion of having the word in their vocabulary have been used.

two and a half to four year olds and the four and a half to six year olds. The implication of this analysis is that, although younger children both undergeneralize and overgeneralize more, they do not necessarily make proportionately more overgeneralization responses than do older children.

Relation of Underextension Responses to Level in Hierarchy

When we were planning this experiment we decided to test children for concepts at different levels of generality. At the back of our minds was the hypothesis that the more general a concept the more likely it would be that children would make more underextension responses. We reasoned that the more specific a concept, the more perceptually homogeneous the instances of that concept would be and, therefore, that if a child could correctly classify one instance of a specific concept he would probably be able to correctly classify other instances since they would be perceptually similar. The more general a concept, the more perceptually diverse the instances of that concept would be, and, therefore, we thought that the child's ability to correctly classify one instance of a more general concept would be no guarantee that he would be able to correctly classify another perceptually dissimilar instance.

However, this hypothesis in retrospect appears to have been somewhat simplistic, for there appear to be cases in which a child will not recognize an instance as belonging to a more specific concept, although he does recognize it as belonging to a more general concept. For example, there were several pictures of tulips which children said were not *tulips* while other children correctly identified these tulips as being *flowers*. In some cases for which a child said that a picture of a tulip was not a *tulip* it appears that he did not have the word in his vocabulary at all and that he was simply guessing, which resulted in negative responses to positive instances. However, in other cases some children seemed to know that only flowers were tulips (they never said that nonflowers were tulips), but still said that several instances of tulips were not *tulips,* whereas they rarely made underextension responses to instances of the concept FLOWER.[4]

What our data on underextension do suggest is that in terms of vocabulary development, as measured by this test of comprehension, there is neither a concrete-to-abstract progression nor an abstract-to-concrete progression, but most often the child is best at identifying instances of some intermediate concepts within a hierarchy of concepts and does not do so well at more specific and more general concepts. For the particular hierarchies of concepts that we used in this experiment children do better on DOG than on COLLIE or ANIMAL, better on FLOWER than on TULIP or PLANT, and better on APPLE than on FRUIT or FOOD. Such a description seems appropriate when only pictures which were tested at each level in a hierarchy are considered. For example, for the ten pictures of collies children gave the greatest percentage of "yes" responses when asked, "Is this a dog?" They gave the next greatest when asked, "Is this an animal?" and the least when asked, "Is this a collie?" For the ten pictures of tulips children did best when asked "Is this a flower?" and next best when asked, "Is this a plant?" They did worst when asked, "Is this a tulip?" For the ten

---

[4] It is easy to show that underextension responses will be made, even by adults, for some quite specific concepts. To demonstrate this to some students who were in a seminar which I was teaching on conceptual development, I showed them a set of pictures of chrysanthemums taken from the April 1973 issue of *Better Homes and Gardens*. I asked them to indicate which of the pictures were of chrysanthemums. Every student could recognize some of the pictures as being chrysanthemums (usually the typical Pom-pom type of chrysanthemum), whereas they all failed to classify a variety of less typical instances such as the White Bonnie Jean Chrysanthemum (which they thought was probably a daisy). The point is that some quite specific concepts include a remarkable diversity of types of which many adults are not aware. These examples illustrate that our initial hypothesis that the more general a concept, the greater the likelihood of underextension is not correct in all cases. I am grateful to R. J. Herrnstein for first pointing out to me the problem with our initial hypothesis.

pictures of apples children did best when asked, "Is this an apple?" They did equally badly when asked, "Is this a fruit?" and "Is this a food?" On the assumption that the ability of children to recognize instances as belonging to various categories is a measure of the order of acquisition of category labels, these results constitute a replication of the basic findings reported in Chapter 2.

DISCUSSION

Although a careful examination of the diary literature will reveal that the child at times does not include all of the instances which an adult does in a given concept, such studies are systematically biased to suggest a predominance of overextension in the child's first terms of reference for reasons which have been discussed (see pp. 102–107). When an experiment is done which is sensitive to both overextension and underextension it is seen that children do in fact make both kinds of responses. Generalization (filling out categories) thus appears to be just as real as differentiation (narrowing down categories) in the early conceptual development of the child. Whether a child will make overextension responses or underextension responses appears to depend upon at least the following three factors: (1) the particular child in question; (2) the concept being investigated; and (3) the nature of the instances and noninstances being tested.

With respect to the child in question some children will overextend certain terms whereas others will underextend those same terms while still others will neither overextend nor underextend them. In general in the two-to-six-year-old range younger children make more "errors" of both kinds than older children. However, as we have seen, the ratio of underextension responses to overextension responses remains roughly constant over this time period, suggesting that it is not the case that younger children overgeneralize relatively more than undergeneralize as compared to older children.

With respect to the concept being investigated, certain concepts are usually overgeneralized by children whereas others are usually undergeneralized. For example, the preschool child's concept of FLOWER often extends beyond the adult's concept of FLOWER since the child often includes several other kinds of plants (nonflowers) in the concept FLOWER. On the other hand, the child's concept of PLANT is often less general than the adult's concept of PLANT since the child will often not include certain kinds of plants (such as trees and sometimes flowers) in the concept PLANT. Thus the concept FLOWER usually becomes more restricted in development whereas the concept PLANT usually becomes more general. The developmental changes in the extension of the concepts FLOWER and PLANT are depicted schematically in Figure 4.7.

This example might suggest to the reader that underextensions will oc-

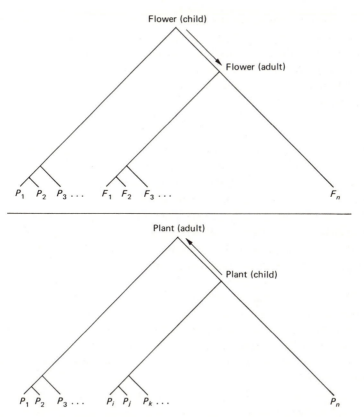

FIGURE 4.7 Schematic representation of developmental changes in the extension of the concepts FLOWER and PLANT. The figure illustrates that whether a child's concept is more or less general than an adult's concept depends upon the particular concept in question. The child's concept of FLOWER often extends beyond the corresponding adult concept whereas the child's concept of PLANT is usually more restricted than an adult's. The arrows in Figure 4.7 indicate the direction of developmental change.

cur only for quite general concepts such as PLANT or ANIMAL or FOOD. This is not the case, however. In this experiment we have seen that the occasional child did not include certain pictures of dogs in the concept DOG and in the next chapter it will be seen that many children fail to include certain somewhat atypical birds (a penguin, a duck, and a hen) in the concept BIRD. Moreover, children and even adults will sometimes not include instances in certain very specific concepts such as TULIP or CHRYSANTHEMUM as was discussed above.

Finally, certain kinds of instances appear to be more likely to produce underextension in children than other kinds of instances, and certain kinds of noninstances appear to be more likely to produce overextension than other kinds of noninstances. Atypical or peripheral instances (see Rosch, 1973, 1975) of a given concept seem more likely to produce under-extension than typical or central instances. The familiarity of the instance may also play a role. At least in some cases young children seem to exclude a familiar instance from a general category because they have another name for that instance ("That's a dog, not an animal") and because they sometimes do not seem to realize that a single object can belong to more than one category or, to put it another way, that a given object has several equally valid names. Three attributes of noninstances may be important in enticing the child to overgeneralize his first terms of reference. In decreasing order of the likelihood of their importance these are: (1) perceptual similarity—the noninstance is perceptually similar to an instance of the category denoted by the term; (2) association through contiguity—the noninstance has been seen in the presence of an instance of the category; and (3) functional similarity—the noninstance serves the same function for the child as an instance of the category.

In the present study it was often difficult to isolate the roles played by peripherality and familiarity in producing underextension and to isolate the roles played by perceptual similarity, association through contiguity, and functional similarity in producing overextension. In Chapters 5 and 6 research will be presented in which we have tried to tease apart the contributions of these various factors in bringing about the child's early referential problems.

Chapter 5

The Determinants of
Underextension in the Child[1]

In the previous chapter it was shown that children sometimes do not include instances in categories which adults do include. For example, when shown a picture of a praying mantis and asked, "Is this an animal?" many children said "no," whereas adults invariably said "yes." Or when shown a picture of a sycamore tree and asked, "Is this a plant?" many children said "no," often adding, "It's a tree, not a plant," whereas adults again always said "yes." The question of real interest concerning the underextension responses in the child is: Why do they make them for certain instances and not for others? An intuitive and *ad hoc* analysis of the stimuli suggested that at least two factors may play a role in enticing a child to make such "mistakes". First, it seemed that children would often make them for instances which intuitively do not seem to be typical instances or good examples of the concept being tested. Thus, for example, although adults will agree that a praying mantis is an *animal,* they will often point out that it is not as good an example of an *animal* as a dog or horse or some other four-legged, furry mammal. Rosch (1973, 1975) has recently made much of the notion that some instances are better examples of concepts than others. She, like several others recently,[2] has argued that the traditional notion of a concept as being comprised of a conjunctive set of

---

[1] I am grateful to Elizabeth Smith for her help in conducting the study reported in this chapter.

[2] See for example Herrnstein and Loveland, 1964; Fodor, 1972; Carey, 1973; Lakoff, 1972; Anglin, 1973; Smith, Shoben, and Ripps, 1974. See also Wittgenstein, 1953, pp. 31–36.

criterial attributes or features is incorrect and that most natural categories do not have well-defined boundaries. Rather she argues that a given concept has "internal structure" by which she means that a given category is composed of a core meaning which consists of the clearest cases or best examples of the category, surrounded by other category members of decreasing similarity to that core. Thus instances of a concept vary along a dimension which she calls "centrality," with the best instances being very central and the worst instances being very peripheral. She has found that adult subjects find it a meaningful task to rate instances according to their degree of centrality to a given concept and that they tend to agree in their judgments of centrality. So, for example, for the concept FRUIT, APPLE is rated by adult subjects as being a good exemplar, whereas FIG or OLIVE are rated as being poor exemplars. ROBIN is rated as a good exemplar of BIRD, whereas CHICKEN or OSTRICH are rated as poor exemplars.

One might speculate, as Rosch in fact has, that children's concepts often start out being comprised of the central instances of the corresponding adult concept and that it is only with development that the more peripheral instances of the adult concept come to be included in the child's. While this hypothesis both overstates its case and does not account for all of the child's underextensions, it does make intuitive sense out of many of the cases of underinclusion which do occur. For example, although we did not have adults rate the pictures in the preceding experiment along the dimension of centrality, it is safe to assume that the picture of a praying mantis would be rated as less central to the concept ANIMAL than, say, a picture of a dog. Also we have had adults rate various kinds of trees for their degree of centrality to the concept PLANT, and in general trees are rated as being rather peripheral. Thus again it would be fairly safe to assume that the picture of the sycamore tree which produced many underextensions in children is probably a peripheral instance of the concept PLANT. Children do not always make underextension responses to the picture of the praying mantis or to the picture of the sycamore tree or to other pictures which one might guess would be rated as peripheral (which is why I said the hypothesis probably overstates its case), but most of the instances of concepts which produced a relatively large number of underextension responses do seem to be atypical, peripheral, or poor examples of the concepts in question. There was one notable exception to this general rule, however. Adults generally rate pictures of human beings as being moderately central to the concept ANIMAL, but as we saw previously, preschool children invariably choose not to classify a picture of a woman as an ANIMAL. Thus adult judgments of centrality will not always provide a predictor of the tendency of the child to exclude an instance from a category, but then again they may very often be predictive.

Rosch (1973) conducted an experiment which in fact did suggest that when a child fails to include an instance in a concept it is often in the case of peripheral instances.[3] She presented words to children and to adults in either true sentences or false sentences and the subject's task was to push a button indicating whether the sentence was true or false. True sentences were of the form "A robin is a bird," "A duck is a bird," "A carrot is a vegetable," and so on. The nouns in the subjects of these sentences were of two types: They were either central or peripheral instances (according to adult ratings) of the categories in the predicates of the sentences. She found, among other things, that neither adults nor children made many errors on the central instances but that children made many errors (about 25 percent) on the peripheral instances whereas adults did not. This suggests that children tend to exclude instances from categories when they are peripheral exemplars of those categories. The children in Rosch's study were nine to eleven years old, much older than the age group with which we have been concerned in this series of studies. In the experiment to be presented we have attempted to see whether two to six year olds will also make underextension responses for instances which have been rated as peripheral by adults more often than for instances which have been rated as central. We have used pictures rather than words, but the basic idea is the same.

In addition to the central-peripheral factor, we also wanted to investigate the role played by another attribute of instances which can be rated by adults: the familiarity of the instance. According to one hypothesis the child would make relatively more underextension responses to unfamiliar than to familiar instances since his lack of experience with such instances might go hand in hand with a lack of knowledge of the categories to which those instances belong. It seemed possible, for example, that children failed to classify a preying mantis as an ANIMAL because they knew nothing of praying mantises, including that they are animals. The problem here is that a praying mantis is both a peripheral and unfamiliar instance of the concept ANIMAL and it is unclear which of these two factors is the important one in determining underextension responses to it. Would the child also make underextension responses to a wombat, or an aardvark, or an anteater, which are presumably unfamiliar to him but which, because they are four-legged furry mammals, are also central to the concept ANIMAL?

Another line of argument suggests that familiar rather than unfamiliar stimuli will sometimes encourage underextension responses, for we noted in the preceding study that the child will sometimes fail to include a familiar kind of object in a general category, quite possibly because he has a more specific name for the object and because he does not realize that a given object can belong to two different categories or be named in two equally valid, different ways. Thus, in the case of the picture of the syca-

[3] See also Saltz, Soller, and Sigel, 1972, and Neimark, 1974.

more tree, when asked, "Is this a plant?" children were often observed to say something like, "No, it's a tree, not a plant." In the case of a picture of a dog, when asked, "Is this an animal?" children occasionally said, "No, it's a dog, not an animal." Inhelder and Piaget (1964) have made similar kinds of observations. For example, they showed a child a group of eight flowers, four of which were primroses. They then asked the child if he would have more if he took all of the primroses or all of the flowers. The child said he would have the same in either case, suggesting that he was not capable of viewing a given object as being an instance of two hierarchically related classes simultaneously.

Such examples illustrate that children sometimes have not mastered the structure of class hierarchy and have trouble interpreting any given object as an instance of more than one conceptual category. According to this view, when the child says of a sycamore tree, "It's a tree, not a plant," his labeling the object with the dominant name *tree* dissuades him from categorizing it as a PLANT at the same time. Presumably such interference will be more likely to occur for familiar objects since he may often have access to names for familiar objects but not for unfamiliar objects. In the study to be presented we have attempted to discern the contributions of the central-peripheral factor and the familiar-unfamiliar factor in determining underextension in the child.

Experiment 5.1

METHOD

Our goal was to investigate the tendency of children to exclude four kinds of instances of concepts from those concepts. Specifically, the kinds of instances we wanted to investigate were: (1) central and familiar; (2) central and unfamiliar; (3) peripheral and familiar; and (4) peripheral and unfamiliar. We did not want to rely on our own intuitions of the degree of centrality or familiarity of the instances since our intuitions might be idiosyncratic or biased for one reason or another. We therefore decided to obtain judgments from several adults of the centrality and familiarity of several instances to several concepts so that we might choose from these instances ones which adults in general tend to rate as being central and familiar, central and unfamiliar, peripheral and familiar, and peripheral and unfamiliar.

We began by taking photographs of several different instances of several different categories. Specifically, we collected a pool of about three hundred pictures of instances which fell into eight different categories: dogs, toys, food, plants, birds, animals, clothing, and vegetables. We then chose from these three hundred pictures a total of one hundred and eighty-eight, with twenty-three or twenty-four pictures in each category which we thought were visually clear and which intuitively seemed to cover a fair range of the centrality-peripherality and the familiarity-unfamiliarity dimensions. We then asked ten adults to rate these pictures according to their degree of centrality to the categories to which they belonged and according to their degree of familiarity. The adult judges, seven females and three males, were all over eighteen years of age, were from the Cambridge area, and were either students at Harvard or otherwise employed. Adult judges were told that they would be asked questions about pictures of instances of the eight concepts: ANIMAL, PLANT, FOOD, DOG, TOY, BIRD, VEGETABLE, and CLOTHING. Specifically, they were told that they would be given a pack of twenty-three or twenty-four pictures for each of these concepts and would be asked to rate each picture for its degree of centrality to the category to which it belonged and also for its degree of familiarity. We spent a few minutes explaining to subjects what we meant by centrality and what we meant by familiarity. Specifically, for the centrality-peripherality dimension we told them, "This dimension refers to how 'close' or 'distant' the object pictured is to the *most typical* instance (or instances) of the concept. In your judgments, first think of the most typical instance (or instances) that you can (the 'doggiest' dog, the most 'clotheslike' article of clothing, etc.). Then as you look through the pictures, rate each one according to its nearness to (centrality) or distance from (peripherality) this typical instance. Some cases are better cases of a concept than others and those which you feel are good instances should be rated as central whereas those which you feel are poor instances should be rated as peripheral." After some discussion subjects seemed to understand what we meant by centrality and the seven-point scale along which they were to rate the stimuli (which I will describe more fully shortly). We then told them that it was possible that for some of the pictures they might feel that the objects depicted were not instances of the concepts under study at all, and if so, they were not to rate the stimulus for its degree of centrality to the concept in question but rather should mark the space provided on the rating sheet with an *X*. We later rejected any of the pictures which were judged not to be instances from the set we finally chose to use with children since we wanted to be sure that when a child made an underextension response it was a genuine one and that adults would not also exclude it from a given concept.

We then told them that for each picture they would also be asked to rate it along a familiarity-unfamiliarity dimension. Specifically, we told them, "For this dimension rate each picture according to how familiar or unfamiliar the *kind of object* pictured is. In this rating, try to be as little idiosyncratic and as much intuitively average as you can. In other words, rate each object pictured by thinking how familiar that kind of object is 'in general' or among the other possible objects in this category. Perhaps you have seen an armadillo frequently, but on the whole an armadillo is less familiar, less well-known, or less frequently seen than, say, a dog." Subjects seemed to have little problem with the idea of familiarity.

They were then shown a seven-point scale along which they were to rate the pictures for both centrality and familiarity. Each of the numbers on the scale was described verbally. Subjects were to choose a 1 if they thought the stimulus was *extremely* peripheral or unfamiliar, a 2 if they thought it was *very* peripheral or unfamiliar, a 3 if they thought it was *quite* peripheral or unfamiliar, a 4 if they thought it was *moderately* central or familiar, a 5 if they thought it was *quite* central or familiar, a 6 if they thought it was *very* central or familiar, and a 7 if they thought it was *extremely* central or familiar. The seven-point scale was placed at the top of each individual rating sheet so the judges could refer to it as they rated the pictures. Subjects were asked to go through all the pictures in a pack and rate them along one dimension. Then they were asked to go through the pictures in that pack again and rate them along the other dimension. Half of the subjects rated the pictures for centrality first and familiarity second; the other half of the subjects rated them for familiarity first and centrality second. The rating process took from forty-five to sixty minutes for each subject. All subjects seemed to understand the task although many of them had questions about its purpose which were answered at the end of the session.

The adult centrality ratings for each stimulus were then averaged, as were the adult familiarity ratings. On the basis of these average ratings we chose twelve pictures for each of four concepts to be used in an experiment with children. The four concepts were ANIMAL, CLOTHING, FOOD, and BIRD. The twelve pictures for each concept were chosen such that three of them had been rated by adults as being central and familiar, three of them as central and unfamiliar, three of them as peripheral and familiar, and three of them as peripheral and unfamiliar. The numerical criteria we were forced to use in light of the averaged adult ratings were as follows: (1) Instances which were rated as greater than 4.5 along the centrality dimension were used as central instances; instances which were rated as less than 4.5 along the centrality dimension were used as peripheral instances. (2) Instances which were rated as greater than 5.0 on the familiarity dimension were used as familiar instances; instances which were rated as less than 5.0 on the familiarity dimension were used as unfamiliar instances. The average centrality rating for central stimuli was 6.11; the average centrality rating for peripheral stimuli was 2.90. The average familiarity rating for familiar stimuli was 6.53; the average familiarity rating for unfamiliar stimuli was 3.15. The instances used in each category and the average adult judgments of centrality and familiarity for each instance are shown in Table 5.1. Consider, for example, the first column of Table 5.1, which shows the ratings for the twelve pictures which were used as instances

TABLE 5.1 Centrality and familiarity ratings for each of the forty-eight pictures of instances used in the underextension study.

Concept	ANIMAL			CLOTHING			FOOD			BIRD		
	Stim	Average centrality rating	Average familiarity rating	Stim	Average centrality rating	Average familiarity rating	Stim	Average centrality rating	Average familiarity rating	Stim	Average centrality rating	Average familiarity rating
C-F	Cow	7.0	7.0	Shirt	6.8	7.0	Bread	6.8	6.9	Prothonotary warbler	6.5	5.5
	Horse	6.9	6.7	Pants	6.6	6.8	Egg	6.8	7.0	English tree sparrow	6.6	6.6
	Cat	7.0	7.0	Dress	6.6	6.3	Chicken	7.0	6.8	Bluejay	6.2	6.0
C-UN	Wombat	5.9	2.9	Kimono	4.9	3.2	Beef kidney	4.8	2.9	Vulture	5.7	4.7
	Aardvark	5.6	3.0	Coptic tunic	5.1	3.1	Codfish	5.8	4.4	Eastern green heron	5.8	4.2
	Anteater	5.5	3.4	1587 suit	5.2	3.5	Tongue	5.9	3.6	Hummingbird	5.7	4.5
P-F	Ant	2.7	6.2	High heel	4.2	6.5	Ketchup	3.0	6.9	Hen	3.8	6.4
	Butterfly	3.1	6.2	Scarf	3.8	6.3	Coffee	2.7	6.8	Duck	4.3	6.7
	Starfish	2.8	5.8	Skates	3.4	6.3	Lollipop	3.0	6.3	Penguin	3.9	6.8
P-UN	Crustacean	1.4	1.2	Lace collar	2.2	2.2	Coffee beans	2.6	4.1	Kiwi	3.1	2.9
	Hydra	1.6	1.3	1715 wood shoe	2.4	2.3	Mint leaves	1.8	2.7	American egret	3.7	4.2
	Centipede	2.0	3.1	Venetian hat	2.5	2.9	Morel mushroom	2.2	2.1	Baby brown pelican	3.3	3.1

NOTE: C-F = central and familiar pictures; C-UN = central and unfamiliar pictures; P-F = peripheral and familiar pictures; P-UN = peripheral and unfamiliar pictures.

Scale used:

PERIPHERAL OR UNFAMILIAR							CENTRAL OR FAMILIAR
1	2	3	4	5	6	7	
extremely	very	quite	moderate	quite	very	extremely	

of the concept ANIMAL. The three central pictures were of a cow, a horse, and a cat. Adult judges had rated these as being both central to the concept ANIMAL and familiar. The three central unfamiliar instances were pictures of a wombat, an aardvark, and an anteater. Adults had rated these pictures as being central to the concept ANIMAL but unfamiliar. The three peripheral familiar instances were pictures of an ant, a butterfly, and a starfish. Adults had rated these pictures as being peripheral examples of the concept ANIMAL, but familiar. Finally, the three peripheral unfamiliar instances were pictures of a crustacean, a hydra, and a centipede. Adults had rated these pictures as being both peripheral to the concept ANIMAL and unfamiliar. Table 5.1 also shows the centrality and familiarity ratings for each kind of instance for the other three concepts which were used in the experiment with children.

Figure 5.1 shows the twelve pictures of animals which were used in the study. In addition to the twelve instances, six noninstances for each concept were also included in our study with children. Thus each child was shown a total of seventy-two pictures, with twelve instances and six noninstances of the four concepts ANIMAL, CLOTHING, FOOD, and BIRD.

Subjects were twenty children between two years, ten months and six years, six months of age from the Living and Learning School in Woburn, Massachusetts (and ten adults to be described later). All children were from middle-income families living in the area. Children were taken from the classroom situation and came quite voluntarily to the "surprise room," a private staff room where there were a table, chairs, and the material for the session. Children were seated to the left of the experimenter who began by asking them for such vital statistics as their names, ages, and how much television they watched. (All children had watched some TV and had seen "Sesame Street" in particular.) Then when the child seemed comfortable *E* turned on the tape recorder and began the session. First the child was asked to define each of the four test categories. With the exception of two children on one word each, it turned out that they could all give some example or definition of the categories which indicated that they had at least some notion of them.[4] Then *E* explained that they would be shown some pictures and would be asked to answer "yes" or "no" to a question about each picture. Also they were encouraged at the outset to name any picture they were shown for which they might know a name.

---

[4] These two children later suggested in their classification of pictures that they had some knowledge of the verbal categories they declined to define. A detailed analysis of the definitions given by the children in this study, as compared with those produced by adults, will be presented in Chapter 7.

See facing page
FIGURE 5.1 Pictures of twelve animals used in the underextension study.

Central and familiar animals

Cow

Horse

Cat

Central and unfamiliar animals

Wombat

Aardvark

Anteater

Peripheral and familiar animals

Ant

Butterfly

Starfish

Peripheral and unfamiliar animals

Crustacean

Centipede

Hydra

Then E showed each picture one at a time to the child and asked, "Is this an animal?" or "Is this clothing?" or "Is this food?" or "Is this a bird?" depending upon which picture was being presented. If the child answered "yes," that answer was recorded, the picture was placed apart for later probing, and E moved on to the next picture. If the child answered "no, it's an X," that entire response was recorded and E moved on to the next picture. If the child answered simply "no," E probed the child immediately, inquiring "What is it?", recorded the entire response, and moved on to the next picture. After testing the child on each of the seventy-two pictures, E again presented to the child all those pictures for which he had responded simply "yes" and asked of each "What is this?" recording the child's name for the picture. Thus for each instance our results included for each child not only a "yes" or a "no" to the question "Is this a _____?" but also the label with which each child chose to name each picture. We wanted to obtain specific identifications of the stimuli from the children in order to understand the nature of any underextension responses that might occur. Specifically, if the child made an underextension response to a stimulus but identified it correctly, then this would be evidence that his underextension was not due to the perceptual ambiguity of the picture but rather was conceptual in origin. On the other hand, if the child misidentified the stimulus with a name that was not an instance of the category being investigated then this might mean that his error was due to the perceptual ambiguity of the picture.

Oftentimes a picture would require considerable discussion to insure that the child definitely meant "yes" or "no" and knew, or at least thought he knew, what the object depicted was. Sessions lasted for about half an hour. The occasional child sometimes grew restless but all finished the task with complete and serious responses. Many of the children seemed to enjoy the task and would ask if they could "do it again." Children were given lollipops as a modest reward for their services at the end of the session.

A group of ten adults was also run in this experiment. This group consisted of five male and five female undergraduate and graduate students between the ages of eighteen and twenty-seven years. They were run in exactly the same way as the twenty children were, as described above, and were paid for their participation.

RESULTS

The main purpose of including an adult group was to be sure that adults do include the instances in the four concepts which were being studied in this experiment. The total number of "no" responses made by the ten adults to the instances (i.e., underextension responses) was 11 out of a possible 480. Thus, the average number of underextensions per adult was 1.1 out of 48. All of the underextension responses made by adults were to peripheral-

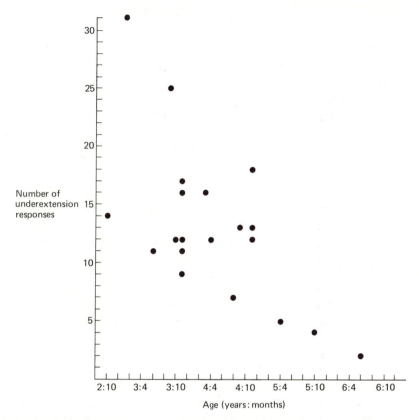

FIGURE 5.2 Total number of underextension responses made by children as a function of age.

unfamiliar stimuli. Six adults said "no" when asked of the picture of mint leaves if it was *food*. Two adults said "no" when asked if the morel mushroom was *food*. And when asked if the lace collar was *clothing*, if the wooden shoe was *clothing*, and if the crustacean was an *animal*, one adult said "no" in each case. With the exception of these few cases, all adults said "yes" to every instance.

In contrast, children made many underextension responses. Figure 5.2 shows the total number of underextension responses (out of forty-eight possible) made by each individual child as a function of age. Figure 5.2 reveals that children make a substantial number of such responses in this study, with three-quarters of the children making more than ten underextensions. Figure 5.2 also reveals that there is an inverse relation between the number of underextension responses made and the age of the child, although the relation is far from monotonic.

For which of the instances did children make the greatest number of underextensions? Table 5.2 shows the total number of underextensions made to each of the four kinds of instances being studied in this experiment: central and familiar, central and unfamiliar, peripheral and familiar, and peripheral and unfamiliar. As Table 5.2 shows, central instances, regardless of whether they are familiar or unfamiliar, produce very few underextensions (17 and 19) compared to peripheral instances (133 and 91). Both kinds of peripheral instances produce many underextensions with familiar peripheral instances actually producing substantially more (133) than unfamiliar peripheral instances (91).

We have performed two statistical tests of significance on the data summarized in Table 5.2. The data for these analyses were the number of errors each child made in judging category membership—the number of

TABLE 5.2 Total number of underextensions made by children for each kind of stimulus (central and familiar, central and unfamiliar, peripheral and familiar, peripheral and unfamiliar) used in the underextension study. Notice that while children make few such responses on central instances regardless of whether they are familiar or unfamiliar, they make many for both familiar and unfamiliar peripheral instances.

	Central	Peripheral
Familiar	17	133
Unfamiliar	19	91

times each child denied that an instance belonged to a conceptual category when it did. These data were analyzed as a five-way factorial design with subjects, conceptual categories, centrality, familiarity, and instances as independent variables. The first test was a repeated-measures fixed- effects analysis of variance in which conceptual categories, instances, centrality, and familiarity were treated as fixed effects. Using this test we found, among other things, that the main effects of centrality and of familiarity and the centrality × familiarity interaction were all statistically significant ($p < .01$). Thus children made significantly more underextensions on peripheral instances than on central instances, and they made significantly more underextensions on familiar instances than on unfamiliar instances. In view of Table 5.2, the significant interaction was a result of the fact that while children did not make more underextensions on familiar instances than on unfamiliar instances when the instances were central to the concepts being tested, they did make more on familiar instances than on unfamiliar instances when they were peripheral. This finding is especially interesting in view of the fact that the few underextension responses made by adults were to peripheral unfamiliar stimuli. Thus we can be confident that if we repeated this experiment testing the same pictures and the same concepts, each of the above mentioned effects would again be significant (see Hayes, 1963, or Winer, 1962, for guidelines in interpreting the results of a fixed-effects analysis of variance).

Can we be confident that if we were to run an experiment similar to the one presented here, but testing different concepts with different pictures that the effects described above would also be significant? As H. Clark (1973b) has recently pointed out, the appropriate analysis when one wants to generalize in this way is the random-effects analysis of variance. So, in our second analysis, subjects, conceptual categories, and instances were treated as random factors and therefore it was necessary to construct quasi F ratios to test the significance of most effects in this analysis of variance (see Winer, 1962). This method provides conservative tests of effects but yields high generality to the conclusions from the analysis (see H. Clark, 1973b). When the analysis was done in this way, of the factors discussed above, the centrality effect was statistically significant ($p < .01$) but the familiarity effect and the centrality $\times$ familiarity interaction were not.[5]

While Table 5.2 gives the over-all pattern of underextension responses made by children in this study, it will require a more detailed examination of the responses produced by children for each of the individual instances of each of the concepts in order to understand and interpret that pattern. Table 5.3 presents the total number of underextensions ("no" responses to instances) and the total number of correct responses ("yes" responses to instances) made by the twenty children to each of the forty-eight instances used in this study. Recall that in addition to obtaining a "yes" or "no" answer to the question "Is this a _____?" children were also encouraged to give a name for the object depicted in each picture as well, if they did not do so spontaneously. Each of the names provided by children for the pictures were assigned to one of four categories: (1) *CC*—correct classification: If the child named the object depicted correctly his name was counted as a correct classification (e.g., *cow* to a picture of a cow, *horse* to a picture of a horse). (2) *RC*—related classification: If the child named the object depicted incorrectly but with a name of an instance of the concept being tested his name was scored as a related classification. For example, if the subject called a picture of a cow a *horse* it was scored as a related classification since *horse* is incorrect but at the same time a kind of ANIMAL. (3) *UC*—unrelated classification: If the child named the object depicted incorrectly and with a name that is not an instance of the category being tested his name was scored as an unrelated classification. For example, if a subject called the picture of a cow a *tree* it was scored as an unrelated classification since it was both incorrect and not an instance of

---

[5] In both analyses there was also a significant category effect ($p < .01$). In this study children made most "errors" on the concept CLOTHING, next most on the concept FOOD, next most on the concept ANIMAL, and fewest on the concept BIRD.

TABLE 5.3 Total number of "yes" and "no" responses for each of the forty-eight instances studied in the underextension experiment.

Concept	ANIMAL			CLOTHING			FOOD			BIRD		
	Stim	Total yes	Total no	Stim	Total yes	Total no	Stim	Total yes	Total no	Stim	Total yes	Total no
C-F	Cow	19	1	Shirt	17	3	Bread	19	1	Prothonotary warbler	20	0
	Horse	19	1	Pants	17	3	Egg	20	0	English tree sparrow	20	0
	Cat	17	3	Dress	16	4	Chicken	19	1	Bluejay	20	0
C-UN	Wombat	20	0	Kimono	15	5	Beef kidney	19	1	Vulture	20	0
	Aardvark	20	0	Coptic tunic	16	4	Codfish	20	0	Eastern green heron	19	1
	Anteater	19	1	1587 suit	16	4	Tongue	18	2	Hummingbird	19	1
P-F	Ant	12	8	High heel	5	15	Ketchup	7	13	Hen	8	12
	Butterfly	12	8	Scarf	10	10	Coffee	4	16	Duck	12	8
	Starfish	10	10	Skates	5	15	Lollipop	14	6	Penguin	8	12
P-UN	Crustacean	15	5	Lace collar	4	16	Coffee beans	15	5	Kiwi	19	1
	Hydra	15	5	1715 wood shoe	6	14	Mint leaves	8	12	American egret	18	2
	Centipede	15	5	Venetian hat	4	16	Morel mushroom	13	7	Baby brown pelican	16	4

the concept ANIMAL. (4) *DK*—don't know: If the child indicated that he did not know a name for an individual picture this was scored as a "don't know" response. Every attempt to name an instance could be classified in one of these four ways.

With the aid of Table 5.3 and the breakdown of the children's names (to be presented in what follows) I would like to consider the responses of the children to each of the forty-eight instances in turn in an attempt to discern the source of their underextension responses. This discussion will be relatively free of theoretical interpretation. After I have examined each of the instances in turn I will try to interpret the results in a more theoretical discussion.

Animals: Central and Familiar

(1) *Cow:* $(C = 7.0; F = 7.0)$: 1 No [*UC*]; 19 Yes [14 *CC*, 3 *RC*, 2 *DK*]

The picture of a cow received nineteen "yes" responses and one "no" response to the question "Is this an animal?" Fourteen of the twenty children correctly identified this instance as a *cow* and also correctly classified it as an *animal*. Thus the availability of a more specific name was not enough to cause children to exclude this instance from the animal category. The one child who did not classify it as an animal identified it as *food* and so his exclusion was therefore in fact consistent with his identification of the stimulus.

(2) *Horse:* $(C = 6.9; F = 6.7)$: 1 No [*CC*]; 19 Yes [18 *CC*, 1 *RC*]

This picture of the horse also received nineteen "yes" responses and one "no" response to the question "Is this an animal?" The one underextension response was associated with the dominant name reaction "No, horsie." This particular child correctly identified the picture as a horse but in spite of this, or perhaps because of it, did not classify it as an *animal*. Eighteen of the children correctly identified the picture as a horse but also classified it as an *animal*. The remaining child misidentified it as a *donkey* and classified it as an *animal*.

(3) *Cat:* $(C = 7.0; F = 7.0)$: 3 No [3 *CC*]; 17 Yes [17 *CC*]

All children correctly identified this picture as a *cat* or *kitty* or the like. Seventeen of these children also correctly classified it as an *animal*. The three children who made underextension responses to this stimulus gave dominant name reactions such as "No, it's a cat (kitty)."

Animals: Central and Unfamiliar

(4) *Wombat:* $(C = 5.9; F = 2.9)$: 0 No; 20 Yes [17 *RC*, 3 *DK*]

No children correctly identified this instance as a wombat. Most of the children guessed that it was a *bear,* a *raccoon,* a *pig,* a *rat,* and so on, but often expressed uncertainty about their guesses. Three of the children simply said that they did not know what it was. Nonetheless all children agreed that it was an *animal*.

(5) *Aardvark:* $(C = 5.6; F = 3.0)$: 0 No; 20 Yes [1 *CC*, 12 *RC*, 7 *DK*]

Every child also agreed that the picture of an aardvark was an *animal*. One child could actually name it *aardvark* since he had seen an aardvark on "Sesame Street." The other children either labeled it with the name of some other kind of animal such as *bear* or *kangaroo* or *anteater* or they admitted that they did not know what it was.

(6) *Anteater:* $(C = 5.5; F = 3.4)$: 1 No [*RC*]; 19 Yes [3 *CC*, 10 *RC*, 6 *DK*]

Nineteen out of twenty children said "yes" to the question "Is this an animal?" for this stimulus. Only three children could identify it correctly as an anteater. Ten of the children gave it some other animal name and six of the children said they did not know what it was even though they had agreed that it was an *animal*.

Animals: Peripheral and Familiar

(7) *Ant:* $(C = 2.7; F = 6.2)$: 7 No [5 *CC*, 2 *RC*], 13 Yes [11 *CC*, 1 *RC*, 1 *DK*]

Seven out of twenty children said that the picture of the ant was not an *animal*. Five of these correctly identified it as an *ant* and two misidentified it as a *spider*. Since for adults both ants and spiders are animals, the "no" responses represent genuine underextensions and are not due to the visual ambiguity of the picture. Thirteen of the children correctly classified this instance as an *animal* and usually identified it as an *ant*. Thus again not all children nor even a majority will fail to classify this instance as an animal even though they can name it more specifically, but a significant minority will.

(8) *Butterfly:* $(C = 3.1; F = 6.2)$: 8 No [7 *CC*, 1 *RC*]; 12 Yes [12 *CC*]

Eight children said "no" when asked if this instance was an *animal*. Seven of these children correctly identified it as a *butterfly* while one child called it a *fly*. Since butterflies and flies are both animals these are genuine underextensions rather than the result of perceptual confusion. The other twelve children classified this stimulus as an *animal* and correctly identified it as a *butterfly*.

(9) *Starfish:* $(C = 2.8; F = 5.8)$: 10 No [8 *CC*, 1 *UC*, 1 *DK*]; 10 Yes [8 *CC*, 2 *RC*]

Ten children said "no" when asked if this instance was an *animal*. One of these children misidentified the stimulus as a *flower* and thus his underextension response was in fact consistent with his identification. One child said he did not know what it was. The other eight children, however, correctly identified it as a *starfish*, which means that their failure to classify it as an *animal* was not the result of perceptual confusion but rather the result of their failure to realize that starfishes are animals. The other ten children said that it was an *animal,* with eight of these correctly identifying it as a *starfish* and two identifying it as a *butterfly* and a *crab*.

Animals: Peripheral and Unfamiliar

(10) *Crustacean: (C = 1.4; F = 1.2)*: 5 No [2 *UC,* 3 *DK*]; 15 Yes [10 *RC,* 5 *DK*]

Five children said "no" when asked if this stimulus was an *animal.* Two of these children identified it as a *tree* and so were consistent in not classifying it as an *animal.* The other three said they did not know what it was. Fifteen children said "yes" it was an *animal* although none of these children could correctly name it. Five of them said they did not know what it was (although they classified it as an *animal*) and ten labeled it with some other animal name such as *bug, spider,* or *octopus.*

(11) *Hydra: (C = 1.6; F = 1.3)*: 5 No [3 *RC,* 1 *UC,* 1 *DK*]; 15 Yes [7 *RC,* 8 *DK*]

Five children said "no" in response to the question "Is this an animal?" While none of these children could name it correctly, three of them named it with animal names—*spider* or *octopus.* The fact that they also declined to classify it as an *animal* suggests that they did not think of spiders or octopuses as animals. Fifteen children did classify it as an *animal.* Of these, eight said they did not know what it was, and seven labeled it with incorrect animal names.

(12) *Centipede: (C = 2.0; F = 3.1)*: 5 No [5 *RC*]; 15 Yes [13 *RC,* 2 *DK*]

Five children said "no" when asked if this stimulus was an *animal.* While none of them was able to correctly identify it, all five of them did label it with an animal name—*caterpillar, spider,* or *bug.* Apparently, for these children caterpillars, spiders, and bugs are not animals. Fifteen children classified this stimulus as an *animal* with thirteen of them labeling it with some incorrect animal name and two of them saying they didn't know a name for it.

Clothing: Central and Familiar

(13) *Shirt: (C = 6.8; F = 7.0)*: 3 No [2 *CC,* 1 *RC*]; 17 Yes [12 *CC,* 3 *RC,* 2 *DK*]

Three children said "no" when asked of this instance if it was *clothing.* Two of these children correctly identified the stimulus as a *shirt* and one of them called it a *dress* and thus their mistakes in not classifying it as *clothing* were genuine underextension responses. Seventeen of the children did classify it as *clothing,* with twelve of these identifying it as a *shirt,* three labeling it with the name of some other article of clothing (*coat, dress, jacket*) and two saying they did not know what to call it.

(14) *Pants:* $(C = 6.6; F = 6.8)$: 3 No [3 *CC*]; 17 Yes [16 *CC*, 1 *DK*]

Three children said "no" when asked if this instance was *clothing.* Each of these three children identified the stimulus correctly as *pants* or *trousers* suggesting that their "mistakes" were genuine underextensions. The other seventeen children classified this instance as *clothing.* Sixteen of these could correctly identify the stimulus as *pants* or *trousers* or *dungarees* while the remaining child said he did not know what it was.

(15) *Dress:* $(C = 6.6; F = 6.3)$: 4 No [4 *CC*]; 16 Yes [15 *CC*, 1 *DK*]

Four children said "no" when asked if this stimulus was *clothing.* Each of these children identified the stimulus as a *dress* and so their mistakes were genuine underextensions. The other sixteen children classified it as *clothing* and all but one of these identified it as a *dress.*

Clothing: Central and Unfamiliar

(16) *Kimono:* $(C = 4.9; F = 3.2)$: 5 No [1 *RC*, 4 *UC*]; 15 Yes [10 *RC*, 5 *DK*]

Five children said "no" when asked if this stimulus was *clothing.* Of these, four identified it with some nonclothing name such as *animal* or *castle.* Thus their mistakes were in fact consistent with their misidentifications. The remaining child called it a *shirt* but still insisted that it was not *clothing.* The other fifteen children said "yes" when asked if it was *clothing.* These children either misidentified it as a *dress* or a *shirt,* and the like, or said they did not know what it was even though they did classify it as *clothing.*

(17) *Coptic Tunic:* $(C = 5.1; F = 3.1)$: 4 No [4 *RC*]; 16 Yes [14 *RC*, 2 *DK*]

Four children said this was not *clothing* even though they identified it as a *coat* or a *dress.* Sixteen children said "yes" it was *clothing* although none of them could correctly name it. Fourteen of them gave some incorrect clothing name, while two of them admitted that they did not know what it was, even though they agreed it was *clothing.*

(18) *1587 Suit:* $(C = 5.2; F = 3.5)$: 4 No [4 *RC*]; 16 Yes [14 *RC*, 2 *DK*]

Four children declined to classify this stimulus as *clothing* even though they identified it as a *coat* or a *dress.* The other sixteen children agreed that it was *clothing* with fourteen of them identifying it as some such article of clothing as *pajamas, dress, jacket,* and with two of them saying they did not know what to call it even though they had classified it as *clothing.*

Clothing: Peripheral and Familiar

(19) *High Heel:* $(C = 4.2; F = 6.5)$: 15 No [15 *CC*]; 5 Yes [5 *CC*]

Fifteen children said "no" in response to the question "Is this clothing?" All of these correctly identified the stimulus as a *shoe* and so their responses were genuine underextensions. The remaining five children classified this stimulus as *clothing* and correctly identified it as a *shoe*.

(20) *Scarf:* ($C = 3.8$; $F = 6.3$): 10 No [7 *CC*, 1 *UC*, 2 *DK*]; 10 Yes [7 *CC*, 1 *RC*, 2 *DK*]

Ten children said this was not *clothing* even though seven of them correctly identified it as a *handkerchief, scarf,* or the like. The other ten children classified it as *clothing* with seven of them identifying it correctly.

(21) *Skates:* ($C = 3.4$; $F = 6.3$): 15 No [11 *CC*, 4 *RC*]; 5 Yes [3 *CC*, 2 *RC*]

Fifteen children said the pair of skates was not *clothing* although most of them identified them as *skates,* with the remaining children identifying them as *shoes* or *boots.* Only five children classified them as *clothing.*

Clothing: Peripheral and Unfamiliar

(22) *Lace Collar:* ($C = 2.2$; $F = 2.2$): 16 No [10 *UC*, 6 *DK*]; 4 Yes [1 *RC*, 2 *UC*, 1 *DK*]

Sixteen children chose not to classify this stimulus as *clothing.* Ten of these children identified it with some nonclothing names such as *picture, design, bridge,* and so their refusal to classify it as *clothing* was consistent with their misidentifications. The remaining six children said they did not know a name for it. Only four children classified it as *clothing.* Curiously, when asked what it was, two of these children identified it with nonclothing names—*fan* and *chicken.*

(23) *1715 Wooden Shoe:* ($C = 2.4$; $F = 2.3$): 14 No [13 *CC*, 1 *UC*]; 6 Yes [6 *CC*]

Almost all children named this stimulus a *shoe* but fourteen children declined to classify it as *clothing.* Six children did answer "yes" to the question "Is this clothing?"

(24) *Venetian Hat:* ($C = 2.5$; $F = 2.9$): 16 No [3 *CC*, 13 *UC*]; 4 Yes [3 *CC*, 1 *DK*]

Sixteen children said "no" this was not *clothing.* Of these, however, thirteen misidentified the stimulus with some nonclothing name such as *hair, horse, tree, grass,* and so on, so that their underextensions were actually consistent with their misidentifications. Three of them correctly labeled this stimulus *hat,* suggesting that for them hats are not articles of clothing. Four children classified this stimulus as an article of clothing, with three of them correctly identifying it as a *hat* and one of them saying he did not know a name for it.

Food: Central and Familiar

(25) *Bread:* ($C = 6.8$; $F = 6.9$): 1 No [*CC*]; 19 Yes [19 *CC*]

All children correctly identified this stimulus as *bread* (one child said *toast* which we counted as correct) and all but one child classified it as *food.* The one child who declined to classify it as *food* gave a dominant name reaction, "No, bread."

(26) *Egg:* $(C = 6.8; F = 7.0)$: 0 No; 20 Yes [19 *CC*, 1 *RC*]

All children said "yes" in response to the question "Is this food? and all but one child correctly identified it as an *egg,* with the remaining child calling it a *pancake.*

(27) *Chicken:* $(C = 7.0; F = 6.8)$: 1 No [1 *UC*]; 19 Yes [15 *CC*, 2 *RC*, 2 *DK*]

Only one child responded "no" to the question "Is this food?" and he identified it as a *girl* and so his underextension was consistent with his odd identification of the stimulus. The rest of the children responded "yes," with most of them correctly identifying the stimulus as *chicken* and with two of them calling it *steak* and *vegetable,* and with two of them saying they did not know a name for it.

Food: Central and Unfamiliar

(28) *Beef Kidney:* $(C = 4.8; F = 2.9)$: 1 No [*RC*]; 19 Yes [1 *CC*, 12 *RC*, 6 *DK*]

Only one child declined to classify this stimulus as *food.* This child named the stimulus *hot dogs* and so his underextension was inconsistent with his misidentification of the stimulus. Although only one of the remaining nineteen children could correctly identify it as *meat,* all of them correctly classified it as *food.* Many of them identified it with some incorrect food name such as *peppers, bread, mushrooms,* and many of them admitted that they did not know a name for it even though they agreed that it was *food.*

(29) *Cod Fish:* $(C = 5.8; F = 4.4)$: 0 No; 20 Yes [7 *CC*, 10 *RC*, 3 *DK*]

All of the children correctly classified this stimulus as *food* although only seven of them could identify it as *fish.* Others misidentified it with other food names such as *chicken* or *meat* or simply said they could not name it even though they had classified it as *food.*

(30) *Tongue:* $(C = 5.9; F = 3.6)$: 2 No [2 *UC*]; 18 Yes [15 *RC*, 3 *DK*]

Only two children declined to classify this stimulus as *food.* These children identified the stimulus as *animal* and *turkey.* Although none of the other children was able to correctly identify the stimulus, they all agreed that it was nonetheless *food.*

Food: Peripheral and Familiar

(31) *Ketchup:* $(C = 3.0; F = 6.9)$: 13 No [12 *CC*, 1 *RC*]; 7 Yes [7 *CC*]

Every child but one (who called it *Coke*) correctly identified this stimulus as *ketchup.* However, thirteen children said "no" in response to the question "Is this food?" Thus all but one of these children recognized what it was but declined to classify it as *food.*

(32) *Coffee:* $(C = 2.7; F = 6.8)$: 16 No [16 *CC*]; 4 Yes [4 *CC*]

All children identified this stimulus as *coffee* or *something to drink*, or the like, but sixteen of them chose not to classify it as *food*. We included this instance since all of our ten adult judges rated this stimulus as a food, a peripheral food but nonetheless a food. Moreover, none of the ten adults whom we tested in the same way as we did the children declined to categorize the coffee as *food*. If the reader is inclined to disagree with our adult judges and subjects, I must say that I sympathize with him. In any event, the data for this particular stimulus can be ignored since they are not crucial for our over-all conclusions.

(33) *Lollipop:* $(C = 3.0; F = 6.3)$: 6 No [5 *CC*, 1 *DK*]; 14 Yes [14 *CC*]

Six children said "no" in response to the question "Is this food?" Five of these correctly identified the stimulus as a *lollipop* or *candy* and so their failures to classify it as *food* represent genuine underextension responses. One child said he did not know what it was. Fourteen of the children correctly identified it as a *lollipop* or *candy* and also classified it as *food*.

Food: Peripheral and Unfamiliar

(34) *Coffee Beans:* $(C = 2.6; F = 4.1)$: 5 No [5 *RC*]; 15 Yes [1 *CC*, 12 *RC*, 2 *DK*]

Five children said "no" when asked if this stimulus was *food*. Three of these children identified the coffee beans as *seeds* so it is unclear whether they were being consistent or inconsistent in their underextension responses since some seeds are edible and others are not. The other two children identified them as *candy* and so their underextensions are genuine. The other fifteen children classified this stimulus as food, often identifying it with such names as *seeds, peanuts, watermelon pits, candy,* and so on. Two children said they did not know what to call them although they classified them as *food*.

(35) *Mint Leaves:* $(C = 1.8; F = 2.7)$: 12 No [10 *CC*, 1 *UC*, 1 *DK*]; 8 Yes [4 CC, 4 RC]

Twelve children responded "no" when asked if this stimulus was *food*. Ten of these children identified them as *leaves*, one as *flowers*, and one said he did not know what they were. Eight children responded "yes," identifying the stimulus as either *leaves*, which they often added were *food*, or as other kinds of food such as *lettuce, mustard greens, chicken,* and so on.

(36) *Morel Mushroom:* $(C = 2.2; F = 2.1)$: 7 No [2 *CC*, 1 *RC*, 3 *UC*, 1 *DK*]; 13 Yes [2 *CC*, 6 *RC*, 1 *UC*, 4 *DK*]

Seven children said "no" in response to the question "Is this food?" Three of these children misidentified the stimulus as a *tree*, a *horse thing*, and *feet* and so their unwillingness to classify this instance as *food* was consistent with their misidentifications of it. On the other hand, two of these children correctly identified it as *mushrooms* and one of them identified it as *salad,* so their names were in fact inconsistent with their unwillingness to classify it as *food.* The remaining child said he did not know what it was. The other thirteen children classified this stimulus as *food* with their identifications being two correct, six other food names, one nonfood name, and four "don't knows."

Birds: Central and Familiar

(37) *Prothonotary Warbler:* ($C = 6.5; F = 5.5$): 0 No; 20 Yes [20 *CC*]
(38) *English Tree Sparrow:* ($C = 6.6; F = 6.6$): 0 No; 20 Yes [20 *CC*]
(39) *Bluejay:* ($C = 6.2; F = 6.0$): 0 No; 20 Yes [20 *CC*]

For each of these stimuli children invariably responded "yes" to the question "Is this a bird?" and usually identified them with the term *bird* or the diminutive *birdie.*

Birds: Central and Unfamiliar

(40) *Vulture:* ($C = 5.7; F = 4.7$): 0 No; 20 Yes [20 *CC*]
(41) *Eastern Green Heron:* ($C = 5.8; F = 4.2$): 1 No [1 *DK*]; 19 Yes [19 *CC*]
(42) *Hummingbird:* ($C = 5.7; F = 4.5$): 1 No [1 *UC*]; 19 Yes [19 *CC*]

Again, apart from one "no" response for the Eastern green heron ("don't know") and one "no" response for the hummingbird (*kiki, cuckoobird*), children responded "yes" to the question "Is this a bird?" and usually identified each as a *bird.*

Birds: Peripheral and Familiar

(43) *Hen:* ($C = 3.8; F = 6.4$): 12 No [7 *CC*, 3 *RC*, 2 *DK*]; 8 Yes [4 *CC*, 3 *RC*, 1 *UC*]

Twelve children when asked "Is this a bird? answered "no" for this stimulus. Seven of these children correctly identified it as a *hen,* a *chicken,* a *cockledoodledoo,* and so forth, and three identified it as a *turkey* or a *rooster.* Thus, for these children, chickens and turkeys are apparently not birds. Two of the twelve children who said "no" for this stimulus said they did not know what it was. The other eight children said "yes," it was a bird, with most of these identifying it as either a *hen, chicken, rooster,* or *duck.* One child said it was a *camel* even though he had correctly classified it as a *bird.*

(44) *Duck:* ($C = 4.3; F = 6.7$): 8 No [8 *CC*]; 12 Yes [11 *CC*, 1 *DK*]

Eight children said "no" when asked "Is this a bird?" Each of these eight children correctly identified it as a *duck.* Thus for these children apparently ducks are not birds. The other twelve said "yes," it was a *bird.* Eleven of these correctly identified it as a *duck,* while one said he did not know a name for it even though he had classified it as a *bird.*

(45) *Penguins:* $(C = 3.9; F = 6.8)$: 12 No [9 *CC*, 3 *RC*]; 8 Yes [5 *CC*, 1 *RC*, 2 *DK*]

Twelve children said "no" when asked if these were *birds*. Nine of these correctly identified them as *penguins,* so apparently for them a penguin is not a *bird*. Three of these children called them *pigeons* or *eagles* and so their underextension responses are conceptual rather than perceptual, since both pigeons and eagles are birds. Eight children said "yes" they were *birds,* with five of them identifying them as *penguins,* one as *ducks,* and two not being able to give them a name.

Birds: Peripheral and Unfamiliar

(46) *Kiwi:* $(C = 3.1; F = 2.9)$: 1 No [*UC*]; 19 Yes [19 *CC*]

Only one child said "no" when asked, "Is this a bird?" for this stimulus. He identified it as a *giraffe* and so his underextension was consistent with his misidentification. All the other children said "yes" to the question "Is this a bird?" and identified it as a *bird*.

(47) *American Egret:* $(C = 3.7; F = 4.2)$: 2 No [2 *RC*]; 18 Yes [15 *CC*, 3 *RC*]

Only two children said "no" when asked of this stimulus, "Is this a bird?" These children misidentified the stimulus as a *duck* and an *eagle*. Since ducks and eagles are actually birds, their responses would appear to be conceptual in origin. The other eighteen children said "yes" it was a bird, with fifteen of these giving a correct identification (usually *bird*), and three identifying it as either a *duck* or an *ostrich*.

(48) *Baby Brown Pelican:* $(C = 3.3; F = 3.1)$: 4 No [2 *RC*, 1 *CC*, 1 *DK*]; 16 Yes [10 *CC*, 4 *RC*, 1 *UC*, 1 *DK*]

Only four children said "no" when asked if this stimulus was a *bird*. Two of these children identified it as a *duck,* one as an *animal,* and one said he did not know a name for it. Sixteen children said "yes," it was a *bird*. Ten of these identified it correctly, usually as a *bird* or *birdie,* four of them called it a *duck* or a *goose,* one of them called it a *comb,* and one of them said he did not know a name for it.

DISCUSSION

Of the two dimensions studied in this experiment, it is clearly the central-peripheral dimension which plays the greatest role in bringing about under-extension responses. The central-peripheral effect was very large and highly statistically significant. Regardless of whether they were familiar or un-familiar, every central instance produced fewer underextension responses than any peripheral instance (with the exception of one tie). This is not to say that the child will always fail to include a peripheral instance in a given concept. But when he does make an underextension response, the chances are quite high that it will be for a peripheral instance rather than for a central instance.

Familiarity appears to be less important in influencing the child to make underextension responses, but it may also be a factor. In this study, for central stimuli, familiar and unfamiliar instances produced approximately the same number of underextensions. However, for peripheral stimuli, familiar instances actually produced more underextensions (about 40 percent) than unfamiliar stimuli.[6] The familiarity effect was not strong enough to reach statistical significance when the results were analyzed by means of a random-effects analysis of variance. However, it was shown to be statistically significant when analyzed by means of a fixed-effects analysis of variance. This means that we may have confidence in the reliability of the finding, at least with respect to the particular pictures (instances) and concepts which were studied. It is possible that the same sort of experiment, but done with different pictures and different concepts, would not produce a significant familiarity effect but I am inclined to doubt it since in other studies, as well as in this one, we have been struck by a tendency on the part of children to exclude from a verbal concept familiar instances for which they have another name ("That's a dog, not an animal"; "That's a tree, not a plant") more than in the case of instances which seem less familiar, for which they do not have another name (see for example, Chapter 4). The significant familiarity-centrality interaction in the case of the fixed-effects analysis of variance suggests that in this experiment at least, the availability of a more specific name only occasionally dissuaded the children from including a central instance in a given concept; however, the availability of a more specific name may have more often been the additional factor which dissuaded them from including a peripheral instance in that concept.

One of the most interesting aspects of the results just considered is that children consistently classify unfamiliar central instances as instances of the various concepts. Thus every child said that the picture of a wombat and the picture of an aardvark were *animals* and all but one child said the picture of an anteater was an *animal*. Some of these children, when asked to identify the pictures, tentatively guessed that they were pictures of *bears* or *kangaroos* or *pigs,* and so on, but a number of them said they did not know what they were, had never seen anything quite like them before, but nonetheless were quite certain that they were *animals*. This behavior testifies to the inferential or generative nature of the child's concepts, for they will consistently include in concepts various kinds of instances which they have never seen before, provided they are central instances.

---

[6] A difference which is more striking in view of the fact that all eleven underextension responses made by adults were made to peripheral unfamiliar stimuli.

For the most part, the underextension responses made by children in this study appear to have been conceptual mistakes rather than the result of perceptual confusion. There were some cases for which the child apparently did not recognize a given picture, would identify it incorrectly, and, consistent with his misidentification, would not include it in a general concept. This happened most often for peripheral unfamiliar instances and the most striking cases were for two of the peripheral unfamiliar instances of CLOTHING—the lace collar and the Venetian hat. Children frequently misidentified the lace collar with nonclothing names such as *picture, design, bridge,* and so forth, and the Venetian hat with such nonclothing names as *hair, horse, tree, grass,* and so on. Their unwillingness to classify these particular stimuli as *clothing* was therefore consistent with their misidentifications. Thus it is possible that the reason why these children did not include these stimuli as instances of the concept CLOTHING was because of the perceptual ambiguity of the pictures for them. If a child really saw the Venetian hat as a horse, then his failure to count it as an instance of CLOTHING results from a perceptual problem. Conceptually he is being consistent by excluding it from CLOTHING, since horses are not articles of clothing.

The majority of underextension responses were not of this nature, however. Children would correctly identify the picture of a butterfly as a *butterfly,* of an ant as an *ant,* and of a starfish as a *starfish,* but would not include them in the concept ANIMAL; they would correctly identify pictures of a high heel as a *shoe* or of a scarf as a *scarf* or of skates as *skates,* but would not include them in the concept CLOTHING; they would correctly identify pictures of ketchup as *ketchup* and of a lollipop as a *lollipop,* but would not include them in the concept FOOD; they would correctly identify a picture of a hen as a *chicken,* of a duck as a *duck,* or of a penguin as a *penguin,* but would not include them in the concept BIRD. For such cases the child's problem clearly is not due to the perceptual ambiguity of the pictures since he can identify the stimuli correctly. Rather, his problem is conceptual in nature. He does not realize that butterflies, ants, and starfish are ANIMALS; that shoes, scarves, and skates are CLOTHING; that ketchup and lollipops are FOOD; and that chickens, ducks, and penguins are BIRDS.

Thus this study reveals that children do not always include all the instances which adults do in a given concept. The child will usually include instances which are rated by adults as being good examples, typical instances or central to the concepts in question regardless of whether those instances are familiar or unfamiliar to him. However, he will often not include instances which are rated by adults as being poor examples, atypical instances, or peripheral to the concepts in question, even though he can often identify those instances correctly with a specific name.

Chapter 6

The Determinants of Overextension in the Child [1]

In Chapter 4 it was observed that children would sometimes include objects within categories which adults would not. For example, when shown a picture of a tomato and asked, "Is this an apple?" many children said "yes" whereas adults invariably said "no." An examination of the pictures which produced the greatest number of overextensions suggested that three factors may play a role in enticing the child to make such "mistakes". In decreasing order of the likelihood of their importance as determinants of such over-extension responses, these were: (1) perceptual similarity—the noninstance is perceptually similar to an instance of the category, the label of which is overextended; (2) association through contiguity—the noninstance (or something like it) has been seen by the child in the presence of an instance of the category; and (3) functional similarity—the noninstance serves the same function as an instance of the category.

In that study it was often difficult to discern which of these three factors were crucial in enticing the child to overextend a given term of reference since the noninstances which produced the greatest number of overextensions often appeared to be both perceptually similar and functionally similar to an instance of the category, or perceptually similar and contiguous, and in still other cases, any one of the three factors may have been involved. For example, the tomato depicted in the picture mentioned above which produced a large number of overextensions seemed to be perceptu-

[1] I am grateful to Elizabeth Smith for her help in conducting the experiments reported in this chapter and to Daniel Klett and Marc Fiedler for their help with the analysis of the diaries.

ally similar to an apple (*apple* was the word overgeneralized), but it was also functionally similar (since both tomatoes and apples are edible objects) and either of these factors (or both) might have been crucial in influencing the child to include it in the category of things comprehended by the term *apple*. Moreover, it could be argued that the child may have seen apples and tomatoes in the same place (in the supermarket, in the refrigerator, on the dinner table, for instance) and therefore that his overextensions were the result of association through contiguity.

Certain other considerations suggested that the most powerful of these three determinants of overextensions was probably perceptual similarity, that the second most powerful was probably association through contiguity, and that the weakest was probably functional similarity, if it was operative at all. For example, the children who classified the picture of a tomato as an *apple* did not classify a picture of a banana as an *apple*. Bananas are presumably just as functionally similar to apples (both dessert foods) as are tomatoes, and just as likely to be seen in the presence of apples as are tomatoes. Thus apparently this degree of functional similarity and association through contiguity is not sufficient to sway the child to overgeneralize, and therefore the crucial attribute of the picture of the tomato was probably its perceptual similarity to an apple.

Nonetheless, perceptual similarity does not seem to account for all of the overextension responses made by young children. For example, in one study Judy Ungerer observed that children would often say "yes" when asked if a picture of a vase was a *plant*. Vases do not look especially like plants, nor do they serve the same function, but plants are often seen in vases. Thus it seems that this may well have been a case of overextension because of association through contiguity. There were no similar cases suggesting that functional similarity alone could produce overextension in the child, which is why I argued above that functional similarity is probably the weakest of these three possible determinants of overgeneralization.

These conclusions, however, were very tentative since there were not many cases which would permit the teasing apart of the relative contributions of these three factors in promoting overextension. It was particularly difficult to establish the relative importance of perceptual similarity and association through contiguity, since for many of the stimuli which evoked a relatively large number of overextension responses arguments could be made for either factor. In the present study our goal has been to investigate the tendency of children to overgeneralize to noninstances which are only perceptually similar (and not functionally similar or likely to be associated through contiguity) to instances of the concept overgeneralized, or when they are only likely to be associated through contiguity with instances of the concept, or when they are only functionally similar to instances of the concept. By investigating the tendency of children to include such noninstances in various concepts our eventual hope has been to discern the relative contributions of these three factors in enticing the child to over-generalize his first terms of reference.

Each of the three factors (perceptual similarity, functional similarity, and association through contiguity) or some combination of them has been advanced as the major determinant of overgeneralization in the child by various authors. For example, although the terminology used varies, some have argued that principles like association through contiguity and per-ceptual similarity are the major determinants of overgeneralization (see Vygotsky, 1962; Moore, 1896).[2] Others have argued for both perceptual similarity and functional similarity (Leopold, 1949a; Bloom, 1973; Nel-son, 1974). Still others have stressed just one of the factors. Specifically, E. Clark (1973, 1974) has contended that perceptual similarity is usually involved. Werner's (1948) argument that overgeneralizations are often based on a "togetherness in the real optical configuration" is similar to an argument for association through contiguity although he preferred not to use this term. And Werner and Kaplan's (1963) argument that in cases of overgeneralization "one frequently finds that the feature common to the phenomena named by the same vocable includes the manner in which the child handles these diverse things" stresses what I have been calling func-tional similarity.

Most of these authors have supported their positions by drawing exam-ples from the diary literature which they felt illustrated the operation of the factor or factors which they were suggesting as crucial. However, with the exception of E. Clark's (1973) analysis, only a few examples were used from the hundreds that could have been used and not surprisingly those few examples tended to be consistent with the position which had been adopted by the theorist who chose them. Even Clark's analysis of the diaries, while by far the most thorough, was not complete. For example, her published records of overextension in the child excluded completely cases which appear to be based upon association through contiguity even though such cases occur in the diaries fairly consistently. In view of this state of affairs it was decided to supplement the results of our experiments with an analysis of all of the cases of overextension of terms of reference found in a number of diaries to see which factors or combination of factors

[2] These authors who have argued for both perceptual similarity and association through contiguity would appear to have a rather eminent ancestry. Most philoso-phers who have advanced the doctrine of associationism, the theory that the mind is made up of simple elements called ideas which come from sensory experience, have argued for two principles by means of which associations are formed: (1) sim-ilarity and (2) contiguity. Occasionally other principles were offered such as con-trast or causality but not nearly so often as similarity (or resemblance) and con-tiguity (or nearness in space and time). Philosophers who have argued for these two principles as governing the formation of associations include Plato, Aristotle, Locke, Berkeley, Brown, J. S. Mill, and Bain, among others.

were most powerful in evoking overgeneralization in the child. The results of this analysis will be described after our experimental studies of over-generalization in the child have been considered.

Experiments 6.1, 6.2, and 6.3

METHOD

The approach we took was analogous to the approach we took to attempt to disentangle the factors determining underextension in the child (see Chapter 5). Again, we collected a large pool of about four hundred pictures from which we chose two hundred and fifty which we thought adults might rate as being either perceptually similar to an instance of a concept or likely to be contiguous with an instance of that concept or functionally similar to an instance of that concept. We began by taking photographs of objects which we thought were perceptually similar or contiguous to instances of the following nine concepts: APPLE, FRUIT, BREAD, DOG, BIRD, HORSE, MONEY, CAR, and FLOWER. (We chose these concepts because we had found earlier that most two to six year olds had some notion of their meanings.) We also took photographs of as many objects as we could that we thought were functionally similar to the four concepts APPLE, FRUIT, CAR, and MONEY. We then enlisted the services of ten adults whom we asked to rate the various pictures along three dimensions: perceptual similarity, association through contiguity, and functional similarity.

Each adult was asked to rate over twenty-five pictures for each concept. A seven-point scale was used again with a 1 representing extremely perceptually dissimilar, extremely uncontiguous, or extremely functionally dissimilar and a 7 representing extremely perceptually similar, extremely contiguous, or extremely functionally similar. Let me illustrate the instructions with reference to the concept CAR. Each adult judge was shown thirty-two pictures and was asked to "rate each of these pictures according to how perceptually similar the objects in the pictures seem to a car. For example, if the object seems extremely perceptually similar to a car, assign it the number '7'; if it seems moderately perceptually similar, assign it the number '4'; if it seems extremely perceptually dissimilar, assign it the number '1', etc." When the adult judge had completed rating each picture for its degree of perceptual similarity to a car, he was given a new rating sheet and was asked to go through the pictures again and to "rate each of these pictures according to how likely you would be to find the objects in the pictures *in the presence* of a car." Finally, when they were finished rating each picture along this dimension, they were given another rating sheet and were asked to go through the pictures again and to "rate each of these pictures according to how *similar in function* the objects in the pictures are to a car." When a subject had finished rating the pictures for one concept along each dimension, he was asked to rate the pictures for the next concept along each dimension, and so on until he had rated the pictures for each of the nine concepts.[3]

After these judgments had been obtained we averaged the ratings for each dimension for each picture over all ten subjects. Our goals were as follows: (1) to obtain for each of the five concepts BREAD, FLOWER, HORSE, BIRD, and DOG pictures of noninstances which were rated by judges as being highly perceptually similar to instances of the concept but unlikely to be associated through contiguity and functionally dissimilar (*PS* stimuli), and pictures which were rated by judges as being highly likely to be associated through contiguity but perceptually dissimilar and functionally dissimilar (*C* stimuli); (2) to obtain for each of the four concepts APPLE, FRUIT, CAR, and MONEY pictures of objects which were rated by judges as being highly perceptually similar but unlikely to be associated through contiguity and functionally dissimilar (*PS* stimuli), pictures which were rated by judges as being likely to be associated through contiguity but perceptually dissimilar and functionally dissimilar (*C* stimuli), and pictures which were rated by judges as being functionally similar but perceptually dissimliar and unlikely to be associated through contiguity (*FS* stimuli).

The average adult ratings of the pictures did not allow us to meet these objectives exactly but we came reasonably close. The two major problems were: (1) For the three animal concepts HORSE, BIRD, and DOG there were no *PS* stimuli. Rather, for these concepts instances which had been rated as highly perceptually similar to instances of the concept had also been rated as "likely to be seen in the presence of instances" of that concept (e.g., butterfly and locust to BIRD) or both high in association through contiguity and functionally similar (e.g., donkey and mule to HORSE). Thus, for these three concepts, we were forced to use *PS+C* stimuli (pictures rated as being both perceptually similar and contiguous) or *PS+FS+C* stimuli (pictures rated as being high on all three dimensions) in addition to *C*

---

[3] For the five concepts BREAD, DOG, BIRD, HORSE, and FLOWER the judgments of functional similarity were not produced by these ten judges, but rather by two different adult judges who were made familiar with all of the ratings made by the ten adult judges and who then attempted to judge the pictures for functional similarity "as consistently as they could" with the ratings produced by the first ten judges. It was not until after we had obtained their judgments that we realized that we should have also obtained judgments of functional similarity from the first set of adult judges on these concepts and so it was necessary to ask two different judges to rate the instances of the concepts as consistently as they could with the average ratings produced by the first ten judges. The two new judges felt fairly confident that their scaling of the pictures was consistent with the ratings produced by the other judges, although it would have been preferable to have obtained these judgments of functional similarity from the first ten judges.

stimuli. (2) The second and more serious problem was that for three of the concepts for which we hoped to obtain *FS* stimuli (MONEY, APPLE, FRUIT) there were no such stimuli. Rather, for these concepts instances which had been rated as high in functional similarity had also been rated as high in perceptual similarity or in association through contiguity. For this reason for these three concepts (MONEY, APPLE, FRUIT) we used only *PS* stimuli and *C* stimuli. For the concept CAR we did use *FS* stimuli, however, in addition to *C* stimuli and *PS+FS+C* stimuli (i.e., pictures which had been rated as high along all three dimensions).

Our criteria were that for a stimulus to be counted as *PS, C, FS, PS+C,* or *PS+FS+C* it had to have received an average adult rating of greater than 4.8 on the relevant dimension(s) and less than 2.6 on the other dimension(s). We also included neutral noninstances (*N* stimuli) which had been rated as less than 2.6 on all dimensions for each concept. Table 6.1 presents a classification of the pictures used in the overextension studies for each concept according to type.

To give the reader a feeling for what the stimuli looked like, Figure 6.1 shows six of the pictures used in the overextension studies, illustrating *PS, C,* and *FS* stimuli. The upper panel of Figure 6.1 shows the pictures of the rubber ball and the balloon (*PS* stimuli) which had been rated as perceptually similar to an instance of the concept APPLE but low on the other dimensions. The middle panel of Figure 6.1 shows the pictures of the saddle and the covered wagon (*C* stimuli) which had been rated as high in association through contiguity with instances of the concept HORSE but low on the other dimensions. Finally, the lower panel of Figure 6.1 shows the pictures of the ship and the sled (*FS* stimuli) which had been rated as functionally similar to an instance of the concept CAR but low on the other dimensions.

Experiment 6.1 (Pilot Study)

In a pilot study we examined the tendency of nine children to make overextension responses to the eighty-eight pictures described in Table 6.1 in a test of comprehension. Subjects were between three years, one month and three years, seven months. The pictures were shown to a child one at a time and for each picture the child was asked, "Is this bread?" or "Is this a flower?" and so on, depending on which picture was being shown. If the child responded "yes" to a given picture, he was asked the question again for that picture at the end of the experiment to see if he really meant "yes," unless he seemed restless, which was sometimes the case. Also, children were encouraged to name and describe the pictures when they made overextension responses.

PS STIMULI (to apple)

Rubber ball

Balloon

C STIMULI (to horse)

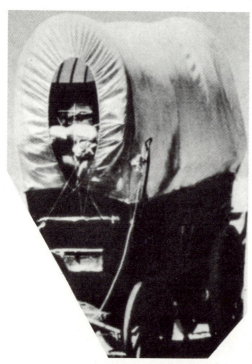

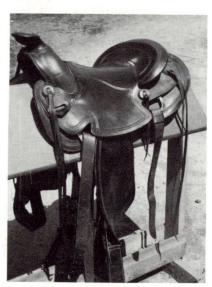

Saddle

Covered wagon

FS STIMULI (to car)

Ship

Sled

RESULTS

Table 6.2 shows the total number of overextension responses made by the nine children for each picture in Experiment 6.1. Table 6.2 reveals that the children (with the exception of one child on one picture) never answered "yes" when asked if a neutral stimulus is an instance of a given concept. On the other hand, children did make overextension responses to some of the other kinds of stimuli. There were thirty-six cases of overextension responses to *PS* stimuli. Specifically, three children agreed that a picture of a mattress was *bread* and five children agreed that a picture of a cork block was *bread;* for two children the picture of a ribbon was a *flower;* all nine children agreed that a picture of animal medals was *money,* and seven of them agreed that a picture of buttons was *money;* for two children the picture of a balloon was an *apple* and for four of them the picture of a rubber ball was an *apple;* two children said "yes" when asked if the picture of balloons was *fruit* and one child agreed that a picture of a mandolin was *fruit.*

Although they were not as frequent, children also made overextensions to *C* stimuli. (There was a total of thirty-six overextensions to *PS* stimuli, twenty to *C* stimuli.) Three children agreed that a picture of a lunch bag was bread; four children, that a picture of a pot was a flower; four children said "yes" when asked if the picture of dishware was *fruit;* one child agreed that a picture of a covered wagon was a *horse,* and three that a picture of a western saddle was a *horse;* two children said "yes" when asked if the picture of a birdhouse was a *bird,* one said "yes" when asked if the picture of a bird cage was a *bird* and finally, two children agreed that a picture of a milkbone was a *dog.* Although children definitely overgeneralized to *C* stimuli, two aspects of their behavior suggested that such overextensions were not as stable as those made to *PS* stimuli. First, children were more prone to reverse their decision on the probe test for *C* stimuli than for *PS* stimuli. Four out of ten children who were probed for their overextensions on *C* stimuli changed their minds, whereas only three out of twenty-six children who were probed for their errors on *PS* stimuli changed theirs. Second, children would occasionally make comments suggesting that their "yes" responses to *C* stimuli were not always responses to the question asked but rather to other questions it suggested to them. For example, when shown a picture of a pot containing dirt and asked, "Is this a flower?" one child said "yes" but then added, "It's for flowers," suggesting that he did not really think it was a flower. Or when asked of a lunch bag, "Is this

---

See facing page
FIGURE *6.1* Six of the pictures used in the overextension studies illustrating *PS, C,* and *FS* stimuli.

TABLE 6.1 A classification of the pictures used in the overextension studies for each concept investigated, according to type. Types include PS stimuli (pictures of objects which were rated as being perceptually similar to an instance of the concept), C stimuli (pictures which had produced high ratings on the association through contiguity dimension), FS stimuli (pictures of objects which were rated as being functionally similar to an instance of the concept), PS + C stimuli (pictures which had produced high ratings on both the perceptual similarity and the association through contiguity dimensions), PS + FS + C stimuli (pictures which had produced high ratings on all three dimensions), and N (neutral) stimuli (pictures which had produced high ratings on none of the dimensions).

Concept	Type	Stimulus	Concept	Type	Stimulus	Concept	Type	Stimulus
BREAD	PS	1. Mattress	DOG	C	33. Dog leash	FRUIT	PS	57. Balloons
		2. Cork block			34. Milk bone			58. Mandolin
	C	3. Lunch bag			35. Dog house		C	59. Dishware
		4. Black lunch pail			36. Dog dish			60. Plate
	N	5. Wheelbarrow		PS+C	37. Sheep		N	61. Eyeglasses
		6. Air force plane			38. Wolf			62. Sandal
		7. Turtle		N	39. Chinese junk			63. Doll
		8. Tricycle			40. Saucepan			64. Chair
FLOWER	PS	9. Feather duster			41. Pins	HORSE	C	65. Cowboy
		10. Ribbon			42. Skis			66. Covered wagon
	C	11. Painted vase			43. Coffee pot			67. Bridle
		12. Pot with dirt			44. Suitcase			68. Western saddle
	N	13. Ice box					PS+FS+C	69. Donkey
		14. Boat						70. Mule
		15. Modern car					N	71. Lamppost
		16. Coffee jar						72. Ship
								73. Spatula
								74. Muffin tin
								75. Chow mein
								76. Grocery

TABLE 6.1 (*continued*)

Concept	Type	Stimulus	Concept	Type	Stimulus	Concept	Type	Stimulus
	PS	17. Animal medals		FS	45. Sled			77. Birdhouse
		18. Buttons			46. Ship		C	78. Bird nest
MONEY	C	19. Plastic black purse		C	47. Meters			79. Bird cage
		20. Cash Register			48. Service station			80. Forest
	N	21. Crane	CAR	PS+FS +C	49. Fire engine	BIRD	PS+C	81. Butterfly
		22. Piano			50. Truck			82. Locust
		23. Ironing board		N	51. Scissors			83. Guitar back
		24. Sawhorse			52. Pencil sharpener			84. Balloon
	PS	25. Balloon			53. Rifle		N	85. Baby carriage
		26. Rubber ball			54. Pail			86. Loafer
	C	27. Knife			55. Hand gun			87. Shishkebob
APPLE		28. Basket			56. Stove			88. Grocery
	N	29. Mailbox						
		30. Wheelchair						
		31. Locomotive						
		32. Typewriter						

NOTE: Scale used:

	1	2	3	4	5	6	7	
PERCEPTUALLY DISSIMILAR	extremely	very	quite	moderate	quite	very	extremely	PERCEPTUALLY SIMILAR
UNCONTIGUOUS								CONTIGUOUS
FUNCTIONALLY DISSIMILAR								FUNCTIONALLY SIMILAR

TABLE 6.2 Total number of overextension responses (out of a possible nine) made by children in Experiment 6.1 for each picture (N = 9).

Concept	Type	Stimulus	Errors
BREAD	PS	1. Mattress	3
		2. Cork block	6
	C	3. Lunch bag	3
		4. Black lunch pail	0
	N	5. Wheelbarrow	0
		6. Air force plane	0
		7. Turtle	1
		8. Tricycle	0
FLOWER	PS	9. Feather duster	0
		10. Ribbon	2
	C	11. Painted vase	0
		12. Pot with dirt	4
	N	13. Ice box	0
		14. Boat	0
		15. Modern car	0
		16. Coffee jar	0

Concept	Type	Stimulus	Errors
DOG	C	33. Dog leash	0
		34. Milk bone	2
		35. Dog house	0
		36. Dog dish	0
	PS+C	37. Sheep	3
		38. Wolf	5
	N	39. Chinese junk	0
		40. Saucepan	0
		41. Pins	0
		42. Skis	0
		43. Coffee pot	0
		44. Suitcase	0

Concept	Type	Stimulus	Errors
FRUIT	PS	57. Balloon	2
		58. Mandolin	1
	C	59. Dishware	4
		60. Plate	0
	N	61. Eyeglasses	0
		62. Sandal	0
		63. Doll	0
		64. Chair	0
HORSE	C	65. Cowboy	0
		66. Covered wagon	1
		67. Bridle	0
		68. Western saddle	3
	PS+FS+C	69. Donkey	5
		70. Mule	7
	N	71. Lamppost	0
		72. Ship	0
		73. Spatula	0
		74. Muffin tin	0
		75. Chow mein	0
		76. Grocery	0

TABLE 6.2 (continued)

Concept	Type	Stimulus	Errors
	PS	17. Animal medals	9
		18. Buttons	7
	C	19. Plastic black purse	0
		20. Cash register	0
MONEY	N	21. Crane	0
		22. Piano	0
		23. Ironing board	0
		24. Sawhorse	0
	PS	25. Balloon	2
		26. Rubber ball	4
APPLE	C	27. Knife	0
		28. Basket	0
	N	29. Mailbox	0
		30. Wheelchair	0
		31. Locomotive	0
		32. Typewriter	0

Concept	Type	Stimulus	Errors
	FS	45. Sled	0
		46. Ship	0
	C	47. Meters	0
		48. Service station	0
CAR	PS + FS + C	49. Fire engine	2
		50. Truck	1
	N	51. Scissors	0
		52. Pencil sharpener	0
		53. Rifle	0
		54. Pail	0
		55. Hand gun	0
		56. Stove	0

Concept	Type	Stimulus	Errors
		77. Birdhouse	2
		78. Bird nest	0
	C	79. Bird cage	1
		80. Forest	0
BIRD	PS+C	81. Butterfly	0
		82. Locust	4
	N	83. Guitar back	0
		84. Balloon	0
		85. Baby carriage	0
		86. Loafer	0
		87. Shishkebob	0
		88. Grocery	0

bread?" one child said "yes" but later remarked, "You put bread in it," again suggesting that he did not really think it was bread and that his affirmative response to our question was more a statement on his part that he saw a connection between the lunch bag and bread.

Children never overgeneralized to *FS* stimuli although we had only included two such stimuli in the experiment because of our difficulties in obtaining them. Children invariably said "no" when asked of a picture of a sled and of a ship if they were *cars*. The results for *FS* stimuli, while only based on two stimuli, when combined with other findings have led us to believe that children will rarely overextend a concept to a noninstance which is functionally similar to an instance of the concept unless that noninstance is also either perceptually similar to, or likely to be associated through contiguity with, an instance of the concept.

A total of twelve overextensions were made by these nine children to the four *PS+C* stimuli. Five out of nine children said "yes" when asked if the picture of a wolf was a *dog* and three said "yes" when asked if the picture of the sheep was a *dog*. The responses of children to the *PS+C* stimuli for the concept BIRD were very interesting and suggest that linguistic factors may play some role in determining whether or not a child will overextend a given term of reference. Four out of nine children responded "yes" when asked if a picture of a locust was a bird, and the two of these children who were probed for their overextensions persisted in making them. However, none of the children responded "yes" when asked of the more or less equally perceptually similar and contiguous butterfly whether it was a *bird*. Rather, they all said "no" and pointed out that it was a *butterfly*. This and other similar observations suggest that when a child knows a name for an object he will be less likely to include it incorrectly in some other category than when he does not know a name for it (see, however, Thomson and Chapman, 1975). The *PS+C* stimuli produced a considerably higher frequency of overextensions than did *C* stimuli, which suggests that for these stimuli perceptual similarity may well have been the stronger factor in bringing about the child's overextensions although association through contiguity may also have played some role.

Finally, there are the *PS+FS+C* stimuli. When shown the picture of a donkey and asked, "Is this a horse?" five out of nine children said "yes" and when shown the picture of a mule seven out of nine children said "yes" when asked if it was a *horse*. The remaining two *PS+FS+C* stimuli were the fire engine and the truck. Just one child agreed that both of these noninstances were *cars* and one agreed that the fire engine was a *car* but not the truck. These few overextensions that do occur on these stimuli may well be primarily due to the perceptual similarity between the noninstances and cars since neither *FS* stimuli nor *C* stimuli for CAR produce any errors. The fact that there are so few errors made on this concept suggests that most three-year-old children have a pretty firm grasp of the extension of CAR which has also been suggested less directly by previous studies (see Chapter 2 of this book; also see Nelson, 1974).

One further point: The results of the probe tests revealed that children were quite consistent in persisting in their overextensions to *PS, PS+C,* and *PS+FS+C* stimuli (only four reversals out of forty-three probes) whereas they were not so consistent in the probe tests for *C* stimuli (four reversals out of ten probes).

Experiment 6.2

METHOD

We thought we should see if we could replicate the basic findings of our pilot study in a full-fledged experiment. The approach we took was basically the same as for Experiment 6.1 except for the following refinements: (1) We decided that for each concept we should add some instances, since without instances the correct response to every stimulus was "no." The child may have anticipated in Experiment 6.1 that since he is being asked to identify *flowers, money, apples,* and so on, there would probably be at least some pictures of flowers, of money, and of apples in the set we showed him, and so he may have been more prone to respond "yes" than if instances had actually been included. We therefore added two photographs of clear instances of each of the concepts we were testing. (2) We did not want to increase by too much the number of pictures in the study since we have found that such studies with more than one hundred pictures are too long for preschool children. We therefore decided to drop the pictures for the concept CAR in Experiment 6.2 since these noninstances were yielding very few overextensions anyway.

Thus in Experiment 6.2 we used the noninstances for each of the eight concepts studied in Experiment 6.1 (BREAD, FLOWER, MONEY, APPLE, FRUIT, HORSE, BIRD, DOG) plus two instances for each of these eight concepts. Specifically, instances were pictures of a piece of oatmeal bread and of a piece of rye bread for the concept BREAD, of a rose and of a daisy for the concept FLOWER, of some coins and of some dollar bills for the concept MONEY, of two different apples for the concept APPLE, of a pear and of a lemon for the concept FRUIT, of two horses for the concept HORSE, of a seagull and an unidentifiable bird resting on a twig for the concept BIRD, and of a black Labrador and of a collie for the concept DOG.

The subjects were twenty children between the ages of two years, five months and five years, one month. Just as in Experiment 6.1 each picture was shown one at a time in a different random order to each child and he was asked "Is this bread?" or "Is this a flower?" and so on depending upon

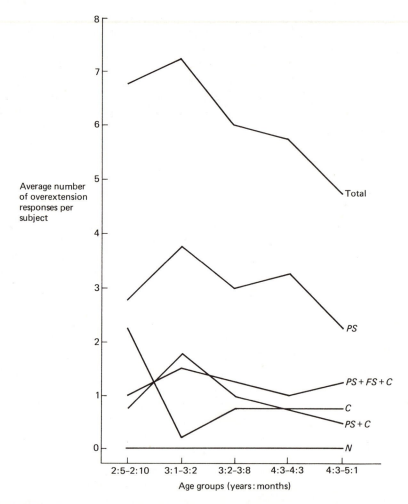

FIGURE 6.2 Average number of overextension responses and each type of error made by children in Experiment 6.2 as a function of age.

which instance or noninstance had been presented. Again children were probed for any overextensions they made and engaged in conversations about the stimuli for which they did so. Sessions were tape recorded.

RESULTS

Figure 6.2 presents a graph showing the average number of overextensions and each type of overextension made by the twenty children in this experiment as a function of age. Each point on the abscissa of Figure 6.2 represents the average performance of four children studied in this experiment. As Figure 6.2 shows, there is a decrease in the total number of overextensions with age although the trend is not quite monotonic (one point is out of line) and the decline with age in the total number of overextensions is not large (from an average of 6.75 errors for the youngest group to an average of 4.75 errors for the oldest group). The decline with age in the average number of each kind of overextension is not striking, with one exception. That exception is for overextensions to *C* stimuli for which the youngest group (ages two years, five months to two years, ten months) made an average of 2.25 such overextensions per child, whereas each of the older groups made an average of less than 1 such overextension per child. The slope of the function showing overextensions to *N* stimuli is 0 since no child made a single error to such stimuli.

Table 6.3 shows the total number of overextensions (out of a possible twenty) made by children in Experiment 6.2 for each picture. Children in this study again fairly often overgeneralized to *PS* stimuli. A total of sixty overextensions were made in all to such noninstances. The *PS* stimuli which produced overextension did so to roughly the same extent as they had in Experiment 6.1.

In Experiment 6.2, although children also made some overextensions to *C* stimuli, they were not as frequent as they had been in Experiment 6.1. A total of nineteen overextensions were made to *C* stimuli by the twenty children in this study compared to the twenty made by only nine children in Experiment 6.1. It is possible that the inclusion of instances in this study discouraged overextensions to contiguous stimuli which would again suggest that errors to *C* stimuli are not as stable as to *PS* stimuli. Again children were not as consistent in sticking with their overextensions to *C* stimuli in probe tests as they were for *PS* stimuli. Four times (out of sixteen possible) children whose errors to *C* stimuli were probed reversed their decision, whereas only two out of fifty-nine reversals occurred for *PS* stimuli and none occurred for *PS+C* stimuli or for *PS+FS+C* stimuli. Also, some of the children's comments again suggested that the overextensions to *C* stimuli were not as stable as for *PS* stimuli. For example, when shown the pot with dirt in it, after one child had said "yes" in response to the question "Is this a flower?" he remarked "Well, you put flowers in it," suggesting that his affirmative response may not have been a direct answer to our question but rather a statement by him that he saw a connection between vases and flowers. Also recall, as noted above, that it is the youngest children who tended to overgeneralize to *C* stimuli—the two to three year olds. The three to five year olds made very few such responses. In contrast, all age groups overgeneralized substantially to *PS, PS+C,* and *PS+FS+C* stimuli.

A total of nineteen overextension responses were made to *PS+C* stimuli. Of such instances the picture of the wolf produced the most overgeneralization. Twelve out of twenty children said "yes" when asked if it was a *dog.*

TABLE 6.3 Total number of overextensions (out of a possible twenty) made by children in Experiment 6.2 for each picture.

Concept	Type	Stimulus	Errors
BREAD	PS	1. Mattress	1
		2. Cork block	4
	C	3. Lunch bag	1
		4. Black lunch pail	0
	N	5. Wheelbarrow	0
		6. Airforce plane	0
		7. Turtle	0
		8. Tricycle	0
FLOWER	PS	9. Feather duster	1
		10. Ribbon	3
	C	11. Painted vase	0
		12. Pot with dirt	3
	N	13. Ice box	0
		14. Boat	0
		15. Modern car	0
		16. Coffee jar	0
	C	17. Cowboy	0
		18. Covered wagon	2
		19. Bridle	0
		20. Western saddle	2
HORSE	PS+FS+C	21. Donkey	6
		22. Mule	18
	N	23. Lamppost	0
		24. Ship	0
		25. Spatula	0
		26. Muffin tin	0
		27. Chow mein	0
		28. Grocery	0

Concept	Type	Stimulus	Errors
FRUIT	PS	29. Balloons	11
		30. Mandolin	1
	C	31. Dishware	1
		32. Plate	0
	N	33. Eyeglasses	0
		34. Sandal	0
		35. Doll	0
		36. Chair	0
DOG	PS	37. Dog leash	0
		38. Milk bone	1
	C	39. Dog house	0
		40. Dog dish	0
	PS+C	41. Sheep	4
		42. Wolf	12
		43. Chinese junk	0
		44. Saucepan	0
	N	45. Pins	0
		46. Skis	0
		47. Coffee pot	0
		48. Suitcase	0

Concept	Type	Stimulus	Errors
MONEY	PS	49. Animal medals	16
		50. Buttons	15
	C	51. Black plastic purse	3
		52. Cash register	2
	N	53. Crane	0
		54. Piano	0
		55. Ironing board	0
		56. Sawhorse	0
APPLE	PS	57. Balloon	4
		58. Rubber ball	4
	C	59. Knife	0
		60. Basket	0
	N	61. Mailbox	0
		62. Wheelchair	0
		63. Locomotive	0
		64. Typewriter	0
	C	65. Birdhouse	2
		66. Bird nest	2
		67. Bird cage	0
		68. Forest	0
BIRD	PS+C	69. Butterfly	1
		70. Locust	2
		71. Guitar back	0
		72. Balloon	0
		73. Baby carriage	0
		74. Loafer	0
		75. Shishkebob	0
		76. Grocery	0

Finally, a total of twenty-four overextensions were made to two $PS+FS+C$ stimuli. Six children agreed that the picture of a donkey was a *horse* and eighteen agreed that the mule was a *horse*. As noted above, none of the overextensions to either $PS+C$ or to $PS+FS+C$ stimuli which were probed resulted in reversals.

To assess the statistical significance of the effects in Experiments 6.1 and 6.2 a set of two tailed, paired *t* tests (see Hayes, 1963, pp. 333–35) were performed on the data. Since such paired *t* tests are not independent we performed a total of only three such tests (only those in which we were most interested) and we set the level at which we would reject the null hypothesis of no difference at a suitably high level ($p < .01$) in all cases. In one test the percentage of errors made by each child to PS stimuli was compared to the percentage of errors made by each child to N stimuli. It was found that significantly more errors were made to PS than to N stimuli ($t_8 = 6.23$ for Experiment 6.1; $t_{19} = 7.96$ for Experiment 6.2; $t_{28} = 9.90$ for the combined data; $p < .002$ for each value of t). In another test the percentage of errors made by each child to C stimuli was compared to the percentage of errors made by each child to N stimuli. It was found that significantly more errors were made to C stimuli than to N stimuli ($t_8 = 3.05$ for Experiment 6.1; $t_{19} = 2.89$ for Experiment 6.2; $t_{28} = 4.10$ for the combined data; $p < .01$ for each value of t). In a final test the percentage of errors made by each child to PS stimuli was compared to the percentage of errors made by each child to C stimuli. It was found that significantly more errors were made to PS than to C stimuli ($t_8 = 5.93$ for Experiment 6.1; $t_{19} = 6.96$ for Experiment 6.2; $t_{28} = 9.08$ for the combined data; $p < .002$ for each value of t).

Table 6.4 represents an attempt to summarize the main findings from Experiments 6.1 and 6.2. Table 6.4 shows the total number of overextensions and the percentage of possible overextensions made by the children for each type of picture. Table 6.4 suggests that with respect to the three attributes of noninstances which have been the focus of this investigation, (1) perceptual similarity is the most powerful determinant of the child's overextension, (2) association through contiguity is weaker and less stable but still does occasionally seem to be a factor in causing younger children

TABLE 6.4 Total number of overextensions and percentage of possible overextensions for each type of picture used in Experiments 6.1 and 6.2.

Type of stimulus	PS	C	FS	PS+C	PS+FS+C	N
Total errors	$96/290$	$39/656$	$0/18$	$31/116$	$39/76$	$1/1,156$
% of possible errors	33.1	5.9	0.0	26.7	51.3	0.09

to include a noninstance in a given concept, and (3) there is no evidence that functional similarity by itself ever entices the child to overgeneralize a given term of reference. Approximately one-third of the time (33.1 percent) that children were presented with *PS* stimuli they included them within the concept for which they were being tested. Only about 6 percent of the time did children overgeneralize to *C* stimuli. None of the time did they overgeneralize to *FS* stimuli although admittedly there were only eighteen opportunities for such responses.

For the stimuli in which more than one of the factors were involved, *PS+C* stimuli produced 26.7 percent and *PS+FS+C* produced 51.3 percent of the possible overextension responses. Since any of the factors or some combination of them might have been involved in producing the overextensions to these stimuli, it would be difficult to know which of the factors were crucial in enticing the child to make such responses if we had no other information. However, in view of the results for stimuli in which only one of the factors was operative it would seem reasonable to conclude that the major determinant of overextension to *PS+C* and to *PS+FS+C* stimuli was the perceptual similarity of the noninstance to an instance of the concept in question although association through contiguity may have been a factor. The neutral stimuli elicited just one error out of a possible 1,156 which suggests to me that if a noninstance is neither perceptually similar to, nor likely to be associated through contiguity with, an instance of a concept then it is a virtual certainty that children will not make the mistake of overgeneralizing the concept to that noninstance, at least in a test of comprehension done along the lines of Experiments 6.1 and 6.2.

Experiment 6.3

Experiments 6.1 and 6.2 were studies of the child's tendency to overgeneralize a term of reference in tests of comprehension. We thought that it would be profitable to study overgeneralization in a test of production as well. That is to say, rather than ask questions of each child such as "Is this a flower?" or "Is this money?" we decided to examine the names that children provided when asked of the various pictures, "What is this?" Our ultimate hope was to see if the factors identified as determinants of overextension in tests of comprehension also appeared to be the important sources of overextension in a test of production.

METHOD

Subjects were five children whose ages ranged from three years, one month to four years, one month. We decided to use the pictures we had used in Experiment 6.1 (excluding the neutral stimuli) since we were curious to see to what extent children would provide the names of the categories which we were studying in that test of comprehension in this test of production. Thus each child was shown a total of forty-four pictures which were presented to him in a random order by the experimenter one at a time. For each picture the child was simply asked, "What is this?" His responses to this question were recorded for each picture as the experiment progressed.

RESULTS

Table 6.5 shows the names given by each child to each of the forty-four pictures used in this experiment. For each picture in Table 6.5 we have tried to classify each response into one of ten categories: (1) correct ($\sqrt{}$): the child's name was a correct name for the object depicted in the picture (e.g., *bag* for lunch bag); (2) perceptually similar (*PS*): the child's name was not correct but the object depicted in the picture was perceptually similar to an instance of the term overgeneralized (e.g., *egg* for ball); (3) contiguous (*C*): the child's name was incorrect but the object in the picture was likely to be experienced in the presence of an instance of the term overgeneralized (e.g., *plant* for pot with dirt); (4) functionally similar (*FS*): the child's name was incorrect but the object in the picture served the same function as an instance of the term overgeneralized (as it turned out, there were none of these); (5) *PS/C:* the child's name was incorrect but the object in the picture was perceptually similar to, and likely to be experienced in the presence of an instance of the term overgeneralized (e.g., *cows* for mules); (6) *PS/FS:* the child's name was incorrect but the object in the picture was perceptually similar and functionally similar to an instance of the term overgeneralized (e.g., *airplane* for sled); (7) *C/FS:* the child's name was incorrect but the object in the picture was likely to be seen in the presence of and was functionally similar to an instance of the term overgeneralized (as it turned out, there were none of these); (8) *PS/FS/C:* the child's name was incorrect but the object in the picture was perceptually similar to, functionally similar to, and likely to be associated through contiguity with an instance of the term overgeneralized (e.g., *guitar* for mandolin); (9) *F:* statement of function—the child's response was a statement of the function of the object depicted in the picture (e.g., *for horses* for the picture of a bridle); (10) don't know (*DK*): the child said he did not know what the object depicted was (e.g., "I don't know" for the picture of a mattress).

Two adult judges went through each of the pictures together and attempted to classify each response of the children into one of these ten categories. In each of the cells of Table 6.5, in addition to the actual name given by a child to a picture, we have included the classification of that name by the two adult judges. The judges felt comfortable in classifying

TABLE 6.5 Names given by five children for forty-four pictures used in the overextension studies. Classification of names into categories is shown for each name.

Stimulus	S₁	(3:1)	S₂	(3:1)	S₃	(3:2)	S₄	(3:2)	S₅	(4:1)
1. Mattress	DK	DK	DK	DK	Pillow for a couch	PS/FS/C	DK	DK	Cookie	PS
2. Cork block	DK	DK	Book	PS	Book	PS	Sponge	PS	Horn	PS
3. Lunch bag	Bag	✓	Bag	✓	Grocery bag	✓	Bag	✓	Bag	✓
4. Black lunch pail	Purse	PS/FS	Lunch box	✓	Purse; Suitcase	PS/FS	Purse	PS/FS	Doctor kit	PS/FS
5. Feather duster	Monkey	?	Round circle and a pen	?	Duck	?	Paint Brush	PS	Brush	PS/FS/C
6. Ribbon	Ribbon	✓	Turtle	PS	Ribbon	✓	DK	DK	Ribbon	✓
7. Painted vase	Bowl	PS/FS	Bowl	PS/FS	Pot	PS/FS	DK	DK	Bottle	PS/FS
8. Pot with dirt	Plant	C	Bowl	PS/FS	Dirt	✓	Dirt	✓	Plant	C
9. Animal medals	Sheep	✓	Balls	PS	Pennies	PS	Seals	✓	Money	PS
10. Buttons	Wheels	PS	Fish	?	Pennies	PS	Buttons	✓	Money	PS
11. Plastic black purse	Purse	✓	Rocking chair	?	Purse	✓	Purse	✓	Purse	✓
12. Cash register	For papers; machine	F	Building	✓	Typewriter	PS	Typewriter	PS	Typewriter	PS
13. Balloon	Balloon	✓	Ball	PS	Balloon	✓	Balloon	✓	Balloon	✓
14. Rubber ball	Ball	✓	Ball	✓	Ball	✓	Egg	PS	Ball	✓
15. Knife	Knife	✓	Stick to hit drum	✓	Knife	✓	Knife	✓	Knife	✓
16. Basket	Basket	✓	Sand	✓	Dirt bowl	PS/FS	Basket	✓	Put dirt inside	F
17. Balloons	Balloons	✓	Birdie	?	Balloons; Ball;	✓ / PS	Balloons	✓	Balloons	✓
18. Mandolin	Egg	PS	Bottle	PS	Guitar	PS/FS/C	Balloon	PS	Guitar	PS/FS/C
19. Dishware	Cups and plates	✓	Table	✓	Cups and plates	✓	Dinner plate	C	House	C
20. Plate	Plate	✓	Table	✓	Plate	✓	Plate	✓	Plate	✓
21. Cowboy	Boy	✓	Cowboy	✓	Cowboy	✓	Man	✓	Cowboy	✓
22. Covered wagon	Tunnel	PS	Owl	PS	Car	✓	Covered wagon	PS/FS	Wagon	✓

No.	Word					
23.	Bridle	Stairs (DK)	Cowboy (√)	Snake (PS)	For reins for horses (F)	For horses; Leash (F; PS/FS)
24.	Western saddle		Owl (DK)	Horse (C)	Saddle (DK)	Saddle (√)
25.	Donkey	Sheep (PS/C)	Rope (PS/C)	Doggie (PS/C)	Horses (PS/C)	Horse (PS/C)
26.	Mule	Cows (PS/C)	Birdie (PS/C)	2 Horses (PS/C)		Horses (PS/C)
27.	Birdhouse	Birdhouse (√)	Horsie (PS/C)	Box on T.V. Post; (PS)	House (√)	Birdhouse (√)
28.	Bird nest	Nest (√)	Water (?)	Nest (√)	Nest (√)	Bird nest (√)
29.	Bird cage	Birdhouse (√)	Box (PS)	Cage (√)	Cage (√)	Bird house (√)
30.	Forest	Trees (√)	Doughnut (PS)	Forest with trees and leaves and sticks	Trees (√)	Trees and forest
31.	Butterfly	Butterfly (√)	Watersink (?)	Butterfly (√)	Butterfly (√)	Butterfly (√)
32.	Locust	Butterfly (PS/C)	Tree (√)	Bat (PS)	Butterfly (PS/C)	Butterfly (PS/C)
33.	Dog leash	DK	Butterfly (√)	Belt (PS)	Belt (PS)	Belt (PS)
34.	Dog house	Monkey cage (PS/FS)	Girl dancing (PS)	Fence; cage; house (√)	Pig house (PS/FS)	Cage-house (√)
35.	Milk bone	Screw (PS)	Belt (PS)	Bone (√)	Bone (√)	Dog bone (√)
36.	Dog dish	Bowl (√)	Birdie; cage for birdie (C)	Bowl (√)	Bowl (√)	Bowl for dogs and cats (√)
37.	Sheep	Sheep (√)	Bone (√)	Lambs (√)	Sheep (√)	Sheep (√)
38.	Wolf	DK	Bowl (DK)	Wolf (√)	Dog (PS/C)	Doggie (√)
39.	Sled	Sled (√)	Parrot (PS)	Roller skate (PS/FS)	Ski (PS/FS/C)	Sled (PS/C)
40.	Ship	Boat (√)	Cat (PS/C)	Boat (√)	Boat (√)	Boat (√)
41.	Meters	DK	Airplane (PS/FS)	Lamp posters (PS/C)	Outside (√)	Street (√)
42.	Service station	For cars (F)	Boat (√)	Gasoline (C)	Station (√)	Gas station (√)
43.	Fire engine	Fire engine (√)	Fence (PS)	Fire truck (√)	Fireman truck (√)	Fire engine (√)
44.	Truck	Truck (√)	Gas station (√)	Truck (√)	Truck (√)	Truck (√)

NOTE: The classifications include: (1) correct (√); (2) perceptually similar (PS); (3) contiguous (C); (4) functionally similar (FS); (5) perceptually similar and functionally similar (PS/FS); (6) perceptually similar and contiguous (PS/C); (7) contiguous and functionally similar (C/FS); (8) perceptually similar, functionally similar, and contiguous (PS/FS/C); (9) statement of function (F); (10) "don't know" (DK); (11) difficult to classify (?).

every response except for nine (out of two hundred and twenty-nine) into one of the ten categories outlined above. These nine responses which were difficult to classify are indicated by a question mark (?) in Table 6.5.

Table 6.6 shows the total number of each type of classification for the names given by the children for all the pictures used in this experiment. There were a total of two hundred and twenty-nine names to be classified since there were nine cases in which a picture was named more than once. Approximately one-half (one hundred and sixteen out of two hundred and twenty-nine) of the names provided by children were correct names. (If a child named something in the background of the picture rather than the object in the foreground it was counted as correct. For example, for

TABLE 6.6 *Total number of each type of classification for the names given by five children for the forty-four pictures used in the overextension experiments. The Classifications used are the same as those used in Table 6.5.*

Type of classification	√	PS	FS	C	PS/FS	PS/C	PS/FS/C	F	DK	?
Total number	116	44	0	7	18	15	5	5	10	9

NOTE: There were nine instances of multiple naming yielding a total of two hundred and twenty-nine (rather than two hundred and twenty) names.

stimulus number 20, a picture of a plate resting on a table, one child said it was a *table* which was counted as a correct response.) Among the overextensions, the most frequent kind were *PS* names. Forty-four overextensions were such that the objects depicted in the picture were judged to be perceptually similar to instances of the term overgeneralized. Examples are *cookie* for mattress; *paint brush* for feather duster; *pennies, money,* and *balls* for animal medals; *typewriter* for cash register; *ball* for balloon; *egg* for rubber ball; *snake, stairs,* and *rope* for bridle; *doughnut* for bird nest; *belt* for dog leash; and so on. There were far fewer *C* errors than *PS* errors (seven versus forty-four). Thus children infrequently overgeneralize concepts to noninstances which are only likely to be experienced in the presence of instances of those concepts, although such errors do occasionally occur. Examples are *plant* for a pot with dirt, *dinner* for dishware, *house* for dishware, *horse* for a western saddle, *gasoline* for a service station, and so forth. There were no *FS* responses at all. Thus children never overgeneralized terms to noninstances which were only functionally similar to instances of those terms. It is important not to confuse *FS* responses with *F* responses which are not really errors but rather statements of the function of the object depicted in a picture. There was a total of five *F* responses. These were "put dirt inside" for a picture of a basket, "for papers" for a picture of a cash register, "for reins for horses" and "for horses" for a picture of a bridle, and "for cars" for a picture of a service station.

There were eighteen cases of *PS/FS* errors (e.g., *bowl* for a picture of a painted vase), fifteen cases of *PS/C* errors (e.g., *cows* for a picture of two mules), and five cases of *PS/FS/C* errors (e.g., *brush* for a picture of a feather duster). It is possible to speculate that perceptual similarity between the noninstance and an instance of the concept overgeneralized played the predominant role in enticing the child to make these responses since in this experiment and in the previous ones, when it has been possible to disentangle the effects of perceptual similarity, contiguity, and functional similarity as determinants of the child's overextension, perceptual similarity has always appeared to be the most powerful factor.

Finally, there were ten "don't know" responses and nine which were difficult to classify. The fact that there are so few "don't know" responses is consistent with the results of previous studies—children seem more inclined to label an unfamiliar object incorrectly than to admit that they don't know what it is. The fact that the number of difficult to classify responses is so low suggests that when children do make overextensions, they will usually be to noninstances which are perceptually similar to or contiguous with instances of the concepts overgeneralized. Children produce very few overextensions where neither of these factors seems to be playing a role.

CONCLUSIONS

This test of production did not usually elicit the exact names of the categories for which the stimuli had been chosen in Experiments 6.1 and 6.2, although in some cases it did (e.g., *money* for animal medals, *horse* for saddle, *dog* for wolf, and so on). Thus the format of Experiments 6.1 and 6.2 involving questions of the form "Is this a flower?" may sway a child to overgeneralize FLOWER, for instance, more than he would if simply asked to name the pictures. This confirms that there are basic asymmetries in the child's proclivity to overgeneralize in studies of comprehension as compared to studies of production, a point made by Huttenlocher (1974) and by Thomson and Chapman (1975). Nonetheless, children do overgeneralize in this test of production and, in general, the factors that appear to be important in enticing the child to do so in naming are the same ones that were seen to be important in the tests of comprehension.

GENERAL DISCUSSION

Each of the three studies on overgeneralization supports the contention that of the factors investigated perceptual similarity was the strongest in bringing about overextension, that association through contiguity was weaker, but nonetheless was sometimes a factor, and that functional similarity was the weakest of the three, if it was operative at all.[4] It might be objected, however, that these results are based entirely upon the child's names of pictures of objects and not upon his names of real objects, and that since a picture of an object is less likely to evoke behavioral assimilation by the child than is a real object, perhaps functional considerations would be less influential in studies like these than in ones involving real objects. In response to this possible objection, two undergraduates in the Department of Psychology and Social Relations at Harvard University [5] and the writer subjected the overextensions found in eight diaries of child speech to a systematic analysis. Specifically, we attempted to assign every overextension reported in those sources into one of the following eight categories: (1) Overextensions based primarily on perceptual similarity between the non-instance and an instance of the concept (*PS* stimuli); (2) overextensions based primarily on association through contiguity (*C* stimuli); (3) over-extensions based primarily on functional similarity (*FS* stimuli); (4) over-extensions to noninstances which were perceptually similar and functionally similar to instances of the term (*PS+FS* stimuli); (5) overextensions to noninstances which were perceptually similar to and likely to be seen in the presence of instances of the term (*PS+C* stimuli); (6) overextensions to noninstances which were functionally similar and likely to be seen in the presence of instances of the term (*FS+C* stimuli; as it turned out, there were no such cases); (7) overextensions which may have been based on all three factors (*PS+FS+C* stimuli); and (8) overextensions based upon any other miscellaneous factors (*M* stimuli). The eight diaries which were analyzed in this way were Chamberlain and Chamberlain (1904a, b), Moore (1896, pp. 115–45), Stern (1930), Lewis (1959), Leopold (1939, 1949b), and Piaget (1962). These diaries were chosen for analysis since the overextensions discussed by their authors occurred in naturalistic settings and were made for the most part to real objects in the child's world. In addition to these diaries we also analyzed in the same way the overextensions discussed in a few secondary sources. Specifically these were Werner (1948), Werner and Kaplan (1963), and Chapter 4 in Bloom's book *One Word at a Time* (1973).[6]

The results are shown in Appendix 3, which presents all of the over-

---

[4] Linguistic factors also appear to play some role in determining whether or not a child will overgeneralize a given term of reference. Specifically, if the child has a correct name for a noninstance, he will be less likely to include it incorrectly in some other category than if he does not know what to call it (See, however, Thomson and Chapman, 1975).

[5] I am extremely grateful to Daniel Klett and to Marc Fiedler for their able assistance in constructing Appendix 3.

[6] Bloom (1973) was treated as a secondary source because in addition to presenting some of her daughter's overextensions and underextensions, she also interprets some other authors' discussions of overextension in early child speech.

extensions found in these sources which fell into one of the eight categories described above. Appendix 3 consists of seven parts labeled A to G.[7] In each of the parts the overextensions occurring in the primary sources are shown first. Below these and separated from them by a line are the overextensions occurring in the three secondary sources.

Throughout Appendix 3 the source of the overgeneralization is shown in the leftmost column.[8] The term overextended is shown in the next column. In some cases the author of a diary attempted to specify the sound of the word as it was said by the child, whether in phonetic script (Leopold, 1939, 1949b) or simply in terms of an orthographic rendition of the sound actually made by the child (e.g., Chamberlain and Chamberlain, 1904a, b). In such cases the actual phonology used by the child is shown in

TABLE 6.7 *Number of overextensions to seven kinds of stimuli by a variety of young children. Data based upon (1) eight diaries (primary sources) and (2) three theoretical discussions of overgeneralization (secondary sources).*

	PS	FS	C	PS+FS	PS+C	PS+FS+C	Misc.	TOTAL
Primary source	113	4	13	23	18	9	16	196
Secondary source	15	1	17	4	1	2	0	40
Total	128	5	30	27	19	11	16	236

parentheses immediately following the term it was thought by the author to mean. In the rightmost column in Appendix 3 the object which the authors had recorded as having produced the overextension is presented.

Table 6.7 summarizes the data in Appendix 3. This table shows the number of overextensions of each kind found in the primary sources and in the secondary sources. It also shows the total number of each kind of overextension found in both kinds of sources.

Appendix 3 and Table 6.7 reveal a distribution of overextensions quite consistent with the results of the experimental studies described earlier in this chapter. More than half of the overextensions were classified as *PS* stimuli. Specifically, 58 percent of the overextensions in the primary sources were to *PS* stimuli, a figure which drops only slightly to 54 percent when based upon both primary and secondary sources. The majority of these appear to be based upon a similarity in shape, or over-all appearance between the object which evoked the response and instances of the term overgeneralized. Examples are *moon* to a half a biscuit, round objects, round

[7] There are only seven parts since there were no *FS+C* overextension responses in these sources.
[8] By *source* is meant the particular diary or theoretical work from which the overextensions have been taken.

candies (Chamberlain and Chamberlain, 1904a); *lettuce* to foliage plants (Chamberlain and Chamberlain, 1904a); *dog* to a lop-eared rabbit (Chamberlain and Chamberlain, 1904b); *papa* to any man (Moore, 1896); *horse* to a large dog (Lewis, 1959); *ball* to a dome on an observatory and to balls of yarn (Leopold, 1939); and *egg* to an egg-shaped rubber ball (Leopold, 1939). Occasionally, however, other factors appear to be involved in the overextensions based upon perceptual similarity. These include similarity of substance or texture (e.g., *bottle* to glass marble [Leopold, 1949b]), similarity of sound (e.g., *firecracker* to thunder [Leopold, 1949b]), similarity of movement (e.g., *bow-wow* to anything moving [Piaget, 1962]), and similarity of size (e.g., *fly* to bits of dust, specks of dirt, toes, and crumbs of bread [Moore, 1896]). These are just the kinds of factors stressed by E. Clark as promoting overextension, which is not surprising since both her analysis and the present one are based upon some of the same diaries. I would only stress that most *PS* overextensions appear to be based upon shape rather than the other factors, although the other factors do occasionally appear to be decisive.

In a number of cases the *PS* overextensions appear to be to objects which are in roughly the right semantic domain from the adult point of view. That is, they appear to be evoked by objects which though not instances of the term according to adults, are nonetheless instances of a closely related superordinate concept in the adult lexicon. Examples are the child's use of the name of a specific animal such as *rabbit, cat (tee)*, or *horse* (*hosh*) to refer to other animals, or *mummy* to refer to other women. However, there are many cases in which the overextension crosses such semantic domains and seems to be based on some more superficial similarity which is usually shape. Examples are *moon* for half a biscuit, cakes of dough, and round cookies; *chocolate* for the metal plates of a door lock; *braid* for twisted doughnuts; *pipes* for telegraph poles; *ball* for a dome of an observatory, and *tick-tock* for the red spool of a fire hose.[9]

Seven percent of the overextensions found in the primary sources were to *C* stimuli, although this figure increases to 13 percent when based on both primary and secondary sources. Examples are *fingernails* for scissors (Chamberlain and Chamberlain, 1904a); *piano* for a piano stool (Leopold, 1939); *sandbox* for sand (Leopold, 1939); *Daddy* for father's rucksack (Piaget, 1962); and *nose* for a handkerchief (Werner and Kaplan, 1963; Stern and Stern, 1928). As in the case of the overextensions based upon association through contiguity which were observed in the experimental studies it is quite possible that in some of these cases the child did not really think that the object which evoked the response was really an instance of the category of things denoted by the term overgeneralized. For

[9] Compare with Bloom's (1973) distinction between what she calls the "nénin" phase and the "doggie" phase in the development of overgeneralization.

example, Piaget's child who said *Daddy* on seeing his father's rucksack may have been doing so since he saw a connection between the rucksack and his daddy (e.g., possession) and his response may have been his way of expressing that connection.

Only 2 percent of the overextensions were classified as having been made to *FS* stimuli. It should be pointed out that by functional similarity is here meant similarity of use, but not of action (see Nelson, 1973a, 1974). The few cases in which overgeneralization appeared to be based upon similarity of action or movement were treated as *PS* stimuli (see E. Clark, 1973). There were only five cases of overgeneralization to *FS* stimuli, four from the primary sources and one from one of the secondary sources. It is even possible that in some of the few cases which were categorized as *FS* stimuli, perceptual similarity was playing some role. For example, one might argue that the airplane which Hildegard called *choo choo* was perceptually similar as well as functionally similar to the trains she had seen. In fact, the only case of overgeneralization to *FS* stimuli for which it would seem to be especially unreasonable to argue for perceptual similarity is the overextension of *door* to a cork in a bottle (Werner and Kaplan, 1963; Stern and Stern, 1928). Thus, as in the experimental studies, the results of this analysis suggest that overgeneralizations based solely on functional similarity are very rare.

Apart from the relatively few cases of overextension in the primary sources which were classified as miscellaneous, all of the other remaining overextensions were made to noninstances which were perceptually similar to an instance of the term overgeneralized. Although these noninstances were also either functionally similar to or likely to be seen in the presence of an instance of the term, or both, given the distribution of the overextensions to noninstances in which only one of the factors was operating, it can be argued that it was the perceptual similarity of these noninstances to instances of the term which was probably often the most powerful determinant of overextension in these cases as well, although association through contiguity may have occasionally been a factor.

Finally, there were a few cases (sixteen out of two hundred and thirty-six) of overextensions in which none of the factors under investigation appear to have been involved in promoting overgeneralization. A few of these are susceptible of interpretation. For example, Hildegard's use of the term *barbecue* to refer to a barber shop and *pyjamas* to refer to a piano (Leopold, 1949b) appear to be based upon a phonetic similarity between the word overextended and the appropriate name. Another interesting case which appears in the miscellaneous category is the use of the word *Mama* (Lewis, 1959) or *Mummy* (Piaget, 1962) when the child wants something. Lewis (1959) presents a particularly interesting discussion of how the term *Mama* is initially an emotionally charged response in the young infant indicating distress or need which only later develops into an objective term of reference for the person who most often alleviates his distress or satisfies his need, his mother. The remaining overextensions in the miscellaneous category are difficult to interpret and it is probably wisest not to try to do so.

CONCLUSIONS

Of the factors we have investigated in the experiments of comprehension, in the experiment of production, and in the analysis of the diaries, perceptual similarity between the noninstance and an instance of the term appears to be the most powerful determinant of overextension in young children. Association through contiguity is a much weaker factor, and errors in which a term is overgeneralized to a noninstance which is likely to be experienced in the presence of an instance of that term appear to be far less stable than errors due to perceptual similarity. Nonetheless, such responses do occur in both comprehension and production. Functional similarity between a noninstance and an instance of a category by itself rarely appears to be enough to entice a child to overgeneralize its label.

Chapter 7

From Reference to Meaning[1]

In the preceding three chapters it has been demonstrated that the child both overgeneralizes and undergeneralizes his first terms of reference relative to adult standards. Although overgeneralization is more obvious in production, and undergeneralization most striking in comprehension, both kinds of responses occur in both performance systems to some degree. While the dimensions along which such "mistakes" are made have been determined, their significance for a theory of semantic development is not obvious, although they raise an interesting possibility.

When the child calls a dome a *ball,* a balloon an *apple,* a pile of buttons *money,* or a vase a *flower,* if his use of the word really indicates that he thinks the object so named is an instance of the category of things denoted by the word, then these responses suggest that the meaning of the word for the child is not the same as it is for the adults who observe him. When he denies that a cookie is *food,* that a tree is a *plant,* that a duck is a *bird,* or that a butterfly is an *animal,* it might be argued again that he does so because the words have a somewhat different meaning for him than for an adult. This might seem like a logical conclusion, although certain problems with such an analysis suggest themselves immediately. Such errors of reference do not occur all the time, they are not always the same from child to child, and they are not always made to the same degree when tested in different ways. Thus, though extension "errors" do occur as has been carefully documented in a number of studies (see for example Leopold, 1939, 1949a, b; Chamberlain and Chamberlain, 1904a, b; Lewis, 1959; Piaget,

[1] I am grateful to Martha Finn, Sophia Cohen, Sara Weiss, Sally Weiskopf, and Marc Fiedler for their assistance in conducting the study to be presented in this chapter. Marc Fiedler and Sophia Cohen helped immensely with the analysis of the results.

1962; E. Clark, 1973; and, of course, the present volume), they are not made quite as frequently or consistently as has been at times suggested (Brown, 1958b; Anglin, 1970; E. Clark, 1973). Although in this book the emphasis has also been on the child's "errors," it must be admitted that the range of referents to which a child will apply a given word, while not identical, nonetheless often overlaps to a considerable degree with the corresponding range of referents to which adults apply these same terms. At least this is true for two to five year olds. Is this degree of correspondence consistent with the proposal that the child's understanding of a word's meaning is radically different from the meaning that word holds for adults?

Another problem is suggested by a different kind of empirical phenomenon from the ones emphasized thus far in this book. It concerns the child's early definitions of verbal concepts. Though there are clearly structural differences in the form in which a child defines category labels,[2] as has been noted especially by Nelson (1973a, 1974), such definitions are often seemingly quite apt ("A hole is to dig," food is "to eat," "a dog is a thing what goes woof"), since the child often mentions the essential use or an almost defining action of instances of the category. In cases in which he is capable of such definitions his extension "errors," it might be argued, are simply obscuring his real knowledge of the word's meaning revealed by another more direct indicator: his facility in defining. Of course, studies of the child's definitions have usually been concerned with children of five years or older so that, taken alone, their relevance for younger preschool children is not entirely clear. However, it was observed in the study of the child's underextension responses (see Chapter 5) that even preschool children sometimes give a reasonable definition of a verbal category. For example young children would sometimes define *food* as "to eat" or *clothing* as "what you wear" even though those same children did not include certain edible objects or articles of clothing in the categories FOOD and CLOTHING in their classification of pictures of objects. If the underextension responses imply that the child does not know the meaning of the word, then why does it seem that he can sometimes define it?

These are the kinds of questions which have led us to the study described in this chapter of what words mean to children. Our approach was a direct one: to encourage the child to describe his knowledge of words (their meaning for him). Obviously such an approach may be limited to some unknown degree by constraints in the child's capacity to perform in the medium involved (i.e., his ability to converse about words). However, given his apparent facility in defining (see above) it was decided to at least

---

[2] Children usually define such words in terms of use or action or description whereas adults more often define them in terms of genus and defining properties. See Feifel (1949); Feifel and Lorge (1950); Wolman and Barker (1965); Al-Issa (1969); Campbell (1975).

try to entice the child to express his knowledge of verbal categories by engaging him in a dialogue and asking him questions about them. The ultimate hope of course was that the knowledge of verbal concepts expressed by children in this sort of dialogue would lead us to an understanding of what they meant to him.

Experiment 7.1

METHOD

Fourteen children ranging in age from two years, eight months to six years, seven months participated in this study. Eight children were from the Living and Learning School in Woburn, Massachusetts, and six were from the Radcliffe Child Care Center in Cambridge, Massachusetts. Three adults, undergraduates at Harvard, were also interviewed in the same way as the children were.

Our goal was to engage the child in a conversation concerning twelve words (specifically, *dog, food, flower, vehicle, animal, apple, rose, car, collie, fruit, plant,* and *Volkswagen,* usually discussed in this order) and to encourage him to tell us all that he knew about these words. In general, we tried to ask five questions about each word in roughly the following order: (1) "What is a _____?" (2) "Tell me everything you can about (a) _____." (3) "What kinds of _____s are there?" (4) "What kind of thing is a _____?" (5) "Tell me a story about a _____?" However, apart from the first one, these questions were not always asked of each child for each word and quite often a variety of other questions were asked. This flexibility was introduced into the interviews since we were guided to some extent by the kinds of statements made by the child. In particular, when a certain line of discussion was providing information about the child's knowledge of a given word we chose to pursue it. When another line of discussion was not developing we dropped it. In general we tried to treat the interview more as a word game than as a test.

Interviews took usually between thirty minutes and an hour. They were tape recorded and later transcribed. If a child seemed uncomfortable, disinterested, or for other reasons reluctant to discuss the words, the interview was ended.

RESULTS

For reasons described above not all children were interviewed in exactly the same way, and, specifically, there was some variability in the questions asked of each individual child. The best way to communicate our findings, therefore, is to present excerpts from conversations with the individual children of different ages and to discuss what their implications might be.

After an extended presentation and discussion of such excerpts, a small set of tables and figures will be presented which summarizes the major trends noted in this study. The tables and figures should be understood in relation to the quality of the individual conversations. Otherwise they would be devitalized and somewhat meaningless statistics.

Conversations with Two Year Olds

We soon discovered that this kind of interview was not appropriate for many two year olds. Although we did manage to entice a few children nearing the end of their third year to enter into this sort of dialogue, most prethree year olds were not comfortable in this situation and for many of them our questions seemed somewhat meaningless and irrelevant. We suspected that our difficulties in engaging the child in such a dialogue stemmed from the abstract format of the situation (i.e., words being discussed out of the context of objects), the social conditions of the interview (i.e., perhaps the child's mother could have had more luck in engaging him in such a conversation), the child's distractibility, and the child's lack of interest in talking about words. Children older than three years seemed to find our word game comprehensible and interesting, but most two year olds did not. Nonetheless, a few children nearing the end of their third year were willing and able to discuss at least a few of the words with us. The youngest child to do so was a boy, Peter, who was two years, eight months at the time. Of the four words discussed with Peter he seemed to have some knowledge of *dog, food,* and *car,* but not of *flower.* By the time we had discussed the fourth word *car* we had reached Peter's saturation point so we cannot be sure about which of the other words he might have had some knowledge, although given that he did not seem to know anything about *flower,* it is likely that he would not have known at least some of the other words. Excerpts from our conversations with Peter follow:

I. Peter (male, 2 years, 8 months)
E: Can you tell me what a dog is?
P: It goes woof, barks.
E: They bark. What else is a dog like?
P: Food.
E: Food?
P: And a dog likes water.
E: And a dog likes food, too.
P: Yeah.
E: What do they look like?
P: Big dogs.
E: Big? What else do they look like?
P: I saw a dog out in the schoolyard.
E: You saw a dog out in your schoolyard, right?
P: Yes. I did. It was big like Martha's dog. It was big like I and Martha.

E: Oh, he was very big . . . ?
P: Like the sky and Martha.
E: What do dogs do, Peter?
P: Eat.
E: Eat? Do they do anything else?
P: They bark and run. Like this (*runs his fists along the table*). They run like this.
E: Oh.
P: Yes. A car goes like this and a truck. (*Peter crawls briefly showing what a dog/car goes like.*)
E: Do they do anything else? They eat and they bark and they run . . .
P: And they don't dive.
E: They don't dive? I guess that's true. I guess I've never seen a dog dive.
P: People dive.
E: That's right. People do dive. When you see a dog, how do you know it's a dog?
P: They don't walk and they don't run.
E: Oh, you're teasing us now.

. . . .

E: OK, can you tell us what kinds of dogs there are?
P: Woofy dogs.
E: Woofy dogs?
E: Are there any other kinds?
P: Martha's dog.

. . . .

Peter's answers are not systematic, reflective, or analytic but he does appear to have a rudimentary base of conceptual knowledge about dogs. He appears to know what a dog does ("it goes woof, barks," it likes food and water, and, later, they eat, bark, run, and "don't dive") and he can recall at least two dogs (one seen in the schoolyard and Martha's dog). When asked what dogs look like, he says, "big dogs," and he has now started to recall particular encounters he has had with particular instances of the concept being discussed. There is a tendency in this child and in other young preschool children, as we shall see, to bring the discussion of a given concept to the level of a particular instance which he can remember having experienced. Thus the very young child's expressible knowledge of a concept, as in this case, often appears to be "instance-oriented" and quite possibly is based to a considerable degree on visual imagery. In this particular child the concept DOG appears to be intimately linked up with his memory of particulars and is not a true generalization yet.

II. Peter (male, 2 years, 8 months)
E: Let's talk about food. Can you tell me what food is?
P: Cereal.
E: Cereal?

E: What else is food?
P: Dessert.
E: Dessert?
P: Yeah.
E: I bet you like that, huh?
P: And I like cookies.
E: Oh.
P: And I like cookies, too.
E: What does food look like?
P: Like (*incomprehensible*).
E: Like what?
P: Potatoes.
E: Potatoes?
P: Chairs.
. . . .
E: Can you tell me what kind of food there is?
P: Woofy dogs.
. . . . (*Child changes topic from food to a variety of other things.*)
E: Peter, can you tell me how you know food when you see it?
P: Eat.
E: Eat?
P: With a poon.
E: With a spoon?
P: All in our tummy.
. . . .
E: Can you tell me a story about food, Peter?
P: I'll tell you about a fire engine.
. . . . (*Child seems to have lost interest in talking about food at this time.*)

In response to the open-ended question "Can you tell me what food is?"
Peter gives an instance of the concept, "cereal." He continues to list instances in the ensuing dialogue—"dessert," "cookies," "potatoes"—even
though he is not being asked specifically what kinds of food there are but
rather more open kinds of questions. Thus this general concept appears to
be based upon knowledge of particulars, is instance-oriented, and may well
involve the use of visual imagery just as had been the case for the concept
DOG. Notice that as he rattles off a list of instances he says "chairs" right
after "potatoes." Now it is quite possible that in saying "chairs" he is just
being playfully perverse. Peter may not really have thought of chairs as
food in view of the fact that he mentions chairs along with potatoes in response to the question about what food looks like and particularly in view
of the fact that later in response to the question "Can you tell me how you
know food when you see it?" he says, "Eat . . . with a poon . . . all in
our tummy." The notion of edibility suggested by this response is in fact
quite close to the adult criterion for whether or not an object is to be
classified as food or not.

It is possible also, however, that even though this child appears to know that food is to eat, edibility is not used by him as a criterion for inclusion in the class FOOD. Chairs may be thought of as instances because he has experienced chairs (his high chair or others) at the dinner table (association through contiguity) and because he has not yet come to use edibility as the *sine qua non* for inclusion in the concept FOOD. The defining property of *food* may not yet have come to govern its extension. This, of course, is only one example and because it is clearly open to other interpretations would not be convincing on its own. However, many of the child's overextension and underextension responses can be viewed in just this way: a failure to coordinate the extension and the meaning of a concept (see also Inhelder and Piaget, 1964). This may be because he is not sure which of the aspects of instances of his linguistic concepts are criterial in determining which objects are instances and which are not and it is not something he has reflected about.

III. Peter (male, 2 years, 8 months)

E: Can you tell me what a car is, Peter?
P: Okay. A car is a truck and a truck is a car (*laughs*).
    . . . .
E: What does a car look like?
P: A truck.
E: A truck? What does a car do?
    (*Peter crawls on hands and knees away from table, demonstrating what a car does.*)
E: Peter, Peter, come on back.
    . . . .
E: Can you tell us what a car does?
P: Voom, voom. (*He demonstrates by acting like a car again.*)
E: It vooms. What else does it do?
P: Yeah.
E: What else does it do?
P: It goes and they run.
E: Oh that's very good, Peter. What does it look like?
P: Voom, voom, voom (*demonstrating again*).
E: Peter, what does a car look like?
P: Voom, voom, voom. (*He acts like a car.*)
E: Peter, OK, why don't you drive back here.
P: No.
E: What kind of cars are there?
P: Trucks, trucks, trucks.
E: Are there any other kinds of cars?
P: Fire trucks. Voom.
E: How do you know a car when you see one?
P: Voom, voom.
    . . . (*Child continues to pretend he is a car.*)

E: Peter, Peter, why don't you drive back over here? Come on Mr. Truck.

P: I'm Mr. Truck. Voom.

. . . .

This conversation illustrates Peter's playful attitude toward our word game and the fact that he would rather pretend he is a car than sit and answer our abstract questions about CAR. However, from the conversation it appears that he knows some things about cars: He knows what they do (they "voom," go, and run); he knows what they look like ("like a truck"). His answer to our question "What kinds of cars are there?" is "trucks . . . fire trucks" which may be again a case of overextension, but it may also be that he was just being playful (see his earlier mention of trucks at the beginning of the conversation) or indicating that he knows that there is a similarity between cars and trucks and fire trucks.

Conversations with Three and Four Year Olds

The preceding conversation and, indeed, each of the conversations with Peter that have been presented indicate the difficulties inherent in this type of format with children under three. Peter often does not answer the questions directly, often digresses into other topics, and seems somewhat bored with the direction the conversation is taking (He would rather pretend he is a car). In fact, this particular child seemed less bored with and puzzled by the nature of our questions than other children of his age for a variety of reasons suggested earlier. Children older than three, however, found the word game more interesting and more comprehensible, so we shall now consider our conversations with them.

IV. Danny (male, 3 years, 4 months)

E: The first word we're going to talk about is *dog*. Do you know what a dog is?

D: No.

E: Tell me, I bet you do. What's a dog?

D: I don't know.

E: Don't know?

D: No, I don't know what, what, what a dog is.

E: Do you know what it looks like?

D: Mm. Mm. Brown.

E: Brown?

D: Yeah.

E: Uh huh.

D: And white.

E: And white?

D: Yeah.

. . . .

E: OK, can you tell me a little story about a dog?

D: Yeah.

E: OK, will you?
 (*Silence.*)
E: When was the last time you saw a dog?
D: I saw it at a playground.
E: Uh huh, and what was it like?
D: Brown and white.
E: Um hum.
D: And at the playground.
E: And what was it doing?
D: It was going away, and we named him Dutch.
 . . . .

This conversation illustrates first of all that this child actually had some knowledge of the word *dog* even though his answers to our initial questions might have indicated that he did not. More significantly, the dialogue indicates that this child in answering questions about dogs seems to be drawing from his memory of a particular encounter with a particular dog. Again his answers appear to be instance-oriented and our impression was that the child was probably relying on visual imagery in producing statements about dogs. Notice that the child answers the question about what dogs look like by telling the experimenter that dogs are brown and white. It becomes clear in a later section of the dialogue that he had previously seen a brown and white dog at the playground and his answers to our questions seem to be primarily based upon this experience. He can think about a particular dog which he has encountered and relate that experience, but he has not yet apparently reflected about dogs in general and it is understandably difficult for him to do so now.

 V. Danny (male, 3 years, 4 months)
E: Well, we're going to talk about flowers now. Do you know what a flower is?
D: No, growing.
 . . . . (*It is difficult to get child to discuss flowers until* . . .)
E: But where do you find a flower?
D: I don't know. In the dirt.
E: In the dirt?
D: Yeah.
E: Uh huh.
D: Yeah.
E: Where in the dirt?
D: Don't know. And I saw one on my dirt, and I found one.
E: Mm hm. What kind of a flower was it?
D: It was pink and white, and it, it, was pink and white. White. And I found one.

Although Danny indicates that he knows that flowers grow, it is difficult to engage him in a conversation about flowers until he is asked where he would find a flower. In answer to this question he responds, "in the dirt," and again he goes on to relate a specific experience he had when he found a pink and white flower in the dirt. Again the child brings the discussion to the level of a particular flower which he has encountered and again, therefore, his knowledge of flowers appears to be instance-oriented. He has some knowledge of particulars but has not yet formulated a general conception which he can verbalize.

VI. Danny (male, 3 years, 4 months)
E: OK, what is an animal?
D: I don't know, a horsie.

This child like many young preschool children defines *animal* not as adults do in terms of a general class and defining property (e.g., "an animal is a living organism which is capable of spontaneous motion") but rather in terms of an instance, in this case "horsie." Again, there is then the tendency in this child to move from the general to the specific and again his knowledge can be described as being instance-oriented.

VII. Danny (male, 3 years, 4 months)
E: OK, what's an apple?
D: I don't know.
E: What do you do with an apple, Danny?
D: Eat it.
E: Uh huh.
D: And chew it.
E: Uh huh.
D: Yeah, tha-tha-that, a- a- and we pick them.
E: Uh huh.
D: And we put 'em in a bag.
    . . . .

Although this child declines to answer the question "What's an apple?" he does answer the question "What do you do with an apple?" by responding "Eat it . . . chew it . . . pick them . . . put 'em in a bag." For this particular concept young children in general and this child in particular seem to be quite good at describing the use to which instances of it can be put or what "you do with" them.

VIII. Danny (male, 3 years, 4 months)
E: What's a car, Danny?
D: It runs, with wheels on it.
E: Anything else?
D: Top on it, and doors.
E: Uh huh.
D: And a trunk in, in, front of, and a trunk on the, on the car.
E: Mm hum. That's right. And what does it do?

D: It moves on the street.
E: That's right.
D: And the wheels go round.
E: Uh huh.
D: Yup.
E: And do you know what kinds of cars there are?
D: No.
E: No? Are all cars the same?
D: No.
E: How are they different?
D: My my my car is blue.
E: Mm hm. OK, and do you know what kind of a thing a car is?
D: No.

Danny seems to be quite familiar with the word *car*. He can tell what a car does ("it runs . . . it moves on the street") and what a car looks like ("wheels on it . . . top on it . . . doors . . . trunk"). Again toward the end of the conversation he leads the discussion back to a specific car, presumably either his toy car or his parents' car when he says, "My car is blue." Questions about subordinates and superordinates are not too meaningful to him although he does know that cars are not all the same.

IX. Danny (male, 3 years, 4 months)
E: What's a VW, or a Volkswagen, do you know?
D: No.
E: What does it look like?
D: I don't know, it moves.
E: It moves. How does it move?
D: It moves on the street.
E: Uh huh, that's right. And what kind of thing is it?
D: I don't know.
E: Are they all the same?
D: No . . . yeah.

In further questioning Danny did not mention that a Volkswagen was a car even though he knew the word *car* as is evidenced by conversation VIII. He also seemed to know something about Volkswagens ("It moves on the street"), but at the least it does not occur to him to mention that it is a car and our further questioning did not indicate that he knew that a Volkswagen is a kind of car. This could be an example of underextension (that is, he does not include Volkswagens in the concept CAR) or it could be a case of the child's difficulty in assigning a concept to a more general category. Superordination often appears to be difficult for children of this age. They can often provide the names of instances of concepts but, even though in cases such as this they appear to have some knowledge of the appropriate superordinate term, they do not use that term spontaneously when discussing the concept and usually questions designed to entice the child to produce the superordinate term are of little help.[3]

X. B (male, 3 years, 6 months)

E: Can you tell me what a flower is?
B: You smell flowers.
E: You smell flowers?
B: Yeah.
E: What kinds of flowers are there?
B: Mmm . . . I don't know.
E: You don't know? You don't know any kinds?
B: No.
E: I bet if you think hard you might be able to think of some.
B: No . . . I know. I know one flower.
E: What?
B: A daffodil.
E: A daffodil is a kind of flower. Are there any other kinds?
B: No, I don't know any more.
E: You don't know any more, but are there?
B: No, no! I know, I know two more.
E: What?
B: No, only one more.
E: What is it?
B: Mmm . . . son of a gun I forgot.
E: (*Laughs*) Oh, OK, well if you remember later you can tell me, OK?
B: (*Pause*) A rose!

This three-and-one-half-year-old child, in addition to knowing that flowers are to be smelled, can, admittedly with great effort, recall the names of two specific kinds of flowers, a *daffodil* and a *rose*. However, in later questioning in which we asked "What kind of a thing is a flower?" and variants of that question, he did not say it is a plant, even though at another point in the interview he indicated that he knew something about the term *plant*.

XI. B (male, 3 years, 6 months)

E: OK, what's an apple?
B: You eat apple.
. . . .
E: What kinds of apples are there?
B: I don't know.
E: Ah, come on, I bet you can tell me some different kinds.

---

[3] It should be noted here that although superordination is often difficult for the child, the degree of difficulty varies with the particular concept being investigated. Of the twelve words studied, the words for which children produced a nominal superordinate (a noun which was superordinate to the concept) most often were: *dog, rose, apple,* and *Volkswagen,* whereas each of the other words produced little superordination and in many cases close to none.

B: No I can't.
E: Are all apples alike?
B: Yeah.
E: Yeah, they are?
B: Well some are red and some are green.
      . . . .
E: What kind of thing is an apple?
B: I don't know.
E: Oh, you can't think . . .
B: It's round.
E: It's round. OK. Can you . . . ?
B: Like this *(shows a circle with his fingers)*.

This dialogue shows that the child knows the use to which apples are usually put ("You eat apple") and with some persistent questioning he indicates that he knows there are green apples and red apples. He also knows that they are round which he illustrates with his hands. However, he does not spontaneously say that an apple is *food* or *fruit* (which older children and especially adults usually do) and he does not produce either superordinate term (of which he has some knowledge) when asked, "What kind of thing is an apple?" although admittedly this question may be too difficult for him to understand.

XII. B (male, 3 years, 6 months)
E: What's fruit?
B: I don't know.
      . . . . *(The questioning gets nowhere until . . .)*
E: What different kinds of fruit can you have?
B: Uh, I don't know.
E: Yeah you do.
B: Grapefruit.
E: Grapefruit? What else?
      . . . .
B: A apple.
E: An apple is fruit. Is there any other kind?
B: Orange.
E: An orange. What else?
B: Uhmmm. I eat snow.
E: You eat snow?
B: Yeah.
E: Is that fruit?
B: No.
E: No. OK. What do you do with fruit?
B: Mmmm . . . Eat it.

The questioning about the word *fruit* gets nowhere until this little boy is asked about different kinds of fruit. At this point he indicates that he knows that a grapefruit, an apple, and an orange are fruit, again suggesting that the names of instances are among the easiest kinds of knowledge for the young child to express for general terms. The child can also say what you do with fruit ("Mmmm . . . eat it") when asked.

XIII. Andy (male, 3 years, 10 months)

E: What's a dog, Andy?
A: Ruff.
E: Ruff? OK . . . tell me everything you know about dogs.
A: They bite us. They bite.
E: Um hum. What else? What do they look like?
A: They look black.
E: What do dogs do?
A: They walk.
E: Anything else?
A: No.
E: No? What kinds of dogs are there?
A: Black.
E: Uh huh. Any other ones?
A: Yayah.
E: What kind are they?
A: They're gold, a cocoa.
E: What?
A: A cocoa.
E: A cocoa?
A: Yeah.
E: That's a dog?
A: Yayah.
E: OK. Any other dogs?
A: No, once when we found in the backyard.
E: Um hm. What kind of a thing is a dog?
A: Uh, I don't know.
E: If I said, what kind of a thing is a child, you might say, well, a child is a kind of person.
A: Yayah.
E: OK. So do you know, like that, what kind of a thing is a dog?
A: Sometimes they are blayack.
E: Oh. Can you tell me a little story about a dog? Using the word *dog*?
A: Yayah.
E: OK.
A: I'm imagining one.
E: Uh huh.
   (*Long silence.*)
E: When you're ready, tell me the story, OK?
A: OK.
E: A little story about a dog.
A: All right.

E: Can you tell me . . . ?
A: Imagining one.
E: OK.
    (*Long silence.*)
E: It can be very short, Andy.
A: I know.
E: Tell me the first thing that comes to your mind about a dog.
A: They're black.

Andy was being playful in his answers but again his dialogue about dogs suggests the use of imagery. He appears to be able to imagine a black dog (as he later tells us he is doing) which he had previously seen. He does mention what dogs do ("ruff . . . they bite us . . . they walk") and he knows that he once saw one in the back yard (presumably a black one), again relating the question asked to a particular experience he has had with one in the past. Deciding to abstain from telling a story about a dog, he prefers to imagine one which in view of the end of the dialogue, again, is probably black. He does not spontaneously mention that a dog is an animal even though a later section of the interview indicates that he has at least some knowledge of the word *animal*. Nor does he tell us that a dog is an animal when asked what kind of a thing it is, although again the question may not have been understood by him.

XIV. Andy (male, 3 years, 10 months)
E: What is food?
A: Food is what you eat.
E: Uh huh, and what kinds of food are there?
A: Uh. Alphabets.
E: Uh huh.
A: Wheaties, Raisin Bran, Froot Loops.

By all counts this child gives quite a reasonable definition of the word *food* ("Food is what you eat") and he also gives a list of cereals as kinds of food. This conversation illustrates the two kinds of knowledge most often expressed by children of this age about *food:* (1) its use (you eat it) and, especially, (2) particular kinds.

XV. Andy (male, 3 years, 10 months)
E: OK, what's a flower, Andy?
A: Uhm, they grow.
E: Uh huh.
A: Like wind.
E: Like wind? Does wind grow?
A: Yayah.
E: And like flowers, flowers grow?
A: I know.
E: OK, what does a flower look like?

A: Um round.

E: Uh huh, and, where do you find them?

A: I found them on the ground.

. . . .

E: What kinds of flowers are there?

A: Sometimes they're round, well, they're round. It's like a star.

E: It's like a what?

A: It's like a star.

. . . .

E: Do you know what kinds of flowers there are? Tell me, what kinds of flowers are there, Andy?

(*Silence.*)

E: If I said what kinds of children are there you might say well, there are boys and there are girls.

A: Yeah.

E: So, can you tell me what kinds of flowers there are?

A: Uh, they're yellow, and they're blue, green, red, black, white, and green and yellow.

E: OK, what kind of thing is a flower?

A: Um, round.

E: It's round? Can you tell me when you last saw a flower?

A: All right.

E: Where did you see a flower?

A: I, I saw a, I walked outside, to milk, for milkman and, but saw a flower and I did that.

E: When you walked outside to go to the milkman . . .

A: Yeah.

Andy knows what a flower does (it grows). He seems to know what a flower looks like and his interesting use of the simile "like a star" again suggests a reliance upon imagery. Moreover, he suggests that he knows that flowers come in different colors ("blue, green, red, black, white, and green and yellow"). He remembers where he has found flowers ("on the ground") and again he can recall an experience he had when he was going outside to see the milkman when he saw a flower.

XVI. Susan (female, 4 years, 0 months)

E: Do you know what a flower is? What's a flower?

s: Flowers look like a tulip.

E: Mm hm. And where do you find it?

s: It grows.

E: Uh huh.

s: In the back yard.

E: Uh huh, and, anything else about flowers?

s: They grow.

E: Mm hm, and, do you know what kinds of flowers there are?

s: Tulips.

E: Uh huh.

s: That's all I know.

. . . .

E: What kind of a thing is a flower?

s: Grows. In the mud.

E: Grows in the mud. OK.

s: You get them from the shops, and weigh them.

XVII. Susan (female, 4 years, 0 months)

E: What's a plant Susan, . . . a plant?

s: Well grows. It's outside in the mud and rain.

E: Uh huh, and what does it look like?

s: I don't know.

E: What kind of plants are there? Do you know any?

s: We have some in our back yard, green things.

Although not asked initially what flowers look like or what they do, Susan tells us immediately that they "look like a tulip" and then that they grow "in the back yard." She knows that tulips are a kind of flower but she does not indicate that she knows that a flower is a kind of plant spontaneously or when asked, even though as Conversation XVII shows, she has some knowledge of plants which she thinks of as "green things." For this child, as well as for others whom we have studied (see Chapter 4) it appears that FLOWER and PLANT are not hierarchically related concepts as they are in adults, but rather mutually exclusive.[4]

XVIII. Susan (female, 4 years, 0 months)

E: What's a Volkswagen?

s: We have one at home, its a car.

This was one of the earliest occurrences of spontaneous superordination which we have observed in preschool children. Notice that the super-ordinate (*car*) is given for the specific concept "Volkswagen." Although we have found that superordination is, in general, difficult for the child, it appears to be less so for some concepts than for others. In particular, as this example illustrates, superordination appears to be easier for certain relatively specific concepts such as VOLKSWAGEN and more difficult for concepts of increasing generality (see Anglin, 1970).

XIX. Susan (female, 4 years, 0 months)

E: What's an apple?

s: An apple is a kind of food to eat.

E: Uh huh, and what does it look like?

[4] Adults will occasionally point out that in some cases a flower is a part of a plant and in other cases it is a plant by itself. However, when asked if individual flowers are plants they will say "yes" and in defining *flower* they will usually say that it is a kind of plant, sometimes noting the above qualification. Children of this age almost never mention *plant* when discussing *flower*.

s: It looks like a um, it's just, it's not anything but it looks like a pear, but it has a little bit there (*indicating top of apple that she is sketching with her hands in the air*) and it grows on trees.

E: Mm hm.

s: Know what? One day we got, we were taking a little walk back to our house and we saw green apples growing on a tree and it wasn't a rainy day.

In addition to knowing the use to which apples are put ("to eat") and to knowing what they look like ("like a pear" but rounder), Susan spontaneously assigns the concept APPLE to the superordinate concept FOOD which is something younger children did not do, although again it should be noted that superordination to APPLE is easier than to two-thirds of the other concepts studied in this investigation.

XX. G (female, 4 years, 3 months)

E: Can you tell me what food is?

G: Food is meat.

E: Meat? and anything else?

G: And bread.

E: And bread?

G: And vegetables and fruits . . . and cheese (*giggles*).

E: And cheese.

G: I'm talking about things on my list.

. . . .

E: Something else.

G: Milk, ice cream. And . . . nothing else on that list.

E: What?

G: Nothing else on that list.

E: OK. Can you tell me anything else about food?

G: And nuts! and nuts! and cereal.

. . . .

E: Can you think of anything else to say about food?

G: Chicken.

In response to a variety of questions about food this little girl gives only instances (and a lot of them, at that) which she apparently knew from her "list."

XXI. G (female, 4 years, 3 months)

E: What's a flower?

G: It is something to make things look pretty.

. . . .

E: OK. What kinds of flowers are there?

G: Daisies, roses and . . .

. . . .

E: Are there any other kinds?

G: Buttercups.

E: Buttercups? Wow. What else?

G: Dandelions.

E: Uh huh. Can you think of anything else?

G: Tiger lilies.

E: (*Laughs*) Oh wow! Anything else?

G: That's a real tall flower with some orange on the top.

Later when we tried to ask what kind of a thing a flower is in a number of ways she did not say *plant* but rather "something to make things look pretty" in spite of the fact that she had some knowledge of plants. (Also, when asked what kinds of plants there are she said, among other things, "flower plants.") Again her responses suggest that subordination is easier for her than superordination, that it is easy to go down a conceptual hierarchy but difficult to go up it. Indeed, this child has an astonishing knowledge of the subordinates of *flower* (daisies, roses, buttercups, tiger lilies, dandelions).

XXII. Sharon (female, 4 years, 7 months)

E: Tell me, what's a dog?

s: I don't know, it has soggy ears that go, that hang down.

E: Mm hm, and?

s: Goes ruff.

E: Uh huh, and?

s: Um, it chases cats.

E: Mm hm.

s: Guess what?

E: What?

s: My cat got bit by a dog.

E: Really.

s: Yeah.

E: Where did the dog bite him?

s: On both sides.

E: Really.

s: He got bit on both sides.

E: Aaa, that's too bad.

s: And his dog is the animal doctor.

E: Uh huh. OK, Do you know what kind of dogs there are?

s: Yeah, um, there are plain doggies, and, let's see, there are, um, there are igloos doggies, let's see, there are scouts doggies, um, there are, there are minuteman doggies.

E: Minuteman doggies? What kinds of doggies do minutemen have?

s: They have ones that um that's, that can get, that go, that is that stay, they um, that go in, that get in the house, that, that man, minuteman doggies are ones, minuteman has, has a doggie in the house.

E: Uh huh, OK. Do you know what kind of a thing a dog is? Like if I say to you, what kind of a thing is a child you might say well, a child is a kind of a person. So do you know what kind of a thing a dog is?

s: It's um, a animal. A animal.

This girl, Sharon, appears to know something about what certain dogs look like ("it has soggy ears that hang down") and what it does ("goes ruff . . . it chases cats"). Again she relates a specific experience she recalls when her cat was bitten by a dog. She cannot give particular names for various breeds of dogs but does seem to know there are different kinds. And although she does not spontaneously say that a dog is an animal she does later when asked what kind of a thing a dog is.

XXIII. Sharon (female, 4 years, 7 months)

E: OK, what's food, Sharon?

S: Its people, it's thing that people, it's things that people eat.

E: Things that people eat. Uh huh. And what kinds of food are there?

S: Animal food, and people food.

E: OK.

S: And . . .

E: And?

S: Ah, let's see, like things that men get, oh let's see, there's meat, and peas, and there's rice, and there's hamburgers, and there's um chicken, and there's turkey. And there's, you can't, you can't have, you don't know the difference between chicken and turkey because they are both alike, right?

E: They're very much alike, yes. But they are a little bit different.

S: My mother said a, a chicken is not the same thing as a turkey.

E: Mm hum. No it's not.

. . . .

E: Just tell me a little bit about food.

S: Oh, there is rabbit food.

E: Mm hum.

S: Carrots, and there is um, there is roast beef, there is um, corn, there is, let's see, there is uh, I don't know what else, uh, there is apples, there is grapes, there is pineapples.

This four-and-a-half-year-old girl gives a very reasonable definition of *food* which is notable since it is presented in terms of genus and differentia ("Things that people eat") and therefore in a form different from that of most definitions produced by preschool children for this general concept FOOD. She appears to know the essential function of food ("eat it") and she knows a variety of kinds (meat, peas, rice, hamburgers, chicken, turkey, carrots, roast beef, corn, apples, grapes, pineapples) and also that some food is for animals and some is for people.

XXIV. Sharon (female, 4 years, 7 months)

E: What's a flower?

S: A flower is what you smell.

E: Mm hum. And what does it look like?

S: It, it looks like rain, or it looks like a little thing that when you're going, like this (*moving her hands*).

E: Um hm, um hm.

s: Looks like this, like this (*showing with hands*).

e: OK, where would you find a flower?

s: In the grass.

e: In the grass. Uh huh. And what kinds of flowers are there?

s: Um, sunflowers and and dandelions, they are weeds, and there are daisies, and there are let's see, there are vegetable flowers that make vegetables and there are, I don't know, there are, there are, there are um, there are lots of kinds of sunflowers.

e: Um hmm. Do you know what kind of a thing a flower is?

s: What?

e: Well, like if I said you are a kind of person. What kind of a thing is a flower?

s: Well it's something that is, that is, that's, what, it's what you smell, and what you um pick, but you don't pick flowers cause they have to grow.

e: That's right.

s: And . . . what's the game we're playing?

e: Well we've been playing "talking about words." That's what we're playing.

s: Oh.

Sharon knows what you should and should not do with flowers (you smell them, you should not pick them). She knows where you find some flowers ("In the grass"). She knows some kinds of flowers (sunflowers, daisies, and "vegetable flowers"). She does not spontaneously say that a flower is a plant and she doesn't respond to the question intended to elicit this superordinate term from her even though in a later section of the interview she indicates that she has considerable knowledge of plants. In that part of the interview about plants she says among other things that roses, dandelions, and daisies are kinds of plants but in this conversation it does not occur to her to mention that flowers are plants. This would therefore seem to be another illustration of the preschool child's difficulty in abstraction or superordination in contrast with her facility in thinking in terms of subordinates or specifics. The child appears to have little trouble in going from general categories to specific categories but greater difficulty in going from specific categories to general categories.

XXV. Sharon (female, 4 years, 7 months)

e: Do you know what an animal is?

s: Yeah, I know.

e: Tell me.

s: An animal is what looks like um, that. A animal is, a, um, a animal is a, a box? Like a box would be in this room, right? And there is, a deer, and lion and a tiger, and a leopard, and um, uh there is.

e: What does an animal look like?

s: Uhhh, it looks, it's something with a tail.

e: Mm hm.

s: And, it, it lives in the zoo and then let's see it's and a bear that's something is, in a factory when it's, when it's very small. Right?

E: Mm?

s: They could be in factories if they're small.

E: Why would they be in a factory?

s: Because of there's the turtles. We have a story of it.

It appeared that Sharon began by attempting a general definition of *animal* and had difficulty in doing so ("what looks like um, that . . . a animal is a, a box?" she asks). What she can express about animals are the names of various kinds of four-legged, furry animals, probably seen at the zoo. (She later shows that she knows that turtles are also animals.) When asked what animals look like she says, "It's something with a tail," and then, "It lives in a zoo." It is possible that she is now attempting to formulate a similarity that would be consistent with the list of animal names she had just given.[5]

But soon she appears to notice that there are small animals ("turtles") which are found not at the zoo but perhaps, she argues, in factories. Thus it appears that this child's knowledge of the concept ANIMAL has a foundation in her recollection of some specific animals she has seen but what she does not seem to know, or at least has not reflected about, are the defining properties of the concept ANIMAL (not surprisingly). It is arguable, however, that she is capable of inference in that she comes up with general properties ("something with a tail," "lives in a zoo") which, while not as close to being defining of ANIMAL as, for example, "is capable of spontaneous motion" is, are reasonable first attempts at discovering what the word *animal* means above and beyond what the term refers to. Thus it appears that this child while not having previously reflected about animals in general, has some knowledge of specific animals including their names and may be capable of inferring similarities among the animals she knows. She seems, therefore, to have at least some capacity for inference which is a prerequisite for discovering the characteristics (or characteristic) that make(s) animals equivalent.

XXVI. Sharon (female, 4 years, 7 months)

E: Do you know what a rose is, Sharon?

s: Yeah.

_____

[5] This is not necessarily true since she may in fact have produced the properties "with a tail" and "in a zoo" simply on the basis of her recollection of a particular animal seen at the zoo. However, she may have been truly attempting (successfully) to produce properties true of each of the animals she has listed. Her use of the subordinate "something" in the phrase "something with a tail" suggests, if only weakly, that she is attributing tails not just to a particular animal but to the animals she has listed in general. Moreover, the two properties that she does choose—"with a tail" and "lives at the zoo"—are quite probably true in her experience of every one of the five animals she has just listed (deer, lion, tiger, leopard, giraffe), a fact which again raises the interesting possibility that she has considered more than just one particular animal in attributing them to animals.

E: What's a rose?

s: Um, it's something that, that you, that bugs sometimes eat. Eat. We planted in roses at our house.

E: Mm hm. And what color are they?

s: Red.

E: Red?

s: We sang a song about roses, you know that?

E: Yes? That's fine. Do you know what kind of a thing a rose is?

s: Yeah.

E: What?

s: Flowers.

E: Uh huh, yes, a rose is a kind of flower.

In this conversation Sharon shows the preschool child's tendency to relate questions about roses to specific ones, the red roses at her house (which "bugs sometimes eat"). At the same time, however, she seems to know that a rose is a flower and says so when asked.

XXVII. Sharon (female, 4 years, 7 months)

E: What is a car?

s: Um, it's well it's um and it's um and it's um, it's something that has a steering wheel.

E: Mm hm.

s: And people drive.

E: Uh huh.

s: And people um test drive with it.

E: Uh huh, what does it look like?

s: It looks like one, one, um, it looks like a big truck.

E: It looks like a big truck?

s: It looks like a little truck.

. . . .

E: What kinds of cars are there?

s: I don't know, um, there are, there are plain cars, and there are taxi cars, and there are truck cars, and there are um, well uh, let's see there's um well there's uh, there are, um, there are, there are junk cars, and there are cars that pull, and there are cars that pull trailers, and there are cars that just go, go, go, go to, go to stores instead of go driving. Right?

E: Mmmm . . . does your family have a car?

s: Yeah.

E: What kind of a car?

s: My daddy's getting a new car. You know that?

E: Mm, what kind of car does he have now?

s: Um, he has a plain car. I think he's getting a taxi car.

E: A taxi car?

s: Yea.

E: Wow . . . Do you know what kind of a thing is a car?

s: What?

E: Well, I'm asking you. Do you know?
S: Yes.
E: What kind of a thing is a car?
S: It has wheels.
E: Uh huh.
S: Um, it has seats.
E: Mm hum.
E: What?
S: And, I don't know anything else, but guess what?
E: What?
S: I know how to swim.
E: Well, that's wonderful.

Sharon knows what you do with a car ("people drive with it"), what it looks like ("like a little truck") and some of its parts (steering wheel, wheels, seats). She doesn't provide the names of specific makes of cars but she does give a list of function-related subcategories of car (taxi cars, truck cars, junk cars, cars for pulling trailers, cars to go to the store). The question about what kind of thing a car is does not elicit a superordinate term but rather properties ("has wheels," "has seats") which, while true of more than just cars, are properties which, in fact, virtually all cars share. She knows an essential function of cars ("people drive") although from her conversation she does not seem to be aware yet that this aspect of cars is crucial.

XXVIII. Sharon (female, 4 years, 7 months)

E: OK, do you know what fruit is?
S: Yeah.
E: What's fruit?
S: There's um grapes, bananas, apples, and pineapples, um pears, and let's see, I don't know any more.
E: OK, and what kind of a thing is fruit?
S: Um, it's what you eat.
E: Uh huh.
S: And it gives juice.
E: Uh huh.
S: And, and it, makes pies, and it makes some pies that are called apple pies sometimes.
E: Uh huh.
S: And, and we had a, we had a movie about um apples and, and, it was about Johnny Appleseed.

Sharon definitely knows the names of a number of instances of FRUIT (grapes, bananas, apples, pineapple, pears) and the uses to which they are put. Note again that Sharon begins by listing instances of this general concept before describing its uses ("what you eat . . . gives juice . . . makes pie").

Conversations with Five Year Olds

The five year olds are rather more sophisticated and adultlike than the younger children whom we have studied. Since only three children in the five-to-six-year-old range were interviewed about the words it is not possible to say with certainty how representative of five year olds in general they are. The ones interviewed, however, appear to have superordination in addition to subordination well within their grasp for many of the words. Moreover, for the first time, children of this age begin to mention, in addition to properties of instances which are the basic concrete ones that younger children mention (such as what instances look like, what they do, what they are used for, and where you find them), less obvious properties such as the internal constituents of instances and the relation of instances to other things in the world. Inference appears to be further developed although, for some of the words, defining properties or essential characteristics have still not crystallized.

XXIX. Keith (male, 5 years, 3 months)

E: So Keith, the first word we're going to talk about is *dog,* OK? What is a dog?

K: Well it's a animal what has, ah, teeth and walks and has dog food and, it does drink water. That's when you run into stories of like what's in Hosea and that kind of thing, you know.

E: OK. What kinds of dogs are there?

K: Well, a poodle and dalmatian. I don't know any other kinds.

E: OK, and what kind of thing is a dog?

K: Well, it's a kind of animal that runs in the water, that's legs work in the water.

E: OK, and can you . . . ?

K: A firedog and, I can't help people under water. I can't help them while they're swimming. That's why I don't go under water, I don't think. Not in the, ah, ocean. Cause I don't dive and swim.

E: OK. Can you tell me a little story using the word *dog?*

K: There once was a poodle named Punch and he had a farm that he helped fertile and the landlord said when he got a farm he had a farmer and so he lost the farmer again and when he found it but then he lost the apple and he threw it up in the tree and then it got caught, and then he took the kite down and then he flew it.

This child, Keith, can produce nominal subordinates of DOG when asked ("poodle," "dalmatian") and he can also say that "it's a kind of animal" when asked what kind of thing it is. Thus productive superordination for the concept DOG is possible for Keith which is not always the case for younger children.[6] His other statements about dogs, while produced impulsively and with little reflection, do suggest that he knows some characteristics of instances—what they have (teeth), what they do (walk), what they eat (dog food), what they drink (water), where they sometimes run (in the water). Only one of these properties is true of dogs and only dogs ("has dog food"), but the child does seem to have a considerably more generalized conception of dog than the three year olds considered earlier.

XXX. Keith (male, 5 years, 3 months)

E: What kind of thing is an apple?

K: Well, its a food and it gots um white stuff inside, the seeds.

This conversation is presented to show that in addition to spontaneously giving the superordinate term *food* for APPLE when asked for it, Keith is capable of describing the inner constituents of an apple ("white stuff inside . . . the seeds") which is not the kind of property given by younger children who when discussing what apples look like tend to produce responses such as "round" and their colors ("red," "green") rather than their constituent parts.

XXXI. Eric (male, 5 years, 7 months)

E: Now, I'm going to ask you a question. What is a dog?

ERIC: A dog is a animal.

E: A animal. OK can you tell me, um, tell me everything you know about dogs?

ERIC: Well they bark.

E: Uh huh.

ERIC: And they chase you, and cats.

E: What does a dog look like?

ERIC: A dog looks like, kinda like a cat.

E: And . . .

ERIC: And a bit different. Um, cats have real big ears and dogs have kinda curved ears.

E: Mm hm.

ERIC: That's all I know about 'em.

E: OK. Where would you find a dog?

ERIC: Well, a pet store.

E: Pet store?

---

[6] Of course, in a test of comprehension younger children may reveal that they appreciate at some level that dogs are animals. For example if you show the young child a picture of a dog and ask him, "Is this an animal?" even three year olds will usually assent. But children of this age frequently do not produce the superordinate term *animal* when describing their knowledge of dogs spontaneously or when asked what kind of a thing a dog is. Thus the advance illustrated by Keith in this dialogue is specifically linked to his inclination and ability to produce superordinates, but nonetheless does seem to represent a real advance, over three year olds at least.

ERIC: Yup.

E: Anyplace else?

ERIC: Well, no, yeah, but I don't know any other place.

E: OK. Now do you know what kinds of dogs are there?

ERIC: German shepherd.

E: Mm hm.

ERIC: Beagles.

E: Uh huh.

ERIC: I know one dog's a bloodhound. Bloodhound.

E: Do you know any more?

ERIC: Yep. Dalmatian, that's all I know. That's all I know.

E: OK. Tell me what kind of a thing is a dog?

ERIC: What kind of a thing, oh, I don't know what you mean.

E: If the word was child, say, and I said, what kind of a thing is a child, then you might say a child is a person. So what kind of a thing is a dog?

ERIC: A dog is a animal.

Eric is a very sharp little boy who knows the words well. His stories (three of which will be presented) are exceptionally well told and funny. In his discussion about dogs he indicates that he knows what they do (they bark), what they look like (like cats, although slightly different) and that a dog is an animal, which he says both spontaneously and in response to the question of what kind of thing a dog is. He also appears to know that dogs are pets since in answer to the question "Where would you find a dog?" he answers, "Well, a pet store." He also knows the specific names of a number of breeds of dogs (German shepherds, beagles, bloodhounds, dalmatians).

XXXII. Eric (male, 5 years, 7 months)

E: What is a flower?

ERIC: What is a flower?

E: Um hm.

ERIC: A flower is a something that you'd like to smell a lot of. And bees flow along and take honey out of it. Mmmmmmmmm.

E: OK. Tell me everything you know about flowers.

ERIC: Well, want me to do it by naming?

E: Sure.

ERIC: Rosies, daisies, dandelion—that isn't really a flower.

E: OK. What does a flower look like?

ERIC: A flower looks, if it, if I can write a picture on the board, I, I would show you.

E: Can you tell me? (*Child shakes head.*) No. OK, where do you find flowers?

ERIC: Find flowers in gardens, and in oats, and in barley.

E: OK, and what kind of thing is a flower?

ERIC: In, what kind of a thing is a flower. Uh. A flower is a kind of thing that you smell.

E: OK. Can you tell me a story about a flower?

ERIC: Once upon a time was a flower that had lots of honey. In a short time three bees come along and buzzed to the flower and the flowers had lots of honey and the bees smelled it. Buzzed. But then they came straight for it and ate it. That's the end.

Eric knows what you do with flowers (you smell them), he knows at least the names of two kinds ("rosies," "daisies"), he seems to know what they look like although he does not or cannot express it, he knows where some can be found ("in gardens"). He does not mention that flowers are plants but does say that they are "a kind of a thing you smell." One interesting aspect of this conversation is that Eric has expressed his knowledge of the way in which other objects interact with flowers ("bees take honey out of it") which is not the sort of property produced by younger children in discussions about *flower*.

XXXIII. Eric (male, 5 years, 7 months)

E: Now, what's an apple?

ERIC: A apple is a food.

E: OK. Tell me everything you know about apples.

ERIC: Well you eat apples, and you also, and you also eat apples off a tree, and, and, if you want you can make apple pies out of 'em.

E: OK. What does it look like?

ERIC: It looks like that (*points to picture of an apple on "surprise box"*)

E: What kind of a thing is an apple?

ERIC: What kind of a thing is a apple. A apple is a kind of thing to eat.

E: OK, and can you tell me a story about an apple?

ERIC: About an apple? Once there was a apple tree with a lonely apple. And the apple was never picked because it would go bad. And one day it fell by itself and a wolf boy came along and picked it up, and he said "This is not an apple, but a barnicoleum!" The end.

In addition to establishing himself as a raconteur of considerable wit, Eric in this conversation shows that superordination is natural for him in defining apple since the first thing he says when asked, "What's an apple?" is "A apple is a food." He also knows the use (you eat them) of instances of the concept and where they come from (trees) and what they look like.

XXXIV. Eric (male, 5 years, 7 months)

E: What is a car?

ERIC: A car is something you can drive in.

E: OK. Tell me what you know about cars.

ERIC: Really? Cars run by motors. And they also run power accessories.

E: Um hm. What does a car look like?

ERIC: A car looks, a car looks kind of like a rocketship. It looks kind of like that (*draws a car in the air*).

E: Um hm. What kinds of cars are there?

ERIC: There are Corvairs, Volvos, um, I don't know any more.

E: OK. What kind of a thing is a car?
ERIC: A car is a kind of a thing, um, drive.

In addition to knowing the essential function of cars (you can drive it), what they look like ("like a rocketship"), and specific makes (Corvairs, Volvos), Eric also appears to know a little about a car's inner parts and how cars work ("Cars run by motors. And they also run power accessories."). This sort of property was never mentioned by younger children when they discussed *cars*.

XXXV. Eric (male, 5 years, 7 months)
E: OK, tell me, what is a plant?
ERIC: A plant? Is something that comes from a seed.
E: OK, tell me what you know about plants.
ERIC: Well plants are things that some animals eat.
E: OK, what would a plant look like?
ERIC: A plant would look like that (*drawing one with hands in the air*).
E: OK, um, what kinds of plants are there?
ERIC: Curved, grey, jewel weed, prickly plant, and I don't know. I don't know.
. . . .
E: OK. That's fine. Can you tell me just a little story about a plant?
ERIC: Once a time upon there was a little, little jewel weed, and it was very sad because it didn't have a mother or a father. And one day, a mother and a father came along and they didn't have any children. And they were, and they were, never ever made one and they wanted one. But then they saw the baby jewel weed with no mother or father so they took him with them to lie in the sun. The Ehehehend.

Eric's very interesting definition of plant ("something that comes from a seed") includes a property dealing with the origins of plant life ("comes from a seed") never mentioned by younger children. He knows the names of specific kinds of plants ("jewel weed," "prickly plant") although notice that he mentions neither *flowers* nor *trees* as instances. Again, however, the most fascinating aspect of the dialogue is Eric's heart-rending story.

XXXVI. G (female, 5 years, 10 months)
E: What's a dog?
G: It's a thing what goes woof woof.
E: It's a thing that goes woof woof? OK. Do you know anything more about a dog?
G: It eats dog food.
E: Mm hmm.
G: It has a tail. It has four feet. It has a body. It has two eyes. It has a mouth. It has a nose. It has hair. It has ears. It has eyeballs.
E: (*Laughs*) It's got a lot of stuff, huh? OK, do you know what kinds of dogs there are?
G: A beagle.

E: That's one, yeah. Do you know any more?

G: Nah.

E: Are there other kinds?

G: Yes.

E: There are. You don't remember the names though. Yeah. The names get kind of long after a while but there are other kinds. OK. If I asked you what kind of a thing a child was, you know, you could say, well it's a kind of person, right? So if I say, "What kind of thing is a dog?" what could you say then? A dog is a kind of a what?

G: Animal.

E: Yup. OK. Do you know anything else about dogs that you want to say?

G: It has eyes. It has a nose. It . . .

E: (*Laughing*) You already said that.

Although she does not define *dog* as "an animal that . . ." as adults usually do, this young girl does present her definition in terms of a general term (in this case the very general *thing*) and an almost defining attribute ("what goes woof woof"). Notice the two attributes she chooses first to characterize DOG. Each of these attributes ("goes woof woof" and "eats dog food") define DOG rather accurately in that most dogs do bark and do eat dog food and most other animals do not. She knows what instances of the concept look like as indicated by the detailed list of body parts she mentions which may have been mediated by an image of a dog or, in the case of the later mentioned parts, by analogy to her own body. She knows well that a dog is an animal since immediately following a rather complicated question designed to see if she had such knowledge she indicates that she does.

XXXVII. G (female, 5 years, 10 months)

E: So, what's food?

G: It's something what I eat.

E: Something that you eat.

G: That I'm eating now. (*Child is eating a graham cracker.*)

E: (*Laughing*) A graham cracker is food then?

G: Mm (*affirmative*).

E: OK. What other kinds of food are there? What other kinds are there?

G: There's graham crackers.

E: (*Laughing*) What else?

G: There's cinnamon crackers. There is meat. Yuck. Spinach. Yuck. There is noodles. There is chocolate bars. There is turkey. There is chicken. There is rice. There's Chinese food. There is eggplant. Yuck.

E: (*Laughing*) You don't like eggplant, huh?

G: Yuck. There's eggnog. There is mayonnaise. There is cottage cheese. There is milk (*laughing*). That isn't a kind of food, it's drink. Um (*short pause, thinking*), there's orange juice. There is peaches. There is oranges. There is pears. There is apples. There is bananas. There is eggs. There is . . .

E: Boy, there is a lot.
G: There is honey.

In response to the question "What's food?" the same young girl gives a semantically precise definition of the concept in terms of genus (something) and essential function ("what I eat"). Although younger children appear to know that food is edible, they sometimes do not mention it and if they do it is very often after they have given a list of instances. This child begins her discussion of the word by going straight to its meaning. She then indicates that she does know many instances which she reels off while interspersing some commentary on the kinds she dislikes. Not only can this child retrieve from semantic memory twenty-two names of particular kinds of foods but there is some discernible clustering of specifically related kinds of foods (crackers, poultry, white dairy products, and fruit). Younger children have also been observed to cluster words in recalling instances as in the case of Andy (three years, ten months; conversation XIV) who, in discussing food produced a list of cereals: "Alphabets, Wheaties, Raisin Bran, and Froot Loops." Other younger children sometimes do not show as much evidence of clustering, however, and none of them remembered this many names of instances.

XXXVIII. G (female, 5 years, 10 months)
E: OK. What's an animal?
G: An animal is something that makes noises and it has sometimes fur an it's a, and it's a frog, it's a rabbit, it's a tiger, it's a wolf, it's a um, a dog, it's a cat, it's a mouse, it's a guinea pig. I have a guinea pig. It is a . . . (*long pause*)
   (E *and* G *laugh*)
G: It's a mouse, it's a . . . kangaroo
E: Oh, that's a good animal.
G: It's a koala bear, koala bear, koala bear. It's a monkey, it's a rabbit. It's a porcupine. It's an ant. It's a bug. It's a . . . But it isn't a human being.
E: It isn't? OK.
G: No, it isn't a person, that's what I meant to say.
E: Is a human being and a person the same thing?
G: (*Pause*) No, I don't think so.
   . . . .
E: What kind of a thing is an animal? That's kind of a hard question.
G: (*Pause*) It's a animal.
   . . . .
E: Can you tell me a little more about what animals look like?
G: Yeah. They look like they have two eyes, they look like they have a nose.
E: Does every animal have a nose?
G: (*Long pause*) Ants don't. I don't think so.
E: (*Laughing*) I wonder if they do? That's a good question. OK, do you know what else they would look like?

G: They would look like they had two arms, and maybe four legs or two . . . four legs or two . . . four legs or two, or two legs.

E: OK, that's pretty much. That's a lot. Will you tell me a story or say a sentence about an animal?

G: I am not a animal.

E: I am not an animal. OK. How about apple? What's an apple?

G: Wait. I am a apple (*both laughing*). Wait. I am a animal.

E: You are? That means a person is an animal?

G: Yeah.

This young girl does not immediately give the names of instances which is what younger children tend to do when answering the question "What's an animal?" but rather attempts to give a general definition of *animal* ("something that makes noises and it has sometimes fur"). The properties of ANIMAL that she provides in her definition are not quite defining, although they are true of many animals. She then gives a long list of the names of instances (with many repetitions) until she finally asserts "not a human being" with some confidence. However, she eventually comes to realize that humans are animals and the steps to this conclusion suggest that she is restructuring her conception of animals on the spot through a process of discovery. After having listed the names of a number of animals she knows she soon mentions some more properties that are often true of many animals and most of the animals she has heretofore listed. That is, in response to the question about what animals look like, she says, "they have two eyes, they look like they have a nose." She shows that she knows that probably some animals don't have noses but this doesn't seem to trouble her and she goes on to continue to list other parts which many animals she knows have ("two arms, and maybe four legs or two . . . four legs or two or two legs"). It appears quite possible that she has started to waver again because it has occurred to her that she herself, and people more generally perhaps also, have eyes and a nose as is the case for the animals with which she is familiar. Struck by this affinity, she mentions a property of people (two arms) in her list of perceptual attributes of animals. She soon, however, shows that she knows that some animals have four legs and not two arms but the possible contradiction appears to puzzle her a bit which leads her back to the question of whether she is an animal. She attempts to resolve this by asserting "I am not a animal." But she is obviously preoccupied by the question and dissatisfied with her initial resolution of it for she says soon thereafter, "Wait. I am a animal," and concludes more generally that "a person is an animal."

Thus, in the course of this dialogue the child has formulated some general properties which while not defining (as for example "is capable of spontaneous motion" is), are true of many of the animals she knows. The articulation of these properties is followed by a restructuring of the extension of the concept ANIMAL, in this case in the direction of greater breadth (i.e., to include humans). This dialogue suggests that the conscious formulation of the properties shared by instances of the concept has been met by a restructuring of the concept's scope; that the child's new awareness of the concept's intension is now being used criterially to govern its extension. Although the intension (properties) arrived at is not quite defining of the adult concept of ANIMAL, it nonetheless is compelling enough to lead her to modify the set of objects comprehended by the term.

Further Analyses of the Conversations

We were guided to some extent in further analyses of the conversations by certain distinctions about word meaning that have been made in the semantic memory literature and in particular by Collins and Quillian (1969, 1972). The most notable of these distinctions is that among (1) subordinates (or subsets) of a given concept, (2) properties of the instances of the concept, and (3) superordinates (or supersets) of the concept, as these were expressed in the conversations. Thus we analyzed the child's discussion of each of the words into three kinds of units: (1) Subordinates: These could be either nominal subordinates, that is, common nouns which name subcategories of the concepts (e.g., *collies, retrievers,* for DOG) or they could be descriptive subordinates, that is, the noun being discussed modified by some descriptive adjective or phrase (e.g., "Martha's dog," "woofy dogs"). (2) Properties: These included any predication on the part of the child true of either all or just some of the instances of a given concept (e.g., "barks" for dogs, but also "black" for dogs). (In later analyses we have subclassified the kinds of properties expressed by children further.) (3) Superordinates: We decided to count as superordinates only nouns produced by the child which were superordinate to the concept being discussed (e.g., *animal* for DOG) but not characteristics which were true of more than just the instances of a given concept (e.g., *moves* for CAR) which were treated as properties.

For each of the children with whom we discussed the words we constructed schematic "molecules of meaning" a few of which are illustrated in Figures 7.1 and 7.3. These figures show the knowledge expressed (as it was expressed) by five children for DOG and FOOD. Figures 7.2 and 7.4 show two molecules for one adult based on the knowledge he expressed for each of these words (presented for comparison with the corresponding figures for children). In these figures subordinates are presented below the label of the category being discussed, properties have been presented to the right of it, and superordinates are presented above it. Also, in Figures 7.1 through 7.4 the question or statement made by the experimenter which was followed by a given item of expressible knowledge by the child is indicated below the molecules of meaning. Figures 7.1 and 7.3 show that children as young as two years, eight months can express some knowledge of the concepts DOG and FOOD although certain progressions are discernible in the structure of the knowledge expressed by the five children. Specifically, in the case of DOG, as Figure 7.1 shows, children younger than four years mention properties which indicate what dogs look like,

Molecules of meaning

Two-year-old boy, age 2; 8

It goes woof, barks.[1]
Likes water, food.[2]
Big dogs.[3]
Eat.[7]
Dog — Run.[7]
Don't dive.[7]
They don't walk and they don't run.[8]
I saw a dog out in the schoolyard[4] ...
Martha's dog.[9]   It was big like Martha's dog. It was big
Woofy dogs.[9]   like I and Martha[5] ... Like the sky and
                     Martha.[6]

1. "Can you tell us what a dog is?"
2. "What else is a dog like?"
3. "What do they look like?"
4. "What else do they look like?"
5. "You saw a dog out in your schoolyard, right?"
6. "Oh, he was very big?"
7. "What do dogs do?"
8. "When you see a dog, how do you know its a dog?"
9. "Can you tell us what kind of dogs there are?"

Two-year-old boy, age 2; 9

It barks.[1]
Sometimes they like me.[5]
Sometimes they fight with me.[5]
Dog — I can jump on them and kick them.[2]
Legs.[3]
A face.[3]
A back.[4]

1. "When you see a dog, what do you see?"
2. "What can you do with them?"
3. "You can't tell me what they look like?"
4. "Anything else about dogs?"
5. "Sometimes it what?"

Three-year-old boy, age 3; 4

Brown and white.[1]
Dog — Runs.[2]
Walks.[2]

1. "Do you know what it looks like?"
2. "What does it do?"

Four-year-old girl, age 4; 3

Animal.[1]
They run.[4]
Dog — Look like an animal.[5]
Hounds.[3]
Poodles.[2]   Spotdogs.[3]
Bulldogs.[2]

1. "Can you tell me what a dog is?"
2. "What kind of dogs are there?"
3. "What else—can you think of anymore?"
4. "What do they do?"
5. "What do they look like?"

Five-year-old boy, age 5; 7

Animal.[1]
They bark.[2]
Chase you and cats.[2]
Dog — Looks kind of like a cat, but different.[3]
Find them in a pet store.[4]
Dalmatians.[5]   German shepherd.[5]
Beagles.[5]
Bloodhounds.[5]

1. "What is a dog?"
2. "Can you tell me everything you know about dogs?"
3. "What does a dog look like?"
4. "Where would you find a dog?"
5. "Do you know what kinds of dogs are there?"

FIGURE 7.1 Representation of expressible knowledge of the meaning of the word *dog* for five children. When questions had been asked which elicited the responses from the children they are indicated in Figure 7.1.

Molecule of Meaning

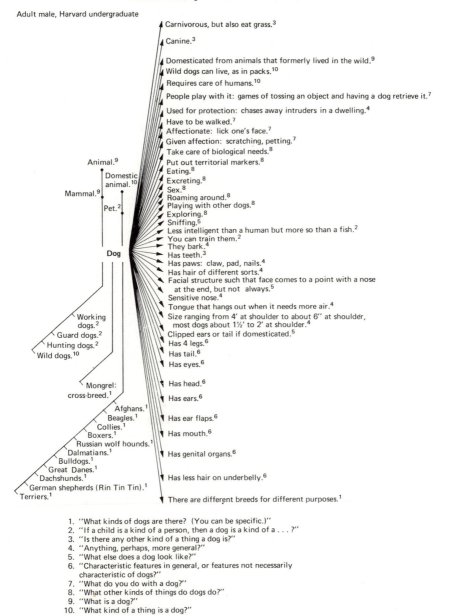

Adult male, Harvard undergraduate

Carnivorous, but also eat grass.[3]

Canine.[3]

Domesticated from animals that formerly lived in the wild.[9]

Wild dogs can live, as in packs.[10]

Requires care of humans.[10]

People play with it: games of tossing an object and having a dog retrieve it.[7]

Used for protection: chases away intruders in a dwelling.[4]

Have to be walked.[7]

Affectionate: lick one's face.[7]

Given affection: scratching, petting.[7]

Take care of biological needs.[8]

Animal.[9]

Domestic animal.[10]

Mammal.[9]

Pet.[2]

Put out territorial markers.[8]

Eating.[8]

Excreting.[8]

Sex.[8]

Roaming around.[8]

Playing with other dogs.[8]

Exploring.[8]

Sniffing.[5]

Less intelligent than a human but more so than a fish.[2]

You can train them.[2]

They bark.[4]

Dog

Has teeth.[3]

Has paws: claw, pad, nails.[4]

Has hair of different sorts.[4]

Facial structure such that face comes to a point with a nose at the end, but not always.[5]

Sensitive nose.[4]

Tongue that hangs out when it needs more air.[4]

Working dogs.[2]

Size ranging from 4' at shoulder to about 6" at shoulder, most dogs about 1½' to 2' at shoulder.[4]

Guard dogs.[2]

Clipped ears or tail if domesticated.[5]

Hunting dogs.[2]

Wild dogs.[10]

Has 4 legs.[6]

Has tail.[6]

Has eyes.[6]

Mongrel: cross-breed.[1]

Has head.[6]

Has ears.[6]

Afghans.[1]

Beagles.[1]

Collies.[1]

Has ear flaps.[6]

Boxers.[1]

Russian wolf hounds.[1]

Has mouth.[6]

Dalmatians.[1]

Bulldogs.[1]

Great Danes.[1]

Has genital organs.[6]

Dachshunds.[1]

German shepherds (Rin Tin Tin).[1]

Has less hair on underbelly.[6]

Terriers.[1]

There are different breeds for different purposes.[1]

1. "What kinds of dogs are there? (You can be specific.)"
2. "If a child is a kind of a person, then a dog is a kind of a . . . ?"
3. "Is there any other kind of a thing a dog is?"
4. "Anything, perhaps, more general?"
5. "What else does a dog look like?"
6. "Characteristic features in general, or features not necessarily characteristic of dogs?"
7. "What do you do with a dog?"
8. "What other kinds of things do dogs do?"
9. "What is a dog?"
10. "What kind of a thing is a dog?"

FIGURE 7.2 Representation of the expressible knowledge of the meaning of the word *dog* for one adult.

what they do, what you can do to them, and where you find them; however, they do not mention nominal subordinates (*poodles, bulldogs,*
etc.) which the two children older than four do, nor superordinates (e.g.,
animal) which again the older children do. In the case of FOOD it can be
seen that even the youngest subject, Peter (two years, eight months), mentions certain nominal subordinates (*cookies, cereal,* etc.) as well as certain
other properties true of some foods, including the essential function of
food ("eat"). It is only the oldest child (five years, seven months) represented in Figure 7.3 whose expressed knowledge of food represented an
advance over the youngest subjects. This child not only mentioned the use

Molecules of Meaning

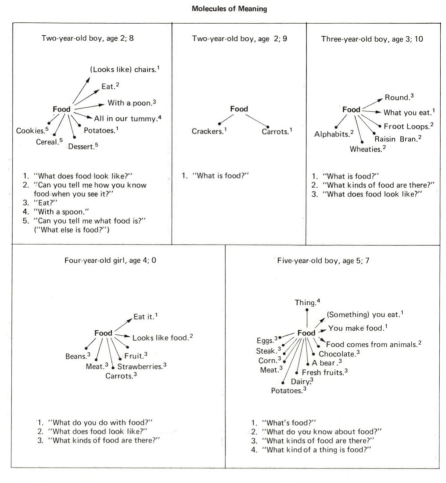

FIGURE 7.3 Representation of expressible knowledge of the meaning of the word
food for five children.

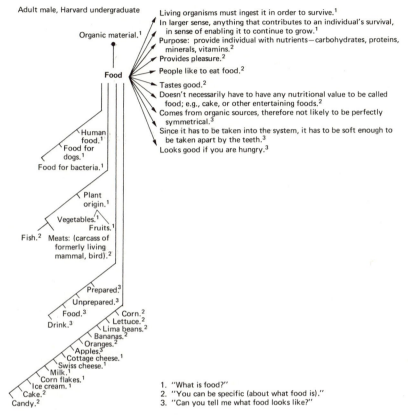

FIGURE 7.4 Representation of the expressible knowledge of the meaning of the word *food* for one adult.

of FOOD ("something you eat") but in addition gave a greater variety of subordinates, produced the very general nominal superordinate *thing,* and also mentioned a property about the origins of some food ("food comes from animals"), which is not the kind of property expressed by younger children. Figures 7.2 and 7.4 show that the adult was capable of describing more knowledge of each kind for each concept. These figures suggest that even though preschool children have a considerable amount to say about DOG and FOOD, the knowledge they can express is limited and less organized in comparison to that of adults.

Table 7.1 shows the number and nature of the items of knowledge expressed by ten of the children and three adults in this study. In Table 7.1 the total number of units of knowledge (subordinates, properties, and superordinates) expressed by each child is shown in the leftmost column.

TABLE 7.1 *Kinds of knowledge expressed by ten children and three adults in the intension study.*

Age	Total properties + subordinates + superordinates	Total properties	L properties	A properties	F properties	E properties	O properties	Number superordinates given / Words known	Number subordinates given / Words known	N Subs	D Subs
3.4	38	32	10	11	6	5	0	$^6/_8$	$^6/_8$	5	1
3.6	37	19	5	5	6	2	1	$^3/_{10}$	$^{15}/_{10}$	12	3
3.10	46	29	9	8	5	5	2	$^9/_{10}$	$^{17}/_{10}$	6	11
4.0	53	35	9	7	8	11	0	$^2/_{10}$	$^{16}/_{10}$	13	3
4.3	55	14	7	6	1	0	0	$^6/_{10}$	$^{35}/_{10}$	26	9
4.7	74	27	11	6	7	3	0	$^3/_{10}$	$^{45}/_{10}$	30	15
5.3	72	28	9	9	3	4	3	$^5/_{10}$	$^{39}/_{10}$	25	14
5.7	83	35	5	8	13	2	7	$^8/_{10}$	$^{40}/_{10}$	37	3
5.10	104	46	30	8	3	4	1	$^7/_{10}$	$^{53}/_{10}$	48	5
6.7	64	30	11	11	8	0	0	$^6/_{11}$	$^{28}/_{11}$	24	4
A_1	452	266	83	56	71	12	44	$^{50}/_{12}$	$^{136}/_{12}$	100	36
A_2	458	252	47	35	98	14	58	$^{25}/_{12}$	$^{181}/_{12}$	142	39
A_3	454	282	86	55	74	26	41	$^{35}/_{12}$	$^{137}/_{12}$	84	53

NOTE: L (look) properties are those which describe what instances of the concept look like; A (action) properties describe what instances of the concept do; F (function) properties describe the uses to which instances of the concept can be put; E (environment) properties describe where one might find instances of the concept; O (other) properties describe aspects of instances of the concept which do not fit into any of the four types outlined above; N *Subs* = the number of subordinates which have been designated by means of a noun which is subordinate to the concept being tested; D *Subs* = the number of subordinates which have been expressed by means of the word being tested, qualified by an adjective or other descriptive phrase.

In the next column the total number of properties is shown. These have been divided in the next five columns into five kinds: (1) *L* (look) properties: those which describe what instances of the concept look like; (2) *A* (action) properties: those which describe what instances of the concept do; (3) *F* (function) properties: those which describe the uses to which instances of the concept can be put; (4) *E* (environment) properties: those which describe where one might find instances of the concept, and (5) *O* (other) properties: those which describe other aspects of instances of the concept. In the next two columns of Table 7.1 the total number of superordinates and subordinates which were given by each child divided by the total number of words known is shown. Finally, the subordinates have been divided into nominal subordinates (*N Subs*) and descriptive subordinates (*D Subs*) in the last two columns of Table 7.1.

Table 7.1 suggests that with increasing age subjects expressed more knowledge of each kind. However, certain kinds of knowledge appear to be expressible even by the youngest subjects whose conversations are summarized in Table 7.1. Specifically, even three year olds often provide *L, A, F,* and *E* properties and both nominal and descriptive subordinates. What the youngest children rarely provide are *O* properties and superordinates.

While these trends are interesting, it is important to consider also this sort of breakdown for each of the individual words studied, for there was some indication that the kinds of knowledge which the child could express varied from concept to concept. Table 7.2 shows the number of properties, subordinates, and superordinates given by each of the ten children for each word investigated in this study. Table 7.3 shows the corresponding statistics for three adults. Table 7.2 shows that the kind of knowledge expressed by children does in fact vary somewhat from concept to concept. For the basic concepts DOG, FLOWER, APPLE, and CAR (*basic* is operationally defined here as the term within each hierarchy that tends to be learned first by children [see Chapter 2]), children give more properties than subordinates and fewer superordinates. For three of the general concepts, ANIMAL, FOOD, and FRUIT (*general* is operationally defined here as terms in the hierarchies which are superordinate to basic terms), children give more subordinates than properties and virtually no superordinates. For one of the remaining five general concepts (PLANT) children give about an equal number of properties and subordinates. For the final general concept (VEHICLE) too few children knew the word to allow any conclusions. Finally, for two specific concepts, ROSE and VOLKSWAGEN, (*specific* is operationally defined here as terms in the hierarchies which are subordinate to basic terms) properties are produced most often followed by superordinates. Only one child knew the specific concept COLLIE at all and so on the basis of this study it is difficult to conclude much about the knowledge first acquired by children about collies, although it is interesting that the one

TABLE 7.2 Number of properties, subordinates, and superordinates given by each of ten children for each word studied in the intension experiment.

	Subject	S_1 3:4			S_2 3:6			S_3 3:10			S_4 4:0			S_5 4:3			S_6 4:7			S_7 5:3			S_8 5:7			S_9 5:10			S_{10} 6:7			Totals		
Age / Word		P	Sub	Super	P	Sub	Super	P	Sub	Super	P	Sub	Super	P	Sub	Super	P	Sub	Super	P	Sub	Super	P	Sub	Super	P	Sub	Super	P	Sub	Super	P	Sub	Super
General ↑	Animal	4	2	0	1	2	0	3	2	0	6	3	0	3	5	0	2	7	0	2	11	0	7	13	0	4	13	0	4	7	0	36	65	0
Basic →	Dog	4	0	0	1	1	1	5	2	0	2	3	0	2	4	0	3	4	1	5	3	1	4	4	1	11	1	1	5	2	2	42	24	7
Specific ↓	Collie	X			X			X			X			0	0	0	X			X			X			X			0	0	1	0	0	1
General ↑	Plant	X			1	0	0	2	0	0	0	0	0	0	2	3	0	2	3	0	2	3	0	2	4	0	4	3	1	3	0	21	19	1
Basic →	Flower	4	0	0	1	2	0	4	6	0	0	1	0	0	5	0	3	4	0	0	2	0	3	3	0	4	3	1	1	2	1	31	27	2
Specific ↓	Rose	X			1	0	1	1	0	0	5	0	0	0	2	0	2	0	1	4	0	0	4	0	0	3	0	1	2	0	0	22	2	7
General ↑	Food	2	2	0	0	6	0	0	4	0	1	5	0	0	10	0	1	15	0	0	13	0	3	10	0	1	22	1	1	3	3	18	77	3
General →	Fruit	2	0	0	0	3	0	2	2	0	3	3	0	0	0	0	0	5	0	0	3	0	0	4	0	1	5	1	3	6	3	20	31	4
Basic →	Apple	4	0	0	2	2	0	0	0	0	0	0	1	3	3	1	3	0	0	3	0	1	3	0	0	3	3	0	1	0	0	30	8	7
General ↑	Vehicle	0	0	0	0	0	0	5	1	0	X			X			X			X			X			X			3	2	0	8	3	0
Basic →	Car	7	1	0	3	2	0	2	0	0	2	1	0	1	3	0	7	7	0	4	4	0	4	2	0	8	3	0	3	4	1	41	27	1
Specific ↓	VW	3	0	0	2	0	1	1	0	0	2	0	1	1	0	0	X			1	0	1	1	0	1	7	0	1	3	0	2	20	0	7
Totals		30	5	0	19	15	0	29	17	0	35	16	2	14	35	6	26	45	3	26	39	5	35	40	8	45	51	7	30	28	6			

NOTE: P = number of properties; Sub = number of subordinates; Super = number of superordinates; X indicates that child did not know the word at all.

TABLE 7.3 Table showing the number of properties, subordinates, and superordinates given by each of three adults for each word studied in the intension experiment.

Subject		S_{A1}			S_{A2}			S_{A3}			Totals		
	Word	P	Sub	Super	P	Sub	Super	P	Sub	Super	P	Sub	Super
General ↑	Animal	21	27	1	15	24	2	30	29	1	66	80	4
Basic →	Dog	50	16	4	39	15	2	39	17	5	128	48	11
Specific ↓	Collie	27	0	7	16	2	2	22	4	3	65	6	12
General ↑	Plant	31	10	2	12	10	1	19	10	0	62	30	3
Basic →	Flower	15	1	3	24	9	2	26	7	3	65	17	8
Specific ↓	Rose	25	3	3	18	2	2	25	3	2	68	8	7
General |	Food	12	27	1	26	30	1	33	19	4	71	76	6
General →	Fruit	11	6	6	26	33	2	21	10	3	58	49	11
Basic →	Apple	16	10	5	33	6	2	19	4	5	68	20	12
General ↑	Vehicle	17	8	3	5	15	3	8	12	1	30	35	7
Basic →	Car	23	22	8	23	29	3	19	19	5	65	70	16
Specific ↓	VW	18	6	7	15	5	3	21	3	3	54	14	13

NOTE: As in Table 7.2, P = number of properties; Sub = number of subordinates; $Super$ = number of superordinates.

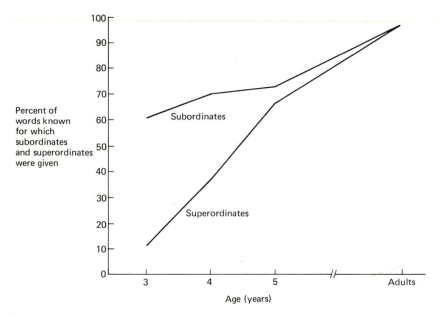

FIGURE 7.5 Percentage of words known for which subordinates and superordinates were given. Data based on conversations with nine children and three adults.

four-year, three-month-old child who indicated any knowledge of this concept mentioned only the superordinate *dog* in his discussion about it. Therefore, as Table 7.2 shows, the kind of knowledge which the child is capable of expressing does vary from concept to concept. Note also in Table 7.2 that the ability to produce a superordinate decreases monotonically with the level of generality of each term within a given hierarchy (see Anglin, 1970). The only exception to this trend is in the case of the collie-dog-animal hierarchy in which only one child produced a superordinate for *collie,* since he was the only child who had any knowledge of the term whatsoever.

Table 7.3 shows that although each adult can produce items of each kind of knowledge for each concept (i.e., there is only one 0 in all of Table 7.3), the relative number of each kind of knowledge (subordinates, properties, and superordinates) does vary from concept to concept in roughly the same way as it had for children.

Figure 7.5 presents two graphs which show the average percentage of words known for which subordinates and superordinates were given by four groups of subjects of different ages (with three subjects per group) in this study. Figure 7.5 is based only on words of which subjects had some knowledge since it would be unreasonable to expect the child to produce either subordinates or superordinates for words unfamiliar to him. Figure 7.5 shows that while both abilities (of subordination and superordination) develop over this age range, the slope of the function for superordination is considerably steeper than the one for subordination. Three year olds produced subordinates for just over 60 percent of the words known in their conversations in comparison to nearly 100 percent for adults. In contrast, three year olds produced superordinates for only about 10 percent of the words known in comparison to nearly 100 percent for adults. Thus Figure 7.5 suggests again that subordination is more within the child's grasp than is superordination (see Anglin, 1970), although, as noted above, there is some variation from concept to concept in these abilities.

Because there were so few children interviewed at each age level and because of the variability in the questions asked of each child in the conversations, it would be unwise to subject the results described thus far in this chapter to tests of statistical significance. Nonetheless it is possible to summarize our impressions of the developmental changes we have observed in the child's ability to express knowledge about the verbal concepts discussed in these conversations.

DISCUSSION

Even three-year-old children have some rudimentary knowledge of most of the verbal concepts which were the focus of this investigation. Adults clearly can express more knowledge of each kind (subordinates, properties, superordinates) about each concept but it is important to give the child credit for the considerable knowledge which he is capable of expressing. For basic concepts he is quite adept at providing properties and, in particular, properties which describe what instances of the concept look like (L properties), what they do (A properties), what you do to them (F properties), and where you find them (E properties). For some general concepts he is most adept at providing the names of instances.

The child's knowledge of these verbal concepts often appears to be instance-oriented and may well involve the use of imagery and the ability to recollect specific encounters with particular instances. The most dramatic advances in the child's expressible knowledge of verbal concepts beyond this rudimentary base include the ability to assign the concept to a superordinate class and the ability to describe characteristics of instances of the concepts other than the basic concrete ones (i.e., O properties in addition to L, A, F, and E properties) which include such characteristics as the relation of instances of the concept to other things in the world, their internal constituents, and their origins.

On the basis of analyses of specific conversations it was also hypothesized that, although they know a considerable amount about the concepts, including at times those properties which adults use to define them, preschool children do not always seem to realize that these properties are defining or, in other words, are the necessary and sufficient criteria for inclusion of instances within the concept. In the last part of this chapter this hypothesis will be subjected to test.

The Relation between Reference and Meaning in the Child's Verbal Concepts

Although the child is capable of describing properties which are true of at least some of the instances comprising the extension of certain verbal concepts (see preceding pages), his discussions often suggest that he is in fact describing attributes of particular instances of the concept which he has experienced. This may be why the attributes he comes up with are often neither true of all nor of only the instances included in the corresponding adult concept (e.g., "black" for DOG). The child, however, in many cases, does mention properties which correspond to the essential function of instances of the concept ("eat it" for FOOD, "drive it" for CAR) and at times certain properties which are almost defining of the instances of the concept (e.g., "bark" for DOG). In such cases it may seem that the word has roughly the same essential meaning for the child as for the adult in spite of less interesting quantitative differences in the amount of knowledge known. However, it is also possible that even though the child is capable of relating these properties they do not always guide his production (or comprehension) of them. That is, the meaning of the concept may not have crystallized yet even though his knowledge at times might include the essential ingredients. The analyses of the child's conversations about words presented in this chapter (see pp. 190–219) often suggested that this might be the case.

For example, even though the child might be able to recall that he has eaten things called *apples* and even though he might mention edibility in his definition of *apple,* this function may not necessarily be a necessary criterion which will always guide his application of the term *apple* to other objects. Since such a criterion has not been formulated by the child as essential, he may use the term to classify objects which, though bearing superficial perceptual similarity to the instances comprehended by the term *apple,* are not considered to be instances of the concept according to adult standards. Such an analysis might explain why children were observed to be willing to classify a balloon and a rubber ball as an APPLE (see Chapter 6).

In fact many of the overextensions made by young children can be viewed in just this way. Similarly, many of their underextensions can be interpreted along the same lines as well. For example, even though the child might know that food is to eat, or that clothing is what you wear, and even though he might mention these aspects when discussing or defining *food* and *clothing,* it is possible that he nonetheless not always uses edibility or wearability as the sufficient condition for his inclusion of instances within the concepts. Thus he might not think of a cookie or ketchup as food or of a shoe or a hat as clothing since he does not always use edibility or wearability criterially in tests of comprehension of these concepts. This line of argument leads to the prediction that the characteristics of instances of a concept described by children in their definition will not always be used by them criterially in classifying objects within those concepts; that since the essential function or defining property of the concept has not crystallized for the child as essential or defining, he will misclassify instances and noninstances in a way that will violate his sometimes seemingly apt definitions; that his expressed meaning of the word will not necessarily control his linguistic behavior when he uses that word to refer to objects spontaneously nor when he classifies objects into categories denoted by the word.

Fortunately, the data collected in one of our previous studies allows for a rather direct test of this possibility. Recall that in the underextension experiment reported in Chapter 5 we had obtained definitions from children of the terms *animal, food, clothing,* and *bird,* in addition to having them classify pictures as being instances or noninstances of the corresponding concepts. In view of the arguments presented above, we decided to see whether or not the child was consistent in his classification behavior with the definition of the concepts which he had provided.

To answer this question we began by examining the definitions of each of the four concepts discussed in Chapter 5 provided by the twenty children and by the ten adults who had participated in that study. Table 7.4 shows a rather detailed classification of the definitions provided by children into fifteen types of definitions. It shows that children tended to define *animal* in terms of examples (e.g., "lion, tiger, dog"); that they tended to define *food* sometimes in terms of examples ("cereal, soup"), sometimes in terms of function ("eat it"), and occasionally in terms of both; that they tended to define *clothing* in terms of function ("you put them on," "people wear") and in terms of examples (e.g., "pants"); and that they tended to define *bird* in terms of the actions of instances of the concept (e.g., "it flies"). It should be noted that there are a number of exceptions to the predominant forms of definitions just described, as can be seen in Table 7.4.

Table 7.5 shows a similar breakdown of the definitions produced by adults. The two most striking differences between the definitions provided by adults and by children are that (1) adults give most (90 percent) of their definitions in terms of a general class and a differentiating property, whereas children give most (82.5 percent) of their definitions without mention of a general class; (2) for the general concepts ANIMAL, FOOD, CLOTHING, there is a strong tendency in children to give a list of examples

TABLE 7.4 *Breakdown of the definitions provided by twenty children in Experiment 5.1*

	E	F	A	P	F/E	A/E	A/P	DK	?	G+D F	G+D A	G+D P	G+D F/E	G+D A/P	G E
Animal	16	0	0	0	1	1	0	1	1	0	0	0	0	0	0
Food	7	5	0	0	3	0	0	0	0	3	0	0	2	0	0
Clothing	5	8	0	0	1	0	0	0	2	3	0	0	1	1	0
Bird	0	0	11	2	0	1	0	1	0	0	3	2	0	0	0
Total	28	13	11	2	5	2	0	2	3	6	3	2	3	0	0
%	35	16.25	13.75	2.5	6.25	2.5	0	2.5	3.75	7.5	3.75	2.5	3.75	0	0

NOTE: E = examples or instances are listed as a definition; F = the functions of instances are given as a definition; A = the actions of instances are given as a definition; P = some other property of the instances of the concept are given as a definition; F/E = both instances and the function of instances are given as a definition; A/E = both instances and action of instances are given as a definition; A/P = both actions of instances and other properties of instances are given as a definition; DK = "don't know"; $?$ = difficult to classify; $G\&D{:}F$ = definition presented as a general class and a differentiating property where the property was functional; $G\&D{:}A$ = definition presented in terms of a general class and a differentiating property where the property was an action of instances of the concept; $G\&D{:}P$ = definition presented in terms of a general class and a differentiating property where the property was neither the function of instances of the concept nor an action; $G\&D{:}F/E$ = definition given in terms of a general class and a differentiating property which was functional and some instances of the concept; $G\&D{:}A/P$ = definition given in terms of a general class and two differentiating properties one of which was an action and one of which was some other property; $G{:}E$ = a definition given in terms of a general class and the names of some instances.

TABLE 7.5 Breakdown of the definitions provided by ten adults in Experiment 5.1.

	E	F	A	P	F/E	A/E	A/P	DK	?	G + D F	G + D A	G + D P	G + D F/E	G + D A/P	G E
Animal	0	0	0	0	0	0	0	0	1	0	4	3	0	1	1
Food	0	0	0	0	0	0	0	0	0	10	0	0	0	0	0
Clothing	0	0	0	0	0	0	0	0	1	9	0	0	0	0	0
Bird	0	0	0	1	0	0	1	0	0	0	0	2	0	6	0
Total	0	0	0	1	0	0	1	0	2	19	4	5	0	7	1
%	0	0	0	2.5	0	0	2.5	0	5	47.5	10	12.5	0	17.5	2.5

NOTE: The typology of definitions is the same as for Table 7.4.

whereas adults never just list the names of instances in defining the term.

But what of the relation between the extension of the class and the definition of the class? To answer this question we have re-examined the classification of pictures by each child in relation to the definition of the concept given by that child and have classified the definitions into three types: (1) those definitions which were consistent with the child's classification behavior (C); (2) those definitions which were not consistent (N); and (3) those definitions which were of indeterminate status (I). To count as consistent (C) the child had to have included all and only the pictures which in our judgment showed instances of the class of things defined in the child's definition. To count as not consistent (N) the child had to have excluded instances (or included noninstances) which violated the definition of the class he had given. When examples were given as definitions, and when in the two cases the child said he did not know how to define the word, these responses were treated as of indeterminate (I) status with respect to the issue of consistency of definition.

In categorizing the definitions in this way we wanted to be sure that the violations of definitions were genuine (i.e., conceptual as opposed to perceptual as described in Chapter 5) and so we took into account the terms the children had used to name the pictures in addition to their classification of them. Thus, in order to count as a violation of a definition, the child must have excluded or included a picture which, in view of his name for it and his earlier definition, he should have included or excluded, respectively. Therefore, if the child had defined *food* as "you eat it" but then had said "no" when asked of the picture of a lollipop if it was *food,* in order for this definition to count as not consistent with his classification behavior, his name for the picture must have been the name of an edible object (e.g., *lollipop, candy*), and not the name of some nonedible object (e.g., *stop sign*).

Table 7.6 shows the resulting breakdown of the eighty definitions produced by children into these three types and also the forty definitions produced by adults which were treated in the same way. Table 7.6 shows that children were rarely consistent in their classification of pictures with the definitions they had provided of the concepts being tested, whereas

TABLE 7.6 *Total number of definitions for both children and adults which were consistent with* (C) *their performance in the underextension experiment, not consistent* (N) *with that performance, and of indeterminant status* (I).

	C	N	I
Children	$\frac{4}{80}$	$\frac{46}{80}$	$\frac{30}{80}$
Adults	$\frac{33}{40}$	$\frac{6}{40}$	$\frac{1}{40}$

adults, usually, though not always, were. A Mann-Whitney U test showed that the adults produced significantly more consistent definitions than did the children ($U = 2$, $p < .001$). Indeed, as Table 7.6 shows, only four out of eighty definitions provided by children were consistent with their classification behavior. While a considerable number of the definitions (thirty out of eighty) were of indeterminate status, more than half (forty-six out of eighty) were violated in their classification of the pictures. Adults, on the other hand, usually produced definitions which were consistent with their classifications (thirty-three out of forty). Moreover, in those cases when an adult did violate his definition, he would sometimes note the violation and point out that his definition should be modified. For example, two adults who had earlier defined *bird* in terms of the capacity for flight, when asked if two penguins depicted in a photograph were birds, said they were but pointed out that their definitions should be modified since not all birds fly. Such observations, combined with the degree of consistency found between the adults' definitions and their classification behavior, suggest that in making judgments about which instances to include in a given concept, the adults often formulate something like a definition of the concept and use that definition as a guide in judging whether a given object is an instance or not.

It is far less likely that children are this reflective or analytic when they first use language to classify objects. They have great difficulty in formulating a definition for some of the concepts (e.g., ANIMAL) and although they sometimes seem capable of formulating reasonable definitions of some other concepts (e.g., FOOD), even in such cases their classification behavior is usually inconsistent with the reasonable definitions that they do provide. Moreover, it was our impression that the child would not have deliberately attempted to formulate a definition on his own had we not asked him to. Thus the child's categorization of the world through language appears to be based upon mechanisms which operate less consciously, less reflectively, and less analytically than is the case for adults. The nature of the more primitive conceptual structure underlying the child's first terms of reference will be considered in the next and final chapter.

Chapter 8

Conclusions:
Implications for a Theory of
Conceptual Development

At the end of Chapter 1, I identified three sets of questions, the answers to which I argued were basic to an understanding of the conceptual structure beneath the child's first terms of reference. The sets of questions concerned the order of acquisition of terms of reference, the extension of those terms of reference in the child, and their intension for him, respectively. Chapters 2 through 7 presented a series of empirical studies which were aimed at providing answers to those questions. We are now at last in a position to draw some conclusions. In this final chapter, at the risk of some redundancy, I shall attempt to review the answers emerging from the empirical studies to the three sets of questions and to characterize the nature of the child's concepts in view of these conclusions.

The objects which the child first learns to name are those with which he first interacts. Some of these objects are related to the fulfillment of his basic biological needs, such as the food he eats, the clothing he wears, and the people who care for him. Others are less intimately related to his survival, such as the toys and games with which he plays. Still others are objects which are simply interesting to look at and listen to which often (though not quite always) move and change in interesting ways in his environment. Prominent among these interesting objects are animals and people.

In Chapter 2 it was shown that among the most frequently occurring names of objects in the vocabulary of Grade 1 children (according to

Rinsland, 1945) the most numerous were the names of animals, of people, of food, of toys, games and sports, of body parts, of clothing, and of furniture and parts of the house. Moreover, it had previously been shown that the frequency of occurrence of words according to Rinsland was an especially good predictor of the order of acquisition of words in the pre-school child. Thus the inference was made that these are just the kinds of terms of reference learned by the child when he first acquires language. This conclusion was consistent with our research in which we examined the child's ability to produce terms of reference in obligatory contexts (see Chapter 2). It is also confirmed by the work of other authors who have recorded and classified the words used first by children in their spontaneous speech (see Leopold, 1939; Nelson, 1973b; Rescorla, 1976).

The words the child first learns to refer to those objects with which he interacts are often terms of an intermediate level of generality which, in the adult lexicon at least, classify the world into categories which are not too big but then again not too small. It is true that among the very first words learned by children are the proper names of specific people and pets which are especially significant in their lives (see Moore, 1896; Huttenlocher, 1974) and the names of especially important specific people such as *Mummy, Daddy,* and *baby* (see Lewis, 1959; Bloom, 1973; Thomson and Chapman, 1975). However, for many of the objects which the child first learns to name, the terms he acquires are at some intermediate level of generality and only later will he acquire more specific and more general terms to denote them. For instance, our studies have shown that typically the child learns the term *dog* before *collie* or *animal, flower* before *rose* or *plant, car* before *Volkswagen* or *vehicle,* and so on (see also Brown, 1958b). Thus there is neither a unidirectional specific-to-general nor a unidirectional general-to-specific progression in the acquisition of category labels. Rather, vocabulary development is characterized by the complementary trends of differentiation and of hierarchic integration which may be processes of cognitive development more generally (see Werner, 1948).

The order of acquisition of terms of reference within a hierarchy is predicted only modestly well by various measures of frequency of occurrence based upon adult use such as Thorndike and Lorge (1944), Kucera and Francis (1967), and Howes (1966). It is predicted extremely well by frequency of occurrence based upon Grade 1 children's spoken and written material according to Rinsland (1945). Since there is neither an invariant specific-to-general progression nor an invariant general-to-specific progression the order of acquisition of terms of reference within a hierarchy is not well predicted by a metric of semantic complexity based solely upon intension, nor one based solely upon extension (see Chapter 2).

As argued in Chapter 2 the failure of either definition of semantic complexity to predict the order of acquisition of English nomenclature is not really that surprising. Each definition generates exactly the opposite prediction and so unless one were all important and the other of absolutely no relevance, neither progression would be followed exactly. Moreover, the definitions were formulated in terms of the "true" extension and the "true" intension of the words but the criterion that was used to establish their order of acquisition did not require that the child understand either their exact scope (extension) or their full meaning (intension). Rather the primary criterion of acquisition of a given word that was used was that the child be able to produce it in certain obligatory contexts which would have been possible without his comprehension of its "true" extension or "true" intension. It was argued that it would be unreasonable to employ criteria of acquisition which required mastery of the exact extension and full intension of any given word since even most adults would not be able to satisfy such stringent criteria. In any event, the likelihood that either definition of semantic complexity would predict the order in which children acquire English nomenclature would seem to be less than if the criterion of acquisition involved complete mastery of the components involved in the definitions. Finally, it was pointed out that the cognitive capacities of the child and the functions of language would militate against either of the unidirectional progressions suggested by the definitions of semantic complexity. For it was argued that, with respect to the words first learned by the child, there would be a pull in the direction of generality to reduce the number of words which would have to be committed to memory and a pull in the direction of specificity to increase the communicative value of the terms learned by him.

For these reasons it perhaps should not surprise us that neither definition of semantic complexity proved to be predictive. However, recently arguments have been made that complexity will prove to be predictive of language development in general (see Brown, 1973; Slobin, 1971) and evidence has been offered to support the contention that semantic complexity in particular is predictive of the order of acquisition of certain domains of linguistic units such as the grammatical morphemes studied by Brown and his colleagues (see Brown, 1973; de Villiers and de Villiers, 1974), of English kin terms (see Haviland and E. Clark, 1974), and of others (see H. Clark, 1973a, E. Clark, 1973). The metrics of semantic complexity which have been used in such studies bear little resemblance to the definition of semantic complexity in terms of extension which we have considered.[1] However, they do often appear to be quite similar to

[1] To my knowledge the only author who seems to have explicitly argued that there is an invariant specific-to-general progression in the order of acquisition of category labels was John Locke (1690, Book III). In the present author's previous monograph

our definition of semantic complexity in terms of intension in that a morpheme or term is viewed as being composed of or requiring control of a number of meaning components and the morpheme or term associated with a set of such components is defined as semantically more complex than a morpheme or term associated with just a subset of those components. Such notions of cumulative semantic complexity seem quite similar to the definition of semantic complexity in terms of intension which has been considered in this book. Indeed, it seems that any definition of semantic complexity in terms of meaning components such as semantic markers, features, criterial attributes, and the like would generate the same prediction that our definition of semantic complexity in terms of intension made—namely, that there would be a unidirectional general-to-specific progression in the order of acquisition of hierarchically related terms. Such a prediction is clearly contradicted by the results presented in this book. This state of affairs raises questions concerning the differences between our studies of the order of acquisition of English nomenclature and those other studies which seem to have shown semantic complexity to be predictive. More broadly it raises questions concerning the generality of the power of complexity to predict the order of language acquisition.

These are extremely complex issues which it will not be possible to resolve completely here. However, some comments would seem to be in order. First, it should be noted that there are a number of differences between the present investigation of the acquisition of English nomenclature and the other studies which have suggested that semantic complexity is predictive, any of which may be responsible for the apparent discrepancy. Three kinds of differences may be especially important. First, there are differences in the domains of linguistic units studied. The present study was concerned with the names of objects. On the other hand, Brown's study, for example, was concerned with fourteen grammatical morphemes (such as the plural *s,* the progressive inflection *ing,* etc.). The study by Haviland and Clark admittedly was concerned with a subset of English nomenclature, namely kin terms, but these are basically relational words unlike those with which we have been primarily concerned in this

---

an argument was made for a concrete-to-abstract progression in the development of the appreciation of the relations among words (Anglin, 1970). That is to say, it was argued that the child is able to appreciate the similarity between *boy* and *girl* before *boy* and *horse, boy* and *horse* before *boy* and *flower, boy* and *flower* before *boy* and *chair,* and so on. I continue to interpret the data presented in that monograph as consistent with a concrete-to-abstract progression in the reorganization of the subjective lexicon. However, the results of the present book rule out the possibility of an invariant specific-to-general progression in vocabulary development. There may be a concrete-to-abstract progression in cognitive development, but there is not an invariant concrete-to-abstract progression in vocabulary development.

book. It is possible that semantic complexity is predictive of the order of acquisition of the linguistic units within certain domains but not others.

Second, it is quite possible that while semantic complexity was correlated with the order of acquisition of the linguistic units being studied in those investigations, it was not responsible for that order of acquisition. For example, in Brown's study a metric of grammatical complexity made roughly the same predictions that were made by the metric of semantic complexity and it is possible that grammatical rather than semantic complexity was chiefly responsible for the order of acquisition of the morphemes. In the study by Haviland and Clark, to take another example, it is quite possible that some other variable such as frequency of occurrence was more directly responsible for the progression.

Finally, it has been noted that in the present study the criterion used to establish whether or not a given term had been acquired did not require complete control on the part of the child of the components involved in the definitions of semantic complexity whereas in the other studies the criteria used (e.g., 90 percent correct use in obligatory contexts in Brown's [1973] work; definitions specifying the components in Haviland and Clark [1974]) often did in fact require their control by the child. This may well have been a crucial difference.

Some developmental psycholinguists are so committed to the belief that semantic complexity determines the order of acquisition of language that they will continually redefine semantic complexity until a definition is found which is at least moderately predictive (e.g., Haviland and Clark, 1974). Often definitions of semantic complexity are formulated after the order of acquisition of a set of linguistic units has been established which makes the semantic complexity hypothesis less convincing. It is possible that there is some alternative metric of semantic complexity for terms of reference that ultimately will be shown to be predictive of their order of acquisition but I am inclined to doubt that any such metric will provide a perfect or even a nearly perfect predictor. There appear to be substantial individual differences in the order of acquisition of English nomenclature even when only a given set of hierarchically related terms is considered. For some hierarchies such as *collie, dog, animal* and *Volkswagen, car, vehicle* most children appear to acquire the terms within the hierarchies in the same order. However, for other hierarchies such as *dime, coin, money,* and *rose, flower, plant* there appear to be greater individual differences in the order in which the terms within the hierarchies are acquired (see Chapter 2). This kind of flexibility alone would seem to bring the hypothesis that a single metric of semantic complexity is invariably predictive of the order of acquisition of hierarchically related terms of reference into question.

Of course our studies were almost entirely concerned with English nomenclature. And as noted above, there may be some domains of linguistic units for which complexity provides a good predictor of their order of acquisition. My suspicion is that complexity may well predict the order of acquisition of the grammatical transformations the child acquires as he develops. However, I suspect that the order of acquisition of vocabulary and specifically content words such as nouns, verbs, adjectives, and the like will not be especially well predicted by any metric of semantic complexity. Rather I think that they will be better predicted by considerations of relevance to the child, function, and frequency of occurrence. Apart from the case of English nomenclature this is primarily speculation on my part. However, this speculation does receive a modest degree of support from our analysis of the words used in tests of definitions in the Stanford-Binet IQ Test. For it was shown that the difficulty of vocabulary is highly correlated with frequency of occurrence of the words according to a number of measures of frequency regardless of whether the vocabulary consisted of nouns or of words from other parts of speech (see Chapter 2).

I am certainly not trying to argue that there is no validity to the hypothesis that the child's semantic system becomes more complex with development. Indeed, our studies have indicated that the child's understanding of a word does become more complex after it has been acquired. For example, the child continues to acquire more knowledge about the verbal concepts that he learns and increasingly he incorporates them into a hierarchic system of concepts. I am not even trying to argue that semantic complexity will play no role in determining the order in which he first acquires vocabulary. However, I am trying to urge that there is another factor which may be even more important in influencing the order in which he first learns words. This other factor has to do with use or function or consequentiality. With respect to English nomenclature I believe that the order of acquisition of this linguistic domain is a reflection of the naming practices of parents, practices which are ultimately based upon their anticipation (whether conscious or unconscious) of the functions of the objects named in the life of the child.

It has been pointed out that the child is somewhat selective in sampling vocabulary from the linguistic input to which he has been exposed (Leopold, 1939; Nelson, 1973b). It has also been shown that there is only a very modest correlation between the frequency of occurrence of grammatical morphemes in the speech of parents to children and the order of acquisition of those morphemes (Brown, 1973; de Villiers and de Villiers, 1974). Nonetheless, as pointed out in Chapter 3, baby talk—the language used by parents when addressing their children—most often includes terms of reference which are kin names, animal names, the names of body parts, the names of games and playthings, and so on. These are just the kinds of terms which children in fact seem to acquire first (see Chapter 2; also see Leopold, 1939; Nelson, 1973b; Rescorla, 1976). Moreover, in our studies it was shown that there was a tendency in mothers to tailor the names they transmitted to their children in the direction of greater frequency and greater generality in comparison to the names they transmitted to other adults. Thus mothers would tend to name a collie a *dog,* a carnation a *flower,* a dime *money,* and so on when addressing their children whereas they were more inclined to use more specific and less frequent terms when addressing adults. The terms addressed to children were just the kinds of terms the studies in Chapter 2 had shown that children acquire first. These findings are consistent with the proposal that to some extent at least the child's first terms of reference are a product of the naming practices of parents.

It was further argued that parents name objects for children in the particular ways they do as a first step in signaling to the child the functions those objects will play in his life. That is to say, they provide the child with words which group together objects toward which he should behave in the same way (see also Brown, 1965).

As a partial test of this hypothesis, after explaining to two groups of adults who were either teachers of children or parents what was meant by "behavioral equivalence", we asked them to rate the terms within a set of hierarchies of nested category labels for their degree of "behavioral equivalence" for the two-year-old child (see Chapter 3). These sets of terms were the same ones for which we had previously determined the order of acquisition in children as described in Chapter 2. The result of both studies was that in seven out of eight hierarchies the adult judges rated the term which children had previously been shown to acquire first as being most behaviorally equivalent for the two-year-old child. Thus, for example, the adults rated *car* as being more behaviorally equivalent than either *Volkswagen* or *vehicle, dog* as being more behaviorally equivalent than *collie* or *animal, flower* as being more behaviorally equivalent than *rose* or *plant, money* as more behaviorally equivalent (for the two-year-old child) than *dime* or *coin,* and *apple* as being more behaviorally equivalent than *fruit* or *food.* I consider these findings to be suggestive evidence in support of the hypothesis that adults will first name, and that therefore children will first learn, terms of reference which group together objects toward which they should behave in the same way.

I should point out that I do not view this study as definitive. One problem was that ratings of behavioral equivalence when produced by adults who were not familiar with children were not as consistent with the order of acquisition of the words by children as when they were produced by parents or teachers of children. This in itself is not that troublesome since the hypothesis really was concerned with adults familiar with children and especially parents, since they are the ones who presumably most often transmit vocabulary to children. However, their very familiarity with children may have made them aware of the kinds of words children actually learn first and it is possible that this knowledge may have influenced their ratings even though the instructions said nothing of the words learned first by children. Nonetheless, parental and teacher ratings of behavioral equivalence of these terms of reference have proved to be more consistent with their order of acquisition than a variety of other dimensions along which we have asked adults to scale them. Thus these results are at least consistent with the hypothesis that parents will initially label objects with names which classify the world into groups of things which will be behaviorally equivalent for the child.

The hypothesis that behavioral equivalence is implicated in the level at which children first learn to categorize objects is related to and fairly consistent with some recent arguments made by Rosch (Rosch, 1976; Rosch et al., 1975) concerning what she calls "basic level objects." In Rosch's work a basic category is empirically defined as the most inclusive category within a hierarchy of categories which according to adult ratings include instances which possess significant numbers of attributes in common, are used by means of the same motor programs, are similar in shape, and can be recognized from averaged shapes of the instances of the category. One of Rosch's conclusions is that they will be the first named by children as they learn language.

Notice that one important element in her definition of basic level objects is in terms of function, specifically motor programs which can be evoked by all of the instances in the category. This emphasis on function or use is very similar to the central element in what I have been calling behavioral equivalence. Indeed, since function is often intimately related to form and to the attributes of objects in the majority of cases, the child's first terms of reference will in fact often be at a level of generality which Rosch calls "basic." However, the argument here is that function is in some sense primary and occasionally the child will first learn to categorize objects at a level which is more specific or more general than Rosch's basic level or at least than the most inclusive level which includes instances which overlap in shape.

For example, it has often been pointed out that among the very first terms acquired by children are *Mummy* and *Daddy* or *Mama* and *Papa* and the like. These terms are more specific than the most inclusive terms which would refer to all objects which are similar in shape to the child's parents. The fact that children seem to learn these specific terms to first designate their parents is consistent with the functional argument that is being advanced here. *Mummy* and *Daddy* are important to the child in their uniqueness and play a different role in his life than the other people he will eventually encounter. Of course the child may not always use the terms *Mummy* and *Daddy* to refer to just his parents. It has often been pointed out that initially he will call other women and other men *Mummy* and *Daddy* respectively. While this tendency to overgeneralize these terms is not quite as prevalent as has often been assumed, it undoubtedly occurs in some children. However, the issue which we are addressing here is what terms enter the child's vocabulary first and not their extension which will be considered shortly. The point is that when a particular object in the child's world is especially functionally significant to him he will often learn a name to denote that object which is more specific than the most inclusive term which refers to objects which are similar in shape.

A similar example is that when there is a pet in the child's home he will often learn its proper name rather than the more generic term which would correspond to what Rosch calls the basic level (see for example Huttenlocher, 1974). Thus the child will often learn to call the family pet *Rover* rather than *dog* or *Morris* rather than *cat*. Such observations are again consistent with the functional argument which has been adopted here. The pet is important in its uniqueness and it is to be treated differently from the other dogs or cats which the child will eventually encounter.

Inversely, there will be occasions in which the child will first learn a term which is more general than the most inclusive term which refers to objects which overlap in shape. Our studies have shown that most often mothers will name a dime *money* rather than *coin* or *dime* and that children most often (though not always) will acquire the term *money* before the alternatives. The most inclusive term which refers to objects which are similar in shape in the dime-coin-money hierarchy is *coin* but our studies indicate that this is the last of these terms typically acquired by children. The fact that *money* is often the first of these terms acquired by children is consistent with the functional argument which is being advanced here. While it is important for adults to know the specific denominations of currency, it is not so important for the child who is learning a first language since he has not yet become entangled in the world of buying and selling. Rather, what is important for him to know as far as his parents are concerned is that he should treat all of the things called *money* with due respect—that is, he should not eat them, nor lose them, but rather put them safely away in Mummy's purse or Daddy's wallet or his piggy bank.

The functional interpretation being presented here carries with it the implication that objects especially significant in the child's life will be named with specific terms for him and that objects of little significance in his life will be named with more general terms. A related cross-cultural implication of this view is that when a given domain of objects is especially significant in one culture, children growing up in that culture will learn to categorize that domain with more specific terms than will children growing up in other cultures in which that domain is of less importance. In support of this contention is the widely cited fact that Eskimos have no generic term for snow but rather a number of specific terms to denote particular kinds of snow (Birket-Smith, 1936; Whorf, 1956). Since there is no general term *snow* it is clear that Eskimo children will first learn to categorize this domain with terms which are more specific than those learned by children growing up in California for example.

It should be emphasized that often children will learn terms at a level of generality which corresponds to the basic level as Rosch defines it.[2] Occasionally, however, children will first learn to categorize an object with a term which is either more specific (e.g., *Mummy*) or more general (e.g., *money*) than this basic level (at least as it is defined in terms of overlap of shape) and often when this is the case the term will be at a level of abstraction which is consistent with the functions of that object in the life of the child.

In conclusion then, the functions served by objects are implicated in both horizontal and in vertical vocabulary development. The child will learn the names of objects with which he interacts whether the interaction fulfills basic needs such as eating food or whether the interaction is less intimately related to his survival such as playing with toys or simply looking at salient objects (see also Leopold, 1939; Stern, 1930; Lewis, 1959; Nelson, 1973b). Moreover, because of the ways in which parents will name these objects for him he will initially learn terms often at some intermediate level of generality which classify them in maximally useful ways in the sense that they group together objects toward which he should behave in the same way (see also Brown, 1958, 1965).

The conclusions described thus far in this chapter are consistent with the conclusions reached by others concerning the order of acquisition of English nomenclature. Specifically, the present conclusions concerning horizontal and vertical vocabulary development involve a kind of synthesis of arguments made previously by Nelson (1973b, 1974) and by Brown (1958b, 1965). However, the child's first words cannot be taken as a direct measure of his concepts since as argued earlier it cannot be assumed that when a child has first acquired a word that it has the same meaning for him as for the adults who observe him. Throughout this book the notion CONCEPT has been defined as all of the knowledge possessed by an

---

[2] In addition to having adults rate the words within the eight hierarchies studied in Chapters 2 and 3 for behavioral equivalence we also had other adults rate the words in terms of the most inclusive level which refers to objects which are similar in shape. The result was that in five out of eight hierarchies such ratings predicted the level at which children first learn category labels whereas ratings of behavioral equivalence predicted in seven out of eight hierarchies.

individual about the category of objects denoted by a term including both knowledge of extension and knowledge of intension. The results reported in Chapters 4 through 7 have indicated that the concepts underlying the child's words differ from the corresponding adult concepts in both their extension and their intension.

The child's first terms of reference do not refer to exactly the same sets of objects as those which are denoted by the corresponding adult terms. This has been pointed out and carefully documented by a variety of authors (see for example Leopold, 1939, 1949a,b; Chamberlain and Chamberlain, 1904a,b; Lewis, 1959; Piaget, 1962; E. Clark, 1973; and of course the present volume). However, in view of our results it would appear that the differences between the extension of the child's term and the corresponding adult term have been to some degree often misinterpreted in two ways. First, the extent of the differences does not appear to be as great as has at times been suggested (see Brown, 1958b; Anglin, 1970; E. Clark, 1973). That is to say, the range of referents to which a child will apply a given word, while not identical, nonetheless often overlaps to a considerable degree with the corresponding range of referents to which adults apply the same term. The reason perhaps that the differences in extension have been overemphasized is that when the child misapplies a word it is both more striking and more interesting than when he applies that term appropriately. Second, the child does not only overextend his first terms of reference as has often been assumed. Of equal importance are cases of underextension. The reason why overextension has been emphasized and underextension has, for the most part, gone unnoticed is probably that conclusions concerning the extension of the child's words have usually been based upon the child's spontaneous production of those words. Although a careful examination of the diary literature does, in fact, reveal cases which can be plausibly interpreted as underextension (see Chapter 4) there are strong biases in favor of overextension and against underextension when the only source of information is the child's spontaneous production. The child's limited vocabulary will virtually force him to overgeneralize a term when he wants to refer to an object for which he does not have a name even though he may not really think that that object is appropriately designated by that term. Of even deeper significance is the fact that if he does not realize that an instance is included in a concept he probably will not name it at all and therefore on such occasions the potential evidence for underextension will go unnoticed since the child has not spoken. If he does name it incorrectly his behavior will be viewed as a case of overgeneralization of the inappropriate term.

Our studies (see Chapters 4 through 6) which for the most part were tests of comprehension rather than production and which therefore circumvented the problems inherent in the diary literature revealed that the preschool child both overgeneralizes and undergeneralizes his first terms of reference relative to adult standards. Indeed, in the study in which we attempted to create an equal opportunity for each kind of response we found that children undergeneralized approximately twice as frequently as they overgeneralized. It is not my intention, however, to argue that the child's propensity to undergeneralize is greater than his propensity to overgeneralize. Rather my position is that he does both (which means, to be slightly simplistic, that overlap of reference is the most common relation between the extension of the child's term and the extension of the same term as used and understood by adults), and that the task for a psychologist is to discern and to try to understand the conditions which will influence him to do either. Our studies have suggested that whether the child will overgeneralize or undergeneralize a given term of reference depends upon a variety of factors, the following four of which appear to be most important.

First, it will depend upon the particular child in question. Some children will overgeneralize certain terms whereas others will undergeneralize those same terms while still others will neither overextend nor underextend them. In general in the two-to-five-year range younger children make both kinds of responses more often than older children. However, in Chapter 4 it was shown that the ratio of underextension responses to overextension responses remains roughly constant over this time period suggesting that it is not the case that younger children overgeneralize relatively more often than they undergeneralize as compared to older children, at least in comprehension.

A second factor concerns the conditions under which the child's terms of reference are studied. Specifically, for reasons which have been described, overgeneralization is more obvious when based upon studies of production. Underextension is more striking when based upon studies of comprehension (see Chapter 4). Huttenlocher (1974) has pointed to this sort of asymmetry between comprehension and production and has even suggested that the child never overgeneralizes in tests of comprehension. However, our studies have in fact shown that the child does at times overgeneralize in tests of comprehension just as he does at times undergeneralize in production. On the other hand it does seem to be the case that overextension is clearer in production and underextension is clearer in comprehension.

A third factor concerns the particular concept being investigated. In general, as argued above, the relation between the extension of the child's concept and the extension of the corresponding adult concept is one of overlap, with the child both overgeneralizing and undergeneralizing relative to adult standards. However, certain concepts appear to be more often overgeneralized by preschool children whereas others are more often undergeneralized. Thus, though by a judicious choice of instances and non-instances a clever experimenter would usually be able to show both overgeneralization and undergeneralization for any given concept, certain concepts do appear to be more likely to be associated with one kind of response than the other. For example, the preschool child's concept of FLOWER often extends beyond the corresponding adult concept since he often includes several other kinds of plants such as elephant's ears, philodendrons, and cacti in the concept FLOWER. On the other hand, the child's concept of PLANT is often less general than the adult's since he will often not include certain kinds of plants such as trees and sometimes flowers in the concept PLANT. Thus the concept FLOWER usually becomes more restricted with development whereas the concept PLANT usually becomes more general.

The more general concepts, such as PLANT, which we have examined usually evoke underextension to some degree. For example, children often would not count as instances of the concept ANIMAL such creatures as butterflies and praying mantises whereas in our studies adults always did. They invariably refused to classify humans as animals whereas again adults always did. Similarly the concept FOOD often appeared to include fewer instances for children since they would sometimes not classify such edible objects as lollipops, cake, and ketchup as FOOD whereas adults would.

Although such general concepts tend to be associated with undergeneralization in the child, it is not the case that more specific concepts are invariably associated with only overextension. The concept FLOWER as discussed above does in fact seem to be primarily associated with over-extension in the young child. However, in Chapter 5 it was shown that the child's concept of BIRD does not always include all the instances which comprise the extension of the adult concept since many children declined to count certain atypical birds such as penguins, ducks, and chickens as instances. In our studies the extension of the concept DOG appeared to be very close to the adult extension with just occasional overgeneralization or undergeneralization (see also Palermo, 1976). This is interesting in view of the fact that DOG has so often been used as the example "par excellence" to illustrate overgeneralization in the child. It might be argued that this apparent discrepancy is based upon the fact that the children studied in our experiments were somewhat older (two to six years) than the children discussed in the diary literature who are usually between one and three years. However, recently Rescorla (1976) has found that even in one to two year olds overgeneralization of *dog* is not universal (although it does appear to occur with greater frequency at this age than in two to five year olds). Even quite specific concepts will not invariably be associated with overgeneralization. As pointed out in Chapter 4 even adults will not include certain instances in some very specific concepts such as TULIP or CHRYSANTHEMUM.

Finally, perhaps the most important factor influencing whether a child will overgeneralize or undergeneralize his first terms of reference concerns the nature of the instances and noninstances of the concept being studied. With respect to the instances of a concept it now appears that the most important factor influencing the child to undergeneralize has to do with the degree of exemplariness or goodness or centrality of those instances to the concepts in question (see Rosch, 1973, 1975). Our study of the determinants of underextension in the child (see Chapter 5) revealed that children almost always included instances which had been rated by adults as being central to a concept regardless of whether they were familiar (e.g., horse or cat to ANIMAL) or unfamiliar (e.g., aardvark or wombat to ANIMAL). On the other hand they often failed to include instances which had been rated by adults as being peripheral regardless of whether they were familiar (e.g., butterfly or ant to ANIMAL) or unfamiliar (e.g., centipede or hydra to ANIMAL). There was in our research only one case of a fairly central instance (according to adult ratings) which promoted a high degree of underextension in children. This case was the picture of a woman. Children invariably refused to classify the woman as an animal, even though we have found that adults generally rate people as being moderately central to the concept ANIMAL. Apart from this one case, however, when children undergeneralize it most often appears to be to instances which are atypical or peripheral members of the concept which is undergeneralized.

A second aspect of the instances of concepts which may also be a factor in enticing the child to undergeneralize a term of reference has to do with the familiarity of the instances. Although the effect was not nearly as strong as the central-peripheral effect, children more often excluded familiar instances from concepts than unfamiliar instances which may often have been a result of the fact that they knew a dominant name for a familiar instance ("That's a butterfly, not an animal") which they did not know for unfamiliar instances such as a centipede (see also Inhelder and Piaget, 1964). It is possible that the case of children's refusal to classify the woman as an ANIMAL mentioned above was in part a result of this factor for they were often observed to say something like "That's a woman, not an animal."

In the majority of cases when the child undergeneralized in our studies his problem appeared to be conceptual in origin rather than a result of perceptual confusion. Children would most often correctly identify the instance but still would not assign it to the concept under study. For example, they showed that they recognized a butterfly since they named it *butterfly* but still they denied that it was an ANIMAL; they could identify a shoe as a *shoe* but still denied that it was CLOTHING; they identified a lollipop as a *lollipop* but still denied that it was FOOD; they could correctly identify a duck as a *duck* but still denied that it was a BIRD. Thus the child will often not include instances in concepts which are rated by adults as being peripheral to those concepts even though he can recognize them and identify them correctly with a specific name.

With respect to the noninstances of a concept it appears that perceptual similarity between the noninstance and an instance of the concept is by far the most important determinant of overgeneralization in the child. In our studies of comprehension, in our study of production, and in our analysis of the diaries perceptual similarity invariably emerged as the most powerful determinant of overextension. In this respect the conclusions of the present book are in substantial agreement with those of E. Clark (1973, 1974) and also with those of Bowerman (in press). In the majority of cases (about three-quarters) in which overgeneralization appears to be based upon perceptual similarity, the noninstance appears to be similar in shape or over-all appearance to an instance of the concept over-generalized. Occasionally, however, other factors seem to be involved in such overextensions. These include similarity of substance or texture, similarity of parts, similarity of sound, similarity of movement, and similarity of size. Sometimes the overextensions are in roughly the right semantic domain from the adult point of view (e.g., *rabbit* to refer to another animal) but often the child crosses such semantic domains in his overgeneralization applying a term to some quite unrelated object from the adult point of view except for a superficial perceptual similarity which is usually based on shape (e.g., *ball* for a dome on an observatory).

Although the overwhelming majority of overgeneralizations appear to be based upon perceptual similarity other factors do occasionally seem to play a role. The most significant of these appears to be association through contiguity as when the child calls a saddle a *horse*. Although such overextensions were observed in our studies of comprehension, in our study of production, and in our analysis of the diaries arguments can be made that such responses are less stable and perhaps more primitive than those based upon perceptual similarity (see also Moore, 1896; Vygotsky, 1962). In our experiments they were most often made by the youngest children who were studied whereas overgeneralization based upon perceptual similarity occurred throughout the two-to-five-year range. Moreover, children were found to be less likely to "stick to their guns" when retested in such cases than when retested for overextensions based upon perceptual similarity. Finally, statements made by the child in such cases sometimes indicated that he perhaps did not really think of the noninstance as being a referent of the term overgeneralized in spite of his overextension. For example, when asked of a lunch bag, "Is this bread?" one child said "yes" but later remarked, "You put bread in it," suggesting that he did not really think it was bread but rather that his affirmative response to our question was more a statement on his part that he saw a connection between the lunch bag and bread.

Our results suggest that functional similarity by itself rarely entices a child to overgeneralize a given term of reference. No such cases were observed in our experiments and only five of the two hundred and thirty-six overextensions found in the diaries appeared to be based upon functional similarity alone. Moreover, in some of these few cases, arguments could be made suggesting that perceptual similarity was also involved. Thus these results run counter to some of the empirical findings of Nelson (1973a) (although they are consistent with some of her theoretical statements implicating form in concept identification) and to theoretical positions which have advocated use as the primary determinant of overgeneralization (see Werner and Kaplan, 1963). Of course form and function are often correlated and when they are it is not possible to tease out the factor most responsible for overextension. However, in our studies in which we attempted to do so it was found that perceptual similarity alone was often enough to evoke overgeneralization (e.g., *apple* to ball) but that functional similarity alone was not (e.g., *car* to sled).

In both our experiments and in the diaries there were cases in which overgeneralization occurred to objects which were both perceptually similar and functionally similar or both perceptually similar and likely to be seen in the presence of an instance of the concept overgeneralized. If we had no other information it would be difficult to establish which factor was most responsible for the overextension. However, in view of our findings concerning overgeneralization when only one of the factors could have been involved it is possible to speculate that perceptual similarity is most often responsible even in cases where the factors are confounded.

Very occasionally overgeneralization appears to be based upon factors other than the ones discussed above. For example, there is the occasional case of overextension seemingly based upon affect or emotion as when the child cries "mama" when he is in distress or wants something (Lewis, 1959; Piaget, 1962). Or there is the occasional case which appears to be based upon a phonetic similarity between the word overextended and the appropriate name as when Hildegard called a barber shop *barbecue* (Leopold, 1949b). However, such cases appear to be quite rare especially in comparison to the large number of overextensions which appear to be based upon perceptual similarity.

In conclusion then the extension of the child's first terms of reference is often not the same as the extension of those same terms as used and understood by adults. However, the differences between the scope of the child's concepts and those of adults is not quite as great as has at times been suggested. Moreover, the child undergeneralizes as well as overgeneralizes his first terms of reference. Whether the child will overextend or underextend these words depends upon a variety of factors the most important of which appear to be the particular child in question, the conditions under which he is observed, the particular terms of reference involved, and the nature of the instances and the nature of the noninstances of the concept being studied.

Our approach to the study of the intension of the child's terms of reference involved an examination of the knowledge which he was capable of expressing about them with a special emphasis on his definitions of them. We adopted this approach because it seemed to be a rather direct method of examining the properties which the child associates with his terms of reference (i.e., their intension for him) and because earlier observations had suggested that even quite young children are willing and able to define or otherwise express their knowledge of the meanings of words. It is possible that our results were biased to some unknown degree by constraints in the child's capacity to perform in the medium involved (i.e., his ability to converse about words) but as it turned out children did, in fact, have quite a lot to say about the words we discussed with them. It is also possible that there are other approaches to the study of the intension of such words in the young child but no obvious approaches would seem to be as direct. Notice that it would not have satisfied our purposes to study the behavior of the child with respect to the objects which were referents of the words we wished to study. For our concern was with the intension or meaning of the words themselves and not with the objects denoted by those words.

Our results suggested that even three-year-old children have some rudimentary knowledge which they are capable of expressing about most of the words which we studied out of the context of specific referents of those words. To be sure adults are capable of expressing more knowledge of every kind about each verbal concept but it is important to give the child credit for the considerable knowledge which he is capable of describing. For basic verbal concepts (i.e., those in any given hierarchy of terms which he learns to name first such as DOG, CAR, APPLE, FLOWER) he appears to be quite adept at expressing certain kinds of properties. Specifically our studies indicate that he is from an early age capable of ascribing four kinds of properties to such verbal concepts: (1) properties which describe what instances of the concept look like; (2) properties which describe what instances of the concept do; (3) properties which describe the uses to which instances of the concept are put; and (4) properties which describe where instances of the concept are found.[3] For

---

[3] Actually children in this study did at times indicate that they knew perceptual properties of the instances of some concepts other than just visual properties and in

some more general concepts such as ANIMAL he appears to be most adept at providing the names of instances.

The child's knowledge of these verbal concepts often appears to be instance-oriented, may involve the use of imagery, and seems to be based upon his ability to recall specific encounters with particular instances.[4] Children in discussing the words often were observed to bring the conversation to the level of particular instances which they had experienced and, as noted above, usually mentioned particular instances when discussing general concepts such as ANIMAL. Such observations led us to describe the child's knowledge of verbal concepts as being instance-oriented and it is this feature of his knowledge which may well lead him to mention properties which are neither true of all nor of only the instances included in the corresponding adult concept (e.g., "brown and white" for DOG). Nonetheless, it must be admitted that in their descriptions of the function of the instances of a concept, and to a lesser extent, the actions of instances of a concept, children were often observed to mention properties which are quite apt from the adult point of view. That is, the child was sometimes capable of specifying the essential function ("eat it" for FOOD) or an almost defining action ("bark" for DOG) of instances of the concept—the kinds of properties that adults in fact use in their definitions of such verbal concepts.

The most dramatic advances in the child's expressible knowledge of verbal concepts beyond this rudimentary base include the ability to assign the concept to a superordinate class and the ability to describe characteristics of instances of concepts other than the four basic "concrete" ones mentioned above. These other more "abstract" characteristics include such properties as the relation of instances of the concept to other things in the world, their internal constituents, and their origins.

Although in discussing the words children were sometimes able to mention the properties which adults use to define them, there were indications that they may not have realized that those properties were defining. For example, one young boy, Peter, did mention that you "eat it" when discussing *food* but he did not mention it until rather late in the conversation and he also mentioned *chairs* in his list of instances of the concept. Such observations are consistent with the hypothesis that even though children often know a considerable amount about a given concept, in-

---

particular the sounds made by instances. For example, some children said that dogs "bark" or that cars go "voom." These were treated as "properties which describe what instances of the concept do" in our analysis but they do indicate that children know auditory properties as well as visual properties of the instances of at least some concepts.

[4] The fact that conceptual knowledge in the child appears to be based upon personal experiences or "episodes" may well mean that semantic memory has its origins in and grows out of episodic memory (see Tulving, 1972).

cluding the properties which adults use to define it, they may not realize that these properties are defining or in other words the criteria which determine what objects are instances and what objects are noninstances of that concept. In other words, the meaning of the child's terms of reference may not have crystallized even though his knowledge may at times include the essential ingredients.

Many of the child's overgeneralizations and undergeneralizations can be viewed in this way. For example, even though the child might recall and express the kinds of things he has done with a ball (e.g., that he has bounced it, rolled it, thrown it) and the kinds of things it has done (e.g., that it has rolled under the couch), neither these functions nor actions will necessarily be the criteria which guide his application of the term *ball* to objects. Since such criteria have not been formulated by the child as essential, he will misuse the term in his spontaneous speech to refer to objects which, though bearing superficial perceptual similarity to the instances appropriately denoted by a given term of reference, are not considered to be instances of the concept according to adult standards. Such an analysis might explain why Leopold's daughter, Hildegard, for example, after having learned a word to refer to a ball (*ba*), applied it on two separate occasions to a dome on an observatory seen in the distance (see Leopold, 1939). According to the present line of argument she may have done so because, although she may have known that she had bounced and rolled some things called *ball,* bounceability and roll-ability were not criterial in her application of the term as yet.

This example should illustrate the major difference between the line of argument being espoused here and that presented by Nelson (1974) for Nelson has discussed the example of BALL in detail to illustrate her theory of early conceptual development. While the argument outlined here shares Nelson's assumption that function as she defines it is in fact often the essence of the meaning of verbal concepts, it differs somewhat with respect to its interpretation of the meaning of words to young children. In Nelson's theory the word is simply appended to a concept which is already well formed on the basis of a "functional core," and no semantic changes in the word's meaning are discussed beyond the child's acquisition of a verbal label, presumably since it is well formed from the outset. According to the present argument, the meaning of the word has not crystallized for the child at the outset, which is why he will overextend it (and underextend it) in production and comprehension.

The same sort of argument might account for the fact that the Chamber-lain's daughter applied the word *moon* to such diverse objects as a half a biscuit, cakes cut out of dough, round marks made on a frosted window, round objects pictured in books, round candies, and so on. It is possible that she could recall that *moon* was used by her parents to refer to a round object shining in the sky but that neither "shining" nor being "in the sky" were criterial for her in her application of the word which is why she applied the term to round candies and the like.

In some cases the essential function may not even be a part of the child's knowledge of a given concept. For example, in our studies children were often observed to agree that a pile of buttons was *money* (see Chapter 6). In this case it seems likely that the younger children to do so may not have even known the role money plays as a commodity of economic exchange. Similarly, Leopold (1939) had observed his daughter Hildegard applying the term *tick-tock* to such objects as a gas meter, a red spool of a fire hose, a bathroom scale, and so on. Again, it seems unlikely that she would have known of the essential function of clocks which is to indicate time (see also Nelson, 1975; Rescorla, 1976). In other cases, however, young children may know that some of the instances denoted by a term are used for certain purposes or act in certain ways but nonetheless not invariably use these functions or actions criterially when using that term to refer to other objects (see the discussion of *ball* above).

The child's underextension behavior may be interpreted in a similar fashion. Sometimes when the child undergeneralizes, his knowledge of the concept may not even include the information which is critical in the adult's definition of that concept. However, at other times his knowledge may include the relevant information but still he may not use it as the criterion which determines membership in a given concept. For example, even though the child might know that he has eaten food or that he wears clothing and even though he might mention edibility and wearability in his definitions of *food* and *clothing,* it is possible that he nonetheless not always uses edibility or wearability as the sufficient condition for his inclusion of instances within the concepts with the result that he may sometimes exclude edible objects (e.g., lollipop) from the concept FOOD and wearable objects (e.g., hat) from the concept CLOTHING.

Such an argument was borne out by our analyses of the child's definitions obtained in the underextension experiment and, in particular, of the relation between their definitions and their classification behavior. The definitions they produced were given primarily in terms of instances (for the concept ANIMAL) or in terms of function and/or instances (for the concepts FOOD and CLOTHING) or in terms of action (for the concept BIRD). The definitions they produced were in general consistent with the kinds of definitions which others have observed children to make (see Feifel, 1949; Feifel and Lorge, 1950; Wolman and Barker, 1965; Al-Issa, 1969; Campbell, 1975) with one exception which was that in our study there was a striking tendency among children to provide the names of instances of some of the concepts (ANIMAL, FOOD, and CLOTHING), a tendency which had not been previously reported. This discrepancy is undoubtedly due to the fact that the other studies never examined the child's definitions of general concepts. The two most striking differences between the definitions provided by adults and those provided by children were that: (1) adults expressed most of their definitions in terms of a general class and a differentiating property, whereas children usually did not mention a general class; and (2) for the general concepts, as noted above, there was a strong tendency in children to list instances whereas adults never just listed names of instances in defining a term.

The child's definitions were at least in some cases quite apt (e.g., "food is to eat," "you wear clothing"). However, when we compared his definitions with his classification behavior it was found that children were rarely completely consistent in their classification behavior with the definitions they had provided even in cases in which their definitions seemed quite appropriate. For example, one child when asked to define FOOD responded "eat it" but in the classification task said that edible objects (which he could correctly identify) such as a piece of bread, a lollipop, and ketchup were not FOOD.

Such observations might seem to pose a problem for any attempt to characterize the nature of the child's concepts. In cases in which the child's definition is appropriate but his classification behavior reveals that he does not include the same instances in a concept that an adult does, it might seem that one is forced to choose one or the other of these observations as in some sense the most valid index of the child's concepts. If one chooses the definition the conclusion might be that his concept is basically the same as that of an adult in spite of differences in the amount of knowledge known. If one chooses the classification behavior, however, it might seem that the child's concept is fundamentally different from that of an adult. However, the notion of a concept as it has been used throughout this book is all of the knowledge possessed by an individual about a given category of objects including both his knowledge of its extension and his knowledge of its intension. The fact that the child's classification behavior is usually inconsistent with his definitions suggests that his concepts are characterized by a lack of coordination between intension and extension (see also Inhelder and Piaget, 1964). Intension and extension may initially have somewhat independent courses of development.[5]

Adults, on the other hand, usually produced definitions which were

---

[5] It may have occurred to the reader throughout this book that even though the child does at times overgeneralize a given term of reference, he may not actually think that the object wich evokes the overgeneralization is really an instance of the concept overgeneralized. For example, when the child calls a balloon an *apple,* he may not necessarily pick it up and eat it. Similarly, when the child undergeneralizes, it may seem that the child might not actually think that the object which he fails to assign to a verbal category is really not an instance of the concept undergeneralized. For example, when the child denies that a lollipop is *food* he still may proceed to pick it up and eat it. Actually, the present line of argument is consistent with such intuitions for this is what is meant by a lack of coordination between extension and intension.

consistent with their subsequent classifications. Moreover, in those cases in which an adult did violate his definition in his classification behavior, he sometimes noted the violation and pointed out that his definition should be modified. For example, as reported in Chapter 7, two adults who had earlier defined BIRD in terms of the capacity for flight, when asked if two penguins were birds agreed that they were but pointed out that their definitions should be modified since they realized that not all birds (such as the penguins before them) do in fact fly. Such observations combined with the degree of consistency found between the adult's definitions and his classification behavior suggest that adults do at least strive to coordinate extension and intension and that in deciding which instances to include in a given concept often have recourse to something like a definition which they can rely upon as a guide in deciding whether any given object is an instance or not.

Preschool children, however, appear to be less reflective and analytic when they first use language to classify objects. They have great difficulty in formulating a general definition for some concepts such as ANIMAL and although they sometimes seem able to formulate reasonable definitions of some other concepts such as FOOD their classification behavior is usually inconsistent with the reasonable definitions that they do provide. In fact children gave little evidence of relying on definitions at all in the under-extension study and we felt that had we not asked them for definitions, they would not have attempted to formulate verbal criteria at all in the classification task.

Thus preschool children do not overtly spontaneously verbalize criterial attributes and, we suspect, do not covertly formulate such criterial attributes consciously in categorizing objects with language, whereas adults often seem to. How then do children categorize the world with language? What mechanism determines the extension of their first terms of reference? [6] Although I think the terms are problematic (see Schwartz, 1968; Goodman, 1968; Fodor, 1975) our findings discussed above and indeed most of our findings concerning the extension of the child's terms of reference (see Chapters 4, 5, and 6) are consistent with the notion that the mechanism for categorization in the child is "iconic" whereas the mechanism for categorization in adults involves an interplay of "symbolic" and "iconic" elements (see especially Posner, 1973, Chapters 3 and 4; see also Bruner, 1964; Bruner, Olver, and Greenfield, 1966; Piaget, 1962, pp. 213–91). Our results on underextension in the child

---

[6] At this point the narrative becomes fairly speculative and it seems possible that future research will show my account of the child's capacity to categorize to be wrong or at least in need of modification. Nonetheless the ensuing account represents my best guess as to the mechanism underlying the child's classification behavior in view of the research reported and reviewed in this book.

bear some affinity to the recent work discussed in Chapter 1 on the formation of schemas or prototypes in adults (see for example, Posner and Keele, 1968, 1970; Posner, 1969; Evans, 1967; Franks and Bransford, 1971; Reed, 1972; see also Rosch, 1973, 1975). These studies have suggested that when presented with a series of instances of a given concept or pattern adults tend to form a schema or prototype which represents the central tendency of the instances presented. Subjects appear to store in memory a prototype along with information about the individual instances of a concept and some notion of the boundaries of the concept which they can later use in identifying instances of that concept. Posner (1973) in reviewing the work on the formation of prototypes argues that it is a relatively primitive process performed by animals as well as by humans and does not require the conscious analysis of a concept into a set of attributes or features which he argues is a more advanced process.

Our findings concerning the extension of the child's terms of reference suggest that their categorization of the world through language may involve something at least analogous to a prototype or perceptual schema as well. The fact that children will usually include instances rated as central to concepts whereas they will often not include instances rated as peripheral (see Chapter 5) is consistent with such an argument. The fact that children's overextensions are predominantly to noninstances which are perceptually similar, and in particular, similar in shape, to instances of the concept overgeneralized (see Chapter 6) is consistent with the notion that in assigning objects to categories they employ their knowledge of the typical form of the instances of a given concept, that is, a prototype. And the fact that children do not seem to attempt to consciously decompose a concept into its criterial attributes when identifying instances of that concept suggests that they are probably relying on some more primitive process in their classification, one which may well involve a prototype or schema (see Posner, 1973, Chapters 3 and 4). These findings while consistent with the notion that children store a prototype of the instances of a concept might only indicate that they store images of specific instances of that concept which they have seen before. However, one of our most intriguing findings is that young children almost invariably recognize totally unfamiliar objects as instances of a concept provided they are central to that concept. For example, twenty out of twenty children in the underextension study identified a wombat and an aardvark as ANIMALS even though they had never seen a wombat or an aardvark before. Such observations clearly indicate that the child's capacity to categorize is based upon a generative or productive mechanism which is capable of classifying novel objects as well as familiar ones. Such observations are also similar to the findings of Posner and Keele (1968, 1970), Franks and Bransford (1971), and others that subjects will recognize a prototype as an instance of a concept or pattern even though they have never seen it before and they suggest that the child's classification of the world through language involves the use of a mechanism which is at least analogous to a prototype rather than just a stored record of specific examples.

One can carry the analogy between the child's classification of the world through language and the classification behavior of subjects studied in the prototype literature only so far however. The research on prototypes has been done for the most part with geometrical figures and random dot patterns whereas when the child first learns language he uses it to classify real objects. In our research on the extension of the child's terms of reference we used materials which we hoped would approximate the kinds of real objects that the child classifies naturally, namely pictures of real objects. Both our studies with pictures of real objects and the diary literature which describes the child's linguistic classification of real objects suggest that the mechanism of classification in children is somewhat more complicated than a straightforward analogy with the prototype literature might suggest. For one thing children in real life can classify objects when seen from different perspectives and also on the basis of just a part of an object. Generally in the research on prototypes the patterns to be classified are all presented on a two-dimensional surface in their entirety and are seen from the same perspective. Moreover, although the majority of the child's overextensions seem to be based on a similarity of shape or typical form, there are undoubtedly occasions in which he overgeneralizes on the basis of some other single striking aspect of the object identified and the instances of the concept overgeneralized such as similarity of a salient part, of size, of texture, of movement, and the like. Indeed, when the child's use of a given term is studied in enough detail it is sometimes found that he will overgeneralize the term not on the basis of one such aspect but on the basis of a number of different ones on different occasions (see Leopold's [1949a] discussion of Hildegard's application of the term *choo choo* to a variety of objects ranging from a train, to a psychological apparatus, to an airplane, to a wheelbarrow, to a streetcar, and to a trunk; see also Thomson and Chapman, 1975). Such observations are reminiscent of Vygotsky's discussion of what he called associative complexes in which the child groups together objects with a nuclear object not on the basis of one single criterion but on the basis of a number of different "bonds" between the nuclear object and the others (Vygotsky, 1962; see also Bruner and Olver's 1973 discussion of "key rings"). Moreover, the child's classification is not always based upon visual information. For example, the child may categorize an object solely on the basis of its sound as in the case of Hildegard who said *firecracker* when hearing thunder or in the case of Piaget's child who overgeneralized the term *tch tch* which had initially been applied to a train to any noise heard on the street (see Leopold, 1939; Piaget, 1962). The research on prototypes has been concerned with visual stimuli only and not with other modalities such as audition. It has also been observed in our studies and in the diaries that children will sometimes overgeneralize a term to an object bearing little perceptual similarity of any kind to the instances of the term overgeneralized but rather to ones which might be seen in the presence of an instance of the term overgeneralized. Such overextensions which seem to be based upon association through contiguity, while not nearly so frequent as those based upon perceptual similarity, do nonetheless occur from time to time among younger children at least. Finally, the child often probably begins to acquire his verbal concepts after only a few pairings of the name with an instance (or instances) and even possibly in some cases with only one such pairing.

The observations described above would seem to rule out the simple kind of template matching discussed by Neisser (1967) as the basis for the child's classification of the world through language. And although much of the evidence tempts me to hypothesize that children form a prototype or perceptual schema and employ it in classifying objects, other aspects of the evidence such as those just discussed force the view that at the least the basis for categorization in the child is more complicated and flexible than the prototypes formed and employed by subjects in the prototype research. One way of viewing the formation and use of the mechanism underlying the child's classification behavior is as follows: As the child is exposed to instances of a concept a perceptual record is laid down in his memory, a record which includes not only information about what those instances look like but, in some cases at least, other kinds of perceptual information such as the sounds they make, how they feel, how they move, and so on, and also the contexts in which they occur. Initially, the child may classify an object as an instance of a concept simply because it looks similar to part of the stored context. Later the child will not categorize an object on the basis of association through contiguity, although information about the context will still be part of his memorial record. From the outset as the child is exposed to instances he will form a conception of their typical form, and in some cases at least their typical sound, their typical movements, their typical feel, and so on, as well as some notion of the variability of which they are susceptible. Thus the child will form something analogous to a prototype but in this case the prototype will be multimodal.

The prototype will initially be based upon the first object which is named in the presence of the child and therefore will consist of whatever perceptual information the child remembers of that object although it may also incorporate other information the child had previously stored about such objects. As the child encounters more instances his prototype will become a more generalized conception, a central tendency. The objects which provide the fuel for the formation of the prototype may well include not only objects which are named in the child's presence but also objects which the child encounters which he believes belong to the class. This belief may well be based upon an innate tendency to generalize to objects which he perceives as being perceptually similar to the stored prototype. Because the child will experience different instances or the same instance from different perspectives, he will form some conception of the variations in orientation which are possible. His memorial record will also include information about specific instances although this information may be subject to more rapid decay or at least may become less accessible than the prototype (see Posner, 1973). According to this account, in classifying objects children will often assign an object to a category if the over-all shape of the object conforms to the typical form of the stored prototype allowing for variations in orientation. In other cases, however, the child will at times classify an object as an instance of a given concept if the object possesses just one striking perceptual aspect in common with the stored prototype such as a similar part, a similar texture, a similar sound, and so on.

With the kinds of modifications indicated in the above admittedly speculative and *ad hoc* description, a view of the child's linguistic classification based upon a prototypelike mechanism will account for most of the data on the extension of the child's terms of reference. Of course, it is clear that children will often know more about a concept than just the perceptual information contained in the prototype and the rest of the perceptual record. Specifically, our studies of the intension of the child's terms of reference and of his definitions of them indicate that he also often knows the function of the instances of many concepts or in other words the uses to which they can be put. This functional knowledge, however, does not appear to play an important role in the process of categorization as our studies on the extension of the child's terms of reference have indicated (see especially Chapter 6). The act of categorization appears to be a fundamentally perceptual process and if the arguments presented here are well formulated may often involve the use of a prototypelike mechanism but one that is complicated along the lines described above.

This account of the child's capacity to categorize with language is at the same time an account of the extension of his verbal concepts, since their extension will consist of the objects which he will categorize with those verbal concepts. As for the intension of his verbal concepts as we have seen the child is often capable of ascribing properties to concepts which specify the functions of their instances. These function-related properties may have their origin in the sensorimotor schemes evoked by instances of the concept in the infant both prior to and during the time that he first learns words to categorize them (see Piaget, 1952, 1962; Inhelder and Piaget, 1964; also see Bruner, 1975). Thus the intension of the child's first verbal concepts seems to be at least partly consistent with the kind of functional model of concept formation discussed in Chapter 1. However, the intension of the child's concepts also often includes perceptual properties which specify such things as what instances of the concept look like, what they do, and where they are found. Thus the intension of the child's concepts appears to have its origin in his perception of their instances in addition to the actions they evoke from him.

Thus, as a first approximation, both the theory of concept formation based upon prototypes and the theory based upon function (described in Chapter 1), with some modifications, have relevance for a complete description of the structure of the concepts underlying the child's terms of reference. The former is implicated in their extension while the latter is implicated in their intension. According to the present account, because of either natural inclinations or constraints in capacity the preschool child does not seem to consciously abstract a conjunctive set of defining attributes in constructing his first concepts, which he uses to guide his classificatory behavior.

As the child grows the conceptual structure underlying his terms of reference will evolve in a number of ways. The number of concepts known will increase. The amount of knowledge known about each of his concepts will also increase so that eventually he will know such things as the relations of their instances to other things in the world, their origins, their internal constituents and so on. The scope of his concepts will increasingly approximate the adult standard. With development, although perhaps not seriously until after he has gone to school, he will attempt to consciously formulate the defining properties of his verbal concepts and will increasingly use those defining properties as a basis for categorizing objects. In other words, more and more he will use the intension of his concepts to determine their extension. Finally, he will increasingly organize his concepts into an interrelated hierarchic system. In adulthood English nomenclature constitutes an organized conceptual system and any given concept gains its meaning at least in part from its particular place within the system. For example, adults appreciate the hierarchic relations among verbal concepts (see for example Collins and Quillian, 1969, 1972; Miller, 1967, 1969; Mandler, 1967; Bower et al., 1969) so that they know for instance that OAKS are TREES and that TREES are PLANTS. Preschool children, however, have not organized their verbal concepts into such a system, at least not consciously. For example, in the classification study described in Chapter 4 they often failed to realize that the objects they called *trees* are also called *plants* and in attempting to define concepts they usually did not assign those concepts to superordinate classes which adults almost always did. The absence of this sort of hierarchic system is a striking feature of the child's concepts. The evidence (see Anglin, 1970; Vygotsky, 1962; Bruner and Olver, 1963) indicates that such a system develops only gradually after the child has gone to school.

A final qualification will bring this inquiry to a close. In this chapter and, indeed, throughout this entire book I have been contrasting the child's concepts with those of adults. This sort of comparative method has been adopted by most psychologists concerned with human growth and, indeed, it is difficult to imagine how else one should proceed in a developmental analysis. However, in the present case this comparative approach may at times have given the reader the impression that my view is that the conceptual behavior of the child is totally different from that of the adult. If at times I have overemphasized the differences and underemphasized the similarities and underlying continuities between the conceptual systems of children and of adults, I did so to indicate the direction of developmental change. In actuality my view is that there are important similarities as well as differences between adult and child, and that there is continuity as well as change in development. I have argued that the child, in categorizing the world with language, employs a mechanism which is at least analogous to a prototype and that adults more often consciously formulate criteria to guide their classification behavior. However, it is clear that adults at times employ a prototypelike mechanism in their classification behavior as well. It is just that more often than children they appear to have recourse to another method of classification. I have argued that the child's concepts are characterized by a lack of coordination between extension and intension and that the concepts of adults are characterized by a greater degree of such coordination. However, extension and intension are not completely uncoordinated in the child's concepts. Nor are they always perfectly coordinated in those of the adult. I have argued that the child's concepts are characterized by less differentiation and less hierarchic integration than the adult's concepts. However, the child's concepts are neither completely undifferentiated nor completely "concrete". Nor are the adult's concepts usually completely differentiated or as "abstract" as they could be.

It was pointed out in Chapter 1 that the natural concepts of adults are often fuzzy around the edges, and that it is often difficult to define them precisely in terms of a single fixed set of criteria. This, in fact, is often the case. Our studies have indicated that in comparison with the concepts of children those of adults are less fuzzy around the edges and that they often at least attempt to define them and use their definitions as a guide in classifying instances. However, it is nonetheless true that even adults have trouble classifying borderline cases, and that sometimes at least, their classification behavior is inconsistent with their definitions.

Perhaps the way to think of the relation between the child's concepts and those of adults is to postulate a continuum of concepts from primitive to scientific with the former being vague, concrete, undifferentiated, and completely lacking coordination between extension and intension and with the latter being precise, abstract, differentiated, and characterized by a complete coordination between extension and intension. On such a continuum the child's concepts would occupy a region closer to the primitive pole than to the scientific pole and the adult's concepts would be somewhere in the middle.

Thus adults do not lose the methods of conceptualization that they used when they were children although they may supplement those methods as they mature. As for children, it has not been my purpose to denigrate their conceptual skills. On the contrary, my intention has been to try to provide a realistic account of their truly remarkable facility in using language to categorize the complex world in which they live.

Appendix 1

Adult modal words and child modal words for each picture used in first order of acquisition experiment. The percentages of adults and of children producing each are included.

Picture	AMW	%A	%C	CMW	%A	%C
Apple₁	apple	75.00	93.33	apple	75.00	93.33
Apple₂	apple	65.00	83.33	apple	65.00	83.33
Apple₃	apple	80.00	83.33	apple	80.00	83.33
Apple₄	apple	65.00	93.33	apple	65.00	93.33
Lemon	lemon	100.00	30.00	lemon	100.00	30.00
Pineapple	pineapple	95.00	50.00	pineapple	95.00	50.00
Apple	apple	100.00	70.00	apple	100.00	70.00
Banana	banana	100.00	93.33	banana	100.00	93.33
Apple	apple	100.00	96.67	apple	100.00	96.67
Lettuce	lettuce	100.00	40.00	lettuce	100.00	40.00
Walnut	walnut	85.00	6.67	peanut	0.00	16.67
Bread	bread	100.00	90.00	bread	100.00	90.00
Rose₁	rose	95.00	30.00	flower	5.00	63.33
Rose₂	rose	95.00	20.00	flower	5.00	70.00
Rose₃	rose	95.00	30.00	flower	5.00	60.00
Rose₄	rose	95.00	26.67	flower	5.00	66.67
Daisy	daisy	65.00	20.00	flower	35.00	56.67
Rose	rose	95.00	30.00	flower	0.00	53.33
Carnation	carnation	95.00	0.00	flower	0.00	60.00
Pansy	pansy	35.00	0.00	flower	25.00	70.00
Elm	tree	100.00	86.67	tree	100.00	86.67
Rose	rose	85.00	13.33	flower	15.00	80.00
Rubber plant	rubber plant	55.00	0.00	plant	40.00	43.33
Cactus	cactus	90.00	13.33	plant	20.00	36.67

Picture	AMW	%A	%C	CMW	%A	%C
VW₁	Volkswagen	100.00	36.67	car	0.00	53.33
VW₂	Volkswagen	100.00	36.67	car	0.00	53.33
VW₃	Volkswagen	100.00	33.33	car	0.00	50.00
VW₄	Volkswagen	100.00	40.00	car	0.00	50.00
Model-T-Ford	old car	30.00	20.00	car	50.00	63.33
Cadillac	Cadillac	45.00	10.00	car	40.00	73.33
VW	Volkswagen	95.00	40.00	Volkswagen	95.00	40.00
XKE	Jaguar/sports car	35.0/35.0	0.0/0.0	car	5.00	76.67
Bicycle	bicycle	100.00	100.00	bicycle	100.00	100.00
VW	Volkswagen	70.00	36.67	car	25.00	50.00
Airplane	airplane	95.00	93.33	airplane	95.00	93.33
Train	train	90.00	96.67	train	90.00	96.67
Dime₁	dime	90.00	36.67	dime	90.00	36.67
Dime₂	dime	85.00	30.00	dime	85.00	30.00
Dime₃	dime	85.00	26.67	dime	85.00	26.67
Dime₄	dime	85.00	26.67	dime	85.00	26.67
Quarter	quarter	100.00	26.67	quarter	100.00	26.67
Dime	dime	100.00	36.67	dime	100.00	36.67
Nickel	nickel	100.00	23.33	nickel	100.00	23.33
Penny	penny	100.00	46.67	penny	100.00	46.67
Quarter	quarter	100.00	16.67	dime	0.00	30.00
$5 bill	$5 bill	70.00	3.33	dollar	0.00	70.00
Dime	dime	95.00	26.67	dime	95.00	26.67
Dollar	dollar	100.00	63.33	dollar bill	45.00	56.67
Collie₁	collie	95.00	3.33	dog	10.00	73.33
Collie₂	collie	95.00	3.33	dog	10.00	66.67
Collie₃	collie	95.00	3.33	dog	10.00	63.33
Collie₄	collie	95.00	3.33	dog	10.00	63.33
Bulldog	bulldog	100.00	10.00	dog	0.00	76.67
German shepherd	German shepherd	90.00	20.00	dog	10.00	56.67
Collie	collie	100.00	3.33	dog	0.00	63.33
Poodle	poodle	100.00	26.67	dog	0.00	56.67
Leopard	leopard	80.00	23.33	tiger	10.00	40.00
Collie	collie	90.00	3.33	dog	10.00	63.33
Toad	frog	100.00	70.00	frog	100.00	70.00
Duck	duck	100.00	70.00	duck	100.00	70.00
Shark₁	shark	95.00	23.33	fish	5.00	60.00
Shark₂	shark	90.00	20.00	fish	10.00	46.67
Shark₃	shark	90.00	23.33	fish	10.00	43.33
Shark₄	shark	90.00	30.00	fish	10.00	50.00
Guppy	fish	55.00	73.33	fish	55.00	73.33
Swordfish	swordfish	70.00	10.00	fish	15.00	60.00
Bass	fish	65.00	83.33	fish	65.00	83.33
Shark	shark	80.00	33.33	fish	15.00	50.00

Picture	AMW	%A	%C	CMW	%A	%C
Rhinoceros	rhinoceros	100.00	30.00	rhinoceros	100.00	30.00
Shark	shark	90.00	26.67	fish	10.00	50.00
Bear	bear	100.00	80.00	bear	100.00	80.00
Turtle	turtle	100.00	86.67	turtle	100.00	86.67
Chimpanzee$_1$	monkey	70.00	76.67	monkey	70.00	76.67
Chimpanzee$_2$	monkey	70.00	90.00	monkey	70.00	90.00
Chimpanzee$_3$	monkey	55.00	83.33	monkey	55.00	83.33
Chimpanzee$_4$	monkey	70.00	93.33	monkey	70.00	93.33
Monkey	monkey	90.00	83.33	monkey	90.00	83.33
Chimpanzee	monkey	60.00	93.33	monkey	60.00	93.33
Man	man	90.00	83.33	man	90.00	83.33
Orangutan	ape	35.00	0.00	monkey	30.00	43.33
Kangaroo	kangaroo	100.00	80.00	kangaroo	100.00	80.00
Pointer	dog	75.00	93.33	dog	75.00	93.33
Chimpanzee	monkey	65.00	83.33	monkey	65.00	83.33
Elephant	elephant	100.00	83.33	elephant	100.00	83.33
Robin	bird	80.00	93.33	bird	80.00	93.33
Piranha	fish	70.00	90.00	fish	70.00	90.00
Fly	fly	85.00	30.00	fly	85.00	30.00
Chimpanzee	monkey	70.00	86.67	monkey	70.00	86.67
Chimpanzee	gorilla	50.00	26.67	monkey	10.00	70.00
Tulip	flower	90.00	90.00	flower	90.00	90.00
Spruce	tree	70.00	86.67	tree	70.00	86.67
Seagull	seagull	75.00	10.00	bird	5.00	63.33
Boy$_1$	boy	84.62	78.26	boy	84.62	78.26
Boy$_2$	boy	84.62	78.26	boy	84.62	78.26
Boy$_3$	boy	92.30	78.26	boy	92.30	78.26
Boy$_4$	boy	84.62	78.26	boy	84.62	78.26
Girl	girl	92.30	82.61	girl	92.30	82.61
Boy	boy	92.30	82.61	boy	92.30	82.61
Girl	girl	92.30	52.18	girl	92.30	52.18
Boy	boy	61.52	76.61	boy	61.52	76.61
Girl	girl	76.92	69.57	girl	76.92	69.57
Woman	old woman	46.15	4.35	grandmother (nana)	7.70	30.44
Man	man	92.31	72.61	man	92.31	72.61
Boy	boy	76.92	69.51	boy	76.92	69.51

NOTE: *AMW* = adult modal word; *CMW* = child modal word; %*A* = percent of adults; %*C* = percent of children. Two words with a slash between them (/) indicate that for that picture two different names were given equally by either group when *AMW* or *CMW* was computed.

Appendix 2

The two hundred and seventy-five most frequently occurring names of objects in Rinsland, Grade 1 (1945), in Thorndike and Lorge's General Count (1944), and in Howes (1966). The words have been categorized by two adult judges into twenty-two semantic categories.

Category	Rinsland		Thorndike-Lorge	Howes
1. *Animals*	(36)		(7)	(5)
	animal	pony	animal	dog
	bear	puppy	bear	fish
	bee	rabbit	bird	fly
	bird	rat	dog	horse
	bunny	reindeer	fish	lobster
	butterfly	robin	fly	
	cat	snake	horse	
	chicken	squirrel		
	cow	sheep		
	dog	tiger		
	duck	turkey		
	elephant	turtle		
	fish			
	fly			
	fox			
	goldfish			
	horse			
	hen			
	kitten			
	kitty			
	monkey			
	mouse			
	pet			
	pig			
2. *People*	(35)		(57)	(73)
	ⓐ *Kin* (16)		ⓐ *Kin* (10)	ⓐ *Kin* (12)
	aunt	mother	brother	sister	brother	mother
	brother	papa	daughter	son	dad	parents
	cousin	sister	family	uncle	daughter	sister
	dad	uncle	father	wife	family	son
	daddy		husband		father	uncle
	father		mother		husband	wife
	grandfather					
	grandma					
	grandmother					
	grandpa					
	mama					
	mamma					
	ⓑ *Nonkin/Description* (11)		ⓑ *Nonkin/Description* (23)	ⓑ *Nonkin/Description* (27)
	baby	people	baby	girl	people	American	fellow	Negro
	boy	woman	boy	human	person	baby	folks	neighbor
	children		child	Indian	woman	boy	fool	man
	friend		children	lady	women	child	friend	men
	girl		enemy	lord	neighbor	children	German	patient
	kid		fellow	man		Catholic	girl	person
	lady		fool	master		Communist	guy	people
	man		friend	member		couple	kid	Russian
	men		gentleman	men		Cuban		woman
						customer		

Category	Rinsland	Thorndike-Lorge	Howes

(People, cont'd)

Rinsland

ⓒ *Occupation* (6)

clown	teacher
cowboy	
doctor	
farmer	
soldier	

ⓓ *Groups* (2)

band
party

ⓔ *Proper names* (0)

Thorndike-Lorge

ⓒ *Occupation* (12)

captain	king	queen
chief	knight	soldier
doctor	officer	
farmer	president	
judge	prince	

ⓓ *Groups* (7)

army	meeting
class	party
club	
crowd	
government	

ⓔ *Proper names* (5)

Arthur	John
George	Mary
Henry	

Howes

ⓒ *Occupation* (17)

boss	freshman	officer
cardinal	governor	president
dentist	instructor	professor
doctor	junior	student
engineer	Marine	teacher
	nurse	
	senior	

ⓓ *Groups* (14)

army	crowd	party
class	faculty	R.O.T.C.
club	fraternity	society
co-op	government	team
corps	Navy	

ⓔ *Proper names* (3)

Kennedy
Khrushchev
Lynn

---

3. Food

Rinsland (27)

apple	cookies	lunch
bread	corn	meat
breakfast	dinner	milk
brownie	egg	nuts
butter	food	orange
cabbage	fruit	pumpkin
cake	grocery	supper
candy	ice cream	toast
carrots	lettuce	vegetables

Thorndike-Lorge (8)

dinner
egg
food
fruit
meat
milk
salt
sugar

Howes (7)

cigarette
coffee
cream
food
milk
sugar
supper

Category	Rinsland	Thorndike-Lorge	Howes
4. *Toys, games, sports*	(24) ball, balloon, bat, bell, bicycle, block, card, doll, drum, football, game, gun, horn, jack-o'-lantern, marbles, scooter, sled, sleigh, swing, toy, tricycle, skate, slide, wagon	(3) ball, game, race	(8) ball, card, doll, equipment, football, game, race, sport
5. *Body parts*	(16) back, ear, eye, face, feet, finger, foot, hair, hand, head, heart, leg, mouth, nose, side, teeth	(25) arm, back, blood, body, ear, eye, face, feet, finger, foot, hair, hand, head, heart, knee, leg, lip, mouth, neck, nose, shoulder, side, skin, tear, wing	(15) arm, back, blood, eye, face, feet, foot, hand, head, heart, knee, leg, muscle, side, teeth
6. *Clothing*	(15) bow, cap, chain, coat, dress, gloves, handkerchief, hat, shoe, stocking, suit, sweater, tie, watch, clothes	(10) chain, clothes, coat, dress, hat, ring, shoe, suit, tie, watch	(6) belt, clothes, outfit, suit, tie, watch
7. *Furniture, parts of house*	(15) bath, bed, chair, door, fireplace, floor, kitchen, porch, room, seat, step, table, wall, window, yard	(14) bed, chair, door, floor, gate, hall, kitchen, room, seat, step, table, wall, window, yard	(13) bed, chair, door, downstairs, floor, kitchen, room, step, table, upstairs, wall, window, yard

Category	Rinsland	Thorndike-Lorge	Howes
8. *Elements*	(13) air, clay, fire, ice, light, rain, rock, sand, snow, water, weather, wind, wood	(22) air, coal, earth, fire, gold, ice, iron, light, oil, rain, rock, silver, smoke, snow, soil, stone, storm, water, wave, weather, wind, wood	(8) air, fire, gas, ice, light, rock, water, weather
9. *Buildings, places of occupation*	(11) ⓐ *General* (11): barn, building, church, farm, home, circus, hospital, house, school, shop, store — ⓑ *Proper names* (0)	(15) ⓐ *General* (15): bank, building, church, college, company, court, farm, home, house, market, office, school, shop, station, store — ⓑ *Proper names* (0)	(28) ⓐ *General* (24): apartment, bank, building, church, camp, court, company, college, factory, home, hospital, hotel, house, lab, library, lodge, market, office, school, shop, station, store, stage, university — ⓑ *Proper names* (4): B.U., Harvard, M.I.T., Northeastern

Category	Rinsland	Thorndike-Lorge	Howes

10. Geographic

Rinsland (10)
 (a) General (10)
  country, garden, ground, hill, park, place, river, spot, star, sun
 (b) Proper names (0)

Thorndike-Lorge (40)
 (a) General (31)
  bay, city, cloud, country, field, forest, garden, ground, hill, island, lake, land, mountain, nation, ocean, place, plain, river, sea, shore, sky, space, spot, star, state, stream, sun, town, valley, village, world
 (b) Proper names (9)
  America, Chicago, England, Europe, France, Germany, London, New York, Washington

Howes (43)
 (a) General (22)
  area, bay, beach, city, coast, country, field, ground, hill, island, lake, land, mountain, overseas, park, place, river, space, spot, state, town, world
 (b) Proper names (21)
  America, Boston, California, Cape, China, Cuba, England, Europe, Florida, France, Germany, Hampshire, Japan, Mass., Massachusetts, Mississippi, Puerto, Rhode, Rico, Russia, York

11. Tools

Rinsland (9)
 bag, basket, box, board, brick, paint, stick, string, wheel

Thorndike-Lorge (8)
 bag, board, box, case, machine, paint, post, stick

Howes (6)
 bag, block, board, case, stick, machine

12. Vehicles

Rinsland (7)
 airplane, boat, car, engine, ship, train, truck

Thorndike-Lorge (4)
 boat, car, ship, train

Howes (9)
 boat, bus, car, engine, plane, ship, trailer, train, truck

Category	Rinsland	Thorndike-Lorge	Howes
13. *Vegetation*	(7) flower grass hay leaf plant seeds tree	(6) branch flower grass plant rose tree	(1) plant
14. *Terms of quantity*	(6) bit lot pair part piece set	(9) amount bit group lot part piece set stock supply	(10) amount bit group lot part piece section set supplies unit
15. *Currency*	(6) bill cent dollar money nickel penny	(5) bill cent dollar money quarter	(5) bill cent dollar money quarter
16. *School items*	(6) desk book paper pen pencil tablet	(2) book paper	(2) book paper
17. *Written communication*	(5) letter newspaper page story valentine	(4) letter note page story	(3) letter newspaper story
18. *Kitchenware*	(5) bowl cup dishes glass stove	(2) cup glass	(0)

Category	Rinsland	Thorndike-Lorge	Howes
19. *Media for travel*	(4) bridge road street track	(3) bridge road street	(5) bridge dock road route street
20. *Media for communication, amusement*	(3) picture radio song	(3) picture record song	(6) picture phone movie record television T.V.
21. *General terms*	(2) kind thing	(8) article being kind material matter object sort thing	(8) article being kind matter sort stuff thing type
22. *Weapons*	(0)	(0)	(2) bomb missile
23. *Difficult to categorize (misc.)*	(13) cage candle color flag hole line name nest number word sentence tickets parade	(20) art circle color cross figure form hole line mark music name number point scene shade shape sign sound square word	(12) cross figure line mark mess name number point sign sound term word

Appendix 3

A classification of all the overextensions found in a number of sources. The overextensions have been classified as based primarily on perceptual similarity (Appendix 3A), as based primarily on functional similarity (Appendix 3B), as based primarily on association through contiguity (Appendix 3C), as overextensions to objects which were perceptually similar and functionally similar to instances of the term (Appendix 3D), as overextensions to objects which were perceptually similar and likely to be associated through contiguity with instances of the term (Appendix 3E), as overextensions to objects which were perceptually similar to, functionally similar to, and likely to be associated through contiguity with instances of the term (Appendix 3F), and as overextensions based on miscellaneous factors (Appendix 3G). By *source* is meant the particular diary or theoretical work from which the overextensions have been taken. Appendix 3 shows for each overextension its source and page number, the word overgeneralized, and the object evoking the overgeneralization.

APPENDIX 3A *Overextensions based primarily on perceptual similarity.*

Source	Word overextended	Object producing overextension
$C+C_1$-265	*moon (mooi, moo, moon)*	half of bisquit, cakes cut out of dough, round marks made on frosted window, water stains on ceiling, round objects pictured in books, round candies, any round mark
$C+C_1$-266	*bridge*	top of staircase, top railing of piazza
$C+C_1$-266	*bubbles*	marbled pattern inside book, patterned fabric
$C+C_1$-266	*chocolate*	metal plates of door lock
$C+C_1$-266	*wrinkles*	film on surface of milk
$C+C_1$-267	*bones*	hard moles on face

Source	Word overextended	Object producing overextension
$C+C_1$-267	flag (*tlag*)	barber pole
$C+C_1$-267	*water*	road in a forest picture
$C+C_1$-268	*lettuce*	foliage plants
$C+C_1$-268	*mouth (mouse)*	hole in the toe of shoe
$C+C_1$-269	*rabbit*	donkey
$C+C_1$-269	*dog*	lop-eared rabbit
$C+C_2$-454	*bath tub*	railroad turntable, wood and coal bin
$C+C_2$-454	*dusters*	long-stem ferns
$C+C_2$-454	*crumbs (trumbs)*	sparks from fireworks
$C+C_2$-454	*sailboat (tail-boat)*	figure 4
$C+C_2$-454	*Christmas tree* (*Chris'm tree*)	firs, pines, all kinds of evergreens
$C+C_2$-454	*mud*	fog clouds
$C+C_2$-455	*feet*	stones under a water pipe
$C+C_2$-455	*bathing hat*	halo of child in picture of Madonna and Bambino
$C+C_2$-455	*lettuce*	bayberry leaves
$C+C_2$-455	*gnats (nuts)*	ants
$C+C_2$-455	*braid*	twisted doughnuts
$C+C_2$-455	*red man*	large red buoy
$C+C_2$-455	*pipes*	telegraph poles
M-140	*bird*	cow, dogs, cats, any animals except flies
M-140	*papa*	any man
M-140	*fly*	bits of dust, specks of dirt, toes, crumbs of bread
M-140	*Mamie*	any lady at a window (was first used for a young lady in neighboring house at a window)
L-96	*mama*	female visitor
L-96	*mama*	picture of a smiling woman
L-133	*horse (hosh)*	large dog
L-133	*cat (tee)*	2 dogs, cows, sheep, 2 horses
S-146	*dolly*	pictures of children
S-146	*wow-wow*	pictures of animals
S-147	*moo-moo*	many animals in picture book, rocking horse
S-194	*goose (goos-goos)*	ostrich, camel, golden-crested wren, sparrow
S-194	*uncle (unkie)*	human skeleton and skull, men in pictures
S-194	*pussy*	bat, eagle-owl
L_1-40	*auto (?auto)*	complicated psychological apparatus, any riding motion
L_1-42	*papa (baba)*	any man
L_1-44	*ball (ba)*	dome of observatory, balls of yarn
L_1-48	*milk bottle (mIk balu)*	bottle with white tooth powder
L_1-80	*egg (?ɛk)*	egg-shaped rubber ball
L_1-114	*snow (no)*	something white on roof
L_1-118	*bottle pieks (balu pik)* (*pieks* was the child's idiosyncratic word for pencil)	medicine dropper

Source	Word overextended	Object producing overextension
L_1-124	*tick-tock (tI-ta)*	gas meter, red spool of fire hose, bathroom scale, machine with round dial, round typewriter eraser
L_1-126	*choo-choo (tʃutʃu)*	picture of psychological apparatus
L_1-131	*wauwau (waʊ waʊ)*	stone lion, soft slippers with dog's face on them, bronze horse book ends, picture of fur-clad old man, elephant-shaped ash tray, porcelain elephant, picture of a sloth, Easter lamb cake
L_1-137	*wheel (wiə)*	ring
L_2-2	*firecracker (waIgagaʃ)*	thunder
L_2-8	*man (mã)*	Mickey Mouse
L_2-8	*monkey (maki)*	Mickey Mouse
L_2-10	*bottle (balu)*	glass marble
P-216	*tch tch* (had been applied to a train)	any noise from street
P-216	*bow-wow*	pattern on a rug (horizontal line crossed by three vertical lines), horse, hens, cyclists, trucks pulled by railway porters
P-216	*daddy*	all sorts of men
P-216	*mummy*	a strange woman
P-217	*daddy*	Jacqueline, who held out her arms to the child as his father had done, male visitor, peasant lighting his pipe, any man who was 15–20 yards away, men in general
P-218	*bow-wow*	hen, cows; anything moving, from an ant to a tractor
P-223	*little man*	doll
P-224	*Uncle Alfred's garden*	another garden
P-225	*the red animal*	all red insects
W-226 (from Lombroso, 1909)	*afta* (drinking glass)	pane of glass, window
W-226 (from Sully, 1903)	*nurse* (had been overextended to sewing machine)	hand organ
	(had been overextended to monkey)	toy rubber monkey
W+K-118 (from Stern and Stern, 1928)	*pin*	breadcrumb, fly, caterpillar
B-73 (from Guillaume, 1927)	*breast (nénin)*	red button on a piece of clothing, point of a bare elbow, eye in a picture
B-73 (from Werner, 1948)	*afta* (drinking glass)	pane of a glass, window
B-78 (from Lewis, 1963)	*cat (tee)*	cow, horses
B-78 (from Lewis, 1963)	*horse (hosh)*	large dogs

Note: The following symbols have been used in the tables to indicate the sources: *Primary Sources:*

$C+C_1$ = Chamberlain and Chamberlain, 1904a
$C+C_2$ = Chamberlain and Chamberlain, 1904b
M = Moore, 1896, pp. 115–45
S = Stern, 1930
L = Lewis, 1959
L_1 = Leopold, 1939
L_2 = Leopold, 1949b
P = Piaget, 1962
Secondary Sources:
$W+K$ = Werner and Kaplan, 1963
W = Werner, 1948
B = Bloom, 1973

APPENDIX 3B   *Overextensions based primarily on functional similarity.*

Source	Word overextended	Object producing overextension
$C+C_1$-266	*bridge*	threshold of a door, wooden edge of a bathtub, window sill
L_1-126	*choo-choo (tʃutʃu)*	airplane
$W+K$-118 (from Stern and Stern, 1928)	*door*	cork

APPENDIX 3C   *Overextensions based primarily on association through contiguity.*

Source	Word overextended	Object producing overextension
$C+C_1$-267	*fingernails (tinger-ales)*	scissors
$C+C_2$-454	*tide*	float to which boats were tied
M-140	*fly*	toad
L_1-42	*piano (ba)*	piano stool
L_1-58	*brief (bitʃ)* (German for letter)	letter slit in door
L_1-94	*sandbox (jabak)*	sand
L_1-111	*nails (nea)*	fingernail file
L_2-9	*picnic (bikinik)*	refreshment stand
L_2-10	*auto Peter (ʔauto pita)* (his auto was important to the child)	Uncle Peter
L_2-24	*candy (tani)*	stick from ice cream bar
L_2-138	*eichhörnchen* (German for squirrel)	acorn
P-217	*daddy*	father's rucksack
P-217	*mummy*	mother's clothes in a cupboard
W-226 (from Lombroso, 1909)	*qua-qua*	water
W-226 (from Darwin)	*quack*	water, all liquids

Source	Word overextended	Object producing overextension
W-226 (from Lombroso, 1909)	*afta* (drinking glass)	contents of glass
W-226 (from Sully, 1903)	*nurse* (*mambro*) (had been overextended to hand organ)	sewing machine, monkey
W-226 (from Egger, 1903)	*papa*	all father's possessions
W+K-118 (from Stern and Stern, 1928)	*nose*	handkerchief
B-73 (from Guillaume, 1927)	*breast* (*nénin*)	picture of mother's face
B-73 (from Werner, 1948)	*qua-qua* (duck)	water
B-73 (from Werner, 1948)	*afta* (drinking glass)	contents of glass
B-100	*dada*	father's bathrobe, father's briefcase, bottles of gin and vermouth

APPENDIX 3D   *Overextensions to objects which were perceptually and functionally similar to instances of the term.*

Source	Word overextended	Object producing overextension
C+C₁-266	*banana* (*mnana*)	yellow string bean
C+C₁-266	*bridge*	stone curbing on street, low retaining wall
C+C₂-455	*skin*	paint on furniture and wall
L-114	*chocolate* (*goga*)	brown crust
L₁-40	*auto* (*ʔauto*)	toy duck on wheels
L₁-44	*ball* (*baI*)	toy balloon
L₁-47	*bike* (*baIk*)	tricycle
L₁-49	*ball* (*bau*)	toy marbles
L₁-48	*bottle* (*balu*)	low jar
L₁-60	*boat* (*bot'*)	airship (dirigible)
L₁-67	*candy* (*da·i*)	cherries
L₁-68	*dolly* (*daI*)	teddy bear
L₁-126	*choo-choo* (*tʃutʃu*)	wheelbarrow, streetcar, truck
L₂-29	*supper*	all meals
M-140	*clock*	watch
M-140	*cork*	bath tub stopper
P-216	*tch tch* (had been applied to a train)	any vehicles
P-218	*bow-wow*	guinea pigs, cat
S-153	*noses* (counted as functionally similar since child liked to pull both)	toes of boots
W+K-118 (from Stern and Stern, 1928)	*nose* (counted as functionally similar since child liked to pull both)	point of a shoe
W+K-118 (from Stern and Stern, 1928)	*door*	tray of a high chair
B-73 (from Guillaume, 1927)	*breast* (*nénin*)	bisquit
B-78 (from Lewis, 1963)	*cat* (*tee*)	small dog

APPENDIX 3E *Overextensions to objects which were perceptually similar to and likely to be associated through contiguity with instances of the term.*

Source	Word overextended	Object producing overextension
L_1-52	*baby* (bebi)	older children
L_1-98	*man* (ma)	women in pictures, women
L_1-137	*wheel* (wiə)	wheelbarrow, toy wagon
L_2-2	*bouch* (bauk)	
	(German for fat tummy)	breast
P-217	*daddy*	father's friend
P-225	*the slug*	all slugs
$C+C_1$-268	*white dandelions*	white daisies
$C+C_1$-265	*moon*	writing on frosted window or paper
$C+C_2$-455	*roses*	wood lilies
M-140	*little girl* (had been applied to a picture of a little girl)	any picture
M-140	*baby frog* (had been applied to a picture of a frog embryo)	any picture in child's father's books any picture child can't identify
M-140	*fly*	all small insects
L_1-52	*baby* (bebi) (had been applied to pictures of children)	pictures of any kind
L_1-131	*wauwau* (waʊ waʊ) (had been applied to picture of a dog) (in one there was a dog pictured, also)	picture book child's baby pictures
W-226 (from Egger, 1903)	*hand*	glove

APPENDIX 3F *Overextensions to objects which were perceptually similar to, functionally similar to, and likely to be associated through contiguity with instances of the term.*

Source	Word overextended	Object producing overextension
S-146	*father* (ahter)	mother
S-152	*dolly*	rag-dog, toy rabbit
L_1-42	*papa* (baba)	mother
L_1-44	*bobby-pin* (babi)	all hairpins
L_1-48	*brush* (ba)	comb
L_1-67	*cake* (keke)	candy
L_1-95	*sunsuit* (jaʃut)	bathing suit
P-217	*mummy*	father
W+K-117 (from Stern and Stern, 1928)	*doll*	small toy rabbit, toy cat

APPENDIX 3G   *Overextensions based on miscellaneous factors.*

Source	Word overextended	Object producing overextension
L-95, 96	*mama* (*mammam* or *mama*)	when lacking something; when reaching for plaything, as if to himself; when searching for an object
L_1-86	*Hildegard* (*haIta*)	her cat
L_2-80	*barbecue*	barber shop
L_2-122	*pyjama*	piano
M-140	*baby frog*	some parallel curves and lines
P-216	*tch tch* (had been applied to a train)	playing bo-peep
P-216	*bow-wow*	woman pushing an open pram, everything seen from child's balcony
P-216	*panana/panena* (had been applied to child's grandfather)	indicates that child wants something
P-217	*mummy*	indicates that child wants something
P-218	*bow-wow*	cowbell
P-221	*frog*	mark on the wall
P-221	*lady*	moon
P-221	*look, dog, bird*	when child watches her food being diluted with milk in a bowl

References

Al-Issa, I. 1969. The development of word definitions in children. *Journal of Genetic Psychology* 114: 25–28.

Anglin, J. M. 1970. *The growth of word meaning.* Cambridge, Mass.: MIT Press.

———. 1973. Introduction to Bruner, J. S. *Beyond the information given,* ed. J. M. Anglin. New York: Norton.

———. 1974. *Studies in semantic development.* Final report of N.I.E. project no. 1–0624–A, U.S. Department of Health, Education and Welfare, Office of Education, E.R.I.C.

———. 1975. On the extension of the child's first terms of reference. Paper presented to the Society for Research in Child Development, Denver.

———. 1976. Les premiers termes de référence de l'enfant. In *La memoire sémantique,* ed. S. Ehrlich and E. Tulving. Paris: Bulletin de Psychologie.

Attneave, F. 1957. Transfer of experience with a class-schema to identification-learning of patterns and shapes. *Journal of Experimental Psychology* 54: 81–88.

Berko-Gleason, J. B. 1973. Code switching in children's language. In *Cognitive development and the acquisition of language,* ed. T. E. Moore. New York: Academic Press.

Berlin, B. 1972. Speculations on the growth of ethnobotanical nomenclature. *Language in Society* 1: 51–85.

Birket-Smith, K. 1936. *The Eskimos.* National Museum Copenhagen. London: Methuen.

Bloom, L. M. 1973. *One word at a time.* The Hague: Mouton.

Bourne, L. E. 1966. *Human conceptual behavior.* Boston: Allyn and Bacon.

Bousfield, W. A. 1953. The occurrence of clustering in the recall of randomly arranged associates. *Journal of Genetic Psychology* 70: 205–14.

Bower, G. H.; M. C. Clark; A. M. Lesgold; and D. Winzenz. 1969. Hierarchical retrieval schemes in recall of categorized word lists. *Journal of Verbal Learning and Verbal Behavior* 8: 323–43.

Bower, T. G. R. 1974. *Development in infancy.* San Francisco: W. H. Freeman.

Bowerman, M. F. In press. Semantic factors in the acquisition of rules for word use and sentence construction. In *Directions in normal and deficient child language.* Baltimore: University Park Press.

Bransford, J. D. 1970. The problem of conceptual abstraction: Implications for theories of learning and memory. Unpublished manuscript, University of Minnesota.

Broen, P. 1972. The verbal environment of the language-learning child. Monograph of American Speech and Hearing Association Vol. 17.

Brown, R. *Words and things.* 1958a. Glencoe, Ill.: Free Press.

————. 1958b. How shall a thing be called? *Psychological Review* 65: 14–21.

————. 1965. *Social psychology.* New York: Free Press.

————. 1973. *A first language: The early stages.* Cambridge, Mass.: Harvard University Press.

Brown, R.; C. Fraser; and U. Bellugi. 1963. Control of grammar in imitation, comprehension, and production. *Journal of Verbal Learning and Verbal Behavior* 2(2): 121–35.

Brown, R., and C. Hanlon 1970. Derivational complexity and order of acquisition in child speech. In *Cognition and the development of language,* ed. J. R. Hayes. New York: Wiley.

Bruner, J. S. 1957. On perceptual readiness. *Psychological Review* 64: 123–52.

————. 1964. The course of cognitive growth. *American Psychologist* 19: 1–15.

————. 1975. The ontogenesis of speech acts. *Journal of Child Language* 2: 1–19.

Bruner, J. S.; J. Goodnow; and G. Austin. 1956. *A study of thinking.* New York: Wiley.

Bruner, J. S., and R. Olver. 1973. Development of equivalence transformations in children. In Bruner, J. S. *Beyond the information given,* ed. J. M. Anglin. New York: Norton.

Bruner, J. S.; R. Olver; and P. Greenfield. 1966. *Studies in cognitive growth.* New York: Wiley.

Campbell, R. 1975 Some remarks on children's definitions. Unpublished paper.

Carey, S. 1973. Research plan. Unpublished paper, M.I.T.

Cassirer, E. 1923. *Substance and function.* New York: Dover Publications.

————. 1946. *Language and myth.* New York: Dover Publications.

Chamberlain, A. F., and J. Chamberlain. 1904a. Studies of a child I. *Pedagogical Seminary* 11: 264–91.

————. 1904b. Studies of a child II. *Pedagogical Seminary* 11: 452–83.

Chomsky, C. 1969. *The acquisition of syntax in children from 5 to 10.* Cambridge, Mass.: M.I.T. Press.

Clark, E. 1973. What's in a word? On the child's acquisition of semantics in his first language. In *Cognitive development and the acquisition of language,* ed. T. E. Moore. New York: Academic Press.

————. 1974. Some aspects of the conceptual basis for first language acquisition. In *Language perspectives: Acquisition, retardation, and intervention,* ed. R. L. Schiefelbusch and L. L. Lloyd. Baltimore, Md.: University Park Press.

Clark, H. 1973a. Space, time, semantics and the child. In *Cognitive development and the acquisition of language,* ed. T. E. Moore. New York: Academic Press.

————. 1973b. The language-as-fixed-effect fallacy: A critique of language statistics in psychological research. *Journal of Verbal Learning and Verbal Behavior* 12: 335–59.

Cole, M., and J. S. Bruner. 1971. Cultural differences and inferences about psychological processes. *American Psychologist* 26(10): 869–76.

Cole, M., and Scribner, S. S. 1974. *Culture and thought.* New York: Wiley.

Collins, A. M., and M. R. Quillian. 1969. Retrieval time from semantic memory. *Journal of Verbal Learning and Verbal Behavior* 8(2): 240–47.

————. 1972. How to make a language user. In *Organization of memory,* ed. E. Tulving and W. Donaldson. New York: Academic Press.

De Paulo, B., and J. D. Bonvillian. 1975. The effect on language development of the modifications in the speech addressed to children. Unpublished paper.

de Villiers, J. G., and P. A. de Villiers. 1973. A cross-sectional study of the acquisition of grammatical morphemes in child speech. *Journal of Psycholinguistic Research* 2: 267–78.

————. 1974. Competence and performance in child language: Are children really competent to judge? *Journal of Child Language* 1: 11–22.

Drach, K. M. 1969. The language of the parent: A pilot study. Working paper no. 14, Language Behavior Research Laboratory, Berkeley.

Dukes, W. F., and W. Bevan. 1967. Stimulus variation and repetition in the acquisition of naming responses. *Journal of Experimental Psychology* 74: 178–81.

Egger, E. 1903. Beobachtungen und Betrachtungen über die Engwicklung der Intelligenz und der Sprache bei den Kindern.

Evans, S. H. 1967. A brief statement of schema theory. *Psychonomic Science* 8: 87–88.

Feifel, H. 1949. Qualitative differences in the vocabulary responses of normals and abnormals. *Genetic Psychology Monographs* 39: 151–204.

Feifel, H., and I. Lorge. 1950. Qualitative differences in the vocabulary responses of children. *Journal of Educational Psychology* 41: 1–18.

Ferguson, C. A. 1964. Baby talk in six languages. *American Anthropologist* 66(6): 103–13.

Franks, J. J., and J. D. Bransford. 1971. Abstraction of visual patterns. *Journal of Experimental Psychology* 90: 65–74.

Fodor, J. 1972. Some reflections on L. S. Vygotsky's *Thought and language. Cognition* 1.1: 83–95.

————. *The language of thought.* 1975. New York: Thomas Y. Crowell.

Goodman, N. 1968. *Languages of art: An approach to a theory of symbols.* New York: Bobbs-Merrill.

————. 1972. On likeness of meaning. In N. Goodman, *Problems and projects.* New York: Bobbs-Merrill.

Guillaume, P. 1927. Les débuts de la phrase dans le langage de l'enfant. *Journal de Psychologie* 24: 1–25.

Haviland, S. E., and E. Clark. 1974. This man's father is my father's son: A study of the acquisition of English kin terms. *Journal of Child Language* 1: 23–47.

Hayes, W. L. 1963. *Statistics for psychologists.* New York: Holt, Rinehart and Winston.

Heidbreder, E. 1946a. The attainment of concepts: I., Terminology and methodology. *Journal of General Psychology* 35:173–89.

————. 1946b. The attainment of concepts: II., The problem. *Journal of General Psychology* 35: 191–223.

Herrnstein, R. J., D. Loveland, and C. Cable. Natural concepts in pigeons. *Journal of Experimental Psychology.* In press.

Herrnstein, R. J., and D. Loveland. 1964. Complex visual concept in the pigeon. *Science* 146: 549–51.

Howes, D. H. 1966. A word count of spoken English. *Journal of Verbal Learning and Verbal Behavior* 5: 522–604.

Hull, C. L. 1920. Quantitative aspects of the evolution of concepts: An experimental study. *Psychological Monographs* 28 (1, whole no. 123).

Huttenlocher, J. 1974. The origins of language comprehension. In *Theories in cognitive psychology,* ed. R. L. Solso. Potomac, Md. Lawrence Earlbaum Associates.

Ingram, D. 1974. The relationship between comprehension and production. In

Language perspectives: Acquisition, retardation and intervention, R. Schiefelbusch. and L. L. Lloyd. ed. Baltimore, Md.: University Park Press.

Inhelder, B., and J. Piaget. 1964. *The early growth of logic in the child.* New York: Norton.

Johnson, D. M. 1972. *Systematic introduction to the psychology of thinking.* New York: Harper and Row.

Katz, J. J. 1975. Logic and language: An examination of recent criticisms of intensionalism. In *Language, mind and knowledge.* vol. 7, ed. K. Gunderson. Minnesota Studies in the Philosophy of Science. Minneapolis: University of Minnesota Press.

Kucera, H., and W. N. Francis. 1967. *Computational analysis of present day American English.* Providence, R.I.: Brown University Press.

Labov, W. 1970. The logical non-standard English. In *Language and Poverty,* ed. F. Williams. Chicago: Markham Press.

———. 1973. The boundaries of words and their meanings. In *New ways of analyzing variation in English,* ed. C. J. N. Bailey and R. W. Shuy. Washington, D.C.: Georgetown University Press.

Lakoff, G. 1972. Hedges: A study in meaning criteria and the logic of fuzzy concepts. *Papers from the Eighth Regional Meeting, Chicago Linguistics Society,* Chicago: University of Chicago Linguistics Department, pp. 182–228.

Leopold, W. F. 1939. *Speech development of a bilingual child: A linguist's record,* vol. 1. *Vocabulary growth in the first two years.* Evanston, Ill.: Northwestern University Press.

———. 1948. Semantic learning in infant language. *Word* 4 (3): 173–80.

———. 1949a. *Speech development of a bilingual child,* vol. 3. *Grammar and general problems in the first two years.* Evanston, Illinois: Northwestern University Press.

———. 1949b. *Speech development of a bilingual child,* vol. 4. *Diary from age Two.* Evanston, Illinois: Northwestern University Press.

Levine, M. 1969. Neo-noncontinuity theory. In *The psychology of learning and motivation,* vol. 3, ed. G. H. Bower and J. T. Spence. New York: Academic Press.

———. 1971. Hypothesis theory and non-learning despite ideal S-R reinforcement contingencies. *Psychological Review* 78: 130–40.

Lewis, M. M. 1959. *How children learn to speak.* New York: Basic Books.

———. 1963. *Language, thought and personality.* New York: Basic Books.

Locke, J. 1690. *An essay concerning human understanding.* London: Routledge.

Lombroso, P. 1909. Das Leben der Kinder. *Padag. Mon.* (Ed. Meumann).

Luria, A. R., and F. Yudovich. 1959. *Speech and the development of mental processes in the child.* London: Staples Press.

Macnamara, J. 1972. Cognitive basis of language learning in infants. *Psychological Review* 79: 1–13.

McNeill, D. 1970. *The acquisition of language.* New York: Harper.

Mandler, G. 1967. Organization and memory. In *The psychology of learning and motivation,* vol. 1, ed. K. W. Spence and J. T. Spence. New York: Academic Press.

Miller, G. A. 1956. The magical number seven, plus or minus two: Some limits on our capacity for processing information. *Psychological Review* 63 (2): 81–97.

———. 1967. Psycholinguistic approaches to the study of communication. In *Journeys in science: Small Steps—Great Strides,* ed. D. L. Arm. Albuquerque: University of New Mexico Press.

———. 1969. A psychological method to investigate verbal concepts. *Journal of Mathematical Psychology* 6: 169–91.

————. 1975. Psycholexicology. Colloquium given at Yale University.

Miller, G. A., and P. N. Johnson-Laird. 1976. *Language and perception*. Cambridge, Mass.: Harvard University Press.

Moore, K. C. 1896. The mental development of the child. *Psychological Review Monograph Supplements* 1 (3).

Neimark, E. 1974. Natural language concepts: Additional evidence. *Child Development* 451: 508–12.

Neisser, U. 1967. *Cognitive psychology*. New York: Appleton-Century-Crofts.

Nelson, K. 1973a. Some evidence for the cognitive primacy of categorization and its functional basis. *Merrill-Palmer Quarterly of Behavior and Development* 19: 21–39.

————. 1973b. Structure and strategy in learning to talk. *Society for Research in Child Development Monographs* 38, (1–2, serial no. 149).

————. 1974. Concept, word and sentence: Interrelations in acquisition and development. *Psychological Review* 81: 267–85.

————. 1975. The conceptual basis for naming. Paper presented at conference on Language Learning and Thought in Infants. McGill University.

Olson, D. 1970. Language and thought: Aspects of a cognitive theory of semantics. *Psychological Review* 77(4): 257–73.

Palermo, D. S. 1976. Sémantique et acquisition du language: Quelques considérations théoriques. In *La memoire sémantique,* ed. S. Ehrlich and E. Tulving. Paris: Bulletin de Psychologie.

Phillips, J. R. 1973. Syntax and vocabulary of mothers' speech to young children: Age and sex comparisons. *Child Development* 44: 182–85.

Piaget, J. 1963. *The origins of intelligence in children*. New York: Norton.

————. 1962. *Play, dreams and imitation in Childhood*. New York: Norton.

————. 1965. *The child's conception of number*. New York: Norton.

Posner, M. I. 1969. Abstraction and the process of recognition. In *The psychology of learning and motivation*, vol. 3, ed. G. H. Bower and J. T. Spence. New York: Academic Press.

————. 1973. *Cognition: An introduction*. Glenview, Ill.: Scott, Foresman.

Posner, M. I., and S. W. Keele. 1968. On the genesis of abstract ideas. *Journal of Experimental Psychology* 77: 353–63.

————. 1970. Retention of abstract ideas. *Journal of Experimental Psychology* 83: 304–8.

Putnam, H. 1975. The meaning of "meaning." In *Language, mind and knowledge,* vol. 7, ed. K. Gunderson. Minnesota Studies in the Philosophy of Science. Minneapolis: University of Minnesota Press.

Quine, W. V. O. 1953. The problem of meaning in linguistics. In *From a logical point of view*. Cambridge, Mass.: Harvard University Press.

Rand, A. 1966–67. *Introduction to objectivist epistemology*. New York: The Objectivist, Inc.

Reed, S. K. 1972. Pattern recognition and categorization. *Cognitive Psychology* 3: 382–407.

Reich, P. A. 1976. The early acquisition of word meaning. *Journal of Child Language* 3: 117–23.

Rescorla, L. A. 1976. Concept formation in word learning. Unpublished Ph.D. thesis, Department of Psychology, Yale University.

Riccuiti, H. 1965. Object grouping and selective ordering in infants 12–24 months old. *Merrill-Palmer Quarterly of Behavior and Development* 11: 129–48.

Rinsland, H. D. 1945. *A basic vocabulary of elementary school children*. New York: Macmillan.

Rosch, E. H. 1973. On the internal structure of perceptual and semantic categories. In *Cognitive development and the acquisition of language,* ed. T. E. Moore. New York: Academic Press.

————. 1975. Universals and cultural specifics in human categorization. In *Cross-cultural perspectives on learning,* ed. R. Breslin, S. Bochner, and W. Lonner. New York: Sage/Halsted.

————. 1976. Classification d'objets du monde réel: Origines et représentations dans la cognition. In *La memoire sémantique,* ed. S. Ehrlich and E. Tulving. Paris: Bulletin de Psychologie.

Rosch, E. H.; C. B. Mervis; W. Gray; D. Johnson; and P. Boyes-Braem. 1975. Basic objects in natural categories. Working paper no. 40. Language Behavior Research Laboratory, University of California, Berkeley, Calif.

Saltz, E.; E. Soller; and I. E. Sigel. 1972. The development of natural language concepts. *Child Development* 43: 1191–1202.

Schwartz, R. 1968. Book review of J. S. Bruner et al. *Studies in Cognitive Growth. Journal of Philosophy* 65: 172–79.

Siegel, S. 1956. *Nonparametric methods for the behavioral sciences.* New York: McGraw-Hill.

Slobin, D. I. 1971. Developmental psycholinguistics. In *A survey of linguistic science,* ed. W. O. Dingwall. College Park, Md.: W. O. Dingwall, Linguistics Program, University of Maryland.

Smith, E. E.; E. J. Shoben; and L. J. Ripps. 1974. Structure and process in semantic decisions. *Psychological Review* 81 (3): 214–41.

Smoke, K. L. 1932. An objective study of concept formation. *Psychological Monographs* 42 (4), whole no. 191.

————. 1933. Negative instances in concept learning. *Journal of Experimental Psychology* 16: 583–88.

Stemmer, N. Cognitive aspects in language acquisition. *Word.* In press.

Stern, W. 1930. *Psychology of early childhood up to the sixth year of age.* New York: Holt.

Stern, W., and C. Stern. 1928. *Die Kindersprache.* Leipzig: Barth.

Sully, J. 1903. *Studies of childhood.* New York: Appleton.

Terman, L. M., and M. Merrill. 1960. *Stanford-Binet intelligence scale: Manual for the third revision: Form L-M.* Boston: Houghton Mifflin.

Thomson, J. R., and R. S. Chapman. June 1975. Who is "daddy" revisited: The status of two-year-old's overextended words in use and comprehension. *Journal of Speech and Hearing.*

Thorndike, E. L., and I. Lorge. 1944. *The teacher's word book of 30,000 words.* New York: Bureau of Publications, Teachers College, Columbia University.

Tulving, E. 1972. Episodic and semantic memory. In *Organization of memory,* ed. E. Tulving and W. Donaldson, New York: Academic Press.

Vygotsky, L. S. 1962. *Thought and language,* (trans. E. Hanfmann and G. Vakar). Cambridge, Mass.: M.I.T. Press.

Wason, P. G., and P. N. Johnson-Laird. 1968. *Thinking and reasoning.* Penguin Modern Psychology Series. Baltimore: Penguin Books.

Werner, H. 1948. *Comparative psychology of mental development.* New York: International Universities Press.

Werner, H., and B. Kaplan. 1963. *Symbol formation.* New York: Wiley.

Weeks, T. 1971. Speech registers in children. *Child Development* 42: 1119–31.

Whorf, B. L. 1956. *Language, thought and reality,* Ed. John Carroll. Cambridge, Mass.: M.I.T. Press.

Winer, B. J. 1962. *Statistical principles in experimental design.* New York: McGraw-Hill.

Wittgenstein, L. 1953. *Philosophical investigations,* trans. G. E. M. Anscombe. New York: Macmillan.

Wolman, R. N., and E. N. Barker. 1965. A developmental study of word definitions, *Journal of Genetic Psychology* 107: 159–66.

Zipf, G. K. 1935. *The psycho-biology of language.* Boston: Houghton Mifflin.

Index

Note: as in the text, concepts are indicated by small caps

Acquisition, *see* Order of acquisition

Adult modal words (*AMW*) in order of acquisition study, 42–44, 51, 59–61, 63–65, 67, 265–67
  computation of, 42, 60

Al-Issa, I., 21, 188*n*, 255

ALL BLACK FIGURES WITH ONE BORDER, as example of nonnatural concept, 6

ALL FIGURES CONTAINING A RED TRIANGLE SURROUNDED BY TWO BORDERS, extension to be attained in, 4

ALL RED TRIANGLES WITH TWO DOTS, as example of nonnatural concept, 6–7

AMW, see Adult modal words

Anglin, Jeremy M., 3, 6, 23, 24, 26, 41, 69, 89, 102, 133*n*, 188, 203, 228, 229, 239*n*, 246, 263

ANIMAL
  in determinants of underextension study, 134–41, 145*n*, 146, 147, 156, 157
    adult centrality and familiarity ratings on, 138–41
    central and peripheral instances of, 134
    implications of results for concep-

tual development theory, 249, 255, 257, 258
    study results, 147–49
  extension of, 4
  in extension study, 107–8, 249
    adult responses to, 116
    discussed, 131
    extension errors made in, 109–10, 112
    familiar and unfamiliar instances of, 126–27
    underextension responses obtained, 118–19, 129
  intension of, 4
  in intension study, 225–27, 253
    relationship between reference and meaning in, 231–33, 235
    responses of five-year-old children to, 218–19
    responses of four-year-old children to, 208
  in order of acquisition study, central instances of, 53, 54, 56
  semantic complexity and, 31–32
  underextension of, 102, 248

APPLE
  in determinants of overextension study
    study method, 161–63, 171
    study results, 167–68, 174
  in determinants of underextension study, 134

291